HOW TO MANAGE PROFIT AND CASH FLOW

MINING THE NUMBERS FOR GOLD

John A. Tracy
Tage C. Tracy

WILEY

John Wiley & Sons, Inc.

Library of Congress Cataloging-in-Publication Data:

ISBN 0-471-64995-3

Printed in the United States of America.

10 9 8 7 6 5 4 3 2 1

PREFACE

John Tracy has been writing books published by John Wiley & Sons for 30 years. Writing this book with his son, Tage, is a very satisfying way to celebrate his thirtieth anniversary with Wiley. John's wife, Fay, suggested that their son Tage, with his many years of business and financial consulting experience, would be a good coauthor. So the old man called and asked him about doing a book together. As it turned out, Tage was thinking of trying his hand at writing a book. He seems to have inherited his father's writing genes, although he got his basketball genes from other members of the family. (He was on the starting five of his high school team that won the 1981 state championship.)

In brief, our book explains the basic financial aspects of managing a business. We pay most attention to making, protecting, and improving profit, as well as generating cash flow from profit. Realistic and easy-to-follow examples are used throughout. The book is written in a serious yet lighthearted style. A little humor helps the reader to remember many points. The book should prove equally useful to budding entrepreneurs and business managers who have been around the track more than once.

The book is divided into three main parts:

1. Birthing a business.

2. Building a business.

3. Selling or burying a business.

Most books of this sort avoid topics concerning the ending of a business venture. Yet, the owners of a business may decide to sell it, or they may find it necessary to shut the doors and close down a business. So our book covers the complete life cycle of a business.

The tables in the book were prepared using the Microsoft Excel©spreadsheet program. We would be pleased to send to you the workbook file of all the examples. You can contact us at our e-mail addresses: tracyj@colorado.edu or tagetracy@cox.net. Comments and suggestions are welcomed.

Finally, we would like to thank the people at John Wiley & Sons who were so helpful in doing this book—executive editor Debra Englander, Greg Friedman, Felicia Reid, and Mary Daniello—as well as copy editor Judith Cardanha. The book is immeasurably better for their advice and assistance.

JOHN A. TRACY
TAGE C. TRACY

Boulder, Colorado
Poway, California
July 2004

CONTENTS

Part One

BIRTHING A BUSINESS

1

MAKING PROFIT: GETTING TO A GOOD BOTTOM LINE

"The numbers have gotta work—let's not sell vision."
—Walter Terry, Senior Vice
President, Wells Fargo
(quoted in the *Wall Street Journal*)

Entrepreneurs generally are strong on vision but not as strong on numbers. In launching a new business venture, you should make sure your vision does not outrun your numbers. Your overall business plan should include a definite profit plan based on realistic numbers for revenue and expenses. You shouldn't shade your numbers to bolster an overly enthusiastic vision. On the contrary, you should temper your vision to fit the numbers.

The driving force behind most business start-ups is a person with an impelling vision—a man or a woman who sees opportunities others do not and who is willing to take the risk of failure. But when the rubber meets the road, your profit numbers have to work. Every entrepreneur wants to build up sales as quickly as possible. But he or she shouldn't simply assume that profit drags along behind sales, like a ball on a chain. It's not as simple as this.

The Profit Plan in Your Business Plan

When you start up a business, your profit plan should be specific and definite, as specific and definite as your marketing plan. Vague statements in your marketing plan about "moving a lot of product" or "taking advantage of competitors' weaknesses" won't cut the mustard. Product categories should be delineated, promotional strategies and pricing tactics should be spelled out, total market demand and the market shares of existing competitors should be quantified as best as possible, how you intend to position your products and your business name should be clearly explained, and the advertising media you intend to use should be identified. These are essential elements of a persuasive marketing plan for every start-up business.

Likewise, your profit plan needs a well-thought-out and convincing profit model: a blueprint that identifies the critical factors that drive profit. You've probably heard the business adage "Nothing happens until you sell it." This is true enough, but once you sell your product, how much profit will you make? Answering this question is the purpose of the profit model. The profit model is the tool that transforms your sales number into a profit (or loss) number. A good profit model takes your sales number and predicts how much your profit or loss outcome will be.

Now, suppose that you have developed a rock-solid marketing plan for your new business venture. Suppose further that you have taken care of the many other things that have to be done to open the door and switch on the lights: hiring employees, leasing space, and so on. And suppose that you have enough money in the bank to get going and to stay going for awhile. You're not certain what your sales will be for your first year of business. So you make forecasts for three sales scenarios: (1) pessimistic, (2) most likely, and (3) optimistic. Table 1.1 presents your sales revenue forecasts for each scenario.

You're hoping for the best of course, but only time will tell. In any case, you're ready to take the plunge and move ahead. Just a minute here. Don't you also need to forecast how much your profit or loss would be for each sales scenario? You've come up with numbers for the top line; you also need to forecast numbers for the *bottom line*: the profit or the loss from sales.

TABLE 1.1—SALES FORECASTS FOR START-UP YEAR

Scenario	Sales Revenue
Optimistic	$1,800,000
Most Likely	1,200,000
Pessimistic	600,000

Two Opposite Cases for Expenses

Between the top line and the bottom line are deductions for expenses, of course. The hard core of mapping a profit model is diagnosing how expenses behave. Some expenses are driven by and vary with the level of sales. When sales are higher, these *variable* expenses are higher; and when sales are lower, these costs are lower. The largest variable expense for businesses that sell products is their cost of products (goods) that are sold. Salespeople's commissions that are based on sales revenue are another common type of variable expense. Packaging and delivery costs are variable expenses.

In contrast, certain expenses of operating a business remain relatively *fixed*—they do not vary with the level of sales over the short run. Once commitments are made, a business cannot scale back fixed expenses—at least not in the short run. Examples of fixed expenses are rent paid under real estate leases, the fixed salaries of employees, property taxes, and insurance premiums.

To contrast the profit effects of each kind of expense, we'll start by looking at two polar opposite scenarios for expenses: (1) the all-variable expenses case, and (2) the all-fixed expenses case. Almost all businesses have both types of expenses, which we will look at later.

All-Variable Expenses Case

For the all-variable expenses case, suppose total expenses are 90% of sales revenue. Therefore, profit is 10% of sales revenue. Your profit model is as simple as could be:

$$\text{Profit} = 10\% \times \text{Sales Revenue}$$

Table 1.2 shows your first-year profit for each forecast sales scenario.

All-Fixed Expenses Case

In the all-fixed expenses case, suppose your total expenses for the year are $1,080,000. In other words, no matter what your actual sales turn out to be, your expenses are stuck at $1,080,000. Table 1.3 presents the profit or the loss result for each sales scenario.

TABLE 1.2—IF ALL EXPENSES WERE VARIABLE

Scenario	Sales Revenue		Variable Expenses at 90%		Profit at 10%
Optimistic	$1,800,000	–	$1,620,000	=	$180,000
Most Likely	1,200,000	–	1,080,000	=	120,000
Pessimistic	600,000	–	540,000	=	60,000

TABLE 1.3—IF ALL EXPENSES WERE FIXED

Scenario	Sales Revenue		Fixed Expenses		Profit (Loss)
Optimistic	$1,800,000	–	$1,080,000	=	$720,000
Most Likely	1,200,000	–	1,080,000	=	120,000
Pessimistic	600,000	–	1,080,000	=	(480,000)

TABLE 1.4—PROFIT COMPARISON FOR ALL-VARIABLE VERSUS ALL-FIXED EXPENSES CASES

Scenario	Sales Revenue	Profit (Loss)		Difference
		All-Variable Expenses Case	All-Fixed Expenses Case	
Optimistic	$1,800,000	$180,000	$720,000	$540,000
Most Likely	1,200,000	120,000	120,000	0
Pessimistic	600,000	60,000	(480,000)	(540,000)

What a difference compared with the all-variable expense case! Or, to be more precise, what a difference for the pessimistic and the optimistic sales scenarios.

Table 1.4 compares profit performances between the two extremes of the expense cases. In the optimistic sales scenario, the large profit is the result of spreading your fixed expenses over the maximum amount of sales. You squeeze every last ounce of sales out of your fixed expenses. In the pessimistic sales scenario, the large loss is the result of too few sales over which to spread too much fixed expenses.

Put another way, in the optimistic sales scenario, you get maximum *leverage* from your fixed expenses. The profit acceleration effect from fixed expenses as sales increase is called *operating leverage*. Operating leverage is a close cousin of *financial leverage*, which refers to using debt in addition to equity (ownership) capital. Interest on debt is a fixed expense for the period and, therefore, has the same effects on profit performance as other fixed expenses.

The all-variable expenses case is like investing in a savings account (or other fixed-income investment). You make a steady 10 cents of profit from every dollar of sales. Profit moves in lock step with sales. The all-fixed expenses case is more like investing in stocks that can fluctuate wildly in value: It has a much higher payoff for the optimistic sales outcome, but it carries the risk of a large loss for the pessimistic sales outcome. If you had your choice between the two expenses cases, which would you prefer? Most entrepreneurs would probably favor the all-fixed expenses case. Anyone willing to start up a new business venture is a risk taker and an optimist.

Basic Profit Model

Virtually all businesses have both variable and fixed expenses. So, our profit model should include both variable and fixed expenses. Notice that for the "most likely" sales scenario, profit is the same for both the all-variable expenses case (Table 1.2) and the all-fixed expenses case (Table 1.3). In both cases, sales revenue is $1,200,000; total expenses are $1,080,000; and profit is $120,000. Suppose total variable expenses equal 60% of sales revenue, or $720,000. Therefore, total fixed expenses are $360,000: ($1,080,000 total expenses − $720,000 variable expenses = $360,000 fixed expenses). Fixed expenses, being fixed, would be the same for both the lower and the higher sales scenarios. In contrast, variable expenses, being variable, would be 60% of sales revenue for both the lower and the higher sales scenarios.

Please Note: We don't mean to suggest that the breakdown between variable and fixed expenses for this example is typical across a broad range of businesses. In fact, the mix of variable and fixed expenses is quite different from industry to industry. The example's 60% ratio of variable expenses to sales revenue is in the ballpark for many businesses, although we would quickly point out that this ratio is generally higher for companies that sell products. (The product costs of many high-turnover retail-ers, without considering their other variable expenses, are 70% or more of sales revenue.)

The profit model for our business example is now a little more complex. Table 1.5 presents the profit model of the business based on its mix of variable and fixed expenses. The operating leverage effect on profit performance is still rather pronounced, although it is dampened down quite a bit. Compare Table 1.5 with Table 1.3: Notice that profit in the optimistic sales scenario in Table 1.5 is only $360,000, as compared with the $720,000 profit in Table 1.3. The counterbalance is that the loss in the pessimistic sales scenario in Table 1.5 is only $120,000, as compared with the $480,000 loss in Table 1.3.

TABLE 1.5—BOTH VARIABLE AND FIXED EXPENSES

Scenario	Sales Revenue		Variable Expenses at 60%		Fixed Expenses		Profit (Loss)
Optimistic	$1,800,000	−	$1,080,000	−	$360,000	=	$360,000
Most Likely	1,200,000	−	720,000	−	360,000	=	120,000
Pessimistic	600,000	−	360,000	−	360,000	=	(120,000)

From the Profit Model to the P&L Report

Shortly following the close of each period (month, quarter, year), business managers receive a profit-and-loss (P&L) report, which summarizes sales revenue and expenses for the period. As you probably know, a company's accountant prepares these profit performance reports, which more formally are called *income statements*, *earnings reports*, or some other title (terminology is not uniform).

In our view, P&L reports to managers should be tailor-made for the decision-making and planning purposes of the managers. However, in most cases, accountants simply copy the format of the income statement that is presented in the external financial reports of the business and use this format for P&L reports to managers, even though the external income statement format is not entirely satisfactory for managers regarding how expenses are reported.

We don't mean to sound critical here, but let's face it: Accountants are not business managers. Accountants are financial scorekeepers, which is an essential function, to be sure. Accountants prepare the income tax returns and the external financial statements of the business. They, quite logically, look to the particular categories of expenses that are required in income tax returns and also consider how expenses are disclosed in external income statements. Expense accounts are set up with these two major demands for information in mind. For example, if the income tax return requires that repairs and maintenance expenses be reported (which it does), then an account for this particular expense is established. In short, expense accounts are established to be a good source of information for preparing income tax returns and external income statements.

Following the path of least resistance, accountants generally do *not* reclassify or regroup expenses for internal P&L reports to managers. In particular, variable expenses are not segregated from fixed expenses in P&L reports to managers. We should mention that much more detail is included in internal profit performance reports to managers. Managers may see more than a hundred separate expense accounts in their P&L reports, and some of these expense accounts are backed up with even more detailed data. But whether an expense varies with sales or is fixed for the period is not made clear in a typical P&L report. The manager may or may not know how a particular expense behaves relative to sales. The standard P&L report does not make this distinction clear, except for one particular variable expense.

For a business that sells products, its "cost of goods (products) sold" expense is reported on a separate line, both in its external income statements and in its internal P&L reports to managers. Cost of goods sold is usually the largest variable expense of a business that sells products. There's no argument about reporting cost of goods sold as a separate expense. It definitely should be the first expense deduction from sales revenue in both the external and the internal profit reports. Managers seem to understand that cost of goods sold is a variable expense. Most businesses have additional variable expenses that collectively are a significant percent of their sales revenue. These additional variable expenses should be reported in a pool separate from the fixed expenses of the business.

In this respect, the typical P&L report to managers falls short of what is needed for their decision-making analysis and for planning for changes in the future. Managers should not be in doubt regarding whether an expense is variable or fixed in nature. A manager should not have to interpret whether an expense is variable (driven by the level of sales) or fixed (not dependent on the level of sales for the period). As we've said before, expenses should be sorted between variable and fixed in internal P&L reports to managers. We return to this important issue in Chapter 5, where we discuss further the design of P&L reports for managers and the different kinds of variable expenses.

We'll keep the P&L report as short as possible at this point, to highlight its essential features. All variable expenses are collected into one pool, and all fixed expenses are assembled in a separate pool. (The variable expense pool includes the cost of goods sold expense, of course.) Table 1.6 presents an abbreviated P&L report for our business example. Essentially this P&L report is a vertical version of the company's profit model. (The profit model in Table 1.5 reads horizontally, from left to right.)

The P&L report shown in Table 1.6 introduces one very important line of information—*margin*.

Margin = Sales Revenue – All Variable Expenses

In our business example the margin ratio is 40% of sales revenue because variable expenses are 60% of sales revenue. We don't include these percents in the brief P&L report (Table 1.6),

TABLE 1.6—P&L REPORT BASED ON PROFIT MODEL

	Sales Forecast Scenario		
	Optimistic	Most Likely	Pessimistic
Sales Revenue	$1,800,000	$1,200,000	$ 600,000
Variable Expenses	(1,080,000)	(720,000)	(360,000)
Margin	$ 720,000	$ 480,000	$ 240,000
Fixed Expenses	(360,000)	(360,000)	(360,000)
Profit (Loss)	$ 360,000	$ 120,000	$(120,000)

but it's a good idea to include these ratios in P&L reports to managers. Margin ratios vary a great deal from industry to industry, as mentioned earlier. A margin ratio less than 20% of sales revenue is rather rare, except for businesses in desperate circumstances.

Margin ratios have to be adequate for a business to survive and to earn a sustainable profit. Whatever type of business you're in—whether you're a retailer, wholesaler, manufacturer, or service business—you have to maintain margins to make enough total margin on sales in order to overcome your fixed expenses and yield a profit. Therefore, the first focus of P&L reports to managers should be on margin—not that fixed expenses are unimportant, of course. Earning an adequate margin is the absolute, essential first step for making profit.

Deciding on the level of fixed expenses for your business, broadly speaking, is the essential second step toward making profit. Your total margin could be adequate. But your fixed expenses may be out of control. Ideally, fixed expenses should not be any higher than they need to be in order to support the level of sales for the period. It's easy to lose sight of this key point.

In Table 1.6, look at the fixed expenses line again. Notice that "fixed expenses" is the same total amount for all three sales scenarios. This means that the business took on fixed expenses high enough to support its optimistic sales forecast. Its fixed expenses are higher than would be needed for the most likely sales scenario and are much higher than would be needed for the pessimistic sales level.

A Closer Look at Fixed Expenses

Fixed expenses are a mixed bag of diverse costs, but they all share one key characteristic: Once you make the commitments to incur these operating costs, it is very difficult to ratchet down any of these expenses over the short run. Fixed expenses are like the old joke about hell: It's easy to get into, but very hard to get out of. It takes a relatively long time to get out from under fixed-expense commitments; these expenses continue whether your actual sales level is good, average, or poor. In short, you're stuck with fixed expenses over the short run. Once you've made these commitments, you can only hope that your actual sales will be high enough to justify your fixed-expense decisions.

For example, suppose you sign a one-year lease for warehouse space. Every month, you have to pay the rent whether you need all the space or not. Suppose you purchase an insurance policy; the insurance premium for the period is the same whether sales are high or low. Many employees are paid fixed salaries that don't depend on the actual sales level. Depreciation expense is recorded each period to spread the cost of buildings, machines, tools, and equipment over their useful lives. You guessed it: Depreciation expense is a fixed amount per period, regardless of your actual sales level for the period. Real estate property taxes are another example of a fixed expense.

The total fixed expenses of a business for a period sometimes is called its "nut." Once the managers of a business commit to a certain amount of fixed expenses for the coming period (hiring fixed-salary employees, renting warehouse space, and so on), the business has to make enough sales and earn enough total margin to cover its nut for the period and still have some residual margin left over for profit. In the "pessimistic" scenario (see Table 1.6), the business earns $240,000 margin, which is $120,000 less than its $360,000 fixed expenses. So, the business suffers a $120,000 loss. (By the way, this loss does not mean that the company's cash balance decreased $120,000 during the year, which Chapter 2 explains.)

Now, let's pose a key question here. For the sake of argument, suppose the pessimistic forecast turns out to be your actual sales for the first year, and assume your variable and fixed expenses are as shown in Table 1.6 for this sales level. So you suffer a $120,000 loss in your first year. Our question is: Why did you incur this loss? We'd bet that you'd be quick to blame your poor sales for the year. Well, not so fast. We could lay the blame for the loss on your fixed expenses instead. You made decisions that committed the business to a $360,000 level of fixed expenses for the year. This amount of fixed expenses would have supported $1,800,000 sales, the maximum sales level forecast. But actual sales turned out to be at the minimum end of your sales forecast. In short, your loss is caused by *excess* fixed expenses.

A manager should translate the level of fixed expenses into a measure of how much *sales capacity* these costs provide for the year. In our business example, the $360,000 fixed expenses provide support for a maximum $1,800,000 sales activity, which is three times actual sales for the first year (at the pessimistic level). If you had known for sure that your first year's sales were going to be only $600,000, you would have committed to a much lower level of fixed expenses, although it's difficult to say how much lower your fixed expenses could have been.

To illustrate this important point, suppose that you had played it safe and committed to only $240,000 fixed expenses for the start-up year (smaller warehouse space, fewer fixed-salary employees, and so on). This amount of fixed expenses would have been adequate to support your $600,000 sales for the year. Sales generated $240,000 total margin, which would exactly cover your fixed expenses for the year. Your profit/loss for the year would be exactly zero, which is called the *breakeven point*. Given the $360,000 fixed expenses, your sales had to be $900,000 just to break even. Your margin would have been $360,000 (40% margin ratio × $900,000 sales revenue), which would have equaled your fixed expenses for the year. In the "most likely" sales scenario, sales revenue is $1,200,000, which is above the breakeven point, and profit is $120,000 (see Table 1.6).

But bear in mind that the $120,000 profit figure would have been higher if your fixed expenses had been better matched with sales for the year. In other words, a level of fixed expenses somewhat lower than $360,000 would have been adequate to support $1,200,000 sales revenue. In our business example, fixed expenses could have supported an additional $600,000 of sales (over the $1,200,000 sales revenue for the most likely scenario). We could argue that you should have kept fixed expenses geared for the most likely level sales scenario instead of going all out and providing for the high end of your sales forecast.

Managers should be equally vigilant and just as hard-nosed about their fixed expenses as they are about their margins. Profit depends on both factors. Managers should take a hard look at their fixed expenses even when sales are good. All too often it takes a steep nosedive in sales to get managers to seriously consider scaling down or cutting back on their fixed expenses. Of course, these are tough decisions, usually involving laying off employees, selling off surplus assets, renting smaller quarters, and so on.

The relative neglect of fixed expenses, compared with the close attention to margins, is due in part to the fact that fixed expenses are not separated from variable expenses in P&L reports to managers. Compounding the problem is the fact that managers do not gauge the sales capacity provided by the level of their fixed expenses. To repeat the key points explained above: Fixed expenses should be clearly identified in P&L reports. And managers should quantify the sales capacity provided by their fixed expenses, which should be compared against actual sales for the period.

Capsule Summary

A business plan is no better than the quality of its profit plan. A profit plan depends on developing a profit model that quantifies how expenses behave relative to sales activity. Some expenses vary with sales activity, and other expenses remain virtually fixed and do not depend on the sales level over the short run. These two types of expenses should be clearly segregated in internal P&L reports to managers.

Sales revenue minus variable expenses equals margin. Enough margin has to be earned to overcome fixed expenses for the period and yield a profit. Making sales and maintaining margins is essential. Equally important, fixed expenses have to be controlled and kept in line with the level of sales. Excess fixed expenses can put a dent in profit as big as that caused by weak sales or inadequate margins.

2

WRINGING CASH FLOW FROM PROFIT: IT AIN'T OVER UNTIL YOU SEE THE MONEY

"If we're in the black, where's the green?"
—Tage Tracy (in a conversation with his father)

From the financial point of view, you're in business to make a profit. This is obvious, isn't it? Or are you in business to make *money*? You see, the two are not the same.

Even though the two expressions *making money* and *making profit* are used interchangeably, they should not be. You should keep in mind that profit is an *accounting* measure. The bottom-line profit number you see in a profit report hardly ever exactly equals the increase in your cash balance from your profit-making activities during the period. In fact, profit and cash flow can be far apart, especially so for the start-up year of a business—and for any business, on occasion. Hardly ever are profit and cash flow from profit exactly the same for the year. Profit and cash flow are identical only if a business uses the cash basis of accounting to record its revenue and expenses.

Cash-Basis Accounting

Many small businesses do not sell products; they sell *services*. A few examples are dry cleaners, physical fitness clubs, movie theaters, travel agents, professional firms, delivery companies, storage rental companies, and trash removal businesses. Scan the Yellow Pages if you want to see the broad variety of service businesses. A service business does not carry an inventory of products for sale that has to be accounted for, which is a major determinant of the accounting system a business should use.

The Internal Revenue Code gives smaller service businesses with annual revenue under $5,000,000 the option to use *cash-basis accounting* for determining their annual taxable income, that is, the profit subject to federal income tax. Cash-basis accounting basically is checkbook bookkeeping. You record actual cash collections from sales to customers as revenue, and you record actual cash payments for the expenses of the business. Cash inflow from revenue minus cash outflow for expenses equals the profit (or loss) for the year. Of course, cash outflows for expenses should include only costs of operating the business, and all cash inflow from sales should be recorded.

Cash-basis accounting is an expedient and practical method for determining taxable income. However, cash-basis accounting is not a good method for measuring the actual, or true, profit for any business—whether it is small or large or sells services or products. As a matter of fact, the income tax law puts restrictions on using cash-basis accounting. Most businesses actually use a *modified* cash basis of accounting; the amounts of cash outlays for certain types of asset purchases must be allocated to expense over several years.

The problems with cash-basis accounting start with recording sales revenue. In many cases, a business has billed customers for services provided to them but has not yet received the customers' payments by the end of the year. Using cash-basis accounting, the amount of earned but uncollected revenue is not recorded as revenue in the year. The revenue account includes only actual cash collections from customers. Put another way, the business has an asset, called *accounts receivable*, that is not recorded on the books by cash-basis accounting. For those service businesses that sell only for cash, checks, or credit cards, this is not a problem. But many service businesses extend credit to their customers, and their year-end uncollected receivables can be sizable.

Cash-basis accounting has serious flaws on the expense side of the ledger as well. When you cut a check, you immediately record the entire amount paid as an expense, with no thought regarding the periods benefited by the outlay. Furthermore, you don't record an expense until you cut a check when using cash-basis accounting, there's no thought of putting expenses in their correct periods, or the periods benefited by the outlays. Expenses are simply recorded when they are paid, and that's that. The result is that some expenses are overrecorded and some expenses are underrecorded in the year they are paid. Therefore, you don't have a true measure of your profit for the year. The income tax law recognizes the wrong timing of expenses by cash-basis accounting. As mentioned earlier, the amounts paid for assets that benefit more than one year cannot be deducted entirely in the year of payment. The costs of these assets must be allocated over more than one year.

Assume that you buy a computer for your business, or a delivery truck, or office furniture and equipment, or whatever. Such assets provide usefulness for several years. Do you really want to expense the entire cost in the year of purchase? The year of purchase would take a big hit, and the other years would escape any charge for using the assets. Doesn't it make more sense to spread the cost of these assets over the several years of their use? Accountants call this *depreciation;* each year is allocated a share of the cost of the asset.

Equally troubling, cash-basis accounting fails to record the liabilities of a business at the end of the year for unpaid expenses. For instance, a business may have utility and telephone charges that have not been paid. Or, at the end of the year, a business may owe commissions for sales made during the latter part of the year. Assume it has collected on these sales. So, the sales revenue has been recorded. Because the commissions haven't been paid, the expense hasn't been recorded. There's an obvious mismatch of revenue and expense here. Many businesses have sizable amounts of unpaid expenses at the end of the year. Cash-basis accounting does not record the liabilities for these unpaid expenses.

Accrual-Basis Accounting:
The Good and the Bad

Cash-basis accounting, as just discussed, has serious shortcomings. Most businesses need a more complete and better accounting system for measuring their annual profit and for recording their assets and liabilities. This more comprehensive record-keeping system is called *accrual-basis accounting*. Basically, the accrual basis goes beyond only recording cash inflows and cash outflows. Accrual-basis accounting records the economic reality of a business (well, within limits).

Sales are recorded when the revenue is earned, regardless of when cash is collected from customers. Expenses are recorded against sales revenue or in the period benefited, regardless of when cash is paid for these costs. The costs of long-lived assets are spread over the several years of their use. And, the costs of products are held in an inventory asset account and are not released to expense until the products are sold to customers. Thereby, the cost of products sold is matched with the revenue from the sale of the products. These are the essential features of accrual-basis accounting.

The "good" of accrual-basis accounting is twofold: (1) You get a much truer and more accurate measure of profit for the year; and (2) the assets and liabilities of the business are recorded, so the financial condition of the business can be determined. When issuing financial statements to outside parties (banks, nonmanagement owners, credit rating agencies, and so on), a business is duty bound to use accrual-basis accounting. If it does not use accrual-basis accounting, a business should clearly include a warning in its financial report that cash-basis accounting (or some other basis of accounting) is used to prepare its financial report. Accrual-basis accounting is necessary for preparing a correct profit report for the year and for preparing a correct statement of financial condition at the end of the year. These are overpowering reasons for using accrual-basis accounting.

However, the accrual basis comes with a price. Accrual-basis accounting is much more complicated than cash-basis accounting, to say the least. Accrual-basis accounting methods are more technical and not as intuitive as those of the much simpler cash-basis accounting. Another disadvantage of the accrual basis is that, well, it's not the cash basis. In particular, accrual-basis revenue and expenses amounts for the year are not the cash inflows and outflows for the year. Because of differences between accrual-basis amounts and cash flows, the bottom-line profit for the year (on the accrual basis) does not reveal cash flow for the year. This is a major inconvenience of accrual basis accounting.

Suppose your business earned $120,000 profit for the year, which we read in your profit-and-loss (P&L) report for the year. We don't have a clue concerning your cash flow from profit for the year. From the profit report itself, you can't tell a thing about cash flow. You could stare at it a long time, but it wouldn't do any good. For instance, sales revenue for the year tells you nothing about the amount of cash collected from customers during the year. You could hazard a guess that the two amounts are not far apart, but you don't really know. A profit report summarizes revenue and expenses for the year, leading down to bottom-line profit for the year. Now here's a neat idea: Why not prepare a cash flow report to go along with a profit report? It would not replace the profit report, nor in any way offer a second measure of profit. No, the cash flow report would simply present a cash flow look at the profit activities for the period.

In fact, accountants do prepare a cash flow report. It summarizes cash inflows and outflows for revenue and expenses of the year, leading down to the bottom-line increase or decrease in cash for the year.

Returning to Our Business Start-Up Example

Chapter 1 introduced three scenarios for a start-up business example. The example is used throughout the chapter to illustrate the differences between variable and fixed expenses on profit. Let's use the "most likely" scenario, in which the business earns a profit for its first year (no small accomplishment, to be sure). Table 2.1 presents the P&L report for this scenario. This profit report is the same as shown in Chapter 1 (Table 1.6), well, with one key modification. In Table 2.1 the cost of goods (products) sold expense is separated from the other variable expenses of the business.

TABLE 2.1—P&L REPORT, SHOWING COST OF GOODS SOLD SEPARATE FROM OTHER VARIABLE EXPENSES

Sales Revenue	$1,200,000
Cost of Goods Sold	(600,000)
Gross Margin	$ 600,000
Variable Operating Expenses	(120,000)
Margin	$ 480,000
Fixed Operating Expenses	(360,000)
Profit	$ 120,000

The cost of products (goods) sold is generally the largest variable expense of businesses that sell products. Accordingly, it is the first expense deducted from sales revenue both in external income statements and in internal P&L reports to managers. Bottom-line profit depends first of all on earning enough *gross margin:* Gross margin equals the sales price of a product minus its cost. (We should warn you that determining the cost of a product is not as straightforward as you might think.)

The spread between sales price and product cost is also called the *markup.* Suppose, for example, you sell a product for $100 and its cost is $60; its markup is $40. The markup is two-thirds, or 67%, of cost: $40 markup ÷ $60 cost = 67%. Alternatively, the markup can be calculated as 40% on the $100 sales price. Be careful which base is used to compute the markup percent.

Showing cost of goods sold as a separate first-line expense (see Table 2.1 again) helps in understanding one major reason why cash flow differs from profit. Cost of goods sold expense for the year is not, we repeat, *is not* a cash outflow amount for the year. The cost of goods sold expense for the year is the total amount removed or taken out of the business's inventory asset account in order to record the cost of products sold and delivered to customers.

Cash outflow depends not on the cost of products sold during the year but rather on the cost of products purchased or manufactured during the year and on when the business pays for these acquisitions. In many cases, a business buys or manufactures considerably more products than it sells during the year. In other words, it increases its inventory. An increase in inventory, to the extent that the inventory accumulation has been paid for, means that cash outflow is larger than the cost of goods sold for the year.

A knee-jerk reaction is to presume that the sales revenue and expense numbers in a P&L report equal the cash flow amounts for the period. But this can't be true; it would mean that a business is using cash-basis accounting instead of accrual-basis accounting. Almost all businesses of any size must use accrual-basis accounting to measure profit performance and to record financial condition. Business managers cannot find cash flows in their P&L reports. They must look to another financial report to learn the cash flows generated by sales and expenses for the period.

Before Moving On, Let's Be Clear about Nonprofit Cash Flows

A friend once asked one of us at a party, of all places, what the term *cash flow* means. Well, the term could be used in a very broad or global sense, or it could be used in a more narrow sense, such as cash flow from making profit. In the broad sense, cash flow refers to all sources of cash inflows and all uses of cash outflows. Assume in our example that early in the start-up year, your business borrowed $300,000, which has to be repaid in the future and on which interest is paid, of course. And assume that you and the other owners invested $300,000 money in the business at the beginning of the year.

You understand that the $600,000 cash inflow from debt and equity (ownership) sources is not included in the company's $1,200,000 sales revenue for the start-up year (see Table 2.1). The $600,000 increases your cash balance. But this is not cash flow from profit-making operations during the year. In summary, your business received $600,000 cash from sources of capital. And your business also received money during the year from customers for sales to them.

Assume, further, that during the start-up year, your business paid a total of $500,000 for the purchase of various long-lived operating assets that will be used for several years. This list includes a building, forklift trucks, shelving, office furniture, computers, delivery trucks, and so on. The $500,000 *capital expenditures*, as these investments are called, are recorded in asset accounts when purchased. The cost of each asset is spread out, or depreciated over, the predicted useful life of the asset. Suppose that $50,000 of the assets' total cost is recorded as depreciation expense in your first year. The $50,000 depreciation expense is included in fixed operating expenses (see Table 2.1). Keep this in mind; it's important for understanding cash flow from profit.

Table 2.2 summarizes the *nonprofit* cash flows of your business for its first year. Cash inflows from debt and equity capital sources were $100,000 more than cash outflows for capital expenditures. So, you have $100,000 in the bank at the end of the year—before taking into account the increase or the decrease in cash from your profit-making activities during the year. Table 2.1 reports that you earned $120,000 profit for the year. However, as harped on earlier, this is not the amount of cash flow from profit.

TABLE 2.2—SUMMARY OF NONREVENUE AND NONEXPENSE CASH FLOWS FOR FIRST YEAR

	Cash Inflow (Cash Outflow)
Borrowings on Interest-Bearing Debt	$300,000
Capital Invested in the Business by Owners	300,000
Investments by Business in Long-Term Operating Assets	(500,000)
Net Cash Flow	$100,000

Now, assume that the business's cash balance at the end of your first year is $90,000. Therefore, your profit-making operations during the year must have had the effect of *decreasing* your cash balance. In other words, cash flow from profit was *negative* for your start-up year. On the one hand, you did very well by earning a profit in your start-up year, and not a bad profit at that. On the other hand, your business suffered a $10,000 decrease to its cash balance, which is not too bad for a start-up year. You're probably wondering why you did so well in making profit but so poor in making money.

A word of warning here: The cash flow from profit during the start-up year of a business usually is negative. But, in many cases, the entrepreneur does not plan for this. Even if a business is able to turn a profit in the first year, more than likely its cash flow from profit will be negative, which means that making the profit will be a drain on the cash balance of the business.

Cash Flow from Profit in Start-Up Year

Managers should understand that during a period of time, revenue and expense cash flows differ from accrual-basis accounting figures for revenue and expenses. This is especially important for the start-up year of a business. In its first year, a business has to build up its inventory of products for sale (assuming it sells products, of course). If the business extends credit to customers, it also has to build up its balance of *accounts receivable*, which is the amount of uncollected sales revenue. Both are cash sinkholes. Well, perhaps "sinkholes" is too strong a word. Inventory and accounts receivable are investments in assets, and these assets are needed for making sales. The cash outlay for inventory accumulation and the cash delay in collecting from credit sales are typically the biggest two factors affecting cash flow in the first year of business. There are other factors at play also.

Table 2.3 presents a combined P&L and cash flows report that discloses the cash inflow from sales and the cash outflows for expenses side by side with sales revenue and the expenses for the start-up year of our business example. In Table 2.3, depreciation expense is separated from the other fixed operating expenses of the business because depreciation is a unique expense from the cash flow point of view.

Caution: There's no standard format for reporting revenue and expense cash flows internally to managers. Indeed, in many businesses, cash flows are not reported to managers—if you can believe it. You don't see a report like Table 2.3 in external financial reports. The statement of cash flows must be included in the ex-

TABLE 2.3—REVENUE AND EXPENSE CASH FLOWS FOR START-UP YEAR

	P&L Report	Cash Flows	Differences
Sales Revenue	$1,200,000	$1,100,000	$(100,000)
Cost of Goods Sold	(600,000)	(680,000)	(80,000)
Gross Margin	$ 600,000		
Variable Operating Expenses	(120,000)	(100,000)	20,000
Margin	$ 480,000		
Fixed Depreciation Expense	(50,000)	0	50,000
Other Fixed Operating Expenses	(310,000)	(330,000)	(20,000)
Profit	$ 120,000		
Cash Flow (Negative)		$ (10,000)	

ternal financial reports of a business (to outside owners and creditors). Most businesses use a different format for presenting cash flow from profit, which is called cash flow from *operating activities*. This format (not shown here) is in accordance with generally accepted accounting principles (GAAP) for external financial reporting. However, the information in Table 2.3 is much more useful for explaining cash flow from the profit-making (operating) activities of a business.

The idea of Table 2.3 is to make it easy to compare sales revenue and each expense in the P&L report with its corresponding cash flow for the year. Cash flows are matched with their accrual accounting basis figures in the P&L report. It is assumed that managers don't have time to delve into all the technical details in the preparation of this report. It is the accountant's job to analyze the accounts and to assemble a concise summary of the cash flows for revenue and expenses of the period.

The following is a brief overview, or executive summary, of why cash flows differ from the revenue and expense figures in the P&L report (see Table 2.3).

Cash Flow Differences from Sales Revenue and Expenses

1. Your year-end balance of accounts receivable is $100,000. You haven't collected this money; your customers should pay early next year. So, you're $100,000 short of cash inflow through the end of the year. Your cash inflow from making sales is $100,000 less than sales revenue for the year.

2. You accumulated inventory of products held for sale. You purchased (or manufactured) more products than you sold during the year. Your out-of-pocket cash outlay during the year for the accumulation of inventory was $80,000. Your ending inventory is actually more than this amount; but through the end of the year, you hadn't paid for your entire ending inventory. You have some accounts payable for inventory at the end of the year. The $80,000 is actual cash paid out for the build-up of your inventory.

3. You did not pay 100% of your variable operating expenses recorded for the year. You have $20,000 of unpaid expenses at the end of the year, which is recorded as a liability (accounts payable). You'll pay for these expenses early next year; but as of the end of the year, you had not written checks for $20,000 of your total variable operating expenses for the year.

4. You bought and paid $500,000 for different *fixed assets*, which provide several years of use (a building, equipment, computers, and so on). The $500,000 cost is recorded in asset accounts; $50,000 of the total cost of these long-lived assets is recorded as depreciation expense in your first year. The $50,000 depreciation expense is not a cash outlay; you already made the cash outlay when you bought the assets. Therefore, the cash effect of recording depreciation expense is zero (see Table 2.3).

5. Your net cash outlay for other fixed operating expenses was $20,000 more than the amount of these expenses for the year. You had to prepay certain of these costs. For example, you wrote checks for insurance policy premiums, but the coverage of these policies extends into next year. The portion of the premium cost that you have used up through the end of the year is recorded as an expense in the year. The asset account *prepaid expenses* holds back the remainder of the insurance premium cost, which will not be charged to expense until next year.

Adding up your revenue and expense cash flows for the year gives a $10,000 net *decrease* for the year (see the bottom line in the cash flows column in Table 2.3). Making $120,000 profit "cost" you a $10,000 cash decrease through the end of the year. The $10,000 negative cash flow from profit is mainly the result of extending credit to your customers and building up your inventory, as just explained. Relative to your annual sales revenue and expenses, your cash flows look reasonable for a start-up year.

You should have forecast the revenue and expense cash flows for your start-up year. The financial plan for the first year should have predicted these cash flows—in particular, that your profit would not provide positive cash flow during the first year. The negative cash flow means that you needed $10,000 cash subsidy from other sources. Evidently, you did a good job of planning for this. You raised $600,000 capital (see Table 2.2), which leaves $90,000 cash balance as you start your second year of business. Congratulations!

Beyond the Start-Up Year

As just discussed, the start-up year is very hard on cash flow from profit (see Table 2.3 again). In our start-up business example, the first year's profit outcome is positive, but cash flow from profit is negative. This is not unusual for the start-up year of a business, during which it accumulates a stockpile of products (inventory) and extends credit to customers. A new business starts from zero and moves up to normal levels of inventory and accounts receivable. A start-up business is an example of quick acceleration, or rapid growth. Generally speaking, rapid growth hinders cash flow; profit does not convert into cash flow during a high-growth year. Cash doesn't flow in due to the accumulation of accounts receivable, and a good amount of cash outflow is needed to accumulate inventory of products held for sale.

In comparison, when a business has moderate or little growth, its profit and cash flows run much closer together—depending on the size of its annual depreciation expense (and any other noncash expenses it records). There are exceptions to this rule, of course. A moderate-growth, or no-growth business could let its accounts receivable and/or inventory get out of hand, either of which can cause a big dent in cash flow.

Table 2.4 shows a P&L and cash flows report for our business example based on the assumption of moderate sales growth for its second year. The example assumes that you kept your accounts receivable and inventory under control. In other

TABLE 2.4—PROFIT AND CASH FLOWS FOR MODERATE-GROWTH EXAMPLE

	P&L Report	Cash Flows	Differences
Sales Revenue	$1,400,000	$1,380,000	$(20,000)
Cost of Goods Sold	(700,000)	(715,000)	(15,000)
Gross Margin	$ 700,000		
Variable Operating Expenses	(140,000)	(135,000)	5,000
Margin	$ 560,000		
Fixed Depreciation Expense	(50,000)	0	50,000
Other Fixed Operating Expenses	(370,000)	(385,000)	(15,000)
Profit (Net Earnings)	$ 140,000		
Cash Flow (Negative)		$ 145,000	

words, you made sure that these two assets increased only moderately, in proportion to your moderate sales growth. Depreciation expense is the same in the second year, which assumes that you did not purchase any additional fixed assets in the second year.

Notice that cash flow from profit in the second year is a little more than profit (see Table 2.4). In this situation, you have a pleasant problem facing you, one concerning what to do with your cash flow. Basically, you have four choices: (1) Pay out some of the cash flow as a distribution of profit to owners; (2) let the cash stay where it is to build up your cash balance so that you can take advantage of opportunities in the future; (3) invest in new assets to expand the capacity of the business or to move in new directions; and (4) reduce the debt and/or equity capital base of your business. Positive cash flow provides a good deal of flexibility for a business.

Good business managers forecast cash flow from profit for the coming year. They don't wait for the cash flow number to be reported to them in the financial reports for the year. They plan ahead so to provide enough lead time for making the critical decisions regarding what to do with the cash flow.

Capsule Summary

Cash flows are not found in a profit report unless the business happens to use cash-basis accounting. Businesses of any size and businesses that sell products don't use cash-basis accounting. They use accrual-basis accounting, which is the gold standard for preparing the financial statements of a business. Unfortunately, cash flows are not transparent in an accrual-basis profit report. There's no way you can divine cash flows from the revenue and expenses in an accrual-basis profit report. Depreciation is not a cash outlay in the period it's recorded as an expense. Otherwise, you're in the dark about cash flows.

The external financial reports of a business include a statement of cash flows. One section in this statement deals with cash flow from profit, or from operating activities, as it is called in the statement. However, from the manager's viewpoint, the presentation of cash flow from profit (operating activities) leaves a lot to be desired. A business manager should instruct his or her accountant to design a report for the cash flows from revenue and for expenses during the period that provides a clear trail down to the net cash increase

or decrease from profit (or loss) for the period. Such a cash flow report for managers is presented and explained in the chapter.

In most cases, rapid sales growth requires equally rapid growth in accounts receivable (unless the business does not give customers credit) and equally rapid growth in inventory (unless the business does not sell products). Steep increases in accounts receivable and inventory suck up cash. Thus, cash flow is much lower than profit for the year. The start-up year is a case in point. A new business starts from scratch and accumulates accounts receivable and inventory. Cash flow can be negative even if a new business earns profit in its first year.

Prepaid and unpaid expenses also affect cash flow from profit. And remember that depreciation is not a cash outlay in the year it's recorded as an expense. In summary, a manager should closely monitor the differences between revenue and expenses in the P&L report and the cash flows of revenue and expenses during the period. The manager needs double vision, as it were, to keep on top of things.

3

INVESTING IN ASSETS: IT TAKES MONEY TO MAKE MONEY

"Money is like muck, not good except it be spread."
—Francis Bacon

One of our relatives used to run a business that was quite unusual. The only assets she owned were a cash register and a little cash in the till. She needed virtually no assets. She sold goods only on consignment, and she rented all the space she needed. It's very unusual to run a business with no assets. Almost all businesses need substantial amounts of assets to make sales and to carry on operations.

The total assets of most businesses are a third, a half, or more of their annual sales revenue. Assets don't come cheap. A business has to raise the capital to invest in its assets. The next chapter examines the sources of business capital that are tapped for the money to invest in assets. This chapter first examines the assets that businesses use in making profit and focuses on the linkages between sales revenue and expenses and their corresponding assets. The size of an asset depends primarily on the size of the revenue or expense that impels the particular asset.

Business Assets: Owned, Leased, Operational, and Nonoperational

You've probably heard the oft-repeated observation that every business is different. This is certainly true regarding the asset profiles of different businesses. Even businesses in the same industry may have different asset profiles, depending, for instance, on whether they own or lease their assets. Assets legally owned by a business are reported in its financial statements, of course. But, as you know, almost any asset can be leased, which includes real estate, machines, tools, trucks and autos, and computers. A leased asset is not reported in the financial statements of a business—*unless* the lease, in substance, is the means to finance (pay for) the acquisition of the asset. This type of lease is called a *capital lease*.

When a lease extends over the largest part of an asset's expected useful life and the business (lessee) has a purchase option for a bargain price at the end of the lease, then the business records the lease as a de facto purchase of the asset. The asset is recorded at a cost figure, and the obligation for future lease payments is recorded as a liability on which interest is charged. The periodic payments under a capital lease are split between interest expense and reductions of the liability balance. The cost of an asset being acquired under a capital lease is recorded to depreciation expense each year over the predicted useful life of the asset.

In contrast, assets being rented under short-term *operating leases* are not recorded as assets and are not reported in a business's financial statements. Rents paid under these short-term leases are recorded to expense in the period the asset is used.

So, what kind of assets do you normally see in a business's financial report? Well, the assets of a bank differ from the assets of an airline, which differ from the assets of an electric or gas utility, which differ from the assets of an auto manufacturer, which differ from the assets of an amusement park, which differ from the assets of a retail supermarket, and so on. You probably get the idea. Some businesses are asset heavy, or *capital intensive*. Other businesses are asset light—they make small investments in assets relative to their annual sales revenue.

Coming up with an asset profile for a typical business is complicated by another factor. A business (except a sole proprietorship) is a separate legal entity, that is, a distinct person in the eyes of the law. Types of legal business entities include corporations, limited liability companies, partnerships, and other forms of for-profit organizations that are enabled by law. As a separate legal entity, a business can own almost any asset that an individual person can. (One exception: Only an individual can own a 401k retirement investment account.) Many businesses invest in assets that are not needed or used in making sales. Wal-Mart, for instance, could invest some of its cash in IBM stock shares.

Generally speaking, assets can be divided into two broad categories: (1) *operating assets*, which are those resources actually used in making sales or generating the mainline revenue of a business; and (2) *nonoperating assets*, which are those resources that a business could do perfectly well without as far as making sales or generating revenue is concerned. A business may hold substantial investments in nonoperating assets; in fact, many do. The range of investments in nonoperating assets is beyond the scope of this book. This chapter focuses on operating assets used in making sales and carrying on the profit-making activities of a business.

We should point out, however, that in their external financial reports many businesses do not make a clear distinction between their operating assets—those assets that are absolutely critical for carrying on the profit-making activities of the business—and their nonoperating assets. In any case, the nonoperating assets of a business should have a legitimate purpose and should provide a good source of income. A business should not carry "excess assets" that don't yield a satisfactory stream of income.

Asset Profile of a Business

This chapter concentrates on a business that sells products. Furthermore, it is assumed that its customers buy on credit. The purpose of using this type of example is to explain two main business assets: (1) products held for future sale that are purchased or manufactured by the business; and (2) receivables owed to the business from credit sales to its customers. A typical business has other assets as well, of course.

In the financial report of a business that sells products you find the following assets.

Typical Business Assets

- **Cash:** Includes checking accounts balances in banks and currency and coins held by a business. (A car wash business keeps a lot of quarters in its change machines, for example, and most retailers keep a fair amount of currency on hand.) *Note:* It's permissible to include in the cash account presented in a financial report "near-cash" items, such as temporary investments in short-term marketable securities that can be immediately liquidated into cash.

- **Accounts Receivable:** The total of receivables from customers for sales made on credit to them. These receivables should be collected early next period.

- **Inventories:** The total cost of products not yet sold to customers. These products are being held for sale, which should occur in the short-term future.

- **Property, Plant, and Equipment:** Includes various economic resources, also called *fixed assets*, owned by the business that are used in its operations. These assets are recorded at their purchase costs, and their costs are allocated over their predicted useful lives, which is called *depreciation*. These assets are not held for sale in the normal course of business.

- **Intangible Assets:** Things that have no physical existence, in contrast to fixed assets that are tangible (having physical substance that you can touch and see). Intangible assets include legally protected rights, such as patents, copyrights, and trademarks. A principal example of an intangible asset is *goodwill*, which generally refers to the competitive advantage that a business enjoys, such as a widely recognized and well-respected brand or business name. Goodwill is recorded only when a business actually pays for it. This purchase happens when one business acquires another business and pays more than what the tangible assets of the business acquired are worth by themselves.

- **Other Assets:** Assets other than the "hard core" basic types just listed; generally much smaller than the basic assets. For example, a business might loan money to its executives or make advances to employees for travel expenses; these receivables are recorded as assets. Many businesses have to put down deposits for such reasons as guaranteeing future performance on contracts. The deposits will be refunded to the business at a future date; such deposits are recorded as assets. A business could have a tax refund coming to it, which is recorded as an asset. This category of "other assets" is rather open-ended—you never know what you will find in it.

One word of advice: A business owner/manager should know which things are parked in the "other assets" account. Not necessarily every last little thing, but the manager certainly should know the larger items included in this asset account, which can become a dumping ground for too many odds and ends that can get out of control over time.

Connecting Revenue and Expenses with Their Assets and Liabilities

The following example sidesteps the last type of assets: It is assumed that the business does not have any "other" assets. The example includes only mainstream assets—cash, accounts receivable, inventories, fixed assets, and intangible assets. (Well, another asset called *prepaid expenses* also has to be discussed.) These are the main assets of the great majority of businesses that sell products.

For this new business example, Table 3.1 illustrates the vital connections between revenue and expenses on the one side and the assets and liabilities that are integral to the profit-making process on the other side. In Table 3.1, cost of goods sold, depreciation, and amortization expenses are shown separately; but all other expenses are grouped together in one amount. The lump sum for other expenses includes operating expenses as well as interest expense and income tax expense. You probably know that interest and income tax are disclosed separately in *internal* P&L reports to managers and in income statements presented in the *external* financial reports of a business. You wouldn't see a profit report like Table 3.1 inside or outside a business.

Table 3.1 highlights the linkages between revenue and expenses

TABLE 3.1—REVENUE AND EXPENSES CONNECTED WITH THEIR ASSETS AND LIABILITIES

Revenue and Expenses for Year		Assets	Year-End Balances
Sales Revenue	$52,000,000	Accounts Receivable	$ 5,000,000
Cost of Goods Sold Expense	33,800,000	Inventory	8,450,000
Depreciation Expense	(785,000)	Fixed Assets (at original cost)	16,500,000
Amortization Expense	(325,000)	Intangible Assets (at original cost)	7,850,000
Other Expenses	(14,448,000)	Prepaid Expenses	960,000
Profit, or Net Earnings	$ 2,642,000		
		Liabilities	
		Payables for Inventory	$ 2,600,000
		Unpaid Expenses	2,400,000

and their corresponding assets and liabilities. The assets and liabilities in Table 3.1 do not comprise all the assets and liabilities of the business. In other words, Table 3.1 is *not* a *statement of financial condition* for the business—commonly called a *balance sheet*—which discloses all its assets and all its liabilities, as well as the sources of its owners' equity. In Table 3.1, only those assets and liabilities directly connected with revenue and expenses are shown. You probably noticed that the asset "cash" is not included Table 3.1. This omission is explained shortly. The year-end balance sheet of the business is presented later in the chapter.

Following the Lines of Connection

The main message of Table 3.1 is that sales revenue and certain expenses of a business drive particular assets and liabilities of the business and that particular assets drive certain expenses.

Connections between Revenue and Expenses and Their Assets and Liabilities

- The business makes sales on credit; thus it has an asset called *accounts receivable*. These receivables are recorded at sales prices charged to customers.

- The business sells products, so it carries a sizable *inventory* (stockpile) of products awaiting sale. Inventory is recorded at cost (not at the sales value of the products). There are different accounting methods for determining cost.

- At year-end, the business has not paid for its entire inventory because it buys most items on credit. It has bills for products on hand in its year-end inventory; these bills will be paid next period.

- The business has purchased several different *fixed assets* (property, plant, and equipment); the costs of these assets are allocated to depreciation expense over their predicted useful lives.

- The business has invested in *intangible assets* (goodwill); the costs of these assets are allocated to amortization expense over their predicted useful lives.

- Certain expenses (such as insurance premiums) have to be pre-paid. The portions of these prepayments that will benefit future periods are held in the asset account called *prepaid expenses;* these amounts will not be released to expense until next period.

- Certain expenses have not yet been paid at the year-end. The liabilities for these expenses are recorded, so that the full amounts of the expenses are recorded in the correct period. In Table 3.1, these liabilities are collapsed into one amount called *unpaid expenses*. In financial statements, these liabilities are reported as accounts payable, accrued expenses payable, and income tax payable (see Table 3.3 later in the chapter for example). You find many variations of these basic account titles in financial reports.

The ratios of the assets' balances at the year-end compared with their revenue or expense amounts for the year are of the utmost importance.

Weeks of Sales in Accounts Receivable: Accounts Receivable Turnover Ratio

Compare the year-end balance of accounts receivable against sales revenue for the year. The business made $52,000,000 in sales during the year, which is an average of $1,000,000 per week. The year-end balance of accounts receivable is $5,000,000, which equals five weeks of annual sales. The flip way of looking at this is as follows: Divide annual sales revenue by accounts receivable to get the *accounts receivable turnover ratio*: $52,000,000 annual sales ÷ $5,000,000 accounts receivable = 10.4 times.

Whether expressed as weeks of sales in accounts receivable or as the accounts receivable turnover ratio, this important measure should be consistent with the credit terms offered to customers. Suppose the business gives four weeks credit to its customers, on average. Some of its customers pay late, and the business tolerates these late payers. Thus, five weeks of uncollected sales (accounts receivable) at year-end is not out of line. If, on the other hand, the business had seven or more weeks sales in accounts receivable, at year-end this would be cause for alarm.

Weeks of Sales in Inventory: Inventory Turnover Ratio

The company's cost of goods sold expense for the year is $33,800,000 (see Table 3.1), which is an average of $650,000 per week. Dividing the company's $8,450,000 cost of year-end inventory by the weekly average reveals that its year-end inventory equals 13 weeks of annual sales. Put another way, the company's *inventory turnover ratio* is 4 (i.e., 52 weeks ÷ 13 weeks inventory = 4, which is also referred to as 4 "turns" per year). A business manager should control inventory, which means keeping it at a proper level relative to sales.

Inventory turnover ratios vary quite a bit from industry to industry. Wal-Mart or Costco would not be satisfied with an inventory turnover of four times per year. They move their products in and out the door more frequently. A full-price retail furniture store, in contrast, may be satisfied to hold products for as long as six months on average before sale, which is an inventory turnover of only two times per year. How long products are in the pipeline varies a great deal from industry to industry.

The line from the "inventory asset" to the "payables for inventory" liability signals that a good part of the company's inventory has not been paid at the end of the year. The ending balance of this liability is about 30% of the cost of its inventory. Because inventory equals 13 weeks of its annual cost of goods sold, this liability equals about 4 weeks of annual cost of sales: 30% × 13 weeks of inventory = about 4 weeks. If the business buys inventory on credit terms of about 4 weeks, this ratio seems right.

Long-Lived Assets Ratios

The costs of fixed assets, or of the long-lived tangible operating assets, of a business are allocated to annual depreciation expense over their predicted useful lives. Each year is allocated a fraction of the cost, which is recorded as *depreciation* expense. The most intuitive allocation method is to charge each year an equal fraction of a fixed asset's total cost, which is called *straight-line depreciation*. For example, one-tenth of total cost would be recorded as depreciation expense each year for a 10-year fixed asset. Alternatively, accounting rules permit higher depreciation amounts to be recorded in the early years and smaller amounts in the later years of a fixed asset's lifespan. This "front-end loading" of depreciation expense is called *accelerated depreciation*. Likewise, the costs of intangible assets, such as goodwill or patents, are allocated over their predicted useful lives (usually by the straight-line method). Each period is charged with a fraction of the cost, which is recorded as *amortization* expense. Table 3.1 shows the lines of connection from these two operating assets to their two expenses.

As just explained, the inventory turnover ratio takes the annual cost of goods expense and divides it by the cost of ending inventory. In like manner an asset turnover ratio *can* be calculated for the company's fixed assets and for its intangible assets. The $785,000 depreciation expense for the year could be divided by the $16,500,000 original cost of its fixed assets. This calculation shows that depreciation expense for the year is about 5% of original cost, which indicates a 20-year average depreciation life for its fixed assets. In the same manner, the average amortization life of its intangible assets is 25 years (give or take a little). What these two ratios reveal is that it takes 20 years on average for the business to recover the costs invested in its fixed assets and 25 years on average to recover the costs invested in its intangible assets.

Prepaid and Unpaid Expenses Ratios

Most businesses have no choice but to prepay certain expenses, as explained earlier. In Table 3.1, see the line of connection from "other expenses" to the "prepaid expenses" asset account. Gener-ally speaking, an "eyeball" review of the prepaid expenses balance relative to total expenses is enough for the manager. In this example, the asset's year-end balance is about 7% of the other expenses for the year. The manager can judge whether this is about right or perhaps too high for the business; 7% seems like it might be too high. The manager should compare this year's ratio with that of past years to reach a conclusion.

Most businesses have not paid 100% of all their expenses by the year-end. In fact, unpaid expenses at year-end can add up to a much higher amount than you might suspect. A typical business buys many things on credit. In the example, unpaid expenses at year-end equal about 17% of the other expenses for the year. Put another way, unpaid expenses are about nine weeks of other expenses for the year. The manager should ask: Is this ratio consistent with the general credit terms extended to the business by its vendors? This liability also includes certain accruals for expenses that have been incurred but not paid, such as sales commissions earned by the sales staff that will not be paid until next period. The nine weeks of unpaid expenses may be consistent with previous years. The manager will have to make a conclusion whether the business is waiting too long before paying its bills. Perhaps the business is short of cash, or perhaps it just waits as long as possible to pay its bills.

Cash Sources and Uses

In Table 3.1, *cash* is the asset missing in action. Now you may be thinking: Don't revenue and expenses flow through cash? Of course they do—although as Chapter 2 explained, these cash flows for the period differ from the accrual-basis accounting revenue and expenses figures for the period. Cash is the universal asset. Virtually *all* activities of a business flow through cash—not just its revenue and expenses. Cash is the master clearing account for almost all the transactions of a business. Table 3.2 summarizes the diverse sources and uses of cash through a business.

TABLE 3.2—SOURCES AND USES OF CASH

Classification	Cash Sources	Cash Uses
Operating Activities	Revenue from sales and other income.	Expenses.
Financing Activities	Borrowing from debt sources.	Distributing profit to owners.
	Raising capital from equity sources.	Paying down debt.
		Returning capital to owners.
Investing Activities	Selling operating assets.	Purchasing operating assets.
	Liquidating investments.	Making other investments.

The accounting profession has adopted a threefold classification (as shown in Table 3.2) of cash flows for external financial reporting:

1. Cash flow from *operating* activities.

2. Cash flow from *financing* activities.

3. Cash flow from *investing* activities.

Accordingly, the statement of cash flows presented in the external financial reports of a business follows this threefold classification scheme. *Operating activities* is the term that refers to the profit-making activities of a business—its revenue and expenses. Any extraordinary, nonrecurring gains and losses that a business records during the period also are included in cash flow from operating activities. Certainly cash is the pivotal asset in the profit-making activities of a business. However, as Table 3.2 shows, more than just profit-making activities cause cash flows. There are also financing activities and investing activities. To get the proper perspective, cash has to be put in the context of the overall financial condition of a business, which is reported in its balance sheet.

Balance Sheet for Business Example

The purpose of a balance sheet is to provide a summary of all the assets and liabilities of a business. The assets of a business should be more than its liabilities, of course. (A business in bankruptcy may have more liabilities than assets.) The excess of assets over liabilities equals the *owners' equity* of a business. This point is expressed in the following version of the *accounting equation:*

Assets – Liabilities = Owners' Equity

Owner's equity arises from two sources: (1) capital invested in the business by the owners, and (2) profit made by the business that is retained and not distributed to the owners. This second source of owners' equity is generally called *retained earnings*. Most businesses do not distribute their entire annual earnings to their owners. Therefore, businesses accumulate a substantial amount of retained earnings over the years. Indeed, for a mature business, retained earnings can be many times the amount of capital invested by owners.

More properly, a balance sheet is called a *statement of financial condition;* and, in fact, this title is used in the financial reports of most businesses. Nevertheless, the informal term balance sheet is very widely used. The term derives from the two-sided nature of this financial statement, which is summarized in the *accounting equation:*

Assets = Liabilities + Owners' Equity

(As just mentioned, liabilities can be subtracted from assets to determine owners' equity, which is another version of the accounting equation.)

A balance sheet is not prepared in a slipshod, arbitrary fashion. The balance sheet is one of the primary financial statements in the *external* financial reports of a business. External financial reports circulate outside the confines of a business; they are issued to its lenders and outside shareowners, as well as to other interested parties. In preparing financial statements for its external financial reports, the chief financial and accounting officers of the business are (or should be!) very aware that the statements should conform with *generally accepted accounting principles* (GAAP). These are the ground rules for the public reporting of financial statements. It would be extremely difficult to justify departures from these financial accounting and reporting standards. Indeed, such departures, if material, constitute prima facie evidence of financial fraud.

Financial accounting reporting standards have been developed over many years. The principal purposes of developing GAAP are to ensure *adequate disclosure* to the outside stakeholders of a business and to achieve *reasonable uniformity* in profit accounting methods and in the valuation of assets and liabilities across all businesses. Table 3.3 presents the balance sheet for the business example introduced earlier in the chapter, in accordance with GAAP, of course.

The balance sheet format in Table 3.3 follows standard

TABLE 3.3—BALANCE SHEET AT END AND START OF YEAR

	End of Year	Start of Year
Current Assets		
Cash	$ 3,265,000	$ 3,735,000
Accounts Receivable	5,000,000	4,680,000
Inventory	8,450,000	7,515,000
Prepaid Expenses	960,000	685,000
Total Current Assets	$17,675,000	$16,615,000
Long-Term Operating Assets		
Property, Plant, and Equipment	$16,500,000	$13,450,000
Accumulated Depreciation	(4,250,000)	(3,465,000)
Cost Less Depreciation	$12,250,000	$ 9,985,000
Goodwill	$ 7,850,000	$ 6,950,000
Accumulated Amortization	(2,275,000)	(1,950,000)
Cost Less Amortization	$ 5,575,000	$ 5,000,000
Total Assets	$35,500,000	$31,600,000
Current Liabilities		
Accounts Payable	$ 3,320,000	$ 2,675,000
Accrued Expenses	1,515,000	1,035,000
Income Tax Payable	165,000	82,000
Short-Term Notes Payable	3,125,000	3,000,000
Total Current Liabilities	$ 8,125,000	$ 6,792,000
Long-Term Notes Payable	$ 4,250,000	$ 3,750,000
Stockholders' Equity		
Capital Stock—800,400 shares at end and 770,400 shares at start of year	$ 8,125,000	$ 7,950,000
Retained Earnings	15,000,000	13,108,000
Total Owners' Equity	$23,125,000	$21,058,000
Total Liabilities and Stockholders' Equity	$35,500,000	$31,600,000

practice. *Current*, or short-term, high-turnover assets are listed first. Longer-term, low-turnover assets are listed second. (In certain specialized industries, such as public utilities, assets are presented in just the reverse order.) The accumulated amounts of depreciation and amortization are deducted from the original costs of these assets, instead of disclosing only the net balances of the assets. Current (short-term) liabilities are listed first, followed by the long-term liabilities. Then the stockholders' (owners') equity sources are presented for the business, which is organized legally as a corporation.

The first three current liabilities reported in the balance sheet (see Table 3.3) are generated by the profit-making activities of the business. These operating liabilities are discussed earlier in the chapter. The total of these three liabilities is $5,000,000. Compared with the company's $35,500,000 year-end assets, there is still $30,500,000 remaining to be accounted for. Where did the $30,500,000 come from? What are the sources of capital that provided this money for the company's assets?

The business's sources of capital are shown in the shaded area of the balance sheet (Table 3.3). In summary, the business borrowed a total of $7,375,000 on short-term and long-term interest-bearing debt. And, it has $23,125,000 total owners' equity at the end of the year. Chapter 4 examines the debt and equity sources that provide capital to businesses for their assets.

Capsule Summary

Businesses that sell products need certain key assets to make sales and to carry on their operations. They need an adequate *working cash balance*. Extending credit to their customers means that they have *accounts receivable*. A product-oriented business carries a stockpile of products awaiting sale, which is called *inventory*. In addition, a business needs a diverse array of long-term tangible assets to carry on its operations, which has the generic name of *property, plant, and equipment*. These *fixed assets*, as they are also called, include land and buildings, vehicles, office equipment, machines and tools. These assets can be leased instead of being bought outright. Long-term-purchase-type leases are recorded and reported as assets. Short-term leases, on the other hand, are not reported as assets in a company's financial report.

The revenue and expenses levels of a business drive the levels of the operating assets that a business needs. Managers need to understand these vital connections in order to plan for and to exercise control over the assets used in the profit-making activities of their business. In other words, the revenue and profit goals of a business determine in large part the asset needs of the business. The asset requirements of a business, in turn, determine the amount of capital that the business must secure from its debt and equity sources. Capital is not a free good, which the next chapter explains.

4

RAISING CAPITAL: THE ULTIMATE SALE

"Show me the money!"
—Cameron Crowe, from the screenplay
for *Jerry Maguire* (1996)

Years ago, the technology industry was launched and driven into the mainstream of the United States economy by such industry giants as Hewlett-Packard, Yahoo!, Microsoft, and Intel. As difficult as it may seem, these companies were all at one time or another small start-up enterprises struggling like most other businesses with managing their business interests and developing economically sustainable models. The ultimate successes of the companies are (needless to say) well-known and have been documented countless times. At the root of their successes was the ability to secure, at the most opportune time, all of the essential ingredients needed to build a business: leadership, vision, talent, planning, determination, the all-important proper amount and type of capital to support the business concept, and a little luck. Big or small, public or private, foreign or domestic, one month new or 20 years old, it really doesn't matter. Securing and managing capital resources represents the lifeline of any company looking to operate in today's challenging economic climate.

Before exploring the process of how capital is secured/raised, it is worthwhile to define what *capital* is. Although there are countless technical and/or theoretical definitions available (to peruse at your leisure), when implementing a new business concept, there really is only one statement that captures the real essence of capital—*"It takes money to make money."* Launching any new business concept, from the aspiring entrepreneur designing a new software product from his or her home office to an executive of a multinational corporation looking to expand foreign distribution channels for new product introductions, requires capital (also known as money, greenbacks, etc.) as a basis to execute the business plan. It's no secret that one of the most common reasons businesses fail is a lack of or inappropriately structured capital resources.

This chapter explores the process of raising capital, the different types of capital available, the sources and risks associated with each type of capital, and the tools needed to successfully secure the almighty dollar and to take an idea from a conceptual stage to a viable business entity. It is important to keep in mind that capital should not be perceived as just the amount of "cash on hand" but rather as the amount of financial resources available to support the execution of a business plan. This point will be clearly illustrated as our discussion on raising/securing capital is expanded.

Tools Needed to Raise Capital

Before all of you aspiring entrepreneurs and corporate ladder climbers can raise capital, it is extremely important that you understand what tools you require. The starting point for raising/securing capital resides in one simple document—*the Business Plan*. This document represents management's foundation and justification for birthing, growing, operating, and/or selling a business based on the economic environment present. Without it, management is left to operate a business in the dark, attempting to guess or intuit the best course of action to pursue. Or, in other words, companies all too often proceed with strategies of "We've always done it like that" or "This is how the industry has operated for the past umpteen years," rather than really evaluating and investigating the economic markets in which they operate.

Business plans come in a variety of shapes, sizes, forms, and structures and often take on the characteristics and traits of the business founder(s). Some sections of the business plan may be developed in depth, whereas other sections may be presented in a quasi-summary format as the needed data, information, knowledge, and so on, is not readily available (for presentation). For example, a founder of a fledgling software company may be able to provide a complete analysis on the software product developed, the underlying code used, and even the product's packaging. However, when asked about the real-market demand for the product, distribution channels available, competition present, and/or the best method to price the product, the founder may

struggle with providing solid, third-party-corroborated information. Herein lies the first lesson of developing a business plan. The business plan should be built from the outside looking in so any reasonable party can clearly, concisely, and efficiently understand the business concept.

As previously noted, business plans come in a multitude of formats and structures and can include a variety of information, data, graphs, charts, reports, financial projections, and so on.

Four Main Elements of a Good Business Plan

1. *Executive Summary:* The executive summary represents a brief overview of the business concept in terms of the market opportunity present, the operational logistics required to bring a product and/or service to market, the management team that is going to make it happen, and the eventual potential economic return available, including the amount of capital needed to execute the plan. This section of the business plan is really nothing more than a summary of the entire business concept presented in a neat and tidy overview of usually not more than five pages (and hopefully shorter). Although the meat of the business plan resides in the remainder of the document, this section is the most critical in terms of attracting capital and financing source interest. Basically, the capital/financing sources must be able to conceptualize, understand, and justify the business concept from the information presented in the executive summary. It must excite the readers, peak their interest, and move them with a sense of urgency to pursue the business opportunity at hand.

2. *Market for the Products or Services:* This section of the business plan is often the most important, in that it substantiates the need for a product and/or service that is not being fulfilled within the current economic environment. Yes, it's hard to believe that the authors of this book, being accountants, would place marketing above finance and accounting issues; but the fact of the matter is that without a viable market present, the only thing left to account for are losses (and we all know how much capital/financing sources love them). Beyond providing information and support on the market size, characteristics, and trends, a clear understanding of the business's competitive niche, target market, and specific marketing strategies must also be presented. Quantifying the size of the market in coordination with qualifying the market need supports the basis of the business concept but represents only half the battle (and often the easier of the two halves). Identifying the specific niche and target market and developing an effective marketing strategy to capitalize on the opportunity present is often more challenging and critical to the future success of the business. In addition, a summary of the marketplace competition is usually provided to identify and properly manage these associated risks.

3. *Company Operating Overview:* This segment of the business plan addresses a number of operational issues, including personnel requirements, technological needs, locations (e.g., office, production/manufacturing, warehouse/distribution), company infrastructure requirements, international considerations, professional/expert counsel resources, and the like. Clearly, the market segment of the business plan drives various business operating elements in terms of the resources needed to implement and execute the plan. For example, if a company is planning on expanding into new foreign markets where the local government still "influences" the distribution channels, then the operating segment needs to address how the product will be distributed and which international partners will be essential to the process. In addition, business plans quite often dedicate a large portion of this segment to providing an overview of the management team in terms of both their past credentials and their responsibilities with the new business concept moving forward. The market may be ripe and capital plentiful; but without a qualified management team, the business concept will more often than not sink.

4. *Financial Segment:* In a sense, this section brings all of the elements of the business plan together from an accounting and/or financing perspective. Financial forecasts or pro formas are prepared to project the anticipated economic performance of the business concept based on the information and data presented in the business plan. The market segment tends to drive the revenue portion of the forecasts, as the information accumulated and presented here substantiates items such as potential unit sales growth (in relation to the size of the market), pricing, and revenue sources by product and service. The expense element of the forecasts is often driven by the operating segment of the business plan, as the business cost structure in terms of personnel, assets, company infrastructure, and so on, is addressed here. When all of the elements of the business plan are put together in this section, not only is the forecast profit-and-loss or income statement produced, but, just as important, the projected balance sheet and cash flow statement are generated as well. And you guessed it, with all of this information now in hand, the capital required to execute the business plan should be readily quantifiable.

As important as the business plan is, two critical issues warrant further discussion in relation to raising capital. The first issue resides in the management team (which was touched on earlier) responsible for executing the business plan. The people behind the opportunity are, in effect, the business plan; that is, financing and capital sources are lured in by business plans and can easily turn over any concept to a slew of professionals for further due diligence, reviews, evaluations, critique, and so on. If a concern is present over the technological basis within a biomedical company, then medical- or technology-based professionals can be brought in to complete additional due diligence and to either approve or can the idea. However, the management team standing behind the business plan and its execution is really where the capital and financing sources invest. The integrity, qualifications, experience, determination, passion, and commitment displayed by the management team are of utmost importance. If there are any concerns with them, the capital and financing sources have their out.

The second issue resides in the notion of selling the concept. In today's economic environment, new ideas and business plans are produced by the tens of thousands each and every year (and those are the ones that actually make it to somewhat of a formal presentation stage). Capital and financing sources are presented with these plans daily and are constantly challenged to focus on the best and brightest ideas. As such, selling or marketing the business concept (to capital and financial sources) becomes the most difficult task in launching the business concept. It's one thing to get people interested in the business plan and a good story. It's an entirely different thing to actually get money committed to the concept. The lead party responsible for securing the needed capital or financing will find that 110% of his or her time will be consumed with this process. And as essential as it is for the party responsible for securing capital or financing to display passion, determination, confidence, reliability, commitment, knowledge, experience, more important is the ability to handle rejection, because it is far easier (and there are far more reasons) for capital sources to say no than yes. Selling the concept, in effect, becomes the greatest sales challenge most business executives will ever face.

Types of Capital

For the sake of simplicity, we'll define *capital* as the amount of financial resources needed to implement and to execute a business plan. Financial resources come in countless forms and structures but basically boil down to two main types: **debt** and **equity**.

1. *Debt* represents a liability to the business because it is generally governed by set repayment terms as provided by the party extending credit. For example, a bank lends $2 million to a company to purchase additional production equipment to support the expansion of a manufacturing facility. The bank will establish the terms and conditions of the debt agreement, including the interest rate (6%), repayment term (60 months), periodic payment, and the collateral required. The company must adhere to these terms and conditions or run the risk of default. Using the aforementioned scenario, the company would be required to support a debt service payment of $38,666 per month to repay the debt per the terms and conditions established.

2. *Equity* represents an investment in the business. It does not have set repayment terms, but it does have a right to future earnings and may be provided dividends or distributions if profits and cash flows are available. For example, a software technology company requires approximately $2 million in capital to develop and launch a new Internet-based software solution. A niche venture capitalist group invests the required capital under the terms and conditions present in the equity offering, which includes

percentage of ownership in the future company, rights to future earnings, representation on the board of directors, preferred versus common equity status, conversion rights, and antidilution provisions. Under this scenario, the company is not required to remit any payments to the capital source per a set repayment agreement, but it has given up a partial right to ownership (which can be even more costly).

So there you have it, simple isn't it, debt or equity, your two types of capital. But let's explore both of these capital types in more depth to expand on how many variations, alternatives, subtypes, and classifications are present within each one. If it were as easy as debt versus equity, there wouldn't be much of a need for bankers, accountants, investment bankers, venture capitalists, and the like (which, of course, to most business owners would be a welcome change).

Debt

Debt is best evaluated by understanding its two most important characteristics: **maturity** and **security.** *Maturity* refers to the length of time the debt instrument has until repayment. In the case of trade accounts payable, vendors will often extend payment terms of "net 30" to their customers, which require repayment within 30 days of receipt of the product or service. Any debt instrument requiring repayment within one year or less would be classified as current or short-term on the balance sheet. Logic would then dictate that long-term debt would be any obligation present with a repayment due of one year or greater. For example, mortgages provided by banks for real estate purchases are often structured over a 30-year period. Hence, any of the debt repayment due past the first year would be considered long-term in nature.

Security refers to the type of asset the debt is supported by or secured with. Using the previous example of a bank lending $2 million to support the expansion of a manufacturing facility, the bank would take a "secured position" in the assets acquired for the $2 million loan; that is, the bank would issue a public notice (generally through the issuance of a Uniform Commercial Code, or UCC, document) that it has lent money to the manufacturing company and that it has a first right to the equipment financed in the case of a future default. This provides the bank with additional comfort that if the company cannot cover its debt service obligations, it (the bank) actually has a tangible asset that it can attach to and liquidate if needed to cover the outstanding obligation. Other forms of security also include intangible assets (e.g., a patent or rights to intellectual property), inventory, trade accounts receivable, real estate, and future cash flow streams (e.g., a future annuity payment stream that guarantees X dollars to be paid each year). It would be logical to assume that most companies that provide credit to businesses would prefer to be in a secured status to reduce the inherent risks present. However, this is logistically almost impossible due to the nature of how most businesses operate on a day-to-day basis. Hence, secured creditors tend to be associated with credit extension agreements that are both relatively large (from a dollars committed standpoint) and cover longer periods of time.

On the opposite end of secured lenders are the unsecured creditors. This type of creditor tends to be the vendors that provide basic goods and services to a company for general operating requirements. Examples of these vendors are professional service firms, utility and telecommunication companies, material suppliers, and general office services. Unsecured creditors obviously take on more risk, in that a specific company asset is not pledged as collateral to support the repayment of the obligation. This risk is mitigated by the fact that unsecured creditors tend to extend credit with shorter repayment terms (e.g., the invoice is due on net 20-day terms) and in lower dollar amounts. In addition, if unsecured creditors are concerned about getting paid, then other strategies may be used, including requiring a deposit or a prepayment to be made.

Beyond the maturity and the security elements of debt are a number of additional attributes, including the use of personal guarantees (i.e., a party outside of the company guarantees the repayment of a debt, similar to how a cosigner works), priority creditors (i.e., certain creditors to a business always achieve a priority status due to the type of obligation present, such as payroll taxes withheld for the Internal Revenue Service), subordination agreements (i.e., a creditor specifically takes a secondary position to a secured lender), default provisions (i.e., in the event of a loan default, statement of the remedies of the parties involved), and lending agreement covenants (i.e., the company must perform at a certain level to avoid triggering a default). Rather than expand on these debt attributes in this segment, a more complete discussion is provided in Chapter 12, which overviews terminating a business and the importance of how debt is structured when a liquidation of business assets occurs.

Equity

Equity is best evaluated by understanding its two most important characteristics: **preference** and **management influence.**

Preference refers to the fact that certain types of equity have preferences to earnings and, if needed, company assets over other forms of equity. For example, a series "A" preferred stock may be issued to investors who have an interest in making an equity investment but want to protect or prioritize their investments in relation to the common shareholders or another series of preferred stock. A series "B" preferred stock may hold a lower preference to the series "A" preferred stock in terms of asset liquidations but may have a slightly higher dividend yield attached or offered with a warrant that allows it to purchase common shares at a later date at a favorable price. Actually, the features built into preferred stock are almost endless and can create a large number of different types of preferred stock (i.e., "A" through "Z").

For common equity, preferences can also exist. Common stock type "A" may have full voting rights and dividends (after the preferred shareholders receive their dividend), whereas a common stock type "B" may have rights to dividends but cannot vote. To list all of the potential preferences and/or features built into equity instruments (the ability to convert, antidilution provisions, cumulative versus noncumulative dividends, voting rights, acceleration clauses, liquidation criteria, etc., etc.) is well beyond the scope of this book. However, the key point to remember is that equity investors will attempt to secure as many preferences and features that protect their interests as possible. While this may be good for them, it may not be in the best interests of the company and may restrict its ability to operate further down the road.

The concept of *management influence* is centered in the fact that when equity capital is raised, the provider of the capital is considered an owner or a shareholder of the company. By its very nature, this entitles the shareholder to have a say in the company's operations (unless otherwise restricted) with the ability to vote for the board of directors and on other critical matters (e.g., approving the company's external auditor or allocating equity to be distributed to company management). This management influence can be extended significantly when preferences are factored into the equation.

It is very common for early-stage equity investors to secure the right to influence the board of directors more actively. For example, if a company has determined that five board members are needed, the early-stage investors may carve out the right to elect two of these board members, and the other investors can elect the remaining three. This provides the early-stage equity investors with additional management control of the business during its critical formation years. If you remember one thing when raising equity capital, it should be this: Be prepared to comanage the business with your new best friends, as your dictatorship will give way to a democracy (hopefully).

So, the real question that needs to be answered is simple: What form of capital, debt, or equity is best suited for a company? Well, this really depends on the company's stage in terms of its operating history, industry profile, profitability levels, asset structure, future growth prospects, and general capital requirements and considered in relation to where the sources of capital lie.

Sources of Capital

In the 1996 movie *Jerry Maguire*, Cuba Gooding Jr., playing a fictitious professional football player named Rod Tidwell, uttered the now somewhat infamous line, "Show me the money!" These four words sum up the capital-raising process as best as any, in that until you have the money in hand, a business concept is really nothing more than the paper on which the business plan is written. And as my dad has always told me, that and $1 should get you a cup of coffee at the local fast-food restaurant (or $5 so you can be covered at Starbucks). So with this in mind, let's look to the potential sources of capital available to launch your new business, open a new product/service niche within a corporate conglomerate, or acquire a pesky competitor. The sources listed are not meant to be all-inclusive but rather provide an overview of the variety of avenues available to raise capital and the pluses and minuses associated with each one.

• *Family, Friends, and Close Business Associates (FF&CBA):* These people have been one of the primary capital sources to launch new business concepts since the beginning of time and will most likely continue to fill this role in the future. These sources range from the business founders tapping their own creditworthiness or resources (i.e., savings, home equity, credit cards) to having Mom and Dad or a trusted business associate step up with the needed seed money to launch the company. Generally, this type of capital tends to be for lower dollar amounts, geared toward equity as opposed to debt (given the uncertain nature of the business and the higher risks present in terms of generating cash flow), and provided to closely held and/or family-operated businesses. However, debt can be effectively utilized with more mature businesses generating solid profitability with some type of security present (such as real estate).

The good news is that raising capital from FF&CBAs can often be completed quickly without a significant amount of "legal paperwork" and/or similar investor creditability issues being present. The bad news is twofold: (1) The amount of capital available from these sources is often restricted. It is one thing to pull together a couple of hundred thousand dollars; but when a business concept needs a million or two, well, not too many FF&CBAs have this type of liquidity available (unless your last name is Dupont or Getty). (2) Having unsophisticated FF&CBAs provide capital to a business carries with it unforeseen risks and emotional elements that can explode.

Reporting back to a seasoned investor that a business concept didn't work and that their investment is worthless may not be the most pleasant task in the world, but at least the investor was aware of the risks. Telling your aunt and uncle that you've just blown through their nest egg and the business has failed . . . well, let's just say that your name may be equated to a four-letter word when spoken in subsequent family gatherings. The external costs of losing a family member's investment can be 10 times the actual internal amount of capital invested.

♦ **Private Capital:** In the business world, a large number of private capital sources are available and include such sources as venture capitalists (VCs), investment bankers, angels or white knights, and similar types of private investment groups. Private capital sources come in a variety of shapes, sizes, and forms; but all tend to gravitate toward a common set of criteria: (1) The dollar size of the capital commitment is generally much larger. These groups are comprised of highly trained and sophisticated professionals responsible for managing large pools of capital and, as such, apply the concept of "economy of scale" frequently. (2) These groups tend to be more risk-based capital sources and look for higher returns from equity-driven transactions. These groups are comfortable with making equity investments in relatively early-stage businesses without proven profitability (but with significant potential) or with structuring risk-based debt facilities to support a "higher risk" business opportunity (e.g., the debt is secured by nothing more than goodwill). Just remember, higher investment returns will be expected for taking on the added risk. (3) These groups are not looking to invest in a company with a revenue potential of $10 million after five years (similar to a solid regionally based construction subcontracting company). With the types of capital these groups have available, the business opportunity must be relatively grand to peak their interest. Although the next Microsoft is not needed, a solid opportunity to produce in excess of $100 million in annual revenue (over a reasonable time) generating solid profits, all combined with an efficient exit strategy, is.

The good news with private capital is that larger capital amounts are available, the groups are generally very sophisticated and can provide invaluable management support, and the capital is often equity-based so that aspiring businesses in need of large capital infusions (e.g., a biotechnology company) have a resource. The bad news is that these groups tend to ask for (and receive) a higher ownership stake in the business and thus can exert a significant amount of management control and influence. In addition, these groups retain highly trained professionals who are very demanding when they are undertaking their investment review/evaluation process. If your case is not ready to be presented, then don't do it, as private capital sources will not even give you the time of day without a business concept or plan that can stand a punishing evaluation.

♦ **Banks, Leasing Companies, and Other Lenders:** Debt capital sources (including banks, leasing companies, government-backed programs [e.g., the federal government's SBA program], hard money lenders, and factoring companies) have evolved over the past hundred years into one of the most sophisticated capital source groups around. For almost any debt-based need, some type of lender is readily available in the market. Once again, these groups, similar to private sources, tend to look for a common set of characteristics when extending capital in the form of debt (but just different): (1) Security of some sort must be present (e.g., an asset or a personal guarantee). Lenders like a secondary form of repayment in case the borrower cannot cover the debt service requirement. (2) Debt providers tend to look for more stable business environments where a company has been in business for an extended period of time and has a proven track record. This is not to say that businesses must generate a profit to secure debt financing but it certainly helps. (3) Debt capital sources are more conservative in nature. Their goal is to ensure that the debt can be repaid while generating an adequate return. Maintaining solid financial returns and strong ratios is more important than watching the company double in size, placing too much pressure on its leverage ratios.

From a positive perspective, debt capital sources cover a broad spectrum of financing requirements ranging from as little as

$50,000 (a niche factoring or a leasing company providing capital to small businesses) to billions of dollars (the world's largest banks providing financing for a multibillion-dollar public company buyout). In addition, management control is not relinquished because debt providers generally do not have a say in an ongoing business. On the flip side, security in some form is usually required, which places business (and potentially personal) assets at risk. Also, the debt must be repaid per the terms and conditions established, regardless of whether the company's performance allows for the repayment. Unlike equity investments, which tend to only generate a distribution of earnings or dividends as the company's performance dictates, debt repayment terms must be adhered to or the company can suffer the wrath of its creditors demanding repayment.

+ ***Public Capital—Wall Street:*** Almost every business owner, professional, and manager is aware of the public markets available to trade stocks and bonds, including the New York Stock Exchange, the Nasdaq, and similar venues. Both equity (e.g., the common stock of Microsoft) and debt (e.g., United States Treasury bills) instruments are actively traded in these open markets. While the allure of the public markets is very appealing to business owners and often is viewed as the endgame (i.e., "I took my company public, and now I am worth X millions of dollars"), the reality of operating in a public market can be very different. As such, public capital sources have developed a unique set of qualifications in terms of making it the most appropriate capital source to pursue.

+ Think big! Public markets are better suited for companies thinking in hundreds of millions or billions than those thinking in mere millions.

+ Think public! Basically, all of your company's information, financial records, activities, and so on will be available for public viewing. You must be prepared not only to disclose the information but also to make sure the disclosure is prepared in the proper format.

+ Understand risk! Consider whether the returns and rewards for being public are adequate in relation to the risks you and your business assume.

Public capital markets' positive attributes include having access to extremely large capital levels, which can tap the widest range of sources available (stretching the globe). There really isn't any deal too big for public markets, as the United States' $7 trillion of outstanding debt clearly displays. The liquidity that public markets offer (i.e., investments can be efficiently bought, sold, and traded), the ability to establish fair market values almost instantaneously, and access to both debt and equity sources also represent positive attributes. But as we all know, there is no utopia from a capital sources standpoint, so there must be a downside to public capital as well. One negative element is the cost. Staying in compliance with all of the public reporting requirements can be extremely expensive. Another negative is the added management exposure. Even when fraud is not present, investors in public debt and equity instruments can turn into a company's worst nightmare when things aren't going as planned. Also negative is the additional burden placed on the management team, which can be extensive and can distract the company from actually running its business. And finally is the misconception about liquidity. Just because your company is publicly traded does not mean that liquidity is present. Smaller companies' (i.e., with less than $100 million of market capitalization) stocks are often not actively traded on the open market, which can make selling or buying a large block of stock more difficult (not to mention the scrutiny insiders received when undertaking these transactions). Although plenty of small companies are publicly traded, public markets are generally best suited for the big boys of corporate America.

So there you have it—FF&CBAs; private capital sources; banks, leasing companies, and other lenders; and public markets. All are viable and accessible capital sources with specific characteristics and traits present providing each source with competitive strengths and weaknesses. However, the sources-of-capital discussion would not be complete if we didn't look a little deeper into three more-creative capital sources that can often be overlooked.

1. *The ability of a company to generate positive internal cash flow and to reinvest this asset internally as needed.* Countless examples of this strategy are present, including a medical company (such as Merck) using positive cash flow from one line of pharmaceutical products to support research and development on a new drug; to a gold mining company (such as Newmont) using its cash flow from a proven gold ore reserve to explore and develop a promising new gold ore reserve; to a temporary staffing company allocating its positive cash flow from a strong staffing technology group in one region to develop a new market in another region. Positive internal cash flow is a real source of capital to finance business operations that is both readily available and, logistically, much easier to secure. However, it should be kept in mind that positive internal cash flow must be managed and invested appropriately within the best interests of the company and its shareholders.

2. *The ability of a company to utilize creative forms of unsecured financing from vendors, partners, customers, and so on, to provide a real source of capital.* In relation to this, the following examples of "creative" forms of unsecured financing have been provided:

- Requiring customers to prepay 20% of their order as a requirement to start the production and future delivery process. In addition, terms such as "20% down, 30% upon half completion, and the remainder due upon delivery" can also be utilized.

- Asking key product suppliers to grant extended terms from 30 days to 90 days during certain seasonal periods (e.g., to support higher sales during the holiday season), which are then brought back to a 30-day term when the cash flow from the increased sales catches up.

- Working with a downstream customer to obtain funding to develop a new product or technology that can greatly improve the customer's future performance. For example, a hardware technology company may need to ensure that software is available for use with their new products. Hence, a capital infusion into the software supplier to develop the technology for which they receive a royalty from future sales may be warranted.

3. *The securing of gifts.* Governments, universities, and non-profit organizations have resources available in the form of grants, loan-interest-rate loans (with limited downside risk), incentive credits, and so on, which are intended to be used for special interests or purposes. The idea is to provide this capital to an organization that will use it in the best interest of the general public. Biotechnology companies often secure research grants for work being completed on disease detection, prevention, and possible cure. Educational organizations may receive grants to help retrain a displaced group of workers or a poorly educated workforce. Under either scenario, the same concept is present in terms of committing the capital for a common good.

The aforementioned additional sources of capital were presented to highlight how many potential sources of capital are actually available and, to a certain degree, how creative companies become when securing capital. And just like the other sources of capital, these three additional sources all come with positive and negative attributes attached. The point is, capital sources come in a variety of sizes, shapes, and forms, which need to be clearly understood prior to approaching and pursuing the appropriate source.

Above all else, don't overlook a potential source of capital. All too often an entrepreneur will not look in places that, in fact, can be good sources of capital. Of course, you should always consider the cost of capital. As you've undoubtedly heard before "there's no such thing as a free lunch." Whoever puts up capital demands to be compensated for the risks of investing in your business. Their demands may be high. You'll have to decide on this relative to what other sources of capital are available to you.

A Business Legal Structure's Influence on Capital

Before bringing all of the elements discussed thus far on raising capital together, a quick review of the different types of legal structures available to operate a business is warranted. Not only are significant tax, cost, and liability issues present when choosing the type of legal business entity to form; but the impact that the business legal entity will have on securing capital must be considered. Certain business forms will limit the type and the amount of capital that can be secured, especially from an equity perspective.

Table 4.1 provides a quick overview of the major types of business entities and the pros and cons associated with each one.

Four key issues really drive the formation of a legal business entity.

1. *How complex and expensive will it be to form the business?* If you want cheap, easy, and simple, try a sole proprietorship or partnership because LLCs and corporations are more complex to form, manage, and operate.

2. *What type of liability protection is desired?* For most, the thought of being able to shield personal assets (to the extent provided by law) from business activities is very desirable. Hence, the corporate or LLC structures are better equipped to address this issue.

3. *What type of tax planning and objectives are being pursued?* If losses at the business level are expected and can be utilized at the personal level, then an LLC, partnership, sole proprietorship, or potentially a subchapter S corporation should be considered.

4. *What type and amount of capital will be needed to support the business?* Having large amounts of capital available from multiple sources would drive the business entity toward the LLC status or, most likely, the regular C corporation structure.

A couple of additional items should be noted when considering the type of legal entity that should be formed. There is nothing that precludes a business from first forming using a simple structure such as a partnership and then changing its legal structure down the road to a regular C corporation. This occurs all of the time, based on how businesses evolve and markets change. Generally, it is easier logistically to move from simple business forms to more complex structures than vice versa. Also, it should be noted that debt capital will be available to basically any legal business type as long as the criteria used by lenders is met. Although the "corporate" status may lend more creditability to the process of obtaining debt, lenders still look to the same fundamentals regardless of the business type (i.e., "Will I get my money back with a reasonable return?").

In closing this brief discussion on the different types of business legal structures, every general manager, owner, executive,

TABLE 4.1—TYPES OF BUSINESS ENTITIES

Business Type	Pros	Cons
Sole Proprietorship and Partnership	Inexpensive, easy, and quick formation possible. Structure is simple to understand and to implement. Certain tax advantages present to owners due to flow-through status.	Legal structure does not provide for liability shield for business claims against personal assets. Equity capital sources will be limited to FF&CBAs (at best).
Limited Liability Company (LLC)	New business form that combines liability benefits of a corporation with flow-through tax benefits. More flexible than a subchapter S corporation in that other legal entities may invest equity in the LLC.	Relatively new business type that is more complex and expensive to establish. Not ideally suited to attract large private equity investments looking for liquidity through public offering.
Subchapter S Corporation	Liability shield present due to corporate structure. Tax benefits available to owners due to flow-through status.	Ownership limited to maximum of 75 individuals. Other legal entities cannot invest in company. Tax restrictions apply to more than 2% owners, which limit some potential tax benefits. Corporate compliance and reporting issues more complex and expensive.
Regular C Corporation	Liability shield present due to corporate structure. Equity capital sources may come from individuals and/or businesses with no restriction on number of types of investors present.	No flow-through tax benefits present as all transactions are taxed at corporate level. Double taxation problems exist with corporate earnings and dividends. Corporate compliance and reporting issues more complex and expensive.

officer, board member, managing partner, and/or other senior-level manager needs to keep the liability issue in perspective. Don't expect the legal structure of the business entity to protect you from personal claims, especially when the willful intent to defraud is present. The current political, social, and business environment is hell-bent on aggressively pursuing white-collar criminals as a result of the high-profile business failures from 2000 through 2003.

The legal system has always been willing to "pierce the corporate veil." In other words, prosecutors and plaintiffs have been able to break through the corporate shield in order to get at those individuals responsible for wrongdoing. The limited liability feature of the corporate form of business organization has a legitimate purpose, of course. However, this feature of the legal entity was never envisioned to protect crooks and fraud perpetrators.

Understanding and Managing Capital's Risks: Bringing It All Together

Raising or securing capital is without question one of the most difficult and time-consuming tasks the executive management team of a company will undertake. Preparing, packaging, marketing, negotiating, and closing the "deal" can easily consume 50% to 100% of an executive's time, depending on the stage of the company. For a start-up operation, chief executive officers (CEOs) and other senior executives often find themselves closing on one round of financing, resting for a day or two, and then starting the process all over again, looking for the next financing source. For a chief financial officer (CFO) of a publicly traded company, the majority of her or his time may be consumed in preparing information for the capital sources and markets and then managing the capital sources expectations, inquiries, and/or other needs. To a certain degree, managing the capital sources, after the capital is secured, can be even more challenging and difficult than raising the capital itself.

Managing this element of capital risks is more intangible in nature, as it is geared toward relationships and communication efforts as opposed to hard financial and accounting data. Now, let's turn our attention toward the more tangible elements of managing capital risks from an accounting and financial perspective. Table 4.2 illustrates these capital risks for an Equity scenario and a Debt scenario.

As is evident from the information provided, all elements of this business are exactly the same except for the way the business was capitalized. Under the equity scenario, a total of $2,000,000

TABLE 4.2—CAPITAL STRUCTURE COMPARISON

XYZ Wholesale, Inc.

Summary Balance Sheet	Equity Scenario FYE 12/31/00	Debt Scenario FYE 12/31/00
Current Assets		
Cash and Equivalents	$ 439,569	$ 94,929
Trade Receivables, Net	1,272,083	1,272,083
Inventory	1,383,391	1,383,391
Total Current Assets	$3,095,043	$2,750,403
Fixed and Other Assets		
Property, Plant, and Equipment, Net	$1,250,000	$1,250,000
Other Assets	75,000	75,000
Total Fixed and Other Assets	$1,325,000	$1,325,000
Total Assets	$4,420,043	$4,075,403
Current Liabilities		
Trade Payables	$1,037,543	$1,037,543
Accrued Liabilities	51,877	51,877
Line of Credit Borrowings	0	0
Current Portion of Long-Term Liabilities	0	300,000
Total Current Liabilities	$1,089,420	$1,389,420
Long-Term Liabilities		
Notes Payable, Less Current Portion	$ 0	$ 900,000
Other Long-Term Liabilities	125,000	125,000
Total Long-Term Liabilities	$ 125,000	$1,025,000
Total Liabilities	$1,214,420	$2,414,420

(Continued)

TABLE 4.2—(Continued)

XYZ Wholesale, Inc.

Summary Balance Sheet	Equity Scenario FYE 12/31/00	Debt Scenario FYE 12/31/00
Equity		
Common and Preferred Equity, $1 per Share	$2,000,000	$ 500,000
Retained Earnings	750,000	750,000
Current Earnings	455,623	410,983
Total Equity	$3,205,623	$1,600,983
Total Liabilities and Equity	$4,420,043	$4,075,403

Summary Income Statement	Equity Scenario FYE 12/31/00	Debt Scenario FYE 12/31/00
Revenue	$15,265,000	$15,265,000
Costs of Goods Sold	11,067,125	11,067,125
Gross Profit	$ 4,197,875	$ 4,197,875
Gross Margin	27.50%	27.50%
Selling, General, and Administrative Expenses	$ 3,251,000	$ 3,251,000
Interest Expense	0	72,000
Other (Income) Expenses	212,000	212,000
Net Profit before Tax	$ 734,875	$ 662,875
Income Tax Expense (Benefit)	279,253	251,893
Net Profit (Loss)	$ 455,623	$ 410,983

Quick Financial Analysis	Equity Scenario FYE 12/31/00	Debt Scenario FYE 12/31/00
Debt-to-Equity Ratio	0.38	1.45
Debt Service Coverage Ratio	N/A	1.10
Return on Equity	14.21%	24.74%
Return on Assets	10.31%	10.08%
Earnings per Share	$0.23	$0.82

of capital was raised, all in the form of equity. Under the debt scenario, a total of $500,000 of equity was raised and $1,500,000 of debt was secured (of which $300,000 was repaid during the year). The Income Statements are exactly the same except for the fact that the debt scenario has interest expense present. The Quick Financial Analysis highlights the key differences and indicates that by using debt the company was able to generate better returns for the equity owners as follows:

- **Returns:** The debt scenario produces a return on equity of 24.74% compared to a return on equity of 14.21% with the equity scenario while the return on assets is almost identical for both scenarios.

- **Earnings:** The debt scenario generates earnings per share of almost four times that of the equity scenario ($.82 per share compared to $.23 per share).

The only real downside lies in the fact that the debt scenario has a much higher debt-to-equity ratio present of 1.45 compared to .38 for the equity scenario in addition to having a debt service coverage ratio of approximately 1.1 (i.e., total earnings of $410,983 divided by the company's total annual debt service including loan principal payment of $300,000 and interest payments of $72,000). While using debt was beneficial in terms of enhancing returns, it placed the company in a higher risk status due to the amount of debt leverage used. This will be clearly illustrated when the next year's operating results are realized as presented in Table 4.3.

The company has gone from having a robust year with strong margins and profitability to having to deal with a recession driving sales and margins lower. While its selling, general, and administrative expenses were reduced as a result of the difficult

TABLE 4.3—CAPITAL STRUCTURE COMPARISON

XYZ Wholesale, Inc.

Summary Balance Sheet	Equity Scenario FYE 12/31/02	Debt Scenario FYE 12/31/02	Summary Income Statement	Equity Scenario FYE 12/31/02	Debt Scenario FYE 12/31/02
Current Assets			Revenue	$12,975,250	$12,975,250
Cash and Equivalents	$ 941,214	$ 263,094	Costs of Goods Sold	9,731,438	9,731,438
Trade Receivables, Net	1,081,271	1,081,271	Gross Profit	$ 3,243,813	$ 3,243,813
Inventory	1,216,430	1,216,430	Gross Margin	25.00%	25.00%
Total Current Assets	$3,238,915	$2,560,795			
Fixed and Other Assets			Selling , General, and Admininstrative Expenses	$ 2,990,920	$ 2,990,920
Property, Plant, and Equipment, Net	$1,000,000	$1,000,000	Interest Expense	0	54,000
Other Assets	75,000	75,000	Other (Income) Expenses	212,000	212,000
Total Fixed and Other Assets	$1,075,000	$1,075,000	Net Profit before Tax	$ 40,893	$ (13,108)
Total Assets	$4,313,915	$3,635,795	Income Tax Expense (Benefit)	15,539	(4,981)
			Net Profit (Loss)	$ 25,353	$ (8,127)
Current Liabilities			**Quick Financial Analysis**	Equity Scenario FYE 12/31/02	Debt Scenario FYE 12/31/02
Trade Payables	$ 912,322	$ 912,322			
Accrued Liabilities	$ 45,616	45,616	Debt-to-Equity Ratio	0.34	1.20
Line of Credit Borrowings	0	0	Debt Service Coverage Ratio	N/A	−0.02
Current Portion of Long-Term Liabilities	0	300,000	Return on Equity	0.78%	−0.49%
Total Current Liabilities	$ 957,938	$1,257,938	Return on Assets	0.59%	−0.22%
Long-Term Liabilities			Earnings per Share	$0.01	−$0.02
Notes Payable, Less Current Portion	$ 0	$ 600,000			
Other Long-Term Liabilities	125,000	125,000			
Total Long-Term Liabilities	$ 125,000	$ 725,000			
Total Liabilities	$1,082,938	$1,982,938			
Equity					
Common and Preferred Equity, $1 per Share	$2,000,000	$ 500,000			
Retained Earnings	1,205,624	1,160,984			
Current Earnings	25,353	(8,127)			
Total Equity	$3,230,977	$1,652,857			
Total Liabilities and Equity	$4,313,915	$3,635,795			

times, it was not enough to enable the company to generate a profit, using the debt-financed scenario. However, under the equity-financed scenario, the company is able to generate a small profit and to produce positive returns on assets and equity while the debt-financed company incurs a loss and negative returns. Making matters even worse is that the debt-financed company may now be in violation of certain debt covenants and in default of the loan agreement. For example, the loan agreement may read that the company needs to maintain a debt coverage service ratio of at least 1.0 and/or to produce profitable results on an annual basis (both common covenants for lending sources).

Because the company may have violated both covenants, it may be in technical default on the loan, a situation that will require a fair amount of management attention moving forward. And just to add a little more insult to injury, the real damage may not be realized until 2002 and beyond. While the equity-financed scenario provides the company with a strong balance sheet and ample financial resources to expand after the recession ends, the debt-financed scenario places the company in the difficult spot of having to restructure its balance sheet to satisfy its creditors. Thus, it may miss significant growth opportunities in 2002 and beyond, costing the company both sales and profits.

In summary, debt and equity financing strategies cut both ways. While debt financing strategies can enhance returns, they also increase the company's operating risks by leveraging its assets. In good times, when profits and cash flows are ample and everyone's making a buck, debt financing strategies look great. When the tide turns and profits dry up and cash flows become restricted, debt financing can look like the evil stepchild that nobody wants around but who must be fed (usually at the expense of some good kids). Remember, debt financing sources are focused on providing loans that generate sound returns and are repaid in a reasonable time frame. You won't get much sympathy from a bank if you ask it to suspend debt payments so you can keep a business unit open on the hopes of an eventual rebound.

Conversely, equity capital offers a chance to strengthen the balance sheet and to help manage the company's operating risks through good times and bad. Maintaining a strong balance sheet can really provide a competitive weapon when expanding a business into new markets or exploring a unique business opportunity. However, having too much equity without being able to generate adequate returns can dampen investor enthusiasm and produce a rather restless group of shareholders and board members. Remember, equity financing sources do not invest capital to watch it generate below-average returns. Equity capital, although representing a lower perceived risk to the company, is by its nature a higher-risk capital source (to the providers) and must produce a satisfactory investment return. If not, the equity capital will find an opportunity that does provide the necessary return.

Raising Capital—Revisited

Raising capital really does represent the ultimate sale in terms of convincing a capital source to actually believe in your business and to then fork over the money. Terms such as "nerve racking," "frustrating," "euphoric," and "riding a roller coaster" will become commonplace, in addition to hair loss, stress, and joy. The following **key points** regarding raising capital capture the essence of the fund-raising process as quickly as possible:

* *Be Prepared:* Like the Boy Scouts of America say, always be prepared. Capital sources expect and demand that the highest-quality information, plans, and underlying support be made available when evaluating an investment opportunity.

* *Be Persistent:* Capital sources are just looking for reasons to say no. The attributes of persistence and determination cannot be emphasized enough when pursuing and securing capital.

* *Qualify the Capital Sources:* Don't waste your time or theirs—make every effort to qualify your capital sources to ensure that the most appropriate avenue is pursued in relation to the operating status of your business. And by all means make sure the capital source is capable and accredited to support the request.

* *Communicate:* Communication efforts are critical to successfully securing and managing capital. It is extremely important to keep the capital sources up-to-date with all relevant information, good or bad.

* *Document and Disclose:* Do not underestimate the importance of properly documenting all capital-raising activities, from the initial communications to the final agreements. In addition, full and complete disclosures are a must in today's litigious environment.

* *Exit Strategies:* Remember that all capital sources will want their money back with a solid return at some point. Offer clear and reasonable exit strategies to provide the capital sources with comfort that a light will be present at the end of the tunnel (hoping that it's not a freight train barreling down in the other direction).

* *Risk/Reward Relationship:* To a capital source, equity investments carry more risk than debt investments do; and, as such, the return realized on the investment must be higher. To a business, debt can expose the company to greater risks but also higher returns. The trick is to find the right balance.

The heart of raising capital lies in a business's ability to generate a profit and positive cash flow. If this sounds familiar it should—cash flow represents the ultimate lifeline of any business operation. Understanding how a business generates and consumes cash represents the single most important item in determining if a company will be economically viable (and gain the interest of capital sources) or die a natural death (and be discarded to the mass grave of dead business plans).

Capsule Summary

A business needs to invest in a variety of assets to carry on its profit-making operations (see Chapter 3). Therefore, a business must raise the capital (mainly money) needed for investing in its assets. This is no easy task, to say the least. A business must persuade others to put their capital in the business, which invariably involves some risk to the capital provider. First and foremost, a business needs a sound business plan to convince sources of capital that it will be a good steward of the capital and will earn operating profit sufficient to pay for the use of their capital. The essential elements of a sound business plan, from the perspective of raising capital, are discussed in the chapter.

Two basic kinds of capital are available to a business: (1) capital supplied under debt contracts and (2) capital invested under equity (ownership) arrangements. The essential features of both types of capital sources are explored in the chapter. Please keep in mind that a business generates liabilities in carrying on its day-to-day operations. Buying things on credit is the main genesis of a business's operating liabilities. The non-interest-bearing operating liabilities of a business are very different from its interest-bearing debt liabilities (such as notes payable). Therefore, operating liabilities are disclosed separately from debt obligations in a business's balance sheet (statement of financial condition).

The chapter identifies where a business goes for debt and equity capital—ranging from family, friends, and close business associates; to private and public institutions that stand ready to provide debt and equity capital; to the issuance of debt and equity securities in the public markets for bonds and stocks. The chapter also looks at certain creative forms of financing, such as requiring deposits from customers when they order products and getting longer credit terms from vendors.

The chapter analyzes business legal entity structures from the perspective of raising capital. The type of legal entity chosen by a business has definite advantages and disadvantages when it comes to raising capital. The chapter also discusses the time and effort a business's executives must spend in managing its sources of capital. This important point is often underestimated. Executives spend a significant amount of time and energy in raising and renewing the business's capital sources. Without adequate capital, a business could shrivel and die. Its senior managers have to get involved and stay involved in the capital side of a business.

Return on capital ratios and other capital performance measures are explained briefly in the chapter. Last, the risks and the rewards of alternative capital sources are examined. Different capital structures are compared that illustrate these important points.

Part Two

BUILDING A BUSINESS

5

GETTING A GRIP ON PROFIT— INSTEAD OF OPERATING BY THE SEAT OF YOUR PANTS

*"When you work with numbers,
a grid of some sort proves to be extremely useful."*
—Dan Bricklin, cocreator of VisiCalc, the first PC spreadsheet

Managers get paid to make profit happen. So how do you make profit? And how do you know the amount of your profit or loss? The second of these questions is easier to answer. One of the main functions of accounting is to record the revenues and expenses (as well as any gains and losses) of a business in order to prepare a report of its profit or loss for a period of time.

Management decisions set in motion the profit-making activities of a business. The profit report is the primary source of feedback to managers on the results of their decisions. To managers, the profit report says: You've made decisions, and here are the outcomes of your decisions. A profit report is historical—backward looking. It presents the collective results of what has already happened. Management decisions are forward looking and are made to affect the course of future events, of course.

In making profit decisions, managers should focus on the relatively few fundamental factors that drive profit—what one could call the "levers of profit." Business managers need a sure-handed grip on these profit levers. This chapter explains profit-analysis techniques that help business managers to gain a better understanding of profit behavior and to make better profit decisions.

Reporting Profit Inside and Outside a Business

Inside a business, a profit report is commonly called the *P&L* (profit-and-loss) *report*. Outside a business, in the external financial reports to its shareowners, a profit report is generally called an *income statement* or *earnings statement*. The purpose of this financial statement is to present a summary of the profit-making activities of a business for a period of time. You probably know that the term *bottom line* refers to the amount of profit or loss for the period, which is the final line of the report.

Table 5.1 shows the basic format of an annual profit report, which steps down from the top line (sales revenue) to the bottom line (profit). A profit report usually includes the previous period's figures so they can be compared with those of the period just ended. In Table 5.1, the bottom line is labeled *net earnings. Net income* is also commonly used for the final profit number. Businesses that sell products disclose cost of goods (products) sold expense immediately under sales revenue in order to show *gross margin* (also called *gross profit*)–see Table 5.1. Interest and income tax expenses are reported separately. Table 5.1 shows a common way of reporting these two unique expenses.

You might have noticed that only one line for all operating expenses is given in Table 5.1. Actually, more lines of operating expenses are reported. A relatively large number of operating expenses are presented in *internal* P&L reports, which may include 20, 50, 100, or more operating expenses.

In contrast, relatively few operating expenses are disclosed in *external* income statements. The standards governing external financial reporting by businesses do not dictate the types or the number of operating expenses that should be disclosed in income statements. This is left to the discretion of each business, and practices vary from company to company. Taking a sample of external income statements would reveal that most businesses disclose about five operating expenses, give or take one or two.

In actual practice, businesses classify and record operating expenses according to an *object of expenditure* basis. Accordingly,

TABLE 5.1—BASIC FORMAT OF ANNUAL PROFIT REPORT

	Fiscal Year 2005	Fiscal Year 2004
Sales Revenue	$28,750,000	$26,587,500
Cost of Goods Sold	18,550,000	17,687,750
Gross Margin	$10,200,000	$ 8,899,750
Operating Expenses	7,200,000	6,383,625
Operating Earnings	$ 3,000,000	$ 2,516,125
Interest Expense	525,000	508,750
Earnings before Income Tax	$ 2,475,000	$ 2,007,375
Income Tax Expense	825,000	669,125
Net Earnings	$ 1,650,000	$ 1,338,250

operating costs are recorded in expense accounts, such as salaries and wages, rent, utilities, maintenance and repairs, insurance, advertising, travel, depreciation, legal, office supplies, entertainment, and transportation. Even a modest-size business keeps a hundred or more operating expense accounts. This detailed level of information is necessary for effective management control. However, a large number of expense accounts can be an obstacle to getting a clear view of the "big picture" that managers need for profit analysis.

Chapter 1 explained that for analyzing profit behavior, a business's *variable* expenses should be separated from its *fixed* expenses. Generally speaking, an expense account title gives a pretty good clue as to whether the expense is fixed or variable. Cost of goods sold expense is a variable expense that depends on the number of units of product sold. Sales commissions are variable expenses. Real estate property taxes are fixed annual expenses. Fire and liability insurance premiums are another example of fixed annual expenses.

Managers could request that operating expense accounts, which have been recorded on the object of expenditure basis, be reclassified as variable or fixed. Distinguishing between variable and fixed operating expenses is not quite as simple as it might appear and takes time, of course. Only the manager can decide if it's worth the effort. Generally it's well worth the effort to separate between variable and fixed operating expenses.

Focusing on Operating Earnings

The following discussion focuses mainly on *earnings before interest and [income] tax* (EBIT). This profit measure is called *operating earnings* or *operating profit*. Interest expense depends on the amount of debt a business uses and, of course, on the interest rates it pays for using this capital. Some businesses are very conservative and use little or virtually no interest-bearing debt. Other businesses are loaded to the gills with debt. The higher the proportion of debt that is used to finance a business, the more the business gains or loses from *financial leverage*, which is discussed in Chapter 6 (page 90).

And then there's income tax expense. Income tax is a unique type of expense, to say the least. When they hear the term *income tax*, most people immediately think of the complexity of the federal income tax law, which can't be denied. For profit analysis, the important aspect of income tax is that it's a *contingent* expense that depends, first, on whether a business earns taxable income and, second, on how much the taxable income is (and, third, where the income is earned and, fourth, what kind of income it

is, and so on). As you undoubtedly know, under the U.S. income tax law, interest expense is deductible from revenue to determine taxable income. In very general terms, taxable income equals operating earnings minus interest expense. (Income tax professionals would cringe at this comment.)

Interest expense and income tax expense are business-wide, or entity-as-a-whole, expenses. Having said this, we should mention that it is common for a business to be organized as two or more separate legal entities, and each one can have its own debt and income tax situation. The main point is that interest and income tax have to be considered at the appropriate entity level.

Management decisions, in contrast, deal with more narrow profit slices of the business. These decisions are made at the microlevel. Managers focus on one separate source of profit at a time, such as a particular product, a product line, or a sales territory. The unit of analysis is not the whole business, but rather a particular segment of the business. The general term for a separate source of profit is *profit center.*

Profit Centers

From a one-person sole proprietorship to a mammoth business like General Motors or IBM, one of the first rules of management accounting is to identify each mainline source of profit and to accumulate the sales revenue and all the expenses for these separate profit hubs, or centers. Can you imagine an auto dealership, for example, not separating revenue and costs between its new car sales and its service department? One auto dealer we audited some years ago made more profit from originating car loans for its customers than it did from selling new and used cars.

Even a relatively small business may have many different sources of profit. In contrast, even a relatively large business may have just a few mainline sources of profit. There are no easy-to-apply general rules for classifying sales revenue and costs for the purpose of segregating sources of profit, that is, for defining the profit centers of a business. Every business has to figure this out on its own. But it has to be done. Clearly, business managers should know where their profit comes from.

Although a business may have a fairly large number of profit centers, one basic profit framework has broad applicability. It focuses on the main variables that drive profit. This basic formula is valid for most profit sources, whether the profit center is a product line, a sales territory, a channel of distribution, or a type of customer. Also, the profit framework can be modified and applied to service businesses.

Framework for Profit Analysis

Please look at Table 5.1 again. Of course the business did not make just one sale during the year just ended in the amount of $28,750,000. The company made thousands of sales during the year. It sells a number of different products and services. Its managers had to set the sales prices and control the costs for all these different products and services. The collective result is that the business made EBIT $3,000,000 for the year.

A logical first question is whether the format of the profit report (Table 5.1) could serve as a good framework for profit analysis. If so, a profit report could be prepared for each profit center. Suppose that the business whose summary-level, company-wide profit report is shown in Table 5.1 sells one main product through a network of distributors. This product accounts for more than one-third of its total annual sales revenue. As you would expect, the product is the largest profit center of the business.

In addition to sales revenue and cost of goods sold expense for the product, assume that the company's accounting system records the operating expenses for each of its separate profit centers. (*Please note:* The accounting system of a business might not be set up to track operating expenses by sales sources.) The profit report for this product, which is one slice of the total business, is presented in Table 5.2 (ending at operating earnings).

TABLE 5.2—PROFIT REPORT FOR PROFIT CENTER

	Fiscal Year 2005	Fiscal Year 2004	Change
Sales Revenue	$10,000,000	$9,555,000	4.7%
Cost of Goods Sold	6,000,000	5,996,250	0.1
Gross Margin	$ 4,000,000	$3,558,750	12.4
Operating Expenses	2,500,000	2,274,400	9.9
Operating Earnings	$ 1,500,000	$1,284,350	16.8

In Table 5.2, the percent of change for each line is included. As you see, sales revenue increased 4.7% and operating earnings increased 16.8% compared with the previous year. This level of profit analysis falls short of the more thorough analysis needed for decision making.

The bare-bones profit report framework shown in Table 5.2 is lacking in three basic areas: (1) It doesn't report *sales volume*—the number of units of product sold. (2) It doesn't distinguish between *variable and fixed* operating expenses. (3) *Unit values* are not included. The profit report presented in Table 5.3 corrects these deficiencies, and then some.

TABLE 5.3—MANAGEMENT PROFIT REPORT

Sales Volume	100,000 Units		97,500 Units	
	Fiscal Year 2005		**Fiscal Year 2004**	
	Per Unit	**Totals**	**Per Unit**	**Totals**
Sales Revenue	$100.00	$10,000,000	$98.00	$9,555,000
Cost of Goods Sold	60.00	6,000,000	61.50	5,996,250
Gross Margin	$ 40.00	$ 4,000,000	$36.50	$3,558,750
Revenue-Driven Expenses	8.50%	850,000	8.00%	764,400
Volume-Driven Expenses	$ 6.50	650,000	$ 6.00	585,000
Margin	$ 25.00	$ 2,500,000	$22.66	$2,209,350
Direct Fixed Expenses		750,000		700,000
Allocated Fixed Expenses		250,000		225,000
Operating Earnings		$ 1,500,000		$1,284,350

Much of the information in the Table 5.3 management profit report is confidential and obviously should not circulate outside the business. Your competitors would love to get their hands on this information. In fact, your competitors might attempt to get this information through industrial espionage and intelligence gathering methods.

Spreadsheet Basis of Profit Report

Table 5.3 is the printout of our spreadsheet. We use the Microsoft Excel spreadsheet program. In fact, all tables in the book are printouts from Excel spreadsheets. (You can get the Excel workbook file for all the examples by contacting us at the e-mail addresses given in the Preface.)

Today, spreadsheets are so widely used and understood that we hardly need to mention the advantages of this analysis tool. However, we should remind you of the "garbage-in, garbage-out" principle. The output of a spreadsheet is no better than the correct coding and accuracy of its inputs. Accordingly, let's be clear on the definitions of the variables in the Table 5.3 profit report.

Sales volume, the first line in Table 5.3, is the total number of units sold during the period, net of any returns by customers. Sales volume should include only units that brought in revenue to the business. Generally speaking, businesses do a good job in keeping track of the sales volumes of their products (and services). These are closely monitored figures, such as in the automobile industry.

Some businesses sell a huge variety of products. No single product or no single product line brings in more than a small fraction of their total sales revenue. For instance, a well-known general hardware store in Boulder, Colorado, carries over 100,000 products. A business may keep count of customer traffic or the number of individual sales made over the year, but it may not track the quantities sold for every product.

Sales revenue is the net amount of money received by the business from the sales of the products during the period. Notice the word *net* here. This business, like most, offers its customers many incentives to buy its products and to pay quickly for their purchases. The sales revenue amount in Table 5.3 is not simply the list prices of the products sold times the number of units sold. Rather, the sales revenue amount is the total after deductions for rebates, allowances, prompt-payment discounts, and any other thing that reduces the amount of revenue received by the business.

Cost of goods sold is the product cost of the units sold during the period. This expense should be net of discounts, rebates, and allowances received by the business from its vendors and suppliers. Manufacturers add together their costs of raw materials, labor, and production overhead to determine product cost. (Accounting for the cost of manufactured products is called *cost accounting*.) For other businesses, product cost basically is purchase cost. A business must choose the sequence in which product cost is charged out to cost of goods sold expense. One choice is the *first-in, first-out (FIFO)* method. The opposite method is the *last-in, first-out (LIFO)* sequence.

One common problem is where to put the cost of *inventory shrinkage*. It may be included in cost of goods sold expense, or it may be included in the volume-driven operating expenses. A manager definitely should know what has been placed in the cost of goods sold expense, in addition to the product cost of units sold during the period.

Table 5.3 separates operating expenses into four classes—two types of variable expenses and two types of fixed expenses. *Revenue-driven expenses* are those that depend primarily on the *dollar amount* of sales revenue. This group of variable operating expenses includes salespeople's commissions that are based on the amount of sales, as well as credit card fees paid by retailers, franchise fees based on sales revenue, and any other cost that depends directly on the amount of sales revenue. Notice in Table 5.3 that these operating expenses are presented as a *percent* of sales price in the per unit column.

Volume-driven expenses are driven by and depend primarily on the number of units sold, or the total quantity of products sold during the period (as opposed to the dollar value of the sales). It includes delivery and transportation costs paid by the business, packaging costs, and any costs that depend on the size and weight of the products sold. Most businesses have both types of variable operating expenses. However, one or the other may be so minor that it would not be useful to report lines for each type to managers for their analysis of profit. Only the dominant type of variable operating expense would be presented, and it would absorb the other type.

Managers may view fixed operating expenses as an albatross around the neck of the business. In fact, these costs provide the infrastructure and support for making sales. The main disadvantage, of course, is that these operating costs do not decline if sales during the period fall short of expectations. A business commits to many fixed operating costs for the coming period. For all practical purposes, these costs cannot be decreased over the short run. Examples of fixed costs are wages of employees on fixed salaries for the period (from managers to maintenance workers), real estate taxes, depreciation on the buildings and equipment used in making sales, and utility bills.

Certain fixed costs can be matched with a particular profit center. For example, a business may advertise a specific product, and the fixed cost of the advertisement can be matched against that product. A major product line may have its own employees on fixed salaries or its own delivery trucks on which depreciation is recorded. A business may purchase specific liability insurance covering a particular product it sells. Table 5.3 reports these costs as *direct fixed expenses.*

In some cases, it's not possible to directly attach company-wide fixed operating expenses to particular products, product lines, or other organization units. General administrative expenses (such as the chief executive officer's annual salary and corporate legal expenses) are incurred on an entity-as-a-whole basis and cannot be connected directly with any particular profit center. Therefore, a business may allocate these fixed costs among its different profit centers. These fixed costs handed down from headquarters are shown as *allocated fixed expenses* in Table 5.3.

Margin—The Catalyst of Profit

Table 5.3 introduces one new line of information—*margin*. Margin is operating profit before operating fixed expenses are deducted. It's not to be confused with *gross margin*, which is profit after the cost of goods sold expense is subtracted from sales revenue, but before any other expenses are deducted. With the information in Table 5.3, the manager can pinpoint the reasons for the unit margin increase—from $22.66 in 2004 to $25.00 in fiscal year 2005. There were two favorable changes: (1) The unit sales price increased, and (2) the unit product cost decreased. The gain in the gross margin per unit was offset by unfavorable changes in both variable operating expenses.

In this example, unit margin increased from $22.66 in 2004 to $25.00 in fiscal year 2005—and the business sold 2,500 more units in 2005. Therefore, total margin jumped $290,650, to $2,500,000 for 2005. The total amount of fixed operating expenses increased $75,000 over 2004, which offsets part of the margin gain. Operating earnings increased a very healthy $215,650 during 2005, which is a 16.8% gain. Most managers would be quite satisfied with this performance.

By the way, the same analysis can be used to explain the variances between actual and budgeted amounts for the period just ended. Actual results would be in the 2005 columns, as shown in Table 5.3. Budgeted amounts for 2005 would be put in the comparison columns on the 2004 side, instead of 2004 results.

The manager's attention should be riveted on unit margin, and the manager should definitely understand the reasons for changes in unit margin. Even a relatively small change in unit margin can have a big impact on operating earnings. For instance, what if unit margin had remained the same at $22.66 during fiscal year 2005? The business sold 2,500 more units than the previous year, which would have increased its total margin $56,650: $22.66 × 2,500 additional units = $56,650 total margin increase.

As you see in Table 5.3, the company's total fixed operating expenses (direct plus allocated) increased $75,000 over the previous period. Therefore, if unit margin had remained the same as in 2004, the company's operating earnings would have decreased. Fortunately, unit margin increased $2.34 (i.e., $25.00 – $22.66 = +$2.34), and this increase more than overcame the increase in fixed expenses and provided a nice boost in operating earnings.

How the Business Made Profit

The management analysis profit report shown in Table 5.3 provides the information we need to answer the question posed at the start of the chapter: How do you make profit? So, how did the business earn $1,500,000 operating profit from this profit center for fiscal year 2005? Actually, there are three answers to the question. Please refer to Table 5.3 in reading each answer.

Answer #1: The business earned a profit margin of $25 per unit, and it sold 100,000 units of the product: $25 unit margin × 100,000 units sales volume = $2,500,000 total margin. The product had $1,000,000 total fixed expenses for the year. Thus, total operating earnings was $1,500,000 for the year.

Answer #2: The company had to sell 40,000 units of the product to reach its *breakeven point:* $1,000,000 total fixed expenses ÷ $25 unit margin = 40,000 units breakeven point. The business sold 60,000 units in excess of the breakeven point. Each unit sold in excess of the breakeven point brought in $25 "pure" profit because the first 40,000 units sold covered fixed expenses. The 60,000 units in excess of breakeven at $25 unit margin provided $1,500,000 operating earnings.

Answer #3: The business spread its $1,000,000 total fixed expenses over 100,000 units sold during the year, which was an average of $10 per unit. This fixed cost per unit is *not* presented in Table 5.3. Fixed costs are monolithic in nature; they are bulk-size costs that are not sensitive to changes in sales volume over the short run. Accordingly, the Table 5.3 profit report does not show fixed costs per unit. However, this third answer for how the business made its profit needs the average fixed costs per unit. The business made $25 unit margin per unit sold, which is $15 more than the $10 fixed costs per unit: $15 × 100,000 units sold = $1,500,000 operating earnings.

Each answer is valid. In a certain situation, one of the three ways for explaining how to make profit is more useful. If you were thinking of making a large increase in fixed operating expenses, for example, you should pay attention to the effect on your breakeven point, so answer #2 is most useful in this situation. If you were thinking of changing sales prices, answer #1, which focuses on unit margin, is most relevant. Likewise, if you're dealing with changes in product cost or variable operating expenses that affect unit margin, answer #1 is the most helpful because it focuses on the "spread," or margin, between sales price and variable expenses.

The Profit Report Framework Is Fine, But . . .

The profit report framework shown in Table 5.3 is a terrific tool for understanding and analyzing profit performance. It's an excellent platform for planning how to improve profit next year (see Chapter 6). The framework can be applied to any business that sells products. With a few modifications, it can also be used by service businesses that don't sell products. But, frankly, it's not the most popular kid on the block; many managers don't use this tool. Despite its utility, business managers may have problems in using this profit report framework.

A major obstacle is that the managers of a business may not be able to get information about variable and fixed operating costs out of their accounting system. Supplying this information is one more demand on the system. A business's accounting system must accumulate a large amount of information needed for preparing its financial statements and its income tax and many other tax returns. Variable and fixed information is not needed for these purposes. Also, a company's accounting system has to provide a wide range of information for its day-to-day operations, including the vital functions of payroll, purchasing, billing and collections, cash disbursements, and property records. Variable and fixed expense information is not needed for these functions either.

The managers of a business could insist that the accounting department compile variable and fixed operating expense information. The computer accounting programs used by most businesses today make much more feasible sorting between variable and fixed expenses. But, clearly this is not done in many businesses. All is not lost, however. Based on his or her experience and close contacts with the profit factors of the business, a manager can make educated estimates for the variable and fixed operating expenses for a particular product or product line or other profit center. You don't really have to use actual accounting data; you can substitute experience-based estimates for the variables.

Managers may have another reason for not using a profit report framework such as the one shown in Table 5.3. They may think that the framework is too cumbersome and would be too time-consuming, especially if they have a large number of different profit sources to manage. Well, this may be true. The one thing a manager never has enough of is time. To make it more time efficient, the framework shown in Table 5.3 can be telescoped into a more compact profit model.

Instead of using the full-blown profit report framework presented in Table 5.3, a manager could use a "mini" profit model. Table 5.4 presents a profit model for the product (for fiscal year 2005). This profit model is a repeat of answer #1 given earlier for explaining how the business made $1,500,000 profit from this product.

Basically the profit model is a shorthand method for thinking about and analyzing profit. For instance, suppose you are thinking of cutting sales price by $5 next year in order to boost sales

TABLE 5.4—PROFIT MODEL FOR PRODUCT

Unit Sales Volume	100,000
Unit Margin	× $25.00
Total Margin	$2,500,000
Fixed Expenses	−1,000,000
Operating Earnings	$1,500,000

volume 10%. Would this be a smart move? Dropping sales price $5 would reduce unit margin $5, assuming product cost and other variable expenses hold constant. So next year you would earn only $2,200,000 total margin on the product: $20 unit margin × 110,000 units sold = $2,200,000 total margin. Bad idea!

Capsule Summary

Managers make decisions toward achieving the profit goals of the business. Managers need feedback on the results of their decisions, of course. The periodic profit reports prepared by the business's accounting department provide the primary feedback to managers. This chapter first introduces and explains the format and the content of a typical profit report. It is noted that internal profit reports to managers contain more information about the operating expenses of the business than do external profit reports to outside shareowners.

The thesis of the chapter is that the framework of conventional profit reports to managers who are in charge of profit centers is not good enough. They need a more informative profit report for analyzing profit behavior. The chapter presents a framework for management profit reports that focuses on the main factors that drive profit—margin, sales volume, and fixed costs. This spreadsheet-based framework is very useful for analyzing change in profit from one period to the next and variances of actual from budget. Furthermore, it's an excellent platform for planning out the details for improving profit.

The chapter closes with a discussion of a compact profit model that would fit on the back of an envelope. It's a very handy tool for doing quick calculations for the impact on profit caused by changes in unit margin and sales volume.

6

SAFEGUARDING AND IMPROVING PROFIT: THE PROFIT POWER OF PRICE VERSUS VOLUME

"After victory, tighten the straps on your helmet."
—Interpretation of an ancient Samurai dictum

Making a profit is hard enough. Doing it again the following year, and, what's more, improving profit is the task facing managers. Nothing can be taken for granted. Every profit factor is subject to change. Managers must keep alert for changes that hurt profit performance. A relatively minor slippage in just one factor can have a devastating impact on the bottom line. Conversely, even a modest improvement in just one factor can cause a significant boost in profit. Getting to a good bottom line is typically a game of inches, not yards.

As the chapter title indicates, there are two themes to this chapter. (1) A good offense requires a good defense. The first job of managers is to safeguard the level of profit they have worked so hard to achieve. Profit can easily slip through their fingers unless they control the key factors that determine profit performance. (2) There is an optimistic side of the same coin: Profit can be improved by making positive changes in the factors that drive profit.

The Business Example

This chapter focuses on a business that is making a satisfactory profit but wants to do better—and certainly does not want to go in reverse. The business is a privately owned corporation; about 20 individuals own its stock shares. There is no trading in the stock shares. Over the years, shares have changed hands occasionally when a stockholder died, when shares were gifted to a son or a daughter, and when shares were transferred to an ex-spouse in a divorce settlement. The business was started several years ago and has had a steady though not spectacular rise in sales. The business has garnered a good reputation with its customers for high-quality products and services.

Key Policies of the Business

The stockholders elect the corporation's board of directors, of course. The chief executive officer, following very clear directions from the board, does *not* plan to grow the business by acquiring other businesses or by entering new markets or opening new locations. Growing the business in those ways would require substantial amounts of additional capital, beyond the annual cash flow provided from profit. The business depends on cash flow from profit for two critical purposes: (1) to replace and modernize its property, plant, and equipment; and (2) to pay cash dividends to stockholders.

The stockholders have made it abundantly clear that they want a healthy cash dividend return on their investment every year. As just mentioned, they are not interested in growing the business through aggressive acquisitions of other businesses or by entering new markets or locations. They think the business should stick to its knitting and continue to do what it knows best. Some might view this strategy as almost "un-American." You often hear the mantra that growth is the main thing a business should do to get ahead in the world. But the owners of many privately owned businesses see the risks and disadvantages of embarking on an aggressive growth strategy. They don't want to go down that road. Furthermore, they may not be able to raise the capital needed to follow a growth strategy.

Financial Profile of the Business

Table 6.1 presents the financial profile of this business. Its most recent three financial statements—balance sheet, income statement, and statement of cash flows—are reduced to as few lines as possible. This financial silhouette of the business avoids the abundance of details reported in its financial statements. The figures from the company's financial statements are rounded off to the nearest hundred thousand in Table 6.1. One purpose of preparing the profile is to keep the three financial sides of the business in view of one another. You must judge a business's earnings relative to the sources and the amounts of capital employed to make that profit. And you

TABLE 6.1—FINANCIAL PROFILE OF BUSINESS

Condensed from Company's Year-End Balance Sheet

Operating Assets (cash, receivables, inventory, and fixed assets)	$17,000,000
Operating Liabilities (accounts payable and unpaid expenses)	(4,000,000)
Capital Raised by Business	$13,000,000
Short- and Long-Term Debt	$ 5,000,000
Owners' Equity (paid-in capital plus retained earnings)	$ 8,000,000

Condensed from Company's Annual Income Statement

Sales Revenue	$26,000,000
Cost of Goods Sold	(16,000,000)
Operating Expenses	(7,900,000)
Operating Earnings (EBIT)	$ 2,100,000
Interest on Debt	$ 300,000
Corporate Income Tax	600,000
Net Income for Owners	1,200,000

Condensed from Company's Annual Statement of Cash Flows

Cash Flow from Net Income	$ 1,900,000
Fixed Asset Outlays	(1,000,000)
Dividends to Stockholders	(800,000)
Cash Balance Increase	$ 100,000
Starting Balance	3,400,000
Ending Balance	$ 3,500,000

should look through to the cash flow generated by that profit and what was done with the cash.

As a stockholder, you should take particular notice of the following points:

- The company's $300,000 interest expense is compared with its $5,000,000 debt, which is a 6.0% interest rate. These days, this interest rate is reasonable.

- The company's $1,200,000 bottom-line profit (net income) is compared with its $8,000,000 stockholders' equity, which reveals that it earned 15.0% annual return on the book (recorded) value of stockholders' equity.

- The short-term and long-term debt sources supplied $5/13$ of the total capital used by the business, or $5,000,000 of its total $13,000,000 capital. However, the debtholders "share" is not $5/13$ of the company's $2,100,000 operating earnings for the year, which would be $808,000 (rounded to the nearest thousand). They are paid $300,000 interest on their capital, and no more. The $508,000 excess over interest enhances the pretax net income for shareowners, which is referred to as a *financial leverage* gain. (If the company had failed to earn at least $300,000 operating earnings, it still would have had to pay $300,000 interest.)

- The business distributed $800,000 cash dividends during the year, which is a two-thirds dividend payout ratio from its $1,200,000 net income.

- The $800,000 annual dividend amount equals 10.0% return on the $8,000,000 book value of owners' equity.

- Deducting the $1,000,000 outlays for capital expenditures, the business had $900,000 remaining cash flow from profit. It used $100,000 of this cash flow to build up its cash balance instead of paying it all out for cash dividends.

- The company's $3,500,000 cash balance is rather sizable compared with its $26,000,000 annual sales revenue, or more than 13%. Many businesses get by on a much smaller working cash ratio. Whether the business is making the best use of its cash is an open question—although holding a relatively large cash balance certainly is conservative.

Table 6.1 is a top-level overview, or an executive-summary financial picture of the business, which almost fits on the back of an envelope. In order to make an adequate after-tax and after-interest profit (net income), a business has to make adequate operating earnings from its sales. Cost of goods sold and operating expenses cannot consume all its sales revenue, of course. In the example, the business squeezed $2,100,000 operating earnings out of its sales revenue, which was the wellspring for paying interest on its debt, paying income tax, and providing net income for its stockholders.

One Thing's for Certain: Profit Will Be Different Next Year

Let's look ahead to next year. Will the company's profit be the same? You know it won't. For sure, profit will be higher or lower than the year just ended. Or, you can look back and say for certain that profit for the year just ended was higher or lower than the previous year. Profit is never the same amount from year to year. The factors that drive profit are always in a state of flux; few factors remain constant very long. Now, we find this intriguing, don't you? Why does profit change? Shouldn't business managers have a good analytical grip on why profit increases or decreases?

One reason that the amount of the annual profit recorded for a business can change year to year is the "noise" in the accounting information system. For example, many businesses deliberately massage their accounting numbers in order to nudge recorded profit for the year up or down so that recorded profit meets certain targets or goals for the year. This is different than "cooking the books," which refers to accounting fraud (such as recording sales revenue when in fact sales have not been made, or not recording expenses and losses that have in fact occurred). Also, an accounting method used by a business—such as an accelerated depreciation method—automatically decreases the expense amount year to year. Then, there's a wide range of odds and ends that cause changes in year-to-year profit. And, one-time events cause spikes in profit.

It's hard to calibrate how much of the profit difference from one year to the next is due to noise and how much is due to changes in the primary factors that drive profit. We would hazard a guess that the noise element can easily cause a 10% or higher year-to-year profit fluctuation for a typical business. If management accounting manipulation is done with a heavy hand, the recorded profit for the year can be affected by more than 10%. In any case, we'll have to put aside the noise factor and move on to changes in the primary factors that drive profit.

You Know How Your Expenses Behave, Don't You?

Unfortunately many business managers would have to answer this question with a resounding "No!" Chapter 5 laid the foundation for how operating expenses should be reported in internal profit-and-loss (P&L) reports. In brief, variable expenses should be separated from fixed expenses. Table 6.2 presents the redesigned P&L report for the business, which classifies operating expenses according to how they behave relative to sales volume and sales revenue.

In Table 6.2, three basic types of variable expenses are shown, which are deducted from sales revenue to get down to the all-important measure of *margin*:

1. *Cost of goods sold expense* is, on the surface, relatively straightforward and simple, being the cost of products sold by the business whose sales revenue is reported on the first line of the P&L report. However, a business must make a choice between different accounting methods for recording this expense. The FIFO (first-in, first-out) method results in a lower expense for the period than the alternative LIFO (last-in, first-out) method when product costs are drifting upward. The loss from write-downs recorded during the period for *inventory shrinkage* (due to customer shoplifting, employee theft and fraud, vendor fraud, mistakes, etc.) may be included in this expense. Furthermore, the expense may include a write-down under the lower of cost or market accounting rule. In short, the cost of goods sold expense may not be as clean as it looks. Roughly speaking, these

TABLE 6.2—P&L REPORT SHOWING HOW EXPENSES BEHAVE

Sales Revenue	$26,000,000
Cost of Goods Sold	(16,000,000)
Volume-Driven Expenses	(1,400,000)
Revenue-Driven Expenses	(2,600,000)
Margin	$ 6,000,000
Fixed Expenses (20% slack estimate)	(3,900,000)
Operating Earnings (EBIT)	$ 2,100,000
Interest on Debt	(300,000)
Corporate Income Tax	(600,000)
Net Income for Owners	$ 1,200,000

additional costs move in concert with the cost of products sold during the period, assuming the business uses consistent accounting methods and practices period to period. Of course, any unusual inventory write-down during the period should be reported separately to managers.

2. *Volume-driven expenses* are those costs that, in addition to cost of goods sold, are driven primarily by the number of units of product sold. The main examples are packaging, handling, and transportation costs. These costs may be immaterial for some businesses and not worth putting in a separate class. In such a case, these costs may be tacked on to cost of goods sold expense, which is also a volume-driven expense. But, in this example, the volume-driven expenses add up to $1,400,000 and are put into a separate class.

3. *Revenue-driven expenses* are those costs driven primarily by the dollar amount of sales made by the business. These expenses include sales commissions based on the dollar amount of sales, credit card fees based on the dollar amount of sales, property rentals that depend on the total dollar amount of sales, franchise fees that are calculated on the total dollar amount of sales, and bad debts (uncollectible receivables from sales on credit) that have to be written off. It's possible that these expenses are negligible and, for some businesses, not worth the effort to distinguish from volume-driven expenses. But, be careful: Many businesses have significant revenue-driven expenses.

Fixed Expenses, or Why Margin Doesn't Equal Operating Profit

Fixed expenses are those costs that for most practical purposes are inflexible and are locked in for the year. These costs of operating a business do not vary with sales volume or the dollar amount of sales during the year. One important component of fixed costs is the *depreciation* recorded for the year. Of the $3,900,000 shown in Table 6.2 for this example, the business recorded $800,000 depreciation on its fixed assets (building, machines, equipment, computers, trucks, autos, etc.) for the year. Recording depreciation expense does not decrease cash; rather, the book values of fixed assets are written down to recognize the use of the resources. The assets have moved one year closer to their eventual replacement.

In contrast, the company's other fixed costs were cash outlays during the year, although the cash payout usually is a little more or less than the amount recorded as expense in the period (see Chapter 2). Examples of fixed costs include real estate taxes, most insurance premiums, employees paid fixed salaries, repair and maintenance expenses, back office expenses (accounting, recordkeeping, and filing many different reports), and legal expenses.

One Key Point: Generally speaking, fixed expenses provide the *capacity* to make sales and to carry on the operations of the business. The business should make an estimate of the percent of its capacity now being used for its sales and operating activities. In this example, the business estimates that it used 80% of its capacity during the year. Therefore, notice in Table 6.2 that 20% slack is reported for its fixed costs, which is the untapped or idle capacity of the business.

Deducting fixed expenses from margin gives *operating earnings (profit)*, which is the amount of earnings (profit) before interest and income tax (EBIT) expenses. As you see in Tables 6.1 and 6.2, operating earnings is "divided" three ways—some to the debt holders of the business, some to the government, and some for the stockholders.

Most businesses use interest-bearing debt for part of their total capital requirements. In the example, the business has borrowed $5,000,000 from short-term and long-term debt sources. Interest expense is the first "take out" from EBIT. As you know, interest is a fixed, contractual payment for the use of debt capital; It's a fixed expense for the period given a certain level of debt. It is deductible for determining taxable income, just as all operating expenses are deductible. (Let's not go into nitpicking details here, such as the deductibility limits on entertainment expenses and so on.) So, roughly speaking, the business's taxable income is its $2,100,000 operating profit minus its $300,000 interest, which comes out to $1,800,000.

In the example, the business is organized legally as a regular, or "C," corporation. So it pays federal income tax based on its taxable income for the year. (Chapter 8 explains pass-through, or non-tax-paying business entities.) As you see in Table 6.2 the business's income tax expense for the year was $600,000. Therefore, its after-tax net income for stockholders is $1,200,000.

From this after-tax net income, the business distributed $800,000 cash dividends to its stockholders, which by the way is taxable in their hands. The federal government gets two bites out of the apple: the first at the corporate level ($600,000) and the second at the individual stockholders' level. Suppose all the stockholders paid the 15% dividend tax rate. In the aggregate, the stockholders would pay 15% of their $800,000 total cash dividends, or $120,000. Please keep in mind that this second layer of individual income taxes on cash dividends is not reported or referred to in the business's financial report.

The Widely Different Results from Changes in Profit Factors

The quote at the start of the chapter is meant to call attention to the wise dictum that managers should avoid hubris in having made a profit and should never let their guard down. Making profit most likely will attract the attention of present and would-be competitors. True, privately owned businesses don't send their financial reports to their competitors. But competitors keep a close eye on one another, and they generally have a fairly good appraisal of how others are doing in the profit department. In any case, your profit performance is vulnerable to many negative changes that can pull the rug out from under your profit success formula. Of course, if you can make positive changes in these factors, you can improve profit. But not all changes in these factors are created equal regarding their impact on profit performance.

For planning and decision-making purposes, we strongly believe that business managers need a profit-analysis tool at their fingertips—one that is handy, easy to use, and as useful as the old slide rule that engineers used to carry everywhere (and some probably still do). We can't offer you a profit "slide rule," but we can offer the brief model that you see in Table 6.2. You can put this in your computer spreadsheet in no time flat. Or you could write it out on a scratch pad quickly. Basically, Table 6.2 is the *profit formula* for the business. The trick is to change one (or more) of the factors and calculate the profit impact of the change.

One very helpful technique is what we call the "10% solu-

tion." Change a factor by 10% and see what happens to profit. This gives you amazing insight into how the profit formula works and why some changes are much more important than others. So suppose the business had sold a 10% lower or a 10% higher quantity of products than it did (without any change in its sales mix, or the proportion of each product in total sales). Sales revenue, cost of goods sold, volume-driven expenses, and revenue-driven expenses would have been 10% lower or higher. Table 6.3 shows the results of these 10% sales volume changes. Notice that Table 6.3 stops at the operating earnings (EBIT) line of profit.

TABLE 6.3—10% CHANGES IN SALES VOLUME

	Changes		
	Lower Volume	Higher Volume	Actual Volume
Sales Revenue	$(2,600,000)	$2,600,000	$26,000,000
Cost of Goods Sold	(1,600,000)	1,600,000	16,000,000
Volume-Driven Expenses	(140,000)	140,000	1,400,000
Revenue-Driven Expenses	(260,000)	260,000	2,600,000
Margin	$ (600,000)	$ 600,000	$ 6,000,000
Fixed Expenses (20% slack estimate)	0	0	(3,900,000)
Operating Earnings (EBIT)	$ (600,000)	$ 600,000	$ 2,100,000

When sales volume changes by 10%, margin moves 10% the same direction. The business has, it estimates, about 20% slack, or unused capacity (see Table 6.3). So fixed expenses should not increase with a 10% jump in sales volume. And due to their sticky nature, fixed expenses would have been about the same if sales volume had been 10% less.

The unchanging nature of fixed expenses (over the short run) causes the percent change in operating earnings (margin less fixed expenses) to be considerably larger than the percent in change in margin. Margin would be 10% lower or higher, but operating earnings would be 29% lower or higher: $600,000 change ÷ $2,100,000 operating earnings = 29%. This much larger percent fluctuation in operating earnings because of fixed expenses is referred to as an *operating leverage* effect.

Suppose that the business had sold all its products at 10% lower or higher sales prices. Sales volume is the same in this scenario. Table 6.4 shows the profit changes at the lower and higher sales prices. Again, fixed expenses are held the same.

The lower sales prices would have more than wiped out all its operating earnings and put the business in the red for the year. Clearly, the business could not afford a 10% price cut across the board on all its products. Even if it were a charitable organization, it could not sell at prices that cause a loss. The key point, as you probably already noticed, is that the $2,340,00 drop in sales revenue (which is net of the offsetting decrease in revenue-driven expenses) is more than its operating earnings.

TABLE 6.4—10% CHANGES IN SALES PRICES

	Changes		
	Lower Prices	Higher Prices	Actual Prices
Sales Revenue	$(2,600,000)	$2,600,000	$26,000,000
Cost of Goods Sold	0	0	16,000,000
Volume-Driven Expenses	0	0	1,400,000
Revenue-Driven Expenses	(260,000)	260,000	2,600,000
Margin	$(2,340,000)	$2,340,000	$ 6,000,000
Fixed Expenses (20% slack estimate)	0	0	(3,900,000)
Operating Earnings (EBIT)	$(2,340,000)	$2,340,000	$ 2,100,000

FIGURE 6.1—COMPARISON OF EFFECTS ON OPERATING EARNINGS (EBIT) CAUSED BY 10% CHANGES IN SALES VOLUME VERSUS SALES PRICES

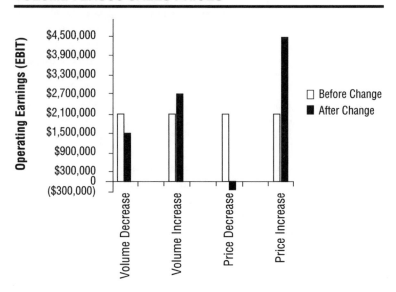

At 10% lower sales prices, all the company's net income would have been wiped out—the business would have reported a loss and could not have paid any cash dividends to stockholders.

Looking on the positive side, a 10% higher level of sales prices would have more than doubled operating earnings. Of course, selling all products at 10% higher sales prices would have been a challenge, to say the least. In any case, the effect on profit caused by sales price changes, compared with sales volume changes, is a much greater swing. Figure 6.1 shows the two scenarios side by side. The moral of the story so far is that a sales price change of a certain percent has a much larger impact than a sales volume change of the same percent.

Sensitivity of Margin to Sales Price Changes

The following example illustrates why sales price changes cause a "boom or bust" effect on profit. Suppose that the business sells a particular product for $2,600. This product is selected because its sales price equals exactly 0.0001 (one ten-thousandth) of the company's $26,000,000 total sales revenue (see Table 6.2). Suppose further that the variable expenses of this product are the perfect average of the expenses of all the products the business sells. Following down the variable expenses in Table 6.2, this product's variable costs per unit are: $1,600, cost of goods sold; $140, volume-driven expenses; and $260, revenue-driven expenses. Subtracting these variable expenses from sales price yields $600, margin per unit for the product. (You can easily visualize this by knocking off the last four zeros from the amounts in Table 6.2.)

Now, suppose the product's sales price had been 10% different. The only variable expense that would have been different is the revenue-driven expense, which in the example equals 10% of sales price. The other two variable expenses would have been the same. If the sales price had been $260 (10% of $2,600) lower or higher, then the revenue-driven expense would have been $26 lower or higher. The margin per unit for the product, therefore, would have been $234 lower or higher.

The key point here is that a $234 difference in unit margin caused by the 10% shift in sales price would have depressed or raised margin by a much larger percent:

$234 Change in Unit Margin ÷ $600 Unit Margin = 39%

There's almost a four-times impact on unit margin! In the example, a 10% change in sales price causes a 39% change in unit margin. In short, profit is much more sensitive to changes in sales prices than to changes in sales volume. By the way, a $234 change in variable costs of the product per unit with no change in the sales price would have the same impact on unit margin, of course.

Raising the Profit Bar for Next Year

Suppose the goal of the business next year is to increase its bottom-line profit 10%. It needs to boost net income $120,000 (or 10% of the $1,200,000 net income for the year just ended). The business keeps only two-thirds of its taxable income (profit after interest) because its income tax equals one-third of its taxable income. So it needs to increase its profit after interest by $180,000. (One-third, or $60,000, of the increase goes to the government; and the company keeps $120,000.) To keep things simple, assume that interest expense will be the same next year and that fixed operating expenses will also be the same. In fact, let's assume that the per-unit costs of all products sold next year will be the same, that the volume-driven per-unit costs will be the same, and that the percent of revenue-driven expenses to sales revenue will be the same.

From the profit model shown in Table 6.2, we can quickly determine how much sales volume would have to increase or how much sales prices would have to change to achieve its profit goal (or a combination of changes in both sales volume and prices

could be used). For instance, if the entire load were put on sales volume (assuming sales prices can't be raised next year), the business would have to boost sales volume 3%. A 3% higher sales volume would increase margin by $180,000 ($6,000,000 margin for the year just ended × 3% higher sales volume = $180,000 increase). Income tax would take one-third of this, leaving a $120,000 increase in net income.

Suppose the business is not able to increase sales volume and will have to increase sales prices to jack up net income next year. The company would have to nudge up sales revenue $200,000. Revenue-driven expenses would increase $20,000, in proportion with the sales revenue increase. Therefore, margin would increase $180,000; income tax would increase $60,000 (or one-third); and net income would increase $120,000. Notice that average sale prices would have to be increased less than 1% (0.77 of 1%, to be precise), or $200,000 additional sales revenue on a base of $26,000,000.

Capsule Summary

A typical business example is used to explore how profit behaves. Its financial statements are reduced to a financial profile of the business, which is very useful to take the measure of its overall financial performance. One thing for certain is that the annual profit of any business is never the same from year to year. Even if all the factors that drive profit keep constant from one year to the next (and we know that they don't, of course), there is a certain amount of "noise" in a business's accounting information system. Managers control some of this noise by massaging their accounting numbers (not that you would do anything like that, of course).

This chapter focuses on changes in the primary factors that drive profit and on the effects of changes in these factors. For this purpose, variable expenses have to be separated from fixed expenses. This separation allows the calculation of margin, which equals sales revenue minus all variable expenses. Margin is an extraordinarily important profit-performance benchmark. A business has to earn enough total margin to cover its fixed costs for the year. The excess of margin over fixed costs equals operating earnings, which is divided three ways—to interest on debt, to income tax (unless the business is a pass-through tax entity), and to residual net income for the shareowners of the business.

Changes in sales volume and sales prices—the big two factors that drive profit—are analyzed and compared in effect. Margin moves in proportion (more or less) with changes in sales volume. But a business's fixed costs cause its operating earnings and net income to fluctuate much more than the change in its margin. This wider swing in operating profit and net income is called the operating leverage effect on profit.

Equal percent changes in sales prices, compared with changes in sales volume, cause a much heavier impact on margin, operating earnings, and net income. If a business decreased its sales prices, say, by 10% or even 5%, all its profit could be wiped out. Even a small increase in sales prices could push up net income by half or more. Put another way, to achieve a 10% growth in net income, a business could increase its sales volume or its sales prices. The example in the chapter demonstrates that it would have to increase sales volume 3%. Increasing its sales prices by less than 1% would yield the same result.

7

GROWING PAINS: FINDING ENOUGH CASH FOR GROWTH

"No profit grows where is no pleasure ta'en;
In brief, sir, study what you most affect."
—William Shakespeare, *The Taming of the Shrew*

Consider three basic sales revenue trend lines for a business: decline, steady state, and growth. (Space doesn't permit discussing cyclical businesses, which have sales trend lines that look like a roller-coaster ride.) Each trend presents a very different kettle of fish regarding cash flow and capital needs. This chapter concentrates mainly on the growth scenario. The major concern is that cash flow from operating activities may not—and, in fact, usually does not—provide all the money needed for growth.

Chapter 2 explains that the amounts of revenue and expenses that are recorded on the accrual basis of accounting to measure a business's profit for the period are different than the amounts of cash flows from revenue and for expenses during the same period. Thus, the bottom-line profit (net income) of a business differs from the cash flow from its profit-making (operating activities) for the period. The following section offers a brief review of cash flow from operating activities, paying particular attention to the cash-flow effect of depreciation expense.

Reviewing Cash Flow from Operating Activities

Accountants divide the cash flows of a business into three types: (1) cash flows from profit-making operations (revenue and expenses, as well as gains and losses that affect the bottom line), which are called *operating activities;* (2) cash flows from investments in long-term and nonoperating assets and from liquidations of these investments, which are called *investing activities;* and, (3) cash flows from raising capital from debt and equity sources, returning capital to these sources, and paying cash dividends to owners, which are called *financing activities.* A business prepares a financial statement called the "statement of cash flows" that summarizes these three types of cash flows for the period. This chapter focuses on the first type—cash flows from operating activities.

Chapter 2 explained that cash-basis accounting is woefully inadequate, except for small businesses that do not extend credit to customers, carry no inventory of products for sale, do not buy things on credit, and do not own long-term operating assets, such as machinery, equipment, and buildings. Virtually all businesses of any size and sophistication use double-entry, accrual-basis accounting. Many different assets and liabilities are recorded in order to keep track of the financial affairs of the business, to recognize economic reality, and to measure the profit or loss for a period. Accrual-basis accounting complicates the cash flow trail, however.

Hopefully, Chapter 2 untangled the cash flow trail and, in particular, marked a clear path to *cash flow from operating activities.*

This refers to the net increase (or decrease) in cash resulting from the profit-making operations (sales and expenses) of a business over a period of time. *Profit* is the net result of the sales and expense operations of a business, so we often use the term *cash flow from profit.* In our view, "profit" has more bite and gut feeling than "operating activities." The term *operating activities* does not immediately conjure up the vision of sales and expenses, but the term *profit* does. Keep in mind that the officially sanctioned term *cash flow from operating activities* is used in financial statements. Assuming you don't mind, we'll use both terms, if for no other reason than for some variety.

Testing Your Understanding of Cash Flow

We're confident that since you have read Chapter 2, you have a good grasp on cash flow from profit. Allow us to put a little test to you here, just to be sure. Refer to Table 7.1, which presents the balance sheet of a business at the end of its most recent fiscal year. The changes in each account during the year are presented. You'll notice that only three accounts changed during the year. No other asset or liability increased or decreased during the year. This is not typical, of course, but it serves the purpose of highlighting the essential aspects of cash flow from operating activities.

The business did not pay any dividends to its stockholders during the year, and there were no disposals or acquisitions of

TABLE 7.1—ENDING BALANCE SHEET, WITH CHANGES FROM START OF YEAR

	Ending Balances	Increase (Decrease) during Year
Cash	$ 785,000	$ 350,000
Accounts Receivable	580,000	0
Inventory	725,000	0
Prepaid Expenses	48,000	0
Fixed Assets, Net of Accumulated Depreciation	$1,450,000	$(150,000)
Total Assets	$3,588,000	
Accounts Payable	$ 325,000	$ 0
Accrued Expenses Payable	385,000	0
Income Tax Payable	3,000	0
Short-Term Notes Payable	500,000	0
Long-Term Notes Payable	750,000	0
Stockholders' Paid in Capital	425,000	0
Retained Earnings	$1,200,000	$ 200,000
Total Liabilities and Owners' Equity	$3,588,000	

fixed assets during the year. From this information and the information in Table 7.1, we address two main questions in the following discussion:

Question #1: What is the amount of cash flow from operating activities for the year?

Question #2: What are the components of this cash flow?

The Two Components of Cash Flow from Operating Activities

A good place to start looking at cash flow from operating activities is the net income earned by the business for the year. In other words, what was its bottom-line profit? Net income is recorded as an increase in the owners' equity account, called *retained earnings*. The business did not distribute any dividends during the year, which would have caused a decrease in retained earnings; so the $200,000 increase in retained earnings is the amount of net income for the year.

Fixed assets (property, plant, and equipment) are the long-term assets used by a business to carry on its profit-making operations. The business did not acquire or dispose of any fixed assets during the year. Yet the balance of this asset decreased $150,000 during the year (see Table 7.1). Fixed assets wear out and become obsolete over time. Therefore, the costs of fixed assets are allocated to expense over their useful lives. Each year, a certain fraction of the total cost of a fixed asset is recorded as a decrease in the asset's book value, and this amount is recorded as depreciation expense in the period.

Depreciation expense is not a cash outlay in the year it is recorded. The business already paid for the fixed assets being depreciated in the year they were acquired (which may be 5, 10, or 20 years ago). In short, recording depreciation decreases net income but does not decrease cash. As you know, net income equals sales revenue minus *all* expenses, including depreciation. Because depreciation is not a cash outlay, the amount of this expense is added to net income to measure cash flow from operating activities.

The $150,000 depreciation plus the $200,000 net income equals $350,000. Cash flow from operating activities was $350,000 for the year. As you can see in Table 7.1, cash increased by $350,000. Net income provided $200,000 of this cash increase, and depreciation provided $150,000. These are the two components of the cash flow from operating activities. The company had no other sources of cash, such as an increase in its short- or long-term debt or an increase in its "stockholders' paid in capital" account.

Cash Cow Nature of a Declining Business

It is difficult to predict how long a declining business can stay in business if its sales continue in a free fall year after year. It may or may not be able to eek out a profit from its steadily falling sales. Almost surely its profit trend line will be as steep as its sales trend line. If it is not able to cut expenses fast enough to stay ahead of its declining sales, it will slip into the loss column. However, from the cash flow point of view, things are not all bad.

Depreciation is a positive cash flow factor, even for a declining business. Furthermore, its accounts receivable and inventory should decline with its declining sales revenue. Its cash flow from operating activities would be positive, unless it suffers a sizeable loss that causes a large drain of cash to pay for the loss (payments for expenses exceed cash receipts from sales). And there's another factor that helps the cash flow of a declining business. A declining business does not need to replace many of its long-lived operating assets, perhaps none at all. In other words, its capital expenditures (investments in new fixed assets) should be minimal or zero. In fact, a declining business may sell off some of its fixed assets to downsize its capacity. This asset attrition generates cash (just as it would if you sold off personal assets you no longer needed).

In summary, a declining business often has more cash flow than it needs. A declining business can become a cash cow. A declining business has to decide what to do with its surplus cash. Taking cash out of the business is no simple matter. (Chapter 12 discusses shutting down a business.)

Steady-State Businesses and Their Capital Expenditures

In stark contrast with a declining business, a steady-state business must replace its fixed assets to continue operating and to improve efficiency. Trucks, machines, tools, and equipment wear out or become obsolete and inefficient. Investments in new fixed assets, which are the long-term operating resources of the business, are called *capital expenditures*. A good deal of thought and planning should go into making capital expenditures decisions, not the least of which is how to pay for them.

First Place to Look for Cash

A business looks first to its cash flow from operating activities to finance (provide cash for) capital expenditures. Assuming it is operating profitably, a steady-state business should generate a fairly decent cash flow from operating activities. The amounts of its accounts receivable and inventory should remain fairly level year to year—although, inflation can drive up these two assets despite the fact that sales volume remains flat. These inflation-driven uplifts in receivables and inventory depress cash flow from profit (operating activities), but they usually don't cause too big a drag on cash. Moreover, the business's accounts payable and accrued expenses should float up because of inflation, and these increases offset the increases in the assets.

Roughly speaking, the amount of cash flow from profit for a steady-state business equals its net income plus depreciation. This is not a perfect measure of cash flow for every steady-state business, to be sure; but it's not too far off the mark for most. In any one year for any one business, several things can happen to cause an up or down spike in cash flow from profit. But as a general rule, "net income plus depreciation" is close enough. It's good enough for government work, as they say.

Depreciation: The Unusual Expense That Increases Cash instead of Decreasing Cash

"Depreciation is a source of cash." This comment always makes us flinch a little. The bookkeeping entry of recording depreciation on fixed assets does *not* generate cash inflow. Sales revenue is the source of cash inflow for a business—not its expenses. The cash inflow from sales revenue reimburses a business for its expenses. Putting it another way, cash inflow from sales revenue recoups the costs of making sales and operating the business, as well as providing a little extra for profit, of course.

When you eat in a restaurant, part of the amount you pay for your meal pays the business for the use of its kitchen equipment, its tables and chairs, its building, and so on. When you take a taxi, part of your fare pays the cab owner for using a few miles of the auto. The depreciation cost component imbedded in sales revenue cash flow reimburses the business for the use of its fixed assets.

Depreciation cost recovery is based on the *historical* cost of the company's fixed assets. Over the useful life of a fixed asset, the business recovers the amount it paid for the asset. However, when the time comes to replace it with a new or better asset, the business most likely will have to spend more for the new asset than it did for the asset being replaced. New delivery trucks cost more than the old ones, construction costs rise over time, and new machines and tools cost more than their predecessors. In short, historical-cost-based depreciation usually does not provide all the amount needed for capital expenditures.

Depreciation Shortfall for Current Capital Expenditures

Consider the situation shown in Table 7.2. The business's depreciation cash flow recovery for the year was $750,000. In addition, the business earned $600,000 net income. As just explained, changes in short-term operating assets and liabilities that affect cash flow are usually minimal for a steady-state business. For all practical purposes, it's acceptable to round off numbers and to assume that net income generated an equal amount of cash flow. Let's not quibble about this. As you see in Table 7.2, the business needed $1,000,000 for its capital expenditures, which was $250,000 more than its depreciation cash flow.

Suppose that the business decided to use $250,000 of its $600,000 cash flow from net income to close its capital expenditures gap. Of course, this decision takes $250,000 out of the pool of cash available for cash dividends to stockholders. Presumably, the stockholders understand the wisdom of this course of action. Alternatively, the business could have increased its debt to fund the additional $250,000 needed for capital expenditures. A steady-state business should think twice about ramping up its

TABLE 7.2—CASH FLOW SOURCES AVAILABLE FOR CAPITAL EXPENDITURES

Cash Flow Sources		Capital Expenditures	
Depreciation	$750,000	$1,000,000	Cost of New Fixed Assets
Net Income	$600,000		

debt. In fact, lenders may be reluctant to loan more money to a business with a flat sales-trend line.

Summing up, a steady-state business often needs to use some of its cash flow from net income for capital expenditures, in addition to its cash flow from depreciation. This limits the amount of cash dividends for stockholders, unless the business increases its debt or lowers its working cash balance. Hopefully, its capital expenditures make the business more productive and improve its profit performance over time.

Funding Capital Expenditures in Growth Situations

We hardly need to tell you that the term *growth* is very popular. However, there's no universally accepted definition or standard for *growth*. Generally, the term refers to sales *volume* increases, although it might refer to a sales revenue uptrend driven by price increases instead of by volume increases. Just how large does the percent increase in sales revenue have to be in order to be called "growth" instead of a more modest descriptor (such as an "increase," or a "rise," or a "step-up" in sales)? Does a 5% increase in sales qualify as growth? Or does it take 10% or higher to classify the business as a growth company? We'll use an example in which the business is planning on a 50% sales revenue increase next year. This meets anyone's definition of a growth business.

A Growth Example

Table 7.3 presents the profit-and-loss (P&L) report of a business for the year just ended and its budget for the coming year. The P&L report shown in Table 7.3 is as brief as possible. Actual P&L reports to managers disclose many operating expenses below the gross margin line, but only two operating expenses are shown in Table 7.3. We need to know the depreciation expense for our present discussion. We don't need a breakdown of the company's "other operating expenses," so they are grouped into one lump sum.

The budget for next year is an ambitious plan, on both the

TABLE 7.3—P&L REPORT FOR YEAR JUST ENDED AND BUDGET FOR NEXT YEAR

	Report for Year Just Ended	Budget for Next Year	Increases	
Sales Revenue	$50,000,000	$75,000,000	$25,000,000	50%
Cost of Goods Sold Expense	30,000,000	42,500,000	12,500,000	42
Gross Margin	$20,000,000	$32,500,000	$12,500,000	63
Depreciation Expense	1,500,000	2,000,000	500,000	33
Other Operating Expenses	14,500,000	21,000,000	6,500,000	45
Operating Earnings	$ 4,000,000	$ 9,500,000	$ 5,500,000	138
Interest Expense	600,000	1,000,000	400,000	67
Income before Income Tax	$ 3,400,000	$ 8,500,000	$ 5,100,000	150
Income Tax	1,200,000	3,000,000	1,800,000	150
Net Income	$ 2,200,000	$ 5,500,000	$ 3,300,000	150

sales and expenses sides of the ledger. Sales revenue is projected to go up 50%, whereas cost of goods sold is scheduled to rise only 42% and other operating expenses 45%. Evidently the business is planning on tighter controls over its product and operating costs. Only time will tell how correct these forecasts will be.

A business can budget one particular expense with a great deal of accuracy: The amount of depreciation expense is predetermined for each year. Depreciation is calculated according to either a straight-line or an accelerated method for allocating the cost of a fixed asset over the years of its predicted useful life. Once a fixed asset is put in place, its depreciation for each future year is known. In Table 7.3, you can see that $2,000,000 depreciation is budgeted for next year.

Forecasting Cash Flow from Operating Activities

The business will make major capital expenditures during the coming year to expand its production and distribution capacity, which will cost several million dollars. Clearly the business should forecast the amount of cash that will be provided from its profit-making (operating) activities. Will this internal source of cash be enough to finance its capital expenditures? Or will the business have to borrow more money from its debt sources? Perhaps the business might have to consider issuing additional shares of stock to raise money from its equity sources of capital.

Surely the chief executive officer (CEO) should not plunge ahead and simply hope that the business will have enough money to pay for its capital expenditures. Without a doubt, the CEO should insist on a forecast of cash flow from operating activities for next year. This source of cash is the foundation for planning the amount of additional external capital the business will need to secure during the coming year. (We won't go into a detailed and technical discussion of cash flow budgeting at this point.)

The accounting staff should carry out the actual budgeting process. Indeed, if they can't do this, the business might consider letting them go. One of the main responsibilities of the Controller or the chief accountant is to implement a good financial planning process, which certainly involves cash flow forecasting. Top-level managers don't have the time to get involved in the mechanics of the budgeting process, but they should have a basic understanding of how cash flow from profit behaves in a rapid-growth situation.

A Balance Sheet for Forecasting Cash Flow

Chapter 3 explained that a business that sells products on credit to its customers makes substantial investments in *accounts receivable* (uncollected sales revenue) and in *inventory* (products awaiting sale). These are nontrivial amounts. Indeed, the total amount tied up in these two assets may even exceed the amount of the company's plant, property, and equipment (fixed assets). Chapter 3 also explained that a business buys inventory on credit and does not pay immediately for many of its expenses. A business has two main types of short-term, non-interest-bearing, operating liabilities: *accounts payable* and *accrued expenses payable*. These liabilities are not the result of borrowing money; rather they arise out of the operating activities of the business.

Table 7.4 presents the summarized balance sheet for this

TABLE 7.4—BALANCE SHEET AT CLOSE OF YEAR JUST ENDED

Assets		Liabilities and Owners' Equity	
Cash	$ 5,000,000		
Short-Term Operating Assets (mainly accounts receivable and inventory held for sale)	12,000,000	Short-Term Operating Liabilities (mainly accounts payable and accrued expenses payable)	$ 5,000,000
Long-Term Fixed Operating Assets (net of accumulated depreciation)	18,000,000	Short-Term and Long-Term Debt	15,000,000
		Stockholders' Equity (invested capital plus retained earnings)	15,000,000
Total Assets	$35,000,000	Total Liabilities and Owners' Equity	$35,000,000

business example. This is not a conventional balance sheet. Not enough details are provided to satisfy financial reporting standards. Table 7.4 is a condensed balance sheet for management analysis purposes, not for external reporting outside the business. You've probably noticed the broken line enclosing one group of assets and one group of liabilities. You never see things like this in a published financial report. But there's a reason for the quarantine around these two components of the balance sheet.

Cash is the pivotal asset of every business; it's in a category by itself. The business had $5,000,000 cash at the end of the year (see Table 7.4). The company's short-term operating assets (mainly accounts receivable and inventory) are collapsed into one amount, which is $12,000,000. On the other side of the balance sheet, the company's short-term operating liabilities (mainly accounts payable and accrued expenses payable) are collapsed into one amount, which is $5,000,000.

Those Assets and Liabilities That Vary with Sales

Elsewhere in the book, we explain the very important point that certain expenses vary in tight formation with changes in sales. Quite logically, these are called *variable* expenses. Short-term operating assets vary with changes in sales, as do short-term operating liabilities. If sales revenue increases, say, by 10%, the amounts of a business's short-term operating assets and operating liabilities would increase by about 10%—perhaps not exactly 10% but reasonably close to 10%.

These are the *variable* assets and liabilities of a business, which behave like variable expenses do in response to changes in sales revenue. In this example, the business has $12,000,000 invested in its short-term operating assets, and it owes $5,000,000 of short-term operating liabilities (see Table 7.4). The net difference between the two is $7,000,000. Changes in the excess of short-term

operating assets over short-term operating liabilities affect cash flow from operating activities, as we shall see.

In contrast with the variable short-term operating assets and liabilities, the fixed assets of a business and its debt levels do not move in synchronization with movements in sales—at least not over the short run. Managers have a great deal of discretion regarding the timing of capital expenditures. The present capacity provided by its fixed assets may be enough to allow for some growth without major new capital expenditures. It's difficult to generalize. Short-term and long-term borrowing policies differ from business to business. Some companies borrow heavily, and some go light on debt. In short, movements in fixed assets and debt levels generally run on a timeline that is different from that for movements in sales.

Suppose in this example, only hypothetically, that the business did not have any short-term operating assets. Its cash position would have been $12,000,000 higher. It would not have used cash to invest in these assets. Suppose in this example, only hypothetically, that the business did not have any short-term operating liabilities. Its cash position would have been $5,000,000 lower. It would have had to pay these liabilities. The net effect would have been a $7,000,000 higher cash balance.

The point is that the business has $7,000,000 of cash invested in its short-term operating assets net of its short-term operating liabilities. This net investment moves up and down with rises and declines in sales. When sales go up, the business has to pump more cash into this area, which reduces the pool of cash available for other uses.

Getting Down to the Calculation of Cash Flow

In the company's budget (Table 7.3), we see that sales revenue is projected to increase 50% next year. Therefore, its short-term operating assets and its short-term operating liabilities should increase 50% next year (give or take a little). Doing the arithmetic, short-term operating assets will increase $6,000,000, and short-term operating liabilities will increase $2,500,000. The net effect of these increases on cash flow from operating activities will be a *negative* $3,500,000. In other words, the business will use $3,500,000 cash to increase its short-term operating assets after subtracting the increase in its short-term operating liabilities.

There's another way to calculate this cash flow effect. Compare the company's $7,000,000 *net* cash investment in short-term operating assets less short-term operating liabilities with its annual sales revenue:

$7,000,000 Net Investment
÷ $50,000,000 Annual Sales Revenue = 14%

This ratio tends to remain fairly stable, unless the business were to make drastic changes in the credit periods offered to its customers or in its inventory holding periods. Assume the business does not intend to make any changes in the normal credit terms offered to its customers and does not intend to change its inventory holding periods next year. Sales revenue is budgeted to increase $25,000,000 next year (see Table 7.3). Assuming the ratio remains the same, the cash effect is figured as follows:

14% Ratio × $25,000,000 Sales Revenue Increase
= $3,500,000 Drawdown on Cash

Given the large increase in sales revenue budgeted for next year, undoubtedly the business will increase its accounts receivable and inventory. And its accounts payable and accrued expenses payable will float up at the higher levels of sales. In short, the $25,000,000 sales revenue increase drives up its net investment in short-term operating assets less liabilities by about $3,500,000. This amount is deducted from net income to determine cash flow from net income.

Summing up, the forecast amount of cash flow from operating activities next year for the business example is calculated as follows (see Table 7.5): The $3,500,000 increase in the business's net investment in its short-term operating assets minus liabilities will take a big chunk out of cash available for other uses, in particular for capital expenditures. The business should expect to have only $4,000,000 available cash from its operating activities next year. Suppose it is planning $10,000,000 capital expenditures next year. Management has the unenviable task of figuring out where to get the other $6,000,000.

TABLE 7.5—FORECAST CASH FLOW FROM OPERATING ACTIVITIES NEXT YEAR

Net Income Budgeted for Next Year	$5,500,000
Increase in Short-Term Operating Assets less Short-Term Liabilities	(3,500,000)
Forecast Cash Flow from Net Income	$2,000,000
Depreciation	2,000,000
Forecast Cash Flow from Operating Activities	$4,000,000

Capsule Summary

The chapter begins with a review of cash flow from operating activities. This is the increase (or decrease) in a business's cash balance attributable to its profit-making operations and activities during the period. The two basic components of this cash flow are depreciation recovery (which is embedded in sales revenue cash inflow) and net income for the period.

Depreciation expense is not a cash outlay during the period. More to the point, cash inflow from making sales includes an amount for depreciation on a business's fixed assets. Each period, a business recoups (or recaptures) part of the money it paid for its fixed assets. Depreciation, even though it's an expense, is a source of cash. The other expenses of a business require cash outlays during (or shortly before or after) the period. Depreciation, in contrast, was "prepaid" when the business bought the fixed assets some time ago.

The cash flow from net income is more complicated to determine, compared with the straightforward cash flow effect of depreciation. For a steady-state business (flat sales year to year), total cash flow from operating activities should approximately equal its net income plus depreciation. This is not a perfect measure of cash flow from operating activities, but it's close enough for most practical purposes.

A declining business (decreasing sales year to year) has a cash flow advantage because two assets—accounts receivable and inventory—should decrease with its declining sales. The business pulls money out of these two assets each year as their balances go down with the fall-off in sales revenue. Moreover, a declining business replaces few or perhaps none of its fixed assets. So, a declining business is a cash cow because it liquidates assets as sales decline.

The amount of cash flow depreciation recovery by a steady-state business usually is not enough to pay for its current capital expenditures. Depreciation is based on the historical costs of fixed assets. The costs of new fixed assets generally are higher than the historical costs of the old assets being replaced. So, a steady-state business usually has to use some of its cash flow from net income to cover the difference.

From the cash flow point of view, a growth business is just the opposite of a declining business. Instead of being a cash cow, a growing business is a cash pit, or sinkhole. An example demonstrates that the short-term operating assets and the short-term operating liabilities of a business vary with changes in its sales revenue. If sales revenue increases by 50%, these assets and liabilities generally increase by about 50%. Therefore, a rise in sales revenue causes a negative effect on cash flow from net income. The negative impact equals the increase in its short-term operating assets in excess of the increase in its short-term operating liabilities. This negative cash flow effect can suck up a large percent of annual net income—and could even be larger than net income, causing a negative cash flow from net income for the year.

A growth business typically makes major capital expenditures for new fixed assets in order to expand its capacity and to open new locations. Depreciation and cash flow from net income sel-dom provide all the money needed for these capital expenditures. The first step should be to forecast cash flow for the coming year from net income and from depreciation. Based on this estimate of available cash flow, the managers can start planning where to find the additional capital needed to grow the business.

8

TAXES AND MORE TAXES: IF IT CAN BE TAXED, IT IS TAXED

"In this world nothing can be said to be certain, except death and taxes."
—Benjamin Franklin, 1789

Ben Franklin certainly was right about what is certain, although business owners might expand on this famous comment as follows: "Nothing can be said to be certain, except death and taxes, *and I'm not sure which is worse*." (We discuss the death of a business in Chapter 12.) The focus of this chapter is structured around the plethora of business taxes and governmentally mandated costs that burden every business today.

Prior to jumping into this subject too deeply, two general thoughts should be kept in mind. *First*, the volume and the complexity of taxation issues with which businesses must deal have exploded during the past 20 years. It has become almost impossible to stay in 100% compliance with every taxing and regulatory authority, including a variety of foreign, federal, state, and local governmental agencies, all of which are desperately searching for funds and new revenue sources to balance budgets, provide basic services, and support infrastructure needs. Hence, it is important to remember that a business is both a taxpayer and a tax collector for foreign, federal, state, and local governments.

Second, a business owner or manager must understand what triggers tax compliance and obligation requirements and what the different types of business taxes are. Executing a business decision as simple as expanding the company's geographical market by adding a new sales representative into a new state is much easier said than done. This decision can carry with it a requirement to comply with a series of new licensing, taxation, and regulatory-mandated costs, which may erode profits and consume scarce management time and resources. By establishing *nexus* (i.e., the presence of a business operation) in a new legal jurisdiction, a company's tax compliance requirements often grow exponentially.

This chapter not only expands on the different types of business taxation and regulatory-mandated costs present, but also provides insight on how best to proactively manage this unavoidable element of operating a business.

Income Taxation: Welcome to the Jungle

The most widely understood (just joking) and commonly referred to form of taxation is the federal income tax. For the more than 100 million Americans required to file an annual income tax return with the Internal Revenue Service (IRS) as well as with various state and local government agencies, the annual process of completing the necessary paperwork and ensuring the returns are filed on time has almost become a national trademark. This is also true for the more than 10 million business entities operating throughout the country that each year must file federal, state, and local income tax returns with the appropriate governing bodies. Big or small, foreign or domestic, public or private, for profit or not, all businesses must file annual income tax returns, regardless of the type of legal business entity and whether it made a profit.

Types of Business Legal Entities

The first step in managing business income tax issues is understanding the type of business legal entity present. From a taxation perspective, there are two main types of business legal entities. One type is known as a *pass-through entity*, which includes Subchapter S (S for small) corporations, general and limited partnerships, and limited liability companies (LLC), a relatively new type of business entity that provides for additional structural and taxation flexibility. These types of entities are not subject to income taxes at the business level but rather "pass

through" the income earned by the business to the individual owners of the company, which are then subject to taxation on their individual tax returns. In contrast, a regular C corporation is a separate entity subject to tax itself. In other words, C corporations are subject to income taxes at the legal entity or business level (rather than the personal level).

The simplified example in Table 8.1 of the income statements for TUV, Inc. and XYZ, Inc., illustrate the difference in taxation principles between the two types of business entities. In the end, the various taxing authorities still get their income taxes with the only real difference being who (i.e., a business or an individual) actually forwards the money.

It is important to note that even though the subchapter S corporation (at the corporate level) has no income tax obligation, the three individual owners of TUV, Inc., must report ordinary taxable income ranging from $164,450 to $59,800 on their personal returns. Assuming each owner is subject to a marginal tax rate of 38% (combined federal and state), the owners pay income tax ranging from $62,491 to $22,724 individually, or $113,620 in total. Hence, the subchapter S corporation will most likely want to make a distribution from net profit to the owners in the amount of at least $113,620 (in total) so that they have sufficient funds available to cover their personal tax liabilities.

The preceding example presents a situation where the taxing authorities receive the same amount of income taxes from either entity, just through different channels. Why use an S corporation

TABLE 8.1—TAXATION OF PASS-THROUGH SUBCHAPTER S CORPORATION VERSUS C CORPORATION

	TUV, Inc., Subchapter S Corporation Year-End	XYZ, Inc., Regular C Corporation Year-End
Income Statement Summary	**12/31/06**	**12/31/06**
Revenue	$15,265,000	$15,265,000
Cost of Goods Sold	11,503,000	11,503,000
Gross Profit	$ 3,762,000	$ 3,762,000
Gross Margin	24.64%	24.64%
Selling, General, and Administrative Expenses	$ 3,251,000	$ 3,251,000
Other (Income) Expenses	212,000	212,000
Net Profit before Tax	$ 299,000	$ 299,000
Income Tax Expense	0	113,620
Net Profit	$ 299,000	$ 185,380
Amount of Net Profit Included in Personal Tax Returns		
Owner A, 55% Ownership	$ 164,450	$ 0
Owner B, 25% Ownership	74,750	0
Owner C, 20% Ownership	59,800	0
Total	$ 299,000	$ 0
Distribution of Net Profit to Cover Personal Income Tax Liabilities		
Owner A, 55% Ownership	$ 62,491	$ 0
Owner B, 25% Ownership	28,405	0
Owner C, 20% Ownership	22,724	$ 0
Total	$ 113,620	$ 0
Net Profit Retained in Business	$ 185,380	$ 185,380

over a C corporation, or vice versa? The answer lies in the ability to utilize proper tax-planning techniques to manage potential income tax obligations over the long term. If earnings are generated and can be passed through to owners at a lower marginal income tax rate (by utilizing a pass-through entity), then tax dollars are saved, and capital is retained in the business—capital that can be used to finance business growth.

In addition, earnings from a pass-through entity are taxed only once, whereas earnings from a C corporation are taxed at the business level and then again at the personal level if any distribution of earnings are made in the form of a dividend (producing a double taxation environment). The list of "technical" tax differences between the two types of business entities is extensive and goes well beyond the scope of this book. However, it is extremely important to understand the pros and cons of the two business types (from a taxation perspective) when establishing and operating a business.

How Income Is Measured

The second issue regarding income taxes is the necessity of understanding how income is measured. The majority of this book has discussed business profitability from a generally accepted accounting principles (GAAP) basis. These accounting principles are applied in recording business transactions to produce financial statements based on complete/full accrual theory. The two main sources of authoritative pronouncements on accounting principles and financial reporting standards are the Securities and Exchange Commission (SEC) and the Financial Accounting Standards Board (FASB).

The national organization of certified public accountants (CPAs)—the American Institute of Certified Public Accountants

(AICPA)—also plays an important role in setting accounting standards. (Until the establishment of the Public Company Accounting Oversight Board by the Sarbanes-Oxley Act of 2002, the AICPA was the preeminent authority for setting auditing standards.) Hence, the majority of financial statements prepared for external distribution are based on accrual-basis accounting principles, and many businesses have their financial statements audited by an independent CPA.

Congress enacts income tax laws, and the Treasury Department and the IRS issue many regulations and rulings governing the interpretation of the Income Tax Code (to say nothing about a large number of court cases that deal with income tax issues). This complex body of income tax law is not in perfect harmony with generally accepted accounting principles (GAAP). The primary differences can be broken down into two areas—*permanent* versus *timing* (temporary) differences.

Permanent and Timing Differences

Permanent differences relate to those transactions that under the Internal Revenue Code are not recorded as income or expense in the determination of annual taxable income. Needless to say, most permanent differences relate to expense deductions that are disallowed by the IRS when calculating taxable income. For example, consider the costs of meals and entertainment of a business. The basic rule is that only 50% of expenses incurred for meals and entertainment can be deducted to determine taxable income. Hence, if a business incurred $100,000 of meals and entertainment expenses during the year, for tax purposes, only $50,000 could be deducted on the tax return. Several other types of permanent differences exist, including certain penalties/late fees and life insurance premiums (depending on how the beneficiary is established). The important thing to remember regarding permanent differences is that no tax benefit or liability will be present with the transaction, and, as such, the company should plan accordingly.

Timing differences relate to when revenue and expenses have to be recorded in calculating annual taxable income, and the period in which the expense or income is recorded differs from the GAAP–based financial statements. The following examples have been provided of some of the most common timing differences:

Timing Differences between GAAP–Based Financial Statements and Taxable Income

• **Depreciation Expense:** For GAAP purposes, a company may elect to use the straight-line method of depreciation and to expense the capital asset over a 60-month period in equal monthly charges. For tax purposes, the IRS provides the opportunity to accelerate the depreciation to expense more of the asset in the first two or three years of its use, thus providing the business a tax incentive.

• **Bad Debt Expense:** For tax purposes, the IRS generally only allows the so-called direct write-off method to be used. Bad debt expense can only be deducted when specific receivables deemed uncollectible are actually written off because no future collection is expected. For GAAP purposes, companies often utilize the allowance for doubtful accounts method to record bad debt expense by estimating how many receivables will become worthless. For example, suppose a business during the year wrote off specific customers' accounts receivable. In addition, based on its past experience, the business estimates that $100,000 of its year-end $5,000,000 accounts receivable will be uncollectible. Accordingly, the business recorded $100,000 bad debt expense for these future write-offs, in addition to the customers' accounts written off during the year. In effect, the income tax law says: Not so fast! You can't deduct bad debt expense until you actually write off specific accounts receivable. The business can deduct the amount of accounts receivable it actually wrote off during the year, but it cannot (yet) deduct the $100,000 estimated future write-offs.

• *Deferred Compensation:* Companies often use deferred compensation plans and programs to provide additional earning potential to employees with pretax dollars; that is, employees can set aside certain earnings in these deferred compensation programs, which are not subject to personal income taxes. While these are a great deal for the employee, the employer often is not allowed to deduct the deferred compensation contribution currently but rather must wait until the employee actually receives the earnings and records it as taxable income (in the year of receipt).

Revisiting Key Points

This next statement may sound far-fetched, but we will go out on a limb anyhow and say, "The volume and complexity of income tax permanent and timing differences are extensive" (translation—"the IRS has killed more than a few trees in producing the complete tax code"). When summarizing income tax issues and providing for a reasonable basis on which to be at least somewhat knowledgeable, the following key points need to be revisited:

Key Points Regarding Business Income Taxation

♦ Know the type of entity that is present for income taxation purposes—pass-through, or nontaxed, entities versus taxed entities.

♦ Understand the basic concept of how taxable income is measured, including timing versus permanent differences.

♦ Comply with all of the various authorities requiring income tax returns to be completed, including federal, state, local, and, if applicable, foreign.

♦ Produce and maintain a sound set of GAAP–based financial statements. This represents the starting point for properly managing income tax issues and for generating the information required to prepare various income tax returns.

♦ Don't be afraid to ask for help and/or to retain professional assistance to manage income tax issues. There is almost no way for a business owner today to stay on top of the multitude of foreign, federal, state, and local income tax issues and still operate a business.

♦ Realize that income tax obligations are not due unless a taxable profit (as defined by the various rules and regulations established) is present. If this is the case, remember that income tax obligations are usually paid in quarterly installments (pay as you go) over the tax period.

The Hidden Dangers of Payroll Taxes

To be successful in real estate, the old saying goes, the three most important considerations are "Location, Location, and Location." When operating a business, the three most important rules for managing tax issues are "Pay your payroll taxes, Pay your payroll taxes, and Pay your payroll taxes." Although payroll taxes are relatively simple to manage and understand in relation to the complexities associated with income taxes, the risks of not properly managing payroll taxes (to the business and its principal owners) can be far greater than those involved with income taxes.

Taxes withheld from employees wages and payroll-based taxes paid by a business must be remitted to various federal, state, and local government agencies on a periodic basis. In almost all cases, wages paid to employees are subject to payroll taxes based on established guidelines, tables, and formulas as determined by those government agencies. Unlike income taxes, which are only due and payable if the business has generated taxable profits, payroll taxes are due when wages (including salaries, hourly compensation, bonuses, commissions, spiffs, and other forms of compensation that are reported as W-2 earnings per the IRS) are paid to an employee. And once again, the various taxing authorities at the federal, state, and local levels all seem to have their hand in the pot.

At the *federal level*, there are four primary payroll taxes: (1) Social Security, (2) Medicare, (3) individual income, and (4) unemployment (a form of insurance). The first three of these taxes are paid by the individual and are withheld from each employee's wages. The fourth, federal unemployment tax, is a burden not on the individual but rather on the employer; thus, no tax is withheld from the employee's wages for this particular tax. It is important to note that Social Security and Medicare taxes tend to be the most burdensome: Not only are these taxes withheld from the employee's wages; but in addition, the employer must match, dollar for dollar, the amount withheld and periodically remit these two payroll taxes to the IRS.

At the *state level*, two types of payroll taxes are generally present: (1) personal income and (2) unemployment. Personal income taxes are withheld from the employee's wages, whereas, similar to the federal unemployment tax, the state unemployment tax represents just the obligation of the employer. Other forms of mandatory withholdings are also present at the state level, including local taxes and disability insurance. However, these vary significantly on a state-by-state basis and are not discussed in any great detail here.

Table 8.2 provides an example of how payroll taxes are calculated for three employees (at different wage levels) from both the employee and the employer perspective.

Social Security taxes are imposed on both employees and employers. Employers withhold Social Security taxes assessed on employees from their wages, as you probably know. Employers are also required to withhold income taxes from their employees' wages. Certain wage-based taxes are paid by employers, but not by their employees.

TABLE 8.2—EMPLOYMENT TAXES FOR DIFFERENT WAGE EARNERS

Employee	Randall S.	Rich E.	Dennis B.
Annual Wages/Earnings	$95,000	$46,800	$6,240
Payroll Tax Withholdings, Employee:			
Social Security	5,394	2,902	387
Medicare	1,378	679	90
Federal Personal Income Tax	19,000	7,020	624
State Personal Income Tax	4,750	1,404	125
Federal Unemployment Insurance	0	0	0
State Unemployment Insurance	0	0	0
Total Withholdings, Employee	$30,522	$12,005	$1,226
Payroll Tax Expense, Employer:			
Social Security	$5,394	$2,902	$387
Medicare	1,378	679	90
Federal Personal Income Tax	0	0	0
State Personal Income Tax	0	0	0
Federal Unemployment Insurance	56	56	50
State Unemployment Insurance	245	245	218
Total Expense, Employer	$7,073	$3,882	$746
Payroll Tax Withheld Plus Tax Paid by Employer:			
Social Security	$10,788	$ 5,804	$ 774
Medicare	2,756	1,358	180
Federal Personal Income Tax	19,000	7,020	624
State Personal Income Tax	4,750	1,404	125
Federal Unemployment Insurance	56	56	50
State Unemployment Insurance	245	245	218
Total Obligation, Employer	$37,595	$15,887	$1,971
Summary:			
Total Expense (Wages and Taxes), Employer	$102,073	$50,682	$6,986
Take-Home Pay, Employee	64,478	34,795	5,014
Total Tax Obligation, Employer	37,595	15,887	1,972
Ratio: Total Tax Obligation/Total Employer Expense	36.83%	31.34%	28.23%

Social Security taxes (used to fund the U.S. national retirement and Social Security program) are applied at a rate of 6.2% on the first $87,900 of wages earned in 2004, which is slightly higher than the 2003 limit used in Table 8.2. (*Note:* The IRS raises this figure annually to account for inflation and other factors.) As is evident from Table 8.2, a business is responsible not just for withholding the Social Security taxes amount from the employee's wages but also for matching the amount and remitting the total to the IRS. This matching requirement represents an expense to the company.

Medicare taxes (used to fund the U.S. national healthcare system for qualifying parties) are applied at a rate of 1.45% of all employee earnings. Similar to Social Security, the business must match the amount withheld and remit it to the IRS on a periodic basis. However, unlike the Social Security component, there is no limit and/or cap on the Medicare tax component—it is applied to all wages earned, including commissions, bonuses, salaries, and hourly wages. This matching requirement also represents an expense to the company.

Federal personal income taxes are withheld just from the employee's wages; there is no company-matching requirement. The federal government bases these taxes on what it estimates the individual will owe in federal personal income taxes at the end of the year. The federal government provides tables to assist employers with calculating the amount of federal personal income tax that should be withheld, depending on the employee's individual tax reporting status, which takes into consideration marital status, number of children/exemptions, and other personal factors. The IRS provides the W-4 form (completed by all employees) to assist with determining what the proper personal income tax withholdings should be.

Federal unemployment taxes (used to support the unemployment insurance payment programs administered by the states to provide supplemental income to unemployed workers) represent just an expense of the company; nothing is withheld from the employee's wages. Currently, the federal government requires 0.8% of an employee's first $7,000 in annual wages to be remitted for this tax. For anyone who struggles with math, this amounts to a whopping $56. These types of taxes tend to be paid during the first two quarters of each year, as once the employee exceeds the base wage level, no further tax is due. However, it is extremely important to note that the wage base level applies on a company identification basis and not to the employee. Hence, if you hire an employee in midyear, at which time they've already earned in excess of $7,000 with their previous employer, the unemployment tax will be due again as the new company has not yet paid any wages to the employee.

At the state level, generally only personal income tax and unemployment taxes are involved. Similar to federal personal income taxes, a state collects these taxes based on what it estimates the individual will owe in personal income taxes at the end of the year. Tax tables are established by the state and provided to employers so that the appropriate amount of taxes can be withheld from the employee's wages and remitted to the state periodically. State unemployment taxes operate in much the same fashion as federal unemployment taxes: A rate is established and applied to the first X dollars of wages. The company absorbs the expense; no withholdings are made from the employee's wages. The main difference between federal and state unemployment taxes is based in the rates used and the wages subject to the rate. Most states use a rate well in excess of 0.8% and wage levels of above $7,000. Hence, the bite at the state level is usually five times (or greater) higher than the $56 at the federal level.

If you remember just one thing about payroll taxes remember this: Payroll taxes are held in trust for the employee by the withholding party (i.e., the business). As such, if the payroll taxes are not paid, the taxing authorities will not only pursue the business in their attempt to secure funds for payment, but will also pierce whatever legal business form is present to collect the taxes. Hence, the officers, board members, check signers, senior managers, and/or any other party aware of the deficiency or of who was responsible for remittance of the payroll taxes can be pursued individually to collect the outstanding obligation. This includes attaching to about any type of personal asset—homes, retirement accounts, college funds, savings, and so on. Needless to say, businesses do not want to find themselves in trouble for unpaid payroll taxes.

Beyond the all-important concept of paying your payroll taxes, the following additional thoughts should be kept in mind concerning payroll taxes:

Additional Points to Remember Regarding Payroll Taxes

- A number of external payroll services (including ADP and Paychexs) and other organizations are available to assist in managing payroll tax issues. These organizations are cheap and reliable, provide quality services, and are one of the best outsourcing values in which a business can invest.

- Payroll taxes are remitted to the various taxing authorities on a periodic basis, depending on the dollar amount of the payroll tax obligation. The larger the periodic amount, the more frequently the business will be required to remit payroll taxes (including being required to transfer funds electronically).

- Payroll tax compliance reporting is essential and is usually completed on both a quarterly and an annual basis (at both the federal and state levels). These reports reconcile the amount of payroll taxes withheld and owed against the amount paid to ensure employers are remitting their obligations in a timely manner.

- The amount of payroll-based taxes remitted to various government agencies (withholdings from employees' plus employers' taxes) is typically about one-third of the total wages including employer taxes. This is extremely important to understand as the nation continues to evolve into more of an employee-based service-orientated economy from a production/manufacturing-based one. Effective management of payroll taxation issues can improve bottom-line performance.

Other Forms of Taxation
(The Fun Is Just Starting)

Now that you're an expert on income and payroll taxes, it's time to move into the third major area of taxation—everything else. It would be almost impossible to address and cover every other type of taxation, due to the volume and variety of federal, state, and local enacted legislation. For example, the hotel/hospitality industry is subject to a room tax passed through to the end customers. For communities dependent on tourism, such as San Diego, Las Vegas, and New York, this represents a significant government revenue source. In the oil and gas industry, federal and state excise taxes are present that significantly raise the per gallon price of gas that a typical motorist pays.

These two examples highlight that it's really not a matter of who pays the ultimate tax (i.e., the end consumer) but rather where the tax is applied and how it is administered. In the hospitality example, the hotel charges the customer the tax (with a clear reference to the tax on the customer's bill) and remits it to the government. In the oil and gas example, the wholesale distributor charges the retail outlet the tax and remits it to the various authorities (thus, the end customer never sees the tax component of each gallon of gas purchased). With this in mind, the remainder of this section will be focused on taxation issues most businesses will need to comply with and manage.

First on the list are the ever-popular sales and use taxes. We will start here because basically every consumer in the United States is subject to this tax. Sales taxes are generally produced from the sale of tangible personal property (from automobiles to

zippers). For example, a retail store that sells jewelry is required to collect sales tax from the customer purchasing a product and to remit it (periodically) to the appropriate taxing authority. Sales tax rules, regulations, and rates are established at the state, local, and city levels, depending on the need for these jurisdictions to generate revenue.

In some instances, no sales tax is due because the specific jurisdiction has opted not to impose a sales tax. For instance, the state of Oregon does not have a sales tax. In other states, certain types of purchases are not subject to sales taxes. For example, Rhode Island and Massachusetts exempt clothing and food from sales taxes. But, almost all states impose a sales tax on most consumer purchases, which provide a significant share of their revenue. It should also be noted that sales tax rates can be a function of multiple government entities as the state, county, city, and other local organizations (e.g., a metropolitan transit authority) all may have a need to generate revenue. Although the state sales tax rate may be 6%, the actual rate charged for a local purchase could be 8% to account for the other governmental agencies.

Accompanying the sales tax is its close cousin the *use tax*. Use taxes are similar to sales taxes (and often administered at the same rates), but they are applied to the organization consuming and/or using the tangible personal property. *Consumption* is the key word here, as property purchased that is subsequently resold is not subject to sales or use tax (e.g., inventory purchases made by a wholesale operation that sells them to a retail store).

The important distinction between sales tax and use tax lies not in the tax rate applied but in who is responsible for paying the tax. The best way to illustrate this point resides in how a number of catalog companies sell their goods. For example, a customer in California orders a piece of clothing from a catalog company located in Maine, pays for the purchase with a credit card, and then receives the product via the U.S. Postal Service parcel delivery service. Because the catalog company in Maine has not established "nexus" in the state of California, it is not required to collect and to remit sales tax. Rather, the end user, or consumer of the product, is obligated to remit a use tax to the government agency where the product is consumed (and we all know how often this occurs). This loss of sales/use tax revenue by various government entities has been an issue for a number of years and is being amplified by the proliferation of purchases over the Internet.

For consumers, the potential risk of not paying use tax on a $100 out-of-state clothes purchase is minimal. For businesses, the story is different, as they must understand the importance of properly accounting for and complying with use-tax rules and regulations. Purchases of property consumed in the normal course of business (ranging from office supplies to tools used in a manufacturing process to inventory that is purchased originally for resale but that is consumed internally) that were obtained without paying sales tax must be reported to the appropriate taxing authority for assessment. If a business fails to do this, audits may be undertaken by the taxing authority, which would trigger not only the use tax due but also penalty and interest charges. It goes without saying that businesses are much easier and bigger targets for the taxing authorities to pursue for tax receipts due.

Property taxes represent nothing more than a tax assessed on the value of tangible/real property owned. For most of us, the most prevalent form of property tax is based on the value of real estate owned (i.e., your primary residence), which is paid either directly or included with a normal monthly mortgage payment (and paid through an escrow account). For businesses, property taxes are most often assessed annually and are based on the value of the tangible/real property owned by a company.

A business is required to complete an annual property tax return that identifies all of the assets owned, leased, and/or in its possession summarized by date of purchase, amount, and type of asset (e.g., computer equipment, office furniture, production tools). This return is then forwarded to the various taxing authorities for review and assessment. Subsequent to this, a property tax bill is forwarded to the company for payment. Generally speaking, property taxes are administered and managed by county tax assessors, as opposed to income, payroll, and sales/use taxes, which are federal and state responsibilities.

Beyond sales, use, and property taxes lay a series of other taxes, which are widely utilized but not nearly as well known and/or understood. Rather than attempt to list and explain every potential tax (which of course would provide grounds for every reader of this book to yell and scream at the authors), the following examples have been provided:

Other Business Taxes to Worry About

◆ *Unclaimed Property Taxes:* Property that is in the possession of a business that rightfully belongs to another party and has never been claimed is not the property of the business; rather, it must be turned over to the appropriate taxing authority for administration. For example, a business does not get to keep the money owed to former employees who never cashed their payroll checks. Rather, an unclaimed property tax return needs to be completed, with the money owed turned over to the taxing authority for eventual "hopeful" distribution to the rightful owner.

• **Head Taxes:** A periodic tax is applied that is based on the number of full-time employees present. For example, a state may assess a $25 per head, per quarter payroll tax. If a company has 100 full-time employees, a $2,500 tax would be due. The state of Nevada has recently implemented the use of head taxes because it has no state personal income taxes generating revenues.

• **Excise and "Sin" Taxes:** These come in all shapes, sizes, and forms and are applied on everything from fuel to liquor and tobacco (i.e., sin taxes) to the rendering of certain services. Yes, certain taxing authorities have begun to tax the rendering of services in their never-ending search for revenue, with an increasing number beginning to look at industries such as personnel staffing to generate additional tax receipts.

• **Incentive Tax Credits:** Amazingly enough, not all taxes represent the outflow of money from businesses. Various federal, state, and local tax laws and regulations provide tax credits as incentives for companies to pursue certain business strategies. Some of the most common incentive tax credits reside in hiring qualified employees (from certain economic classes) and using environmentally friendly energy sources.

In summarizing the various other forms of business taxation issues present, three critical issues should be kept in mind. (1) Educate yourself to understand how these types of other taxes apply to your business and can influence economic decisions. Missing even the slightest tax issues can result in significant added costs. (2) Proper tax reporting and compliance is once again extremely important. The bigger the dollars, the more frequent the reporting and the more closely your business will be monitored. (3) Understand that a number of these taxes are held in trust (similar to payroll taxes) for the government. If they are not paid, be prepared for the taxing authority to disregard the business's legal structure and to pursue the persons responsible for the taxes at the individual level.

Government-Mandated Costs
(We're Not Done Yet)

As much fun as we've had in attempting to discuss the plethora of business taxation issues, this fun pales in comparison to the sheer enjoyment we're going to have discussing other government-mandated costs. (You might detect a note of sarcasm here.) This cost area within a business has become one of the most problematic for employers to manage; and it only looks to get worse as federal, state, and local governments attempt to "fix" the problem by burdening companies with more and more costs. The good news, however, lies in the fact that this cost area represents a significant opportunity for employers to proactively manage risks within the organization to reduce expenses and to gain competitive advantages.

First, let's discuss the wonderful world of *workers' compensation* insurance. Workers' compensation insurance is basically required in every state of the country. This form of mandated insurance is charged to the employer to cover costs of potential employee injuries, accidents, and similar types of events. Workers' compensation insurance is designed to cover both medical-related costs (e.g., a worker falls and breaks his ankle requiring medical services to be rendered) as well as lost wages/earnings (e.g., the same worker is laid up for two weeks, during which time he cannot work and earn a paycheck). In addition, workers' compensation insurance premiums also cover the related administrative costs associated with managing this form of insurance as well as other potential costs, such as legal fees.

State laws, rules, and regulations dictate the types of workers' compensation insurance benefits that will be provided to the injured worker. The actual workers' compensation insurance premium charged to the employer is generally based on the level of risk the employees are undertaking as they work. For example, a construction worker operates in a much higher risk environment than does a paper-pushing accountant. Although both may earn $20 per hour, the workers' compensation insurance premium for the construction worker may average 15% of this hourly rate (i.e., $3.00 per hour) whereas the premium for the accountant may be only 1% of the hourly rate (i.e., $0.20 per hour). Clearly a significant difference, but one that is designed to account for the increased risk associated with a construction worker getting hurt on the job.

Because states mandate that the employer carry workers' compensation insurance, state-operated programs are made available to employers to secure coverage. Hence, a business basically has the option of either securing workers' compensation insurance coverage from a quasi-governmental agency, such as the State Compensation Insurance System in California, or going to the open market and obtaining insurance from carriers willing to "write" (i.e., extend) these types of coverages. In some states, carriers openly provide quotes and aggressively pursue business, as state laws tend to be "employer friendly."

In other states (let's pick on California for a moment), carriers apply strict underwriting criteria and guidelines, as the states tend to be employee friendly. Needless to say, the differences between state coverage levels can vary widely because a workers' compensation insurance claim in one state may run $2,000, whereas the same claim in another state may reach $10,000 or more. It's not too hard to figure out why businesses locate certain operations (e.g., a manufacturing plant) in one state over another, given the potential added workers' compensation insurance expenses present.

Business owners and managers should keep some key issues in mind with workers' compensation insurance. (1) If you don't have the coverage, penalties assessed by the states can be severe and actually may include criminal charges in certain situations (against the officers/owners of the business). (2) State-operated and -supported workers' compensation insurance programs are often inefficient, expensive, and burdensome. If your company has the resources, private coverage should definitely be pursued. (3) Properly and proactively managed workers' compensation insurance programs can provide your business with a competitive weapon. Investing internally in the needed corporate infrastructure for risk-management tasks can often produce substantial returns.

Beyond workers' compensation insurance, health/medical insurance represents the next most pressing "potential" regulatory-mandated business cost. We use the term *potential* because health/medical insurance is still generally provided to employees at the option of the employer. However, California has taken the lead in requiring businesses of certain sizes, starting in 2006, to provide mandated employee health/medical coverage or pay a premium to the state for similar coverage. Clearly, states are experiencing significant economic discomfort from the past three-plus years of annual double-digit increases in health/medical costs, which show no signs of abating soon. States once again are looking to pass the economic burden of rising expenses on to businesses rather than attempting to manage the issue internally with limited/inadequate resources. Business owners and managers will need to stay on top of this issue in the years to come, as having to absorb medical/health insurance costs internally, which can easily exceed 10% of an employee's base compensation, could significantly change economic operating models.

And finally, let's spend a moment discussing the various *fees*, *licenses*, and *permits* a business must obtain in order to operate in certain local jurisdictions (e.g., cities and unincorporated county locations). If a business has established nexus (or presence) in a local jurisdiction, chances are that a periodic license, permit charge, or fee will be due. This can range from a one-time annual flat fee (which depends on the number of employees a company has) to a fee based on the amount of receipts generated within that jurisdiction (sounds like another tax). The easiest rule of thumb to apply here is really quite simple: If you have a business presence in a local jurisdiction, assume a license, fee, and/or permit will need to be obtained and paid for in order to "legally" operate.

Taming the Business Taxes Beast

Thus far the emphasis of this chapter has been centered on discussing business taxation and regulatory-mandated costs from more of an informational perspective; that is, an effort was made to provide a basic overview of the major types of business taxation and regulatory-mandated costs present, the underlying logic inherent within each one, and the associated compliance requirements (with each one). In addition, various tips and suggestions were provided that offered management ideas on how to proactively tackle this increasingly complex and burdensome business area. In an effort to summarize the issues covered in this chapter and to draw some sort of logical conclusion on how to manage this area, the following reference points are provided:

Final Checklist for Managing Business Taxes

- *Accounting Books and Records:* Development and maintenance of a sound set of accounting books and records is essential to the management process. The data and information needed to properly administer business taxation and regulatory-mandated costs are located here.

- *Knowledge and Education:* Business owners and managers must obtain a base knowledge/education (however tough this may be) with this subject matter. It is very difficult for business plans and economic models to be developed and understood without it.

- *Nexus and Compliance:* If you proactively manage nexus and compliance requirements, you will save countless hours and dollars down the road. If you don't, working with a taxing authority in a reactive mode (i.e., letting them find you) will undoubtedly waste valuable company resources.

- *Professional Support:* Retaining professional support to assist with the management of business taxation and regulatory-mandated costs is often worth every penny spent. Experts abound in this area, due to the volume and the complexities of the issues present.

- *Economic Opportunities:* Numerous opportunities are present to enhance a company's performance by actively managing these issues. A decision as simple as locating a business just on the other side of a state border (let's say from California to Nevada) may save business countless dollars due to differences in workers' compensation laws, state income tax rates, and related expenses. It's no wonder that certain states and foreign countries maintain such strong competitive positions.

- *Strategic Planning and Company Management:* Business taxation and regulatory-mandated costs should be an active part of a company's strategic planning process. Adequate business resources (internal or external) need to be dedicated to this function.

• *State and Local Taxing Authorities:* Most people recognize the IRS as the predominant taxing authority in this country. From a collection standpoint, this is true, as the federal government is the single largest taxing authority in the country. However, states, counties, and cities often represent a bigger business-management challenge because of the different types of taxes present, the volume of compliance issues, and the agencies' aggressiveness (in collecting tax receipts). Remember that almost every state in the country is experiencing budget problems and, as such, is looking to generate as much tax receipts (and as quickly) as possible.

• *Added Liabilities and Risks:* Finally (and if you haven't picked up on this yet), numerous of the aforementioned business taxation and regulatory-mandated costs will pierce the company's legal structure and may attach to the officers, directors, and senior managers at the personal level. The last thing you want to have happen is a taxing authority attaching to your personal assets to collect obligations due. It's not a pretty sight.

Capsule Summary

This chapter surveys business taxes and certain other legally imposed costs on businesses (in particular, workers' compensation insurance). Taxes are not the favorite topic of business managers, of course. However, business owners/managers ignore taxes at their own peril. Failure to fully comply with tax requirements can cause serious business problems and could leave its owners vulnerable to legal action against them as individuals and against their personal assets.

The chapter is not an exhaustive treatise on the federal income taxation of business entities. Just bare fundamentals are covered, including the important distinction between businesses that are taxed as a separate entity (regular "C" corporations) and pass-through tax entities. Regular corporations are subject to tax on their annual taxable income. If any portion of after-tax net income is distributed to stockholders, the dividend income is subject to individual income tax in the hands of the stockholders. In contrast, a pass-though entity does not pay income tax itself, as a separate entity. Instead, its annual taxable income is allocated among its owners, and the owners must include their individual shares in their annual personal income tax returns— whether or not any of the business's taxable income was distributed to them.

Unfortunately, certain accounting methods and restrictions under the income tax law differ from the accounting methods used to prepare the financial statements of businesses. These are either permanent differences or timing differences; examples of both types are provided in the chapter. The chapter spends a fair amount of time discussing payroll-based taxes—both on employees and employers. The responsibility of the business employer to withhold Social Security, Medicare, and income taxes from employee wages is explained. The total amount remitted to government agencies (withholdings plus taxes paid by an employer) is a significant percent of the basic labor cost of a business. Looking at this more broadly, the soundness of our Social Security and Medicare programs depends on business employers carrying out their responsibilities in these areas.

In addition to income and payroll taxes, a business pays many other types of taxes and must comply with workers' compensation insurance requirements. Also, businesses play a vital role in the collection of sales taxes for state and local governments. A business should take the lead and determine every tax it has to collect and pay. Then it must file all the required forms and returns on time. Many businesses need the advice and expertise of professionals such as certified public accountants on tax matters. Like many other areas in managing a business, the devil is in the details. Tax laws are plagued with a bewildering amount of details, that's for sure. But, this should not prevent taking a proactive approach to minimizing the tax cost of a business.

9

PREVENTING FRAUD AGAINST BUSINESS: CONTROLS FOR COMBATING FRAUD ATTACKS

"There's only one way to deal with student cheating—prevent it!"
—Sage advice given to John Tracy early
in his teaching career by a senior professor

The senior professor quoted was absolutely right, of course. Once a professor catches a student cheating, you are in a quandary. The student knows what he did was wrong (at least you don't have to explain that to him. Should you give him an F on the exam or an F for the course? Should you report this to the Dean? Should you call his mother? Would he possibly consider suicide if you came down too hard on him? Should you offer him a second chance and give him a makeup exam?

Suppose a professor catches one person cheating on the exam. How many others cheated that were not caught? In hindsight, the professor should have done more to prevent students from cheating. However, designing and enforcing anticheating controls take time. If the controls are too intrusive, they may violate the rights of students. On the one hand, you can't strip-search students to make sure they don't have crib notes with them. On the other hand, you can forbid cell phones and PDAs (personal digital assistants) in the exam room. The student-cheating example provides a parallel to the problems facing managers in preventing and dealing with *business fraud*.

Business fraud has been around for a long time. At its core there's very little new about business fraud. Only the devices and the methods for doing it are different today from those in the past. This chapter takes an unflinching look at business fraud and offers suggestions on how to prevent fraud—or at least how to minimize its effects. The chapter takes a no-holds-barred approach. Business managers are not exempt from criticism in the chapter.

Business Fraud and Its Two Basic Types

In the chapter, the term *fraud* is used in its broadest and most comprehensive sense; the word covers the waterfront. It includes all types of cheating, stealing, and dishonest behavior by anyone inside the business and by anyone outside with whom the business deals. The fraud may be illegal; or even if it isn't illegal, it is immoral, unethical, or unacceptable. Examples of fraud range from petty theft and pilferage to diverting millions of dollars into the pockets of high-level executives. Fraud includes shoplifting by customers, kickbacks by vendors to a company's purchasing managers, embezzlement by trusted employees, inflated expense reports submitted by salespeople, deliberate overcharging of customers, and so on. A comprehensive list of business fraud examples would fill an encyclopedia.

Speaking as a business manager, there are two types of business fraud:

Type 1: The kind you *don't* want to happen because it damages the business and may raise questions about your competence in not having prevented the fraud.

Type 2: The kind you *do* want to happen, or the kind you do nothing to stop even though you have to hold your nose while the fraud goes on.

In other words, there is fraud *against* the business and fraud *by* the business. Type 1 fraud can be classified by who does it. It includes all kinds of schemes and scams by vendors, by employees, by customers, and even by a business's own managers. Unfortunately, a business is vulnerable to all kinds of fraud attacks from virtually everyone it deals with. And, we regret to say, the business may engage in fraudulent practices, too.

Fraud Perpetrated by Businesses

Accounting and business finance articles and books dealing with business fraud focus almost exclusively on Type 1 and either side-step or downplay Type 2. However, you can't do justice to the topic without mentioning that some businesses engage in Type 2 fraudulent practices. Most experienced business managers would agree with us on this point, in private if not on the record.

Most frauds perpetrated by businesses are illegal under various state and federal statutes. Also, restitution for damages suffered from the fraud can be sought under the tort law system. No one advocates this type of fraud, of course. Very few people make the argument that this type of fraud is a necessary evil, which, viewed in a larger frame of reference, has to be tolerated in order to achieve the overall benefits from our economic system. In other words, the "for the greater good" argument doesn't carry water when it comes to fraud by business.

In any case, the evidence is clear that many businesses deliberately and knowingly engage in fraudulent practices and that their managers do not take action to stop it. Indeed, the managers are complicit in the fraud. They initiate a fraud; or for fraud going on in the business, they look the other way. The managers may not like fraud and not approve of it, but they live with it. Sometimes a manager is convicted of being part of a fraud conspiracy. However, over their careers, few managers are ever prosecuted for fraud.

You read about Type 2 fraud all too often in the financial and business press. Examples include bribing government and regulatory officials, knowingly violating laws covering product and employee safety, failing to report information that is required to be disclosed, misleading employees regarding changes in their retirement plans, conspiring with competitors to fix prices and divide territories, condoning misleading advertisements, and discriminating among employees on grounds of gender and race. One "duty" of a manager is to keep quiet and to cover up and prevent publicity regarding fraud by the business. Managers are under pressure to follow the "three monkey" policy: See no evil, hear no evil, speak no evil.

And then there is the whole area of *accounting fraud* and *fraudulent financial reporting* by a business's executives and its financial and accounting officers. These topics require a separate chapter—Chapter 10. This present chapter focuses on Type 1 fraud, which managers do not want to happen and should take actions to prevent. Other than what has already been said, Type 2, or "management complicity" fraud, is not discussed further in this chapter—except to make one final point: Fraud condoned by management makes a business more vulnerable to Type 1 fraud by employees. The literature and official pronouncements on business fraud stress the key point that preventing fraud depends first and foremost on the "tone at the top." Employees generally are aware of what's going on in the business. When they see fraudulent practices in the business that are sanctioned by its top-level managers, then some employees might be more inclined to adopt an "entitlement" attitude and commit some fraud on their own. And they may be very good at it.

Antifraud Controls

Businesses handle a lot of money, have a lot of valuable assets, and give managers and other employees a lot of authority. So it's not surprising that a business is vulnerable to fraud. The 2003 Fraud Survey by the Big Four CPA (certified public accountant) firm KPMG, for example, includes the following types of fraud against businesses:

+ Diversion of sales.

+ Duplicate billings.

+ Extortion.

+ False invoices and phantom vendors.

+ Inventory theft.

+ Kickbacks and conflicts of interest.

+ Loan fraud.

+ Theft of intellectual property.

The main advice offered in the professional literature on fraud against a business is to put into place and to vigilantly enforce preventive controls. The literature has considerably less advice to offer regarding the course of action managers should take once an instance of fraud is discovered, other than to say that the manager should plug the hole that allowed the fraud to happen.

The KPMG Fraud Survey found that the companies in its survey took the following actions:

+ Begin an investigation.

+ Immediately dismiss employees who commit fraud.

+ Seek legal action.

+ Notify a government regulatory agency or law enforcement.

An Example of Lack of Controls

Just as we were starting this chapter, the local paper reported a case of business fraud that serves as an excellent example to illustrate several key points. The police charged a young woman who worked as a hostess in a restaurant and who was in charge of the cash register with stealing $115,000 over a period of five years. The owner, who evidently was not an "on the premises" manager, noticed that sales peaked during the two weeks that the woman took a vacation.

In the past, the owner had noticed that sales seemed to be lower during the shifts she worked. Some of the employees told the police they had suspected that she was not ringing up all sales and that she also was stealing tips. The police investigation found that the woman and her husband lived a lifestyle beyond their combined incomes. To top it off, the police found the woman had a rap sheet that included jail time for similar offenses.

Certain basic controls, had they been in place, would have prevented this fraud. First, the background of all new employees, especially those who will be handling money, should be checked to determine whether they have a criminal record. Second, every business should have strong controls over cash receipts because cash is the preferred asset to steal. Cash transactions are a high-risk area.

Many restaurants, for example, have a conspicuous sign at the cash register that your meal is free if you don't get a receipt. Prenumbered order forms should be used, and all numbers should be accounted for to make sure that all sales are rung up. A video surveillance camera could have been used to watch cash register activities. If the owner had some questions regarding the hostess, he could have had a friend or two eat at the restaurant and closely observe whether the hostess rang up their cash. The owner could have hired a private investigator to discreetly look into the situation.

The owner should have noticed early on the mismatch between the sales revenue and expenses in the monthly or quarterly profit-and-loss (P&L) reports. A business owner/manger should develop a profit model for the business against which actual results are compared. For a certain level of sales revenue, the owner/manager should know how much expenses should be. The owner should have noticed that sales revenue was too low for the recorded expenses or that the two were out of kilter.

The restaurant owner comes off looking rather dim-witted or naïve in this case. Still, you have to give the owner some credit for noticing the variation in sales when the hostess was on duty versus when she was off duty. Finally, one other possibility comes to mind. Perhaps the owner was also skimming some cash and not reporting all sales revenue in the income tax returns for the business and in his tax returns. This might help explain why the owner took five years to take action.

The Twofold Purpose of Internal Accounting Controls

Antifraud controls are generally called *internal controls* or *internal accounting controls*. The accounting department of a business is delegated the responsibility for most antifraud controls. These controls consist of required forms that must be used and procedures that should be followed in authorizing and executing transactions and operations. The accounting department records the financial activities and transactions of a business, so it is natural that the accounting department is put in charge of designing and enforcing internal controls. The accounting profession has a long history in designing and using internal controls.

Most internal accounting controls have both an antifraud purpose and an accounting-reliability purpose. Keep in mind that the accounting system of a business is the source of information for its financial statements, tax returns, and management reports. The accounting purpose of internal controls is to eliminate (or at least to minimize) errors in capturing, processing, storing, and retrieving the large amount of detailed information needed in operating a business. Many controls are needed to ensure the accuracy, completeness, and timeliness of information held in the accounting system of a business.

Controls have to keep up-to-date with changes in a business's accounting system and procedures. For example, a whole new set of internal controls had to be developed and installed as businesses converted to computer-based accounting systems. This was a difficult transition for many businesses.

Internal Control Guideposts for Managers

Accountants have a large repertoire of internal controls from which to choose. This book is directed to business managers, not accountants. Therefore, we will not delve into the details of a large number of specific controls. Rather, we'll discuss a relatively few general guideposts for managing internal controls that apply to all businesses.

Internal Control Checklist for Managers

♦ *High-Risk Areas:* Strong and tight controls are needed in high-risk areas. Managers should identify the areas of the business that are the most vulnerable to fraud against the business. The most likely fraud points in a business usually include the following areas (some businesses have other high-risk areas, of course):

♦ Cash receipts and disbursements.

♦ Payroll (including workers' compensation insurance fraud).

♦ Customer credit and collections, and writing off bad debts.

♦ Purchasing and storage of inventory.

♦ *Legal Considerations:* Pay careful attention to the legal aspects of internal controls and to enforcing the controls. For example, controls should not violate the privacy rights of employees or customers. Needless to say, a business should be very careful in making accusations against an employee suspected

of fraud. Of course, the absence of basic controls possibly could expose a manager to legal responsibility on grounds of reckless disregard for protecting the company's assets. A legal opinion may be needed on your internal controls, just to be safe.

♦ *Separation of Duties:* Where practicable, have two or more employees involved in the authorization, documentation, execution, and recording of transactions, especially in the high-risk areas. This is called the *separation of duties*, the idea being that it would require the collusion of two or more persons to carry out and conceal a fraud. For instance, two or more signatures should be required on checks over a certain amount. Or the employee preparing the receiving reports for goods and materials delivered to the company should not have any authority for issuing a purchase order and should not make the accounting entries for purchases. Instead of the concentration of duties in the hands of one person, duties should be divided among two or more employees, even if there is some loss of efficiency.

♦ *Surprise Audits:* Make use of surprise counts, inspections, and reconciliations that employees cannot anticipate or plan for. Of course, the people doing these surprise audits should be independent of the employees who have responsibility for complying with the internal controls. For instance, a surprise count and inspection of products held in inventory might reveal missing products, unrecorded breakage and damage, products stored in the wrong locations, mislabeled products, or other problems.

Several such problems tend to get overlooked by busy employees. The inventory errors could be evidence of theft. Many of these errors should be recorded as inventory losses, but they may not be if surprise audits are not done.

♦ *Whistle-blowing:* Encourage all employees to report suspicions of fraud by anyone in the business (which has to be done anonymously in most situations). Admittedly, this is tricky. You're asking people to be whistle-blowers. Employees may not trust upper management; they may fear that they will face retaliation instead of being rewarded for revealing fraud. On the one hand, employees generally don't like spying on each other; but on the other hand, they want the business to take action against any employees who are committing fraud.

♦ *Audit Trails:* Insist that good audit trails be created for all transactions. The documentation and recording of transactions should leave a clear path that can be followed back if it is necessary to do so. Supporting documents should be organized in good order and should be retained for a reasonable period of time. The Internal Revenue Service publishes recommended guidelines for records retention, which are a good point of reference for a business.

♦ *Access to Accounting Records and End-of-Year Entries:* Strictly limit access to all accounting records to accounting personnel, and require that no one other than the accounting staff be allowed to make entries or changes in the accounting records of the business. Also, managers are well advised to keep a close eye on end-of-year accounting entries that are made to close the books for the period. Managers need to provide critical information for these entries, which may have a large effect on the amount of profit recorded for the period. (Providing the information to their accountants for these entries provides the managers with the opportunity to massage the financial statement numbers, which Chapter 10 explains.)

♦ *New Employee Background Checks:* Make thorough background checks on all employee applicants, especially those who will handle money and work in the high-risk fraud areas of the business. Letters of reference from previous employers may not be enough. A business may have to consider more extensive background and character checks, possibly using private investigators, when hiring mid- and high-level managers. Studies have found that many manager applicants falsify their resumes and list college degrees that they have not earned. Databases are available to check on a person's education, credit history, driving record, criminal record, workers' compensation insurance claims, and life insurance rejection record.

♦ *Periodic Audits of Internal Controls:* Consider having an independent assessment done on your internal controls by a CPA or other professional specialist. This might reveal that critical controls are missing or, conversely, that you're wasting money on ineffectual controls. If your business has an annual financial statement audit, the CPA evaluates and tests your business's internal controls. But you may need a more extensive and critical evaluation of your internal controls that looks beyond just the accounting-oriented controls.

♦ *Regular Appraisals of Key Assets:* Schedule regular "checkups" of your business's receivables, inventory, and fixed assets. Generally speaking, over time, these assets develop problems that are not dealt with in the day-to-day bustle and pressures on managers and other employees. Receivables may include seriously past due balances, but these customers' credit may have not been suspended or terminated. Some products in inventory may not have had a sale in months. Some items in fixed assets may have been abandoned or sold off for scrap value, yet the assets are still on the books and are being depreciated.

- **Computer Controls:** Be particularly vigilant regarding computer controls. Computer hardware and software controls are extremely important, but most managers don't have the time or the expertise to get into this area of internal controls. Obviously, passwords and firewalls should be used, and managers know about the possibility of hackers breaking into their computers and about the damage that computer viruses can cause. Every business has to adopt internal controls over e-mail, downloading attachments, updating software, and so on. If the business is not large enough for its own IT (information technology) department, it will have to bring in outside consultants. There is one good piece of news. The business accounting and enterprise software packages that are available today generally have strong security features—but you can't be too careful.

- **Special Rules for Small Businesses:** Be sure that internal controls are in place. The lament of many small business owners/managers is, "We're too small for internal controls." This is not true. Even a relatively small business can enforce certain internal controls that are effective. Among these are the following:

  - Require that the owner/manager sign all checks, including payroll checks. This forces the owner/manager to keep a close watch on the expenditures of the business. Under no conditions should the accountant, bookkeeper, or Controller of the business be given check-signing authority.

This person could easily conceal fraud if he or she has check-writing authority.

  - Require that employees working in the high-risk fraud areas (generally cash receipts and disbursements, receivables, and inventory) take vacations of two weeks or more, and, furthermore, make sure that another employee carries out their duties while they're on vacation.

  - Although separation of duties may not be practicable, consider the job-sharing approach such that two or more employees are regularly assigned to one area of the business on alternate weeks, or some other schedule.

  - Without violating their privacy, keep watch on the lifestyles of your employees. If your bookkeeper buys a new Mercedes every year and frequently is off to Monte Carlo, you might ask where the money is coming from. You know the salaries of your employees, so you should be able to estimate the sort of lifestyles they can afford.

In addition to internal controls, most businesses need what are generally referred to as *security measures*. Some of these are obvious, such as locking the doors when the business is closed and limiting access to areas where products are stored. Other measures may or not be needed, such as security guards, surveillance cameras, motion detectors, ID cards for employees, and security tags and devices on products. Generally these practices are not under the authority of the accounting department. Larger businesses employ a director of security. In a smaller business, the general manager may have to take on this duty.

Control Guidelines for Accepting New Customers and Clients

One area where internal controls are needed but are often overlooked by many businesses concerns taking on new customers—especially if the business extends credit to its customers. Of course, most businesses put a high priority on securing new customers. But the wrong kind of customer can cause large losses instead of yielding additional profit. Some new customers may be out-and-out crooks who never intended to pay for their purchases from the business. Other new customers may have good intentions but may be on thin ice financially and end up not being able to pay their accounts on time, or may not pay them at all. A business should have controls guiding its sales staff for sorting out the wheat from the chaff.

An internal memo to the sales staff of a California business provided the following guidelines for making an assessment of the financial integrity and viability of new customers. It has been condensed and edited to protect the identity of the business.

Macrolevel Business Credit Risk Flags

• **Related Parties:** No, we're not talking about visits from the dreaded in-laws during the holiday season but rather the risk inherent in conducting business with an entity that transacts with a number of closely associated entities. Various entity forms (corporations, LLCs [limited liability companies], partnerships) are available to structure businesses and to protect assets that are legal and represent legitimate and viable strategies. However, multiple related parties can be hidden in a maze of legal entities that can pose all types of problems. No one needs to look any further than the recent disaster with Enron Energy to understand why related-party transactions should be viewed as a red flag. On the flip side, understanding all of the related parties involved with an account may offer new leads.

• **Concentration Risk:** Accounts that generate high volumes of sales with only a few customers (or just one) have always been singled out as having increased business risks. This concentration risk (as it is referred to in the banking world) can be a major problem for accounts that rely heavily on only a couple of customers to generate significant revenue. Cash flow problems, profitability issues, and so on all increase as a result of this business model. Also, the concentration risk works both ways: If the customer is dependent on a key supplier or vendor to operate and produce products/services, then if that supplier/vendor experiences problems, so will the customer.

- **The Consummate Salesperson:** Simply put, if the customer spends the majority of the time "selling" the business (rather than discussing the operating issues with which they're confronted), then a flag should be raised. Although it is important to understand the business of your customer, being constantly "sold" on why the business is so good and has so much potential should raise an eyebrow. I think most of the management team would agree that we are generally retained to support the customer and to help manage an operational issue. We are not there to invest in the company and/or to help promote its legitimacy.
- **Industry Association:** One should always be keenly aware of the general characteristics of industry within which the customer operates. Different risks and operating standards are present within various industries that when understood may help us evaluate the risks present. For example, companies that operate in the health/medical care industry are often subject to lengthy billing and cash-receipt cycles (e.g., 90 days) as a result of how the insurance sector works. This is vastly different from a retail operation, which generates most of its sales in cash at the point of contact (but which has much larger inventory issues to manage).
- **The Hot New Business:** Without question, this has been one of the most difficult credit and collection issues for our company during the past year. Needless to say, Dot.Com to Dot.Bomb companies are a perfect example of this. However, other companies in other industries represent just as big a risk. These types of companies tend to be very young, in rapid employee ramp-up stages, make references to additional capital/investments being needed, are prerevenue, and so on. The length of time a business has been in operation should be an important focal point. A company that has been in business for 10 years, weathered an economic downturn, and built a solid reputation helps ease some anxiety, as opposed to a company that is simply riding a short-term economic wave, which almost always crashes.
- **Recent Material Event:** A significant and recent material event with a customer may be cause for concern or optimism. For example, if your customer was recently acquired by another organization, then payment cycles may change, usage levels may fluctuate, and so on. Other common references to events such as these may include a corporate restructuring, senior management terminations, awarding of a large contract, and ramping up for production. Once again, a recent material event shouldn't be viewed as a negative but rather as a business risk that needs to be proactively managed.
- **The Management Team/Reputation:** The importance of a qualified and reputable management team (at the customer) cannot be emphasized enough. The problem for our company is how to gain an understanding of this issue in relation to understanding business risks. I think most management team members would agree that once you've operated in a market for a while, some amount of common knowledge is obtained as to whom we want to work with. What is more difficult is to evaluate the management team of the company in a very short period. Key points of reference with this issue may include identifying information on the availability of organization charts, family members involved in management, titles of key management members, qualifications of the management team, availability of basic operational and financial information, use of external professionals (e.g., a CPA firm, banking relations, an insurance company) to support the operation. In addition, the ability of the management team to clearly communicate issues and problems to us (on a proactive basis) is critical. This displays an attitude that our company is a partner rather than just another vendor.
- **Instinct:** Last but not least is the issue regarding following your sense, gut, and/or instinct. If something smells like you-know-what, looks like you-know-what, feels like you-know-what, and tastes like you-know-what, it probably is you-know-what. This doesn't mean that our company wouldn't conduct business with the account, but rather that further evaluation and investigation may be needed to manage the business and credit risks present. Sometimes, just touring a facility or observing simple employee actions can provide a great deal of information about the account.

Important Note: It is extremely important to understand that the guidelines just noted do not mean that we will not conduct business with the customer just because flags are raised. Conversely, it may provide us with even greater business opportunities. However, how we manage the risk with a particular customer may change as a result of the flags raised.

(Continued)

Questions and/or Customer Inquiries

Needless to say, hundreds of potential questions could be listed to assist our company's management team in performing inquiries of the customer. Rather than list all of the questions, we've broken them down into the following five main segments/areas:

1. **Business Stability:** How long has the company been in business? Has it moved recently? If so, why did it move? Has the management team remained intact, or has there been turnover in the managers? How many customers does the company have? Do any customers represent significant accounts (e.g., over 10% of total sales)? What industry would you classify the company as operating in? What issues are currently impacting the industry?

2. **Growth Potential:** How has the company's overall head count changed during the last year (or three years or five)? Has the mix between temporary staff and permanent staff changed? Is the company expecting any near-term change (increase or decrease) in business? If yes, how will the company manage it (e.g., adequate financing, personnel strategies, etc.)?

3. **Management Qualifications and Strategic Focus:** What is the total number of years of management experience on board? Has the management team incurred recent turnover? Does the company prepare a business plan? Does the company utilize forecasts/projections? Is this a family-owned-and-operated business? If yes, what type of succession plan is in place (i.e., will the kids take over the business)? What type of training and/or human resource skills are available to the company (internal and external)? Does the company have an active board of directors (or similar type of supporting group)?

4. **Financial Resources:** How has the company performed financially during the past three years (i.e., has revenue increased, decreased, or remained flat)? Is the company operating at a profit, at a loss, or at the breakeven level? Is the company currently relying on external financing to fund operations, or is it self-sufficient? Are audited/reviewed financial statements available? How often are internal financial statements prepared? How have the company's key financial ratios trended recently (e.g., debt to equity, current ratio, etc.)?

5. **Material Events, Transactions, and Relationships:** Does the company have any significant partners? If yes, what is the basis of the relationship? Has the company acquired or sold any business interests recently? If yes, what was the strategic objective of these transactions? Who owns the company? What is the legal structure of the company? Is the company private or public?

In summary, we wouldn't expect that all of the preceding guidelines should be applied to every situation. Certain of the guidelines may not be appropriate and/or feasible (or, conversely, other guidelines not mentioned may need to be applied). Rather, the guidelines were prepared to provide the senior management team of our company with an additional tool to assess business and credit risks. Also, a number of alternatives are available to us for better protecting our business interests when a material business risk is detected (i.e., guarantees, prepayment options, letters of credit, UCC [Uniform Commercial Code] security interest filings, etc.). These strategies/tools have not been presented in this memo, as they are often very technical. Our finance/accounting and legal corporate service groups should be contacted to evaluate the appropriateness of these strategies/tools.

The guidelines presented in this "memo" illustrate how one business deals with the issue of avoiding taking on new customers and clients that may prove troublesome and may cause serious problems and losses. An ounce of prevention is worth a pound of cure, as they say. Every business has to adopt its own individual set of rules for new customers.

In this connection, it's very interesting to note that CPA firms are bound under their professional standards to establish policies and procedures for deciding whether to accept or continue a client relationship and whether to perform a specific engagement for that client. The main purpose is to minimize the likelihood of association with a client whose management lacks integrity. One of the key characteristics that CPA firms list is that the client should have "appropriately comprehensive and sound internal controls that are consistent with the size and organizational structure of the business" (AICPA, "Acceptance and Continuance of Clients and Engagements," January 2004, *Practice Alert*, J1-2). So, if your business contacts a CPA, you should be aware that the CPA firm will be doing a check on how good your internal controls are.

Policies and Problems Concerning Internal Controls

A good deal of business is done on the basis of trust. Internal controls can be viewed as a contradiction to this principle. Yet in a game of poker among friends cutting the deck before dealing the cards is not viewed as a lack of trust. Most people see the need for internal controls by a business or by card players—at least up to a point.

Many businesses, especially smaller ones, adopt the policy that some amount of fraud simply has to be absorbed as a cost of doing business and that it's not worth the time and cost of instituting and enforcing an elaborate set of internal controls. This mind-set reflects the fact that business by its very nature is a risky venture. Despite taking precautions, you can't protect your business against every possible risk. This is true but it is also true that a business invites trouble and becomes an attractive target if it doesn't have basic internal controls. Deciding how many different internal controls to put into effect is a tough call.

Internal controls are not free. Internal controls take time and money to design, install, and use. It's difficult to measure or to estimate the costs of an internal control or of a related group of related internal controls in one area of the business—such as purchasing, or cash receipts, or payroll, or customer credit.* Fur-

---

*One exception to this general comment is the cost of fidelity insurance. The insurance company quotes a definite cost for premiums per period under these policies. Also, it should be noted that the insurance company will do a background investigation on each employee being bonded under a policy, which is a good internal control.

thermore, there can be serious side effects from some internal controls. Customers may resent certain internal controls, such as checking backpacks before entering a store, and take their business elsewhere. Employees may deeply resent entry and exit searches, which may contribute to low morale.

It's very difficult to estimate the number of instances of fraud prevented by the internal controls used by a business and the damage that would have been done by the frauds. Where do managers look for information about fraud, then? Well, for one thing, they read articles in newspapers about frauds. Also, managers trade information with business associates. Business trade associations provide information about frauds in the industry in formal reports. At regional and national meetings, managers swap stories about fraud. Some cases of fraud are truly astonishing.

You wouldn't think the perpetrator could have gotten away so long with the fraud or could have stolen such a large amount without being noticed. We remember newspaper stories years ago reporting that a long-time, trusted bookkeeper had stolen virtually half of the assets of a small bank in the Midwest. This happened to more than one bank, as a matter of fact. The bookkeeper realized that many of the savings accounts in the bank were owned by older depositors and were inactive. The bookkeeper also knew that the bank officers never took a close look at these accounts.

So the bookkeeper "withdrew" money from these savings

accounts and sent monthly statements to the depositors that reported their original balances. Because the bookkeeper prepared the depositor statements, it was easy to falsify the balances. The simple internal control of separating the duty of preparing depositor statements from the duty of recording deposits and withdrawals in the accounts would have prevented the fraud, unless the two employees colluded. Of course, the bank's officers should have been held accountable for not keeping a close eye on inactive savings accounts.

Keep in mind that internal accounting controls are not 100% foolproof. A disturbing amount of fraud still slips by these preventive measures. How are these frauds found out? Well, the 2003 Fraud Survey by KPMG reported that common methods for uncovering frauds included:

- Internal controls
- Internal audits
- Notification by an employee
- Accident
- Anonymous tip
- Notification by customer
- Notification by regulatory or law enforcement agency
- Notification by vendor
- External audit

One test of a good internal control is that it will detect a fraud if it fails to prevent it. Of course, this is like closing the barn door after the horse has escaped. Still, it's critical to learn what fraud has happened in order to close the loophole in the system.

An internal control may fail because it is not carried out conscientiously or because it is done in a perfunctory manner. In theory, managers should not tolerate such a lackadaisical attitude toward internal controls by employees. But until something serious happens, managers may let this attitude slide. Sometimes a manager intervenes and overrides an internal control. This sets an extremely bad example and, in fact, might be evidence of fraud by the manager.

Fraud by high-level managers is particularly difficult to prevent and detect. By the very nature of their position, these managers have a great deal of authority and discretion. Their positions of trust and power give them an unparalleled opportunity to commit fraud and the means to conceal it. If you have any doubt about this, look in the financial press over the past few years and read the many articles describing the gross abuses by top executives of many corporations. Evidently their huge salaries and stock options were not enough. One commentator said it's not just about money, but rather about hubris—meaning that these individuals did not consider themselves bound by normal rules of behavior and they had to demonstrate that they could break the rules. Good old-fashioned greed seems behind most of the corporate scandals, however.

Public Companies and Internal Controls

As you probably remember there was a plethora of high-profile business fraud cases over recent years—Enron, WorldCom, Waste Management, Rite Aid, HealthSouth, and many more. Then came along the mutual fund scandals of 2003. I've lost count of the number of high-level executives that have pleaded guilty to extremely serious fraud charges. Many have gone to jail. One result of these many scandals was passage of the Sarbanes-Oxley Act of 2002, which sailed through Congress and was immediately signed by President George Bush. The act had a major impact on the CPA auditing profession, including establishing the Public Company Accounting Oversight Board to oversee the auditing profession.

One section of the Sarbanes-Oxley Act deals with internal controls of public companies. PricewaterhouseCoopers, one of the Big Four CPA firms, ran a full page ad in the *Wall Street Journal* (March 12, 2003, A20) under the main title "Internal Control Is No Longer Just Internal." Three paragraphs describe the act's impact on internal controls:

> The Sarbanes-Oxley Act of 2002 includes several important sections related to internal control for public companies—the spirit of which is to improve the completeness, accuracy and transparency of financial reporting and to foster compliance with laws and regulations.
>
> Section 404, a key part of Sarbanes-Oxley, requires an annual assertion by management regarding the effectiveness of internal control over financial reporting, as well as an attestation by the company's auditors on management's assertions.

> Many public companies have long relied on control procedures to guard against fraud, unethical behavior and honest human error. But now management not only will be asked to acknowledge its responsibility for having in place an adequate internal structure, it will need to assess the effectiveness of that structure, publicly report that assessment, and subject that assessment to attestation by the company's auditors.

The act applies to publicly owned businesses, which include approximately 10,000 corporations whose securities (stocks and bonds) are traded in public markets. These are large businesses, of course. Roughly speaking, a business needs to have a market cap of $25 million or higher to be affected by the regulations under Sarbanes-Oxley. One concern is whether there might be a "trickle down" effect on small businesses.

States and other regulatory agencies might use the act as a model to pass similar laws that cover businesses domiciled in their states. It seems more likely, however, that states will be more interested in other features of the act—especially the sections dealing with which services CPAs should be prohibited from providing their audit clients in order to ensure the independence of CPAs for doing audits.

Large businesses have one tool of internal control that is not practical for smaller businesses—*internal auditors*. Most large businesses, and for that matter most large nonprofit organizations and governmental units, have internal auditing departments. The internal auditors have broad powers to investigate any of the organization's operations and activities, and they report their findings to the highest levels in the organization. Small businesses cannot afford to hire a full-time internal auditor. But even a relatively small business should consider hiring a CPA to do an assessment of its internal controls and to make suggestions for improvement. In fact, this might even be of more value than having a CPA audit its financial statements.

Why Did They Do It?

The easy and quick answer is that people commit fraud for the money. However, this shallow answer does not get to the root causes of why people take risks and engage in fraud. Good internal controls should make it difficult for employees and anyone else with whom a business deals to carry out a fraud. But internal controls are lacking in many situations, or the controls are not enforced. In many situations, people so inclined see the opportunity and devise all sorts of ways to steal money and other assets from a business. Do they need the money that bad? Don't they see the risks of getting caught?

Well, many people seem to think that business is a fair target because businesses rip them off every day. Or they might commit fraud to get even with the owner of a business. I was passing through an airport recently and got talking with a man working in one of the stores in the airport. He asked what I did, and I told him I was a retired professor of accounting and that I had written several books on accounting and financial business management. We got talking and he told me that he had served time in the state penitentiary for fraud. Of course, I asked why he did it.

He was the accountant for a business. He said that the owner of the business was arrogant and treated him with contempt. So, to get even as it were and to prove that he could do it, he embezzled $300,000 over a period of years. However, he was caught and convicted. He didn't go into details regarding how he was caught. Ironically, he had just returned from being a guest speaker at a national convention of forensic accountants and fraud specialists. (He showed me the permission letter signed by his parole officer to travel to Los Angeles for his talk.) Of course, I think he did it for the money, but the other factors probably played a role also in his fraud.

How do people that commit fraud rationalize or justify their actions in their minds? A line from the *Seinfeld* comedy series offers a clue. In one episode, when Jerry asked George, "How do you beat a lie detector test?" George responded "Remember, it's not a lie if you believe it's the truth." Fraud often originates as a result of a number of different complex business factors that are often misunderstood and, worse yet, difficult to detect. Fraud involves a variety of business, personal, emotional, and other factors that can encourage even the most honest, hard-working person to push the limit of what's legal and reasonable to what's illegal and dishonest.

Fraud driven by the need to survive probably is far more commonplace and represents a much greater risk to the average business than fraud driven by greed alone. How far will a business owner push the envelope to survive? The business owner views his or her company as a part of the family and will do almost anything to ensure its survival. Wouldn't you do the same for one of your children?

A simple adjustment or revision to an estimate may be all that's needed to make the company's financial statements look much better. The mentality of "I'll make up for it next quarter or next year" is prevalent. An employee in a bind (health, spousal layoff, etc.) may push the envelop by simply "borrowing" an asset for a while with the intent to repay. An employee may feel he or she should receive a bonus for hard work and takes advantage of a simple control lapse to reap an added benefit.

Businesses should know that their employees and managers will sometimes have problems paying their bills on time, to say nothing about all the other financial pressures caused by divorce, health problems, medical emergencies, kids going to college, drug addiction, and on and on. You can make the argument that a business is responsible for having good internal controls that prevent its employees and managers from committing fraud. Good internal controls are not only good business, but also good for everyone.

Capsule Summary

Most people are honest most of the time. Businesses have to deal with the exceptions to this general rule. A business cannot afford to assume that all the people with whom it deals are honest all of the time. Fraud against business is a fact of life. One function of business managers is to prevent fraud against their business. It goes without saying that managers should not commit fraud on the behalf of the business. (But some do, of course.)

A business is vulnerable to many kinds of fraud from many directions—customers who shoplift, employees who steal money and other assets from the business, vendors who overcharge, managers who accept kickbacks and bribes, and so on. The threat of fraud is present for all businesses, large and small. No one tells a business in advance that they intend to engage in fraud against the business, of course. Compounding the problem is the fact that many people who commit fraud are pretty good at concealing it.

Every business should institute and enforce controls that are effective in preventing fraud. An ounce of prevention is worth a pound of cure. And a business needs many accounting controls to ensure that its financial records are accurate, timely, and complete. Otherwise, its financial reports and tax returns may be seriously mistaken and misleading. The terms *internal*

controls and *internal accounting controls* generally refer to both antifraud controls and antiaccounting error controls. Nevertheless, it's useful to keep in mind the difference between controls designed primarily to stop fraud (such as employee theft) and procedures designed to prevent errors creeping into the accounting system.

The chapter provides examples of frauds that cost a business hundreds of thousands of dollars. Internal control guideposts for managers are explained, which they can use as a checklist to assess the adequacy of their business's internal controls. One company's guidelines for accepting new customers and clients are presented in the chapter. Controls for this area are often overlooked by many businesses.

Problems in managing internal controls are discussed, including cost/benefit trade-offs and what to do when fraud is uncovered. The responsibilities of top management of public companies for internal controls under the Sarbanes-Oxley Act of 2002 are explained briefly. This act was the direct result of the plethora of high-profile corporate fraud over the past few years. Finally, the chapter briefly explores the question, "Why did they do it?" It's not just the money, although greed is certainly a motivating factor.

MANAGING YOUR PROFIT ACCOUNTING: YOU MIGHT MASSAGE THE NUMBERS, BUT DON'T COOK THE BOOKS

"Accountants would rather be precisely wrong than approximately correct."
—Kenneth Boulding, late economist who had a well-known sense of humor

The quoted one-liner by Ken Boulding plays off the caricature green-eyeshaded accountants so obsessed with details that they lose sight of the main purpose of what they're doing. As in most humor, there's an element of truth in this quip. Accountants tend to view accounting as an end in itself. Business managers look at accounting as the means to an end—the means to assist in operating the business and to help in achieving its financial goals. Accountants like to stick closely to the rules. Business managers are willing to bend the rules if necessary. Accountants think that profit depends on the facts. Business managers argue that profit depends on how you look at the facts.

This chapter takes the business manager's viewpoint. One main theme is that managers should be intimately involved with the profit accounting of their business. Being managers, they call the shots and make the final decisions. Managers depend on the expertise and experience of their accountants, of course. Business managers should work closely with their accountants so that both are on the same page and singing the same tune. But we're reminded of the adage, "War is too important to be left to the generals." Likewise, profit accounting is too important to be left to the accountants.

Business managers need a basic understanding of profit accounting—not the debit-and-credit bookkeeping mechanics of accounting, but the way that choices of methods and estimates affect the profit and the financial statements of the business. Managers should be clear on the difference between massaging the numbers and fluffing the pillows (which are accounting manipulations tolerated in the financial world) and accounting fraud and cooking the books (which are practices that are not tolerated and might land you in jail).

The Nature of Profit Accounting

One primary function of accountants is to prepare the financial statements of the business in order to report its profit (or loss) for a period and its financial situation at the end of the period. Table 10.1 presents an illustrative income statement and balance sheet for a midsize business. These two financial statements are not the whole of a financial report. The statement of cash flows and footnotes to the financial statements are included in a financial report. This is not the place to delve into the differences between financial reports of public and private companies and between larger and smaller private companies. Profit accounting issues and problems are largely the same for all businesses.

As you probably know, the income statement for a period reports the revenue minus the expenses of a business for that period. The bottom-line profit is usually labeled "net income" or "net earnings." You might quickly read down the company's income statement in Table 10.1. The company reports $2,642,000 net income for the year. Is this key figure correct? Is its sales revenue figure true and correct, and is every one of its expenses true and correct?

Chapter 9 emphasized that every business needs good internal accounting controls to eliminate (or at least to minimize) honest and unintentional accounting errors. Business managers should keep alert for possible errors in their accounting systems. Errors are not the concern here. Rather, the purpose of raising these questions is to direct attention to the nature of profit accounting and its inherent, unavoidable problems.

Is profit accounting comparable to measuring the size of a parcel of land, or is it more like judging an athlete's performance in a gymnastics competition? Well, it has elements of both. Sometimes profit accounting is referred to as "scorekeeping." This analogy assumes that the scoring rules for the business profit game are clearly defined and that there's an impartial referee to make the calls. Such is not the case.

A profit report, such as the income statement in Table 10.1, appears to be factual and precise. A profit report depends first and foremost on the accounting methods used to record revenue and expenses. These accounting methods are not singular and uniform but involve choices among alternatives. Moreover, many estimates and assumptions are made that have the result of tilting the accounting numbers one way or the other.

TABLE 10.1—EXAMPLE OF INCOME STATEMENT AND BALANCE SHEET FOR A BUSINESS

Income Statement for Year

Sales Revenue	$52,000,000
Cost of Goods Sold	33,800,000
Gross Margin	$18,200,000
Depreciation Expense	785,000
Amortization Expense	325,000
Other Operating Expenses	12,480,000
Operating Earnings	$ 4,610,000
Interest Expense	545,000
Earnings before Tax	$ 4,065,000
Income Tax Expense	1,423,000
Net Income	$ 2,642,000

Balance Sheet at End of Year

Assets			Liabilities and Owners' Equity		
Cash	$ 3,265,000		Accounts Payable	$ 3,320,000	
Accounts Receivable	5,000,000		Accrued Expenses	1,515,000	
Inventory	8,450,000		Income Tax Payable	165,000	
Prepaid Expenses	960,000		Short-Term Notes Payable	3,125,000	
Current Assets		$17,675,000	Current Liabilities		$ 8,125,000
Property, Plant, and Equipment	$16,500,000		Long-Term Notes Payable		4,250,000
Less Accumulated Depreciation	4,250,000	12,250,000	Stockholders' Equity:		
Goodwill	$ 7,850,000		Capital Stock (800,400 shares)	$ 8,125,000	
Less Accumulated Amortization	2,275,000	5,575,000	Retained Earnings	15,000,000	23,125,000
Total Assets		$35,500,000	Total Liabilities and Owners' Equity		$35,500,000

Different Strokes for Different Folks

Someone must decide which particular methods to use for recording the recurring stream of revenue and expenses of a business. Deciding on accounting methods may be delegated to the business's chief accountant. A small business may depend on an outside certified public accountant (CPA) for advice regarding which accounting methods to adopt. In any case, managers should not abdicate their responsibility here. Managers should be intimately involved in making the key accounting decisions for the business—they should either make the final decisions on accounting methods or at least review and put their stamp of approval on the methods. Whatever their role in making accounting decisions, managers definitely should understand that different methods cause different results in their financial statements, especially the income statement. Profit depends on which methods are used to record the revenue and expenses of a business.

For revenue and for many expenses, there is not just *one and only one* method that has to be used, but rather there are *alternative* methods to select from. One of the alternatives has to be used; the choice is left to the business. The alternatives are equally acceptable under established financial accounting standards. One method does not dominate the other(s) on theoretical grounds, or according to the authoritative pronouncements on accounting standards, or by the particular circumstances of a business. Accountants have not whittled down the alternatives to just one method that all businesses should use.

These alternative accounting methods differ regarding *when* revenue and expenses are recorded. Compared with the alternative(s), one method records revenue or an expense either sooner or later. In other words, the differences between alternative accounting methods are *timing* differences. The term *conservative* accounting means that the profit accounting methods used by a business, in normal circumstances, record revenue later and expenses sooner. Thus, profit is reported later rather than sooner. The term *aggressive* accounting means just the opposite: The business records revenue sooner and expenses later causing the result that, in normal circumstances, profit is reported sooner rather than later.

Once specific profit accounting methods have been chosen, a business sticks with these methods consistently over time. (Well, a business may occasionally change from one method to another, although switching methods is not common and is frowned upon.) The selection of basic revenue and expense accounting methods is the first decision point in the profit accounting process of a business. But this is not the end of the story. There are other accounting decision points, which are much more dicey.

Before closing its books for the period, a business should take a hard, critical look at its assets and liabilities, as well as at any other financial problems that may be lurking in the bushes. The business should take a final look at its accounts to determine whether it should make *end-of-period adjustments* to its revenue and expense accounts for the period. And the business should decide whether it should record any *unusual or extraordinary losses or gains*. Like choosing among the alternative revenue and expense methods, the end-of-period accounting problems are essentially *timing* questions: Should certain adjustments and certain gains or losses be recorded *now*, or should the effects be deferred until *later*?

Bad Debts, Inventory Shrinkage, and Product Warranty Liability

Most businesses have accounting problems with two assets in particular: (1) accounts receivable and (2) inventory. The problem with accounts receivable concerns *bad debts*—customer balances that the business will be able to collect only in part or not at all. Deciding exactly *when* and *how much* of these particular balances to write off and charge to expense is rather arbitrary. Different businesses follow different rules for recording bad debts expense.

One method is to charge off all customer balances that become, say, 60 days past due or 90 days past due. Or a business may wait until a customer actually declares bankruptcy or skips town. Another approach is to decide bad debt write-offs or write-downs on a customer-by-customer basis; each receivable is evaluated on its own merits.

The problem with inventory concerns what generally is called *inventory shrinkage*. In its balance sheet at year-end, the business reports $8,450,000 in inventory (see Table 10.1). The handling and storage of products usually results in some amount of breakage, deterioration, damage, theft, obsolescence, and losses from other causes. One important internal accounting control is doing a regular physical count and inspection of products being held in inventory in order to determine the extent of inventory shrinkage.

A good time to do this is at the end of the accounting year. Of course, the cost of products missing from inventory is recorded as an expense. And the loss of value caused by products that have been damaged or that have deteriorated, as well as the loss in market value of products that cannot be sold at normal prices, should be recorded. These inventory write-downs from their original costs depend on evaluations by managers regarding the salability and likely sales prices of the products.

Accounts receivable and inventory are typically the two biggest end-of-period accounting problems, but a business can have other problem areas as well. For instance, a business may have to service products after the sales to its customers under warranty and guarantee provisions. In its balance sheet at year-end, the business reports $1,515,000 for its accrued expenses liability (see Table 10.1). A significant component of this amount is the cost of fulfilling its warranties and guarantees for products already sold. Estimating the future costs of fulfilling these obligations is not cut-and-dried, as you might imagine. As with accounts receivable and inventory, managers play a key role in deciding the costs of these future obligations that are recorded as expense. Usually, this type of expense is recorded by an end-of-year adjusting entry.

In summary, adjusting accounting entries—such as for bad debts, inventory shrinkage, and product guarantee costs—can have a huge impact on the recorded profit (or loss) for the period. In making or approving these accounting decisions, managers can lay a heavy hand on the profit (or loss) for the period.

The income statement presented in Table 10.1 does not report any unusual or extraordinary losses or gains for the year, such as a one-time write-off of fixed assets that have been abandoned or sold off for salvage value, or a large legal settlement that was in favor of the business. Many public businesses disclose in their income statements "asset restructuring" and employee severance charges running into the billions of dollars. It's not unusual for a public company to write off a big chunk of its intangible assets—just wipe them off its balance sheet in one fell swoop.

The whole area of recording extraordinary, nonrecurring losses and gains is beyond the scope of this book. Suffice it to say that many businesses record these losses too often, apparently to clear the decks of future expenses. This is a very troublesome aspect of financial reporting by public companies, which causes serious problems for security analysts and investors trying to get a bead on the normal, recurring profit performance of a business. (You can read more on this topic in John A. Tracy, *How to Read a Financial Report*, sixth ed. [New York: John Wiley & Sons, 2004], starting on page 169.)

Timing Discretionary Expenses to
Lift or Lower Profit

As you can see in Table 10.1, the company reports $12,480,000 "other operating expenses" for the year. This composite total includes many different kinds of expenses, including payroll and payroll taxes, employee health and medical insurance benefits paid by the business, contributions by the business into the retirement plans for employees, advertising and sales promotion costs, casualty and general liability insurance premiums, gas and electricity bills, real estate and personal property taxes, back office costs (accounting, computing, recordkeeping, etc.), delivery and transportation costs, repair and maintenance expenditures, employee training costs, and many other expenses.

Consider two operating expenses: (1) salaries and wages and (2) rent. On a regular basis—every week, or two weeks, or month—these expenses are paid and recorded. The business does not have discretionary latitude over when these expenses are recorded. Many operating expenses are of this character, such as gas and electric bills, insurance premiums, and real estate taxes. In contrast, business managers have discretion over the timing of several expenses: advertising, employee training, repair and maintenance, sales incentive programs, and so on. Business managers decide *when* these expenses are incurred, which impacts profit for the period. For example, a manager could decide to spend more on repair and maintenance toward the end of this year, rather than waiting until early next year when the building normally would be painted, or when its equipment would nor-

mally be overhauled, or when new tires would normally be put on its delivery trucks, and so on. By the timing of discretionary expenditures, a manager can boost expenses this year and thereby depress the amounts of taxable income and profit recorded this year. The reverse effect on profit is rendered if a manager delays making such expenditures until next year.

Generally, a manager has a fair amount of slack regarding the timing of several expenses. There's nothing illegal about moving these expenses forward or back in time for the primary purpose of depressing or boosting profit for the year. The business's CPA auditor may not like this sort of profit manipulation, but there's little he or she can do about it, unless expense shifting between years gets out of hand.

We have worked on audits where a business changed its bottom line 20% by using these tactics. It's hard to prove, but we would say that almost any business can move its bottom line up or down by at least 10% by manipulating one or more of its discretionary expenses. If managers are really good at this sort of thing, our guess is that the bottom line of most businesses could be shifted up or down by 25% or more.

Keep in mind the "robbing Peter to pay Paul" effect of expense timing. Suppose you hold off and don't do certain repair and maintenance work during November and December, the last two months of your fiscal year. This work would have cost $25,000. Your expense this year would be $25,000 less of course. But, presumably, this work should be done and will be done early next year; so next year's expenses are hit with an extra $25,000—unless you do the same thing again during the final two months of next year. Of course, this works in reverse as well. If you had accelerated $25,000 of repair and maintenance work in December, your expenses would have been $25,000 higher this year but would escape this $25,000 of expenses next year.

As you probably know, a business does not disclose in its financial report whether it is manipulating its expenses. CPA auditors do not comment on this practice, unless the auditor judges that the manipulations are excessive and beyond reasonable limits that are tolerated in the business world. You might argue that business managers should not manipulate the timing of their expenses (or revenue either, for that matter) and that they should let the chips fall where they may. But managers get paid to make profit happen; and if they need to, many managers are willing to do a little massaging of their expense numbers, unless the chief executive makes it very clear that he or she will not tolerate any tinkering with the accounting numbers.

Summing Up So Far: Three Ways Managers Control Profit Accounting

Summing up briefly, managers can take three bites out of the profit accounting apple.

1. They can decide which accounting methods to use for recording the ongoing stream of revenue and expenses of the business. In making these choices, managers can implement either a conservative or an aggressive accounting policy for their business.

2. Managers can play a critical role in recording adjusting entries to recognize such things as uncollectible accounts receivable (bad debts), inventory shrinkage write-downs, and liability for future costs required under product warranties.

3. Managers can decide to delay or to accelerate several discretionary expenses in order to push up or press down the profit that is recorded for the period.

The evidence is fairly convincing that many public companies manipulate the timing of their expenses to smooth out the fluctuations and perturbations in the year-to-year profit numbers that would have to be reported if they did not intervene in the accounting process. The purpose is to report a more steady profit performance trend line, which stock investors seem to prefer. This is called *income smoothing*, or the *management of earnings*. It is more difficult to gather evidence regarding whether *private* businesses engage in income smoothing. They may have less reason to do so, although their owners may also prefer a steady earnings trend rather than a zigzag, year-to-year profit line.

Despite the opportunity, many managers do not jump into the profit accounting fray. They steer clear of this aspect of the business. Clearly, many business managers have an aversion to anything accounting. And accountants are not anxious to have managers looking over their shoulders. They would just as soon be left alone in making the profit accounting decisions for the business. But accountants don't necessarily know everything that managers do. Some of the missing information could have a bearing on the estimates for accounting adjusting entries.

Accountants can intimidate managers with their technical jargon. And accountants make frequent reference to their "generally accepted accounting principles," as if these official rules constitute the holy grail of profit accounting. If you are a manager, don't let your accountants bluff you on this. Profit accounting is in fact very subjective and flexible. This does not mean that a business and its managers are free to do whatever they please.

For preparing its financial statements that are released outside the business, the basic revenue and expense methods used by a business must be consistent with established standards, which are called *generally accepted accounting principles* (GAAP). The GAAP rulebook is written for professional accountants. Nonaccountants can't really wade through the technical language of these official pronouncements. Moreover, the rules change somewhat over time. Managers have to rely on their accountants to keep the business within the boundaries of GAAP.

A business would invite all kinds of trouble if it were to issue a profit report (income statement) that was in material violation of GAAP. This is very much like saying that a business should not violate the law. Staying within the boundaries of the law still leaves a business a great range of choices regarding how it operates. Likewise, staying within the boundaries of GAAP still leaves a business a range of choices regarding how it accounts for profit. Managers should take charge of their profit accounting, like they take charge of most everything else in the business. Otherwise, they are only passengers on the profit ship instead of being the captain.

Two Profit Pictures for One Business

Please refer to the profit report (income statement) for the business in Table 10.1. This is not the only profit report that could have been prepared by the business. As was explained earlier, the business could have used different accounting methods, and it could have made different estimates for recording adjusting entries. Also, the business could have spent more or less for certain discretionary expenses. Therefore, the business could have recorded different figures for its sales revenue and expenses during the year. The business uses moderately aggressive accounting methods, which are within the boundaries of GAAP. Instead, it could have chosen to use more conservative accounting methods and estimates. Table 10.2 presents the business's yearly statement that discloses sales revenue and expenses that would have been recorded if the business had used more conservative profit accounting methods. The first (left) column shows the figures based on the aggressive accounting methods actually used by the business (which are the same figures as shown in Table 10.1, of course). The second (right) column presents the sales revenue and expense figures and the bottom-line profit number that would have been recorded if the business had adopted more conservative profit accounting methods.

The business could have used a slightly different method for recording its sales revenue. The difference has to do with exactly when a sale is considered final. For instance, customers may have a week or two during which the products can be returned with no questions asked. The business could book the sale as soon as the

TABLE 10.2—TWO INCOME STATEMENTS FOR SAME YEAR

	Aggressive Accounting	Conservative Accounting
Sales Revenue	$52,000,000	$51,500,000
Cost of Goods Sold	33,800,000	33,875,000
Gross Margin	$18,200,000	$17,625,000
Depreciation Expense	785,000	870,000
Amortization Expense	325,000	375,000
Other Operating Expenses	12,480,000	12,725,000
Operating Earnings	$ 4,610,000	$ 3,655,000
Interest Expense	545,000	545,000
Earnings before Tax	$ 4,065,000	$ 3,110,000
Income Tax Expense	1,423,000	1,088,000
Net Income	$ 2,642,000	$ 2,022,000

products are delivered, or it could wait for the sales return period to expire. Another business may install products sold to its customers, which may require a second or third visit to a customer's premises to compete the installation and to have the customer sign off on the sale. The business could wait until the installation is finally completed before recording the sale, or it could record the revenue when the first round of installation is done.

The business could have used a different method for recording the cost of products it sold during the year, which would have caused a higher amount for the cost of goods sold expense reported in its income statement. The difference has to do with the sequence in which the costs of products manufactured or purchased are charged to expense. If product acquisition costs don't vary during the period, there's no difference. Typically, however, acquisition costs drift upward over time. (Of course, some product costs go down or fluctuate over time.)

One method, called *first-in, first-out* (FIFO), uses the first-in, or earliest, cost recorded into inventory as the first cost to charge to expense, then the next cost, and so on in chronological order. The alternative method, called *last-in, first-out* (LIFO), uses the last in, or most recent, costs into inventory as the costs to charge to cost of goods sold expense. Basically, LIFO follows the reverse chronological order sequence for picking costs to charge to cost of goods sold expense.

By using a different method, the business's depreciation expense for the year would have been higher. This has to do with how quickly the costs of a business's fixed assets (its long-term operating assets) are charged off to expense. The so-called *accelerated method* adopts a relatively short useful-life estimate for a fixed asset and loads most of depreciation expense in the front end of its useful life. The *straight-line method*, in contrast, uses longer useful-life estimates for fixed assets and spreads depreciation evenly over the years.

To amortize the cost of intangible assets, such as goodwill, accountants use only the straight-line allocation method. However, the business could have used shorter economic-life estimates for amortizing the costs of its intangible assets. The business could have been more conservative in making adjusting entries for bad debts and for inventory shrinkage. So, its "other operating expenses" would have been higher, as shown in Table 10.2.

Interest expense depends on the amount borrowed, which would have been the same regardless of the accounting methods used by the business. So, "interest expense" for the year is the same in both scenarios. Generally, a business uses the same basic accounting methods for determining both its taxable income and its earnings before tax reported in its income statement. Therefore, as you see in Table 10.2 the "income tax expense" would decrease in proportion to the decrease in "earnings before tax."

As you see in Table 10.2, the business could have reported $2,022,000 bottom-line profit instead of the $2,642,000 net income it did report. The difference is $620,000, or 23% less than its reported profit. Does the difference make any difference? The profit figure reported by a small business definitely influences the amount of cash dividends from net income that are distributed to its stockholders. For a public company, its earnings-per-share amount (net income divided by the number of shares outstanding) is the most important number affecting the market value of its capital stock shares.

We present an alternative profit accounting scenario in Table 10.2. But we don't mean to suggest that a business keeps two sets of books—one for public consumption and the second being the real story, as it were. Some people seem to believe that a business keeps the true numbers hidden from prying eyes and that only management insiders know the true state of affairs about its profit and financial condition. Not many, if any, businesses go to the trouble of keeping a complete second set of books (i.e., making a second series of accounting entries for all the transactions of the business that are posted in a second set of accounts). Keeping a second set of accounting records would be a nontrivial task, to say the least.

But managers have, or should have, a good idea of how different their profit number would be if they had made different estimates in their end-of-year adjustments. Also, as explained earlier, a manager may deliberately delay or accelerate making certain discretionary expenditures in order to lift profit up or push it down for the year. In these situations, the manager certainly has a profit-effect number in mind.

In short, a business does not have a second set of books to refer to for an alternative profit number. But its managers should be able to estimate approximately how much "play," or elasticity, there is in its profit number for a period. In their financial reports, businesses do not disclose more than one bottom-line profit number.

The only other profit number you occasionally see in a financial report is a so-called "pro forma" profit figure. Often this term refers to a profit measure before a special, nonnormal charge or gain is taken into account. Sometimes the term is used to refer to the combined profit of two companies—as if two had been merged before they will be merged in fact. Or the term may refer to the past profit of a business as if it had disposed of a segment before it did in fact. Don't confuse a pro forma profit figure with the bottom-line profit figure in an income statement.

Asset and Liability Effects of Revenue and Expenses

Different accounting methods and adjusting entries cause differences in the amounts of revenue and expenses that are recorded, as just explained. Different accounting methods and adjusting entries also cause differences in the amounts (balances) in assets and liabilities, which are reported in the company's balance sheet at the end of the period. In recording sales revenue, either cash or accounts receivable is increased. (Some businesses receive cash from customers in advance of delivering products or services to them; in recording sales revenue, the liability for revenue collected in advance is decreased.) In recording expenses, an asset account is decreased, or a liability account is increased. The assets and liabilities affected by sales revenue and expenses are generally called *operating* assets and liabilities.

The operating assets and liabilities for the business example are shown in the shaded areas of Table 10.3. These year-end balances would have been different if the business had used different accounting methods and had made different estimates for its year-end adjusting entries. For instance, accelerated depreciation results in higher amounts in the accumulated depreciation account, which is deducted from the cost of fixed assets—property, plant, and equipment (see Table 10.3). Therefore, the book value of fixed assets (i.e., the undepreciated cost of the assets) is lower than if the business used straight-line depreciation.

The LIFO inventory cost reported in the balance sheet is considerably lower than the FIFO inventory cost (assuming product costs have risen steadily over the years). The amount reported for accounts receivable would be lower if the business had estimated that more of its accounts receivable would turn out to be bad debts than it did. Cash would be higher if discretionary expenditures had been delayed to next year. Or perhaps accounts payable is lower because these expenditures are generally purchased on credit. The liability for accrued expenses would be higher if the business had been more conservative in estimating its future costs for product warranty and guarantee work.

In general, the main purpose of massaging revenue and expense numbers is not to manipulate the asset and liability balances reported in the company's balance sheet,* but to control the amount of profit reported for the period. But you can't

---

*One accounting trick called "window dressing" is used to increase a company's year-end cash balance or to improve the appearance of its short-term solvency. Cash receipts from customers in payment of their accounts receivable that are not actually collected until after the end of the year are recorded as if the money were received on the last day of the year. The cash balance is increased, and the accounts receivable account is decreased. There are other reasons for holding the books open a few days in order to capture transactions that actually take place after the close of the year.

TABLE 10.3—OPERATING ASSETS AND OPERATING LIABILITIES (IN SHADED AREA)

Balance Sheet at End of Year

Operating Assets (All assets in this example)

Cash	$ 3,265,000	
Accounts Receivable	5,000,000	
Inventory	8,450,000	
Prepaid Expenses	960,000	
Current Assets		$17,675,000
Property, Plant, and Equipment	$16,500,000	
Less Accumulated Depreciation	4,250,000	12,250,000
Goodwill	$ 7,850,000	
Less Accumulated Amortization	2,275,000	5,575,000
Total Assets		$35,500,000

Operating Liabilities

Accounts Payable	$ 3,320,000	
Accrued Expenses	1,515,000	
Income Tax Payable	165,000	$ 5,000,000

Debt Sources of Capital

Short-Term Notes Payable	$ 3,125,000	
Long-Term Notes Payable	4,250,000	7,375,000

Equity Sources of Capital

Capital Stock (800,400 shares)	$ 8,125,000	
Retained Earnings	15,000,000	23,125,000
Total Liabilities and Owners' Equity		$35,500,000

change profit without also changing the balance sheet. Sophisticated financial statement analysts search for red flags in the balance sheet that reveal that a business may be using questionable profit accounting. The balance sheet serves as a "whistle-blower" by providing pointers to possible accounting problems or even accounting fraud.

Cooking the Books (Accounting Fraud)

By using the means previously explained, the managers of a business can control the amount of profit recorded for the year. Using these accounting tricks and techniques to manipulate profit is referred to as *massaging the numbers*. Most businesspeople, bankers, and professionals know that this goes on, although it's difficult to know for certain whether a particular business is manipulating its profit numbers or not. One danger is that a business may cross the line and do more than just massage its profit numbers. A business may engage in out-and-out accounting dishonesty with the intent of misleading those who rely on its financial statements.

Businesses in desperate situations may do desperate things. It should not be surprising that when a business finds itself in dire straits, it may resort to distortion and falsification of its profit performance and financial condition. A business resorts to these extreme tactics to buy time, hoping that it will be able to work itself out of its troubles. Or its motive may not be so innocent. The deliberate distortion and falsification of financial statements is popularly called *cooking the books*. Prosecutors call it *accounting fraud*, or *financial reporting fraud*.

Accounting fraud is subject to both civil and criminal law. You are most likely aware of the many high-profile accounting fraud cases that were reported in the press over the past several years. The widespread accounting fraud at some companies (Enron, Waste Management, and HealthSouth come to mind) would take a book to explain fully. The growth of accounting fraud has spawned a new professional specialty, *forensic accounting*.

Accounting fraud may be part and parcel of a fraudulent business scheme. The fraudulent accounting is done to cover up business fraud—such as recording bribes and kickbacks paid by a business as payments for consulting fees. Or fraudulent accounting may be done to artificially pump up the profit reported by a public corporation in order to inflate the market price of its stock shares so that its executives can make millions of dollars off their stock options or so that managers receive bonuses that are based on the profit performance of the business. Audits by CPAs have a poor track record in discovering accounting fraud in financial statements, even though this is one of the main reasons for having an audit.

Large public companies get most of the press coverage, but accounting fraud is found in businesses that are public and private, large and small. Private businesses, as well as those individuals who suffered losses as the result of accounting fraud, frequently want to keep it out of the press. A private business may engage in accounting fraud to depress the valuation of the business in order to minimize estate taxes when the principal owner dies. Accounting fraud may be done to overstate the valuation of a business when the business is put up for sale. Or a private business may engage in accounting fraud when securing a loan from its bank or in raising capital from its stockholders.

Suppose a business decided on a course of accounting fraud and ordered its accountant to cook the books. The accountant had to decide whether to go along with the scam. We would think that many accountants made the decision not to be involved in the fraud and quit the company. But actual cases have shown that accountants at many businesses did not quit and were active in carrying out the fraud, which made them coconspirators. We read one deposition of an accountant who was under investigation by the Securities and Exchange Commission (SEC). He was accused of participating in an accounting fraud by a business—it was a sad story.

There are many accounting "recipes" for cooking the books. Many accounting frauds consist of overstating sales revenue. A business may concoct a scheme to record substantial amounts of sales revenue sooner than it should or sales revenue for nonexistent sales. The schemes are endless. Here are just a few examples of sales revenue fraud:

- Products are shipped before scheduled shipment dates without the customers' consent but are recorded as sales.

- Customers are sent invoices for goods that are still in the process of being manufactured (sales should not be recorded until products are completed and delivered, of course).

- A business holds its books open to record sales but shipments are not made until after the close of the year.

- Duplicate shipments are deliberately sent to customers and recorded as sales, even though the business knows the second shipment will be returned.

- Shipments are sent to public warehouses, bogus sales invoices are prepared, and sales revenue is recorded.

Many businesses commit accounting fraud by understating some of their expenses or by not recording certain expenses at all. One business did not depreciate its fixed assets, if you can believe it. Another business refused to write off certain of its assets that were obsolete and worthless. A business may not record its liability for a lawsuit that legal counsel has said it will have to pay. A business could have a huge future obligation for environmental damage it has caused over the years, but it may not record this liability. A business could deliberately make wrong estimates for its obligations under its employee retirement plan.

Massaging the numbers involves nudging up or down the recorded profit for the year. Cooking the books, in contrast, involves gross distortions of the facts or the complete falsification of facts. Massaging the numbers puts a spin on the profit message. Cooking the books is a flat out lie. But beware: One person's spin may be another person's lie. History teaches that business and accounting fraud has been around a long time. In the late nineteenth and early twentieth centuries, business fraud was widespread, and accounting rules were practically nonexistent. Businesses and accountants are held to higher standards of conduct today.

Capsule Summary

This chapter is not meant to be a "how-to" manual but rather a "watch-out" guide. It deals with the nefarious side of accounting—massaging the numbers and cooking the books. Business managers should be involved in all aspects of making profit, including the accounting for profit. The starting point is understanding the basic accounting methods of the business. However, profit accounting consists of more than selecting which accounting methods to use for recording the revenue and expenses of a business.

The final profit or loss figure for the year depends on estimates and assumptions provided by managers to record the end-of-year adjusting entries, which is the last step in closing the books for the year. The final profit or loss number also depends on the extent to which managers have accelerated or delayed certain discretionary expenditures in order to control the amount of expenses recorded in the year.

Some businesses adopt conservative accounting methods, use conservative estimates for their year-end adjusting entries, and prohibit their managers from timing expenditures to manipulate expenses for the year. Other businesses adopt an aggressive accounting policy. They choose accounting methods that record revenue sooner and expenses later, so that profit is reported as soon as possible. They use optimistic estimates and assumptions for making their year-end adjusting entries. And their managers may defer certain expenditures until next year to keep expenses lower this year.

Tinkering with or tweaking the estimates and assumptions used in making end-of-year adjusting entries and timing discretionary expenditures to control expenses generally are referred to as *massaging the numbers*. Examples are given to illustrate how revenue and expenses can be manipulated. In the business and financial world, massaging the numbers is viewed as a venial sin, or as an accounting misdemeanor. Few like it, and many rant and rave that it shouldn't go on; but as a practical matter, not much can be done about it.

The main lesson to be learned from the general practice of massaging the numbers is to be more cautious about accepting the bottom-line profit or loss reported by a business. You should realize that this one figure is not the only profit number that could have been reported. Take a profit number with a grain of salt, and keep in mind that the reported profit could have been higher or lower. The quote at the start of the chapter from Ken Boulding makes an important point. The best we can hope for is that a profit number is approximately correct.

Accounting fraud, generally called *cooking the books*, is a different matter altogether. Accounting fraud involves the deliberate distortion and/or falsification of a company's accounting records, usually to report profit that the business has not yet earned, and may never earn. The purpose is to mislead those who rely on the financial statements of the business. A few examples of revenue and expense accounting fraud are provided in the chapter. The only good thing about cooking the books is that eventually these accounting frauds are found out, although the lid may not blow off for many years.

In closing, we take note of the alarming number of high-profile accounting frauds that have come to light over the past few years. These could indicate a moral decay in our society at large. Perhaps this is so. But we see a breakdown in one particular mechanism that was in place and that should have prevented these accounting frauds. Businesses have audits of their financial reports by outside, independent CPAs. The main purpose is to have the auditor pass judgment on the accounting and disclosure by the business. The CPA auditors failed to discover these accounting frauds. Hopefully the newly established Public Company Accounting Oversight Board will raise the level of performance of CPA auditors.

Part Three

SELLING OR
BURYING A BUSINESS

11

BUSINESS VALUATION:
THE ENDGAME

"Time is the most valuable thing a man can spend."
—Theophrastus (died 278 B.C.)

Each and every day throughout the world, hundreds or thousands of businesses are bought and sold. From megamergers handled by the power brokers on Wall Street to the local dry cleaning operation being sold after 50 years of family ownership, selling and buying companies represents big business. But how are the values for these transactions determined? Is it similar to residential real estate, where comps (comparables) and appraisals are used? Or is it closer to a retail environment, where the cost of the product or service is calculated and then a profit component added? This chapter explores commonly applied models and concepts used to generate business valuations and the most critical underlying element in the business valuation process—cash flow. By this we mean *cash flow from operating activities* or *cash flow from profit*. (You might go to Chapter 2 for a refresher on this very important topic before continuing this chapter.)

Why Businesses Are Valued

Before exploring how a business is valued, understanding *why* business valuations are critical to managing an operation is needed. On the surface, the answer to this would appear fairly obvious: How much is this business worth, and (more important) how much will I make from owning all or a portion of this business? Everyone has heard the stories about the young entrepreneur, we'll say Harvey Smindlap, starting a business in his garage, selling it years later for millions of dollars, and living the good life in sunny Southern California (of course hoarding his wealth and not bestowing any of his windfall on his children). There is no question that calculating an owner's value in a business represents a useful piece of information, but this is just one of the many uses of this all-important data point. The "why" part of valuing a business (beyond the obvious) is often more important than the "how," which the following examples and situations illustrate.

Business Management

Business valuations represent an essential element of almost any employee equity participation plan. Businesses often provide long-term compensation incentives to their employees via the utilization of various forms of stock option or equity participation plans. Basically, the goal is to provide the employees with an opportunity to generate future income and compensation in exchange for committing their services to the company for an extended period of time. Discussing these plans in detail is beyond the scope of this book, but it is important to note that business valuations are essential to ensuring the plans work efficiently.

For example, SAIC, a multibillion-dollar governmental contracting and technology company headquartered in San Diego, California, establishes a fair market value for its stock on a quarterly basis. This is undertaken to ensure that all of its employees, investors, and other interested parties have a fair basis on which to base investment decisions. If an employee needs to liquidate shares owned and sell them back to the company, a fair value or per-share price is readily available. Determining the business valuation (in this instance) supports an invaluable management tool.

Strategic Business Decisions

In today's economic environment, a change in business direction, for whatever reason, can occur almost overnight. A market that once looked like it held all the promise in the world (e.g., providing workers' compensation insurance to California businesses in the late 1990s) can quickly change, resulting in the need to liquidate or terminate the business unit. As such, having a reliable business valuation available can assist management with making important and timely decisions that may impact a company in numerous ways (e.g., losses or gains that may be realized from selling a business or a division could impact accounting reporting, tax planning, investor relations, etc.).

Business Insurance

All businesses bind various forms of insurance to manage operating and legal risks the company is exposed to. It is hard to find a business that goes completely naked and self-insures against every loss it could incur. The most widely used insurance types are general liability (to protect against a customer claiming damages from using the company's product or service), workers' compensation insurance (mandated by almost every state in the country to cover injuries suffered by employees), directors' and officers' (to provide additional liability coverage to the directors and officers of the business), and medical/life (to provide coverage to employees for health-, medical-, and death-related claims).

In addition, almost every business will utilize property and causality insurance to protect the company's assets from damage and/or loss of use. The basis for determining the property and causality insurance premium is a function of both tangible (e.g., what is the replacement cost of all the equipment in the office?) and intangible (e.g., what is the value of the business' cash flow stream?) assets. Understanding the value of a business will assist in securing the proper type, form, and amount of property and casualty insurance, which includes the value associated with "loss of use." Companies often mismanage this issue in an effort to reduce expenses (i.e., lowering insurance expense to increase the bottom line) at the risk of exposing the organization to lost income and cash flow streams. Improper insurance coverage can cost a company mightily in terms of impairing its business value.

Life Insurance and Business Planning

Most businesses operating throughout the world are privately held by a family, a small group of owners, or an individual. Quite often, a need arises to value the business for planning purposes. For example, a corporation may be owned by three partners, all of whom are married. In the event one of the owners dies, the remaining owners may want to purchase the deceased owner's interest in the company from the surviving spouse, rather than having the surviving spouse become a partner (which can often lead to significant management problems).

Often, companies will purchase term life insurance on each owner to provide enough coverage to purchase the interest held. Hence, if a company was valued at $10 million and the deceased partner owned 25%, term life insurance of approximately $2.5 million would be required. Rather than utilize internal resources (which the company may not have or the use of which would place it in a difficult operating environment) to purchase the interest, life insurance could be used to help protect all of the parties' interests (including the business itself and the individual owners). Clearly, having a business value established becomes an essential part of the planning and management process.

Individual Estate Planning

Just as, in the previous discussion, business valuation is relevant to life insurance and business planning, valuation is necessary for an individual's estate planning. Large, illiquid, individually held investments can wreak havoc with estate planning and taxation issues if not properly planned for and understood. Having a firm and fair business valuation both supports the estate management process (i.e., there are no delays as different parties squabble over the value of the assets) and provides for a solid data point for financial planning purposes (i.e., the amount of life insurance needed to cover the potential estate tax burden). The failure to plan for estate taxes is not only a problem for the estate, but may be even more of a problem for the business itself as a result of a forced or premature sale. If the estate cannot secure the necessary funds to cover the estate taxes, it may have no other option than to sell its interests in the business, which may result in new partners/investors or, worse yet, a complete business liquidation.

The "whys" it is important to value a business could be expanded upon. The aforementioned examples highlight that the need to value a business goes well past just "looking to cash out" or determining "what I'm worth." Business valuations represent an extremely important piece of information supporting a company's strategic business planning process and management functions. So, before we let our egos direct us toward answering the question "How much am I worth?" we need to answer the real issues: why this information is needed and how it can be used to better plan for the future.

How Are Businesses Valued?

This discussion will be easy. Or perhaps we should say that the discussion of the fundamentals of how a business is valued is straightforward, although it can devolve into many technical details if you're not careful. A business's valuation is based on the present value of its future cash flows, in particular its operating cash flows from its profit-making activities (as opposed to, say, selling off some of its long-term operating assets). No matter what valuation model, methodology, logic, concept, technique, and/or guiding principle is used, it all comes back to the company's ability to generate cash flow from profit (i.e., its operating activities). Even when a company is being liquidated, the end value is based on how much cash will be left over for the equity investors. Simply put, cash flow reigns as king when valuing a business.

Although countless business valuation models, techniques, and concepts can be utilized, this section will be geared toward keeping the discussion simple and will be focused on the basics, with two of the more common business valuation techniques examined—"Main Street" and "Wall Street."

Cash Flow Multiple—Main Street

Under this method, a simple cash flow multiple is applied to a company's expected future "adjusted" cash flow stream. This adjusted cash flow stream is most commonly referred to as EBITDA (earnings before interest, taxes, depreciation, and amortization).

Generally speaking, the cash flow multiple ranges from 2 to 5 (but can be higher or lower) for private businesses that are not the size of IBM. This key ratio, or multiple, depends heavily on the company's perceived risk and forecast growth factors. In addition, historical cash flow information tends to be used as a basis or starting point when calculating the expected/future "adjusted" cash flow stream. For example, if a company's average EBITDA for the past three years has been $750,000 annually and a multiple of 4 is applied, the business's value would be approximately $3,000,000. This business valuation method is more widely utilized by "Main Street" due to the nature of how these companies operate (i.e., a high volume of relatively small and unsophisticated businesses, as compared to corporate America as represented by Wall Street).

Price Earnings Multiple—Wall Street

Using this technique, a business valuation is derived from taking the net after-tax earnings of a company and multiplying that number by a market-driven factor. For businesses that enjoy the prospects of high growth rates, which translate into potential significant future cash flows, a multiple of 20 or more may applied. For businesses that are more mature with relatively steady cash flow streams, a lower multiple may be applied, such as 10. This is one (but certainly not the only) reason why a company such as Microsoft may be valued using a factor of 30, whereas Exxon may be valued using a factor of only 13. This technique is most prevalent with publicly traded companies listed on the New York Stock Exchange, the Nasdaq, and other markets. The market quickly and efficiently establishes the total value of the company (i.e., its market capitalization), which is readily available at any point in time.

Table 11.1 illustrates these two valuation techniques, which, although different, come to the same general valuation conclusion in the example given. As you can see in Table 11.1, both techniques essentially value the company at approximately $4,000,000. In other words, a potential acquirer would provide $4,000,000 of consideration to generate a potential operating cash flow of approximately $661,000 per year (i.e., net profit of $410,983 plus depreciation expense of $250,000), producing a simple investment return of approximately 16.5%.

Also note that the valuation derived is approximately one times the company's gross profit generated of roughly $4.2 million. You will often find that within certain industries, common valuation reference points are made such as X times revenue, Y times gross profit, or Z times book value. For example, in the banking world, business valuations are often based in terms of the multiple achieved on the bank's net book value (or net equity). Although this valuation technique may appear to be different, if you look closely enough and apply the lessons of valuing a business on its ability to generate cash flow, you'll quickly understand why one bank will sell for two times its book value and another for one times—its ability to generate cash flow.

So in summary, business valuations are really based on two critical pieces of information: (1) the expected or future cash flow the company has the ability to generate, and (2) the multiple applied to the expected or future cash flow stream (by the market). Both of these issues will be explored in more detail as our discussion on business valuations continues.

TABLE 11.1—COMPARISON OF BUSINESS VALUATION METHODS

XYZ Wholesale, Inc.

Summary Income Statement	Cash Flow Multiple FYE 12/31/00	Price Earnings FYE 12/31/00
Revenue	$15,265,000	$15,265,000
Cost of Goods Sold	11,067,125	11,067,125
Gross Profit	$ 4,197,875	$ 4,197,875
Gross Margin	27.50%	27.50%
Selling, General, and Administrative Expenses	$ 3,001,000	$ 3,001,000
Depreciation Expense	250,000	250,000
Interest Expense	72,000	72,000
Other (Income) Expenses	212,000	212,000
Net Profit before Tax	$ 662,875	$ 662,875
Income Tax Expense (Benefit)	251,893	251,893
Net Profit (Loss)	$ 410,982	$ 410,982
EBITDA	$ 984,875	N/A
Cash Flow Multiple	4.00	N/A
Business Value	$ 3,939,500	N/A
Net Earnings	N/A	$ 410,982
Price Earnings Multiple	N/A	10.00
Business Value	N/A	$ 4,109,820

What Drives Business Valuations?

The hard thing about valuing a business lies in the great unknown of future cash flows. Although historical operations can provide a sound starting point to determine future cash flows, they can also be very misleading. For example, a biotechnology company in an early stage of clinical trials has no historical positive earnings or cash flows, but it may hold an extremely high market valuation based on the promise of future cash flows from the eventual production and sales of a new drug. Conversely, a cemetery operation may have a one-time (nonrecurring) event due to a liquidation of (long-held) real estate holdings. Hence, future cash flows can be distorted by historical events that are nonrecurring (positive or negative). The key lies in the ability to calculate a core, or operating, cash flow figure on which to base the valuation.

Exploring further, the following common situations and issues regarding how cash flows are determined are provided. These are not meant to be all-inclusive but rather are offered to give you a sense for how cash flows are and should be "adjusted" when used as a basis for determining business value.

Common Cash Flow "Adjustments" for Business Valuation Purposes

• *Expense Savings:* A company may be interested in acquiring a business that offers tremendous expense savings opportunities via implementing the concept of economies of scale. By combining the two entities, a once unprofitable business may now actually produce a positive cash flow (which has value).

• *Added Expense Removal:* Pushing through other or personal expenses in closely held businesses has been around as long as the Internal Revenue Service (IRS). Generally, these are not necessary expenses for the ongoing business to operate, but the owners take advantage of getting the tax break. Removing these expenses to increase cash flows will lead to higher business valuations.

• *Potential Cost Increases:* Certain companies may be at a stage where a significant reinvestment in capital equipment, assets, and so on is required to continue to support and generate cash flows. These one-time expenditures will need to be factored into a business valuation model to reflect the impact on future cash flows.

• *Hidden Assets:* Certain assets may have a significant value present, external to the core business. For example, years ago a company may have purchased real estate (for future business expansion) that is no longer needed internally. To an outside party, the value may be substantial, and as such, this hidden value needs to be reflected in the complete business valuation.

• *Intangible Assets and/or Intellectual Property:* Brand names, research in process, patents, trademarks, contracts for retail shelf space, and similar assets have the ability to generate significant cash flows if managed properly. While one company may struggle with generating adequate cash flows, another may prosper by applying its marketing or financial muscle to their assets.

♦ *Lost Future Business:* In service organizations, a business valuation may decrease as a result of a key principal leaving or retiring. Anyone who has evaluated an acquisition within the service industry knows how critical this issue can be in terms of negatively impacting future cash flows. If a partner of 30 years leaves, chances are a portion of his accounts will also leave.

This sort of list could fill a book. The issue of importance is that in valuing a business, all elements and facts of importance must be evaluated in terms of determining what is the most reasonable future cash flow stream that can be expected.

Step two in the business valuation process is based in how the multiple applied to the cash flow or earnings stream is determined. The following factors all play a role in determining the multiples used:

Factors Affecting Multiples Used in Business Valuation

♦ *Concentration or Diversification Risks:* The higher the concentration or diversification risk, the lower the multiple. Two like companies with the same cash flow stream operating in the same industry may receive different valuations because one company generates its revenue equally from 100 accounts and the other from just 10 accounts (equally). The impact of losing 1 account in 10 is far greater than 1 in 100 and increases the concentration risk.

♦ *Interest Rates:* Interest rates, simply stated, represent the cost of capital. Higher interest rates produce lower valuation multiples. Today's low-interest-rate environment provides for higher multiples; but when the Federal Reserve Board even mentions that rates may rise, well, it should come as no surprise that valuations may be pressured.

♦ *Growth Potential:* Higher growth opportunities, which translate into stronger future cash flow potential, will demand higher multiples. Just ask the dot-coms of the late 1990s and early 2000s about how they received astronomical valuations based on the premise of extremely high future-growth rates.

♦ *Length of Cash Flow Stream:* Cash flow streams that are longer and more secure, or reliable, will produce higher valuation multiples than shorter, uncertain cash flow streams. If a company has patent production in place for the next 10 years (supporting the cash flow stream) versus 3 years, it's safe to say the valuation multiple will be favorable.

♦ *Liquidity:* If an investment is readily liquid with multiple buyers available, a higher multiple will generally be provided. Illiquid investments with limited market appeal increase risks and drive down valuation multiples.

♦ *Management Continuity:* This issue works both ways. Eliminating poor management may actually help the valuation multiple, whereas losing key executives may hurt it. However, if poor management was in place, it's safe to say the historical cash flow stream was not as strong as it might have been.

The valuation multiple really boils down the risks present (perceived and actual). Needless to say, the higher the risks, the lower the valuation multiple received.

In summary, it should be stressed that there are no set rules in the business valuation game. Whereas a seller may want to maximize cash flows and lower the risks (thus increasing the value), the acquirer may want to deflate potential future cash flows and increase the perceived risks (thus decreasing the value). Conversely, an estate may want to justify a lower valuation to reduce potential estate taxes, whereas the IRS may be more aggressive and increase the valuation for obvious reasons. While the basics in the business valuation process remain the same—cash flow and multiples—how these figures are "managed" or "manipulated" represents the real basis of valuing a business. Quite clearly there's a fair amount of "wiggle room" in coming up with the figures on which the valuation of a business is based. Honest and fair-minded people can and do disagree on cash-flow forecasts and the appropriate multiples for setting a value figure. At the same time, there's a point beyond which the good faith of a party to the negotiation can be questioned.

Quick Review of Business Acquisitions

Thus far, the chapter has focused mainly on the why, how, and what of business valuations. We've not said anything about how a business acquisition is undertaken and structured. It would be impossible to overview all of the attributes of a business acquisition, as documenting the legal issues alone might kill a couple of trees. Rather, a quick review of some key elements of business acquisitions have been highlighted to provide a map of some sort from the business valuation process to an acquisition.

Business acquisitions tend to come in one of two types: (1) *asset deals* or (2) *stock deals*. Under an *asset deal*, specific assets of a business are acquired, with the remaining legal entity left intact either to wrap up its affairs or to continue with another business opportunity. This deal may mean buying just the ongoing business operations (including inventory; property, plant, and equipment; and the intangible assets [e.g., customer lists, patents, trade names, etc.]) and leaving the remaining assets (such as trade receivables, prepaid expenses, and cash) with the old legal entity. The acquiring company purchases the assets and then integrates them into its operation for the purpose of realizing economic gain (i.e., produce cash flow). The selling company is left to finalize its business affairs by liquidating the remaining assets, paying off the creditors, and hopefully having a return available to the owners or shareholders. It should be noted that in a variety of situations, the selling company may still have an ongoing operation intact, as the sale may involve only one division or segment of the business. Hence, the selling business continues its operations as usual, with the exception of having one less division to manage. Asset deals tend to be associated with smaller businesses or companies looking to shed a specific business interest.

Under a *stock deal*, instead of purchasing specific assets of the selling company, the stock or equity of the selling company is purchased at fair market value with all assets being acquired and all liabilities assumed. The acquired company usually survives as a legal entity and continues to operate as subsidiary of the acquiring company or is in some capacity merged into a new entity formed for the specific purpose of acquiring the target company. Generally, the equity owners of the acquired company sell their holdings (i.e., stock, LLC membership interests, etc.) for cash, equity or stock in the acquiring company, a note payable, or a combination of these items. Stock deals tend to be associated with larger, publicly traded companies (as well as the larger privately held businesses) that have ample liquid resources and freely traded stock to complete the transaction.

As you probably would surmise, there are certain key advantages and disadvantages that determine whether to use an asset deal or a stock deal. However, the same premise usually holds under either transaction, in that the general business interests of the acquired company are maintained on an ongoing basis because the acquisition was based on the premise that an economically viable operation is present.

Once the acquisition value and deal type have been selected, the structuring of the transaction can be undertaken. The following structuring issue examples have been presented to provide some basic insight as to how business acquisitions are put together.

Business Acquisition Structuring Issues

• *Forms of Consideration:* It should go without saying that the acquiring company will need to remit payment to the selling company. This usually is in the form of cash, stock or equity, debt (such as a note payable), or a combination of these items. For sellers, the preference is to get cash or liquid stock/equity in hand. For acquirers, the tendency is to conserve cash and manage the financing element of the transaction with some debt or restricted stock/equity.

• *Restrictive Agreements:* A number of restrictive agreements are usually required, the majority of which tend to fall on the seller. For example, the acquiring company will want to ensure that the selling company or its founders do not compete against it in the future. This will trigger the use of a noncompete agreement. When stock is provided as consideration, the acquiring company will often place a restriction period on when and how much of the stock can be sold after the fact to avoid too much of their stock being dumped on the open market at once (driving down the price).

• *Representations and Warranties:* Both parties will be required to provide representations and warranties that the business being acquired is viable and that the acquiring business is of sound "mind and body." In this day and age of fraud, deceit, and misrepresentations, both parties will want to ensure that added legal protection is in place to prevent the "take the money and run" attitude from prevailing.

• *Variable Acquisition Control Features:* A number of business acquisitions will place controls on the valuation and consideration paid by implementing such elements as variable debt payments (or "earn-outs"), continued employment agreements for key management, meeting future operating performance objectives, and others. The general idea is that some future event needs to occur (e.g., management needs to stay intact for three years, X number of stores need to be opened, or the acquired business needs to produce Y cash flow) before additional consideration will be remitted. This tends to favor the acquiring company, but it can also benefit the seller in that added deal kickers can be put in place if the acquired business actually performs better than expected.

This concludes our abbreviated discussion on acquisition types and structuring issues. We haven't even touched on the issues of courting business acquisitions, due diligence, packaging the business for sale, and how friendly the attorneys can become. Hopefully, this has provided you with a little more insight on the acquisition process. Remember that all this is for naught if an economic value (i.e., cash flow) cannot be justified.

Final Thought on Business Valuations

More than one person has asked us why the owners' equity in the most recent balance sheet of a business is not a good measure of its value. Or, putting it another way: Shouldn't the value of a business equal its total assets minus its total liabilities? This is called its *net assets*, which equals the book value of its owners' equity. Why not use this number, which is conveniently available? Well, this sounds like a simple answer. But this makes sense if, and this is a mighty big IF, the assets and liabilities reported in the balance sheet were based on their current market and replacement values and if accountants recorded the values of the experienced work force of the business, its reputation with customers, its well-known brand name, and so on. But accountants don't record these assets.

Accountants, following generally accepted accounting principles, use the historical cost basis for preparing a business's financial statements. Accountants do not record the "intangibles" or "invisible assets" behind the numbers reported in the financial statements of a going business. The historical cost basis of accounting is backward looking; accountants record the financial history of a business. Business valuation is forward looking. The most recent financial statements of a business are an invaluable point of departure, but they are just the starting point for looking into the future, which has both predictable and unpredictable elements.

Capsule Summary

This chapter explores the whys and the how of putting a value on a business, with some advice thrown in for good measure. This relatively short chapter cannot do full justice to the broad topic of business valuation. Just fundamentals are presented in the chapter, but these are essential building blocks that business managers, as well as sellers and buyers of a business, definitely should understand.

Even if there is no prospect or likelihood of putting a business on the market, its managers are well advised to determine the value of the business. Employee equity (ownership) participation plans need a sound business valuation basis. When a business decides to shed a major segment, it needs a reliable valuation for that piece of the business. Deciding on business insurance coverage needs a valuation for the business that takes into account all resources that contribute to its success, including intangibles such as customer loyalty and its experienced employees. Valuation of a business is needed to determine the appropriate life insurance amounts on the lives of the principal owners of a business. The value of the interest of a deceased shareholder is based on the valuation of the business as a whole.

Putting a valuation number on a business can get rather technical. Most valuation methods focus on the future cash flows of the business as far out as can be forecast and apply a multiple times the cash flow stream to determine value. The most appropriate multiple is a matter of judgment, of course. The chapter compares two basic valuation methods, which we call the "Main Street" and the "Wall Street" methods, to distinguish between privately and publicly owned businesses. In either case, future cash flows are always uncertain to one degree or another. Projecting cash flows can be done with more certainty for some businesses than for others.

The historical pattern of cash flows of a business is normally used as the point of departure for forecasting its future cash flows. Instead of drawing a simple trend line into the future, adjustments usually have to be made to the historical pattern of cash flows. These modifications include projected changes in expenses, the way established brand names and established products will fare in the future, and key personnel changes that might happen if new ownership takes over. Also, factors such as concentration of customers, interest rate changes, the growth potential of the business, and the length of cash flow streams should be considered.

The chapter also covers business acquisitions, which are divided into two types: asset deals and stock deals. A buyer may want to take control of the assets of a business. Or the buyer might want the stock shares of the business in order to continue the business as before. Structuring the acquisition is very important. When and how the money will be paid over, restrictive agreements, and several other key points have to be ironed out in business acquisition negotiations.

The chapter also explains that the amount reported for owners' equity in the balance sheet of a business usually is significantly different from the market value of a business. The book value of owners' equity is the result of recording the history of transactions over the years that have affected the owners' equity. In contrast, the market value of a business is forward looking. The price a buyer is willing to pay for ownership of a business may be quite a bit higher (or lower) than the book value of owners' equity that is reported in its balance sheet.

Finally, keep one thing in mind above all others. The price you pay for a business does not in any sense drive its future cash flows. Just the other way around: The future cash flows of a business should determine the price you are willing to pay for a business. The future cash flows will be the same regardless of the price you pay for the business. Don't pay too much; but to be fair, you shouldn't pay too little either.

12

TERMINATING A BUSINESS: WHEN THE DOG NO LONGER HUNTS

"O! that a man might know
The end of this day's business, ere it come."
—William Shakespeare

It is fitting that this book should be brought to a close by exploring a subject matter that is more relevant than most people think in relation to managing business interests, but one that is not well understood by the business community—*terminating a business*. On the surface, it would be easy to assume that terminating a business is as simple as locking the doors, shutting off the phone and utility services, and turning off the lights (without even having the courtesy to leave a forwarding phone number or address). Conversely, one might think that electing to pursue entering bankruptcy is a more viable option in terms of letting the lawyers handle the final company affairs. Yes, both of these avenues are utilized to help close the 80%-plus of all businesses that fail within the first five years of their lives, and both will be briefly touched on within this chapter.

The objective of this chapter, however, is not to simply review the options available for terminating a business but rather to delve into how the termination process actually works and ties back to all of the accounting and financial concepts discussed throughout this book. From the initial birth of the business to its almost certain death (at some point), the same accounting, financial, and business principles need to be applied to ensure that a proper burial is achieved. If a business termination is not properly managed, well, let's just say the ghosts of past business failures have come back to haunt more than a few aspiring entrepreneurs.

Voluntary versus Involuntary Business Terminations

As discussed in the previous chapter on business valuation, companies are usually sold using one of two different methodologies: an asset sale or a stock sale. Under a stock sale, the acquired company usually survives as a legal entity and continues to operate as a subsidiary of the acquiring company or is in some capacity merged into a new entity formed for the specific purpose of acquiring the target company. Under either scenario, the general business interests of the acquired company are maintained on an ongoing basis because the acquisition was based on the premise that the business is economically viable.

This assumption of a viable going business also holds true for an asset sale, as it is deemed that the assets acquired have some economic value to the acquiring company. The major differences between these types of transactions were presented in the previous chapter, one of which directly feeds into understanding why properly managing a business termination is so critical. Under an asset sale, the legal entity, which sold the assets, still remains and either continues to operate as a business entity or needs to be formally terminated to ensure that proper closure is brought to all company affairs.

Stock sales and asset sales are generally considered *voluntary* terminations; that is, the selling party or parties have an interest or a desire to liquidate their holdings in a fair market value transaction with the acquiring party or parties. The good news with a voluntary termination is that an orderly close of the business is undertaken with both creditors and equity investors usually on board with the process. Hence, the biggest hurdle to face is managing the administrative process of closing the business, which can be accomplished either internally (retain a close down management team to finalize the business's affairs) or externally (hire professional support to finalize the business's affairs).

On the flip side of the voluntary termination process is the ever-so-popular (yet unfortunate) involuntary termination. Involuntary business terminations tend to get more of the headlines because they are usually centered on an unfortunate event leading to a high-profile failure (which of course the press loves to report on). This type of termination is usually brought on by external parties (e.g., creditors, shareholders, government agencies) protecting their interests in a failing business. Generally, the heart of the problem lies in the inability of the business to grasp the extremely important concept of "positive cash flow and net income." The dot-com darlings of the 1990s quickly learned that a business must actually produce net income and positive cash flow to stay in business for an extended period of time (hardly a novel concept in a capitalist society). Most involuntary business terminations are managed under the context of bankruptcy proceedings and/or equivalent processes, such as an Assignment for the Benefit of Creditors. As such, the federal court system, trustees assigned/retained to support the process, and/or business creditors are the ones who generally manage and control involuntary business terminations.

Whether a business termination will be voluntary or

involuntary, one critical element must be remembered: The business's owners, founders, entrepreneurs, and/or key executives often have a difficult time accepting the economic reality of the situation and the proximate end of the business. These individuals will often pursue any course of action to keep the doors open and to not let their business concept (i.e., their child) die. As noted in the discussion on fraud, the emotional state of these individuals may push them to make decisions that to external parties are clearly crossing the fraudulent line but to them are still within the bounds of acceptable accounting and business practices.

What these individuals fail to realize or simply don't want to accept is that the business enterprise's cash flow (or lack thereof) does not and will not support a competitive economic model. To an external party, a quick review of the business plan and/or economic model may clearly project an unviable operation. To an internal party, however, he or she may be self-deluded into believing the economic model does work. How? By increasing revenue assumptions, reducing expenses unreasonably, and/or presenting information (actual or forecast) to capital sources that is not supportable. Being realistic is just as important in the life of the business as in its death.

A Quick Review of Bankruptcy Protection

Bankruptcy filings by individuals and businesses have reached all-time highs during the past decade. It's almost impossible to have missed such high-profile bankruptcy actions as K-Mart, Enron, Johns-Manville, United Airlines, FAO Schwarz, and Zales Jewelry; and the list goes on and on. In some cases, the bankruptcy filing results from an economic model that is no longer viable (e.g., K-Mart's inability to compete in the highly intense mass-merchandising market) or a one-time event that burdens the company with an unreasonable monetary obligation (e.g., claimants being awarded huge sums of money against Johns-Manville for asbestos-related claims). In others, bankruptcy results from outright fraud (e.g., Enron). Whatever the cause, bankruptcy filings by businesses have been and will continue to be utilized as an effective strategy to manage a company's affairs in difficult economic times.

Most of the high-profile bankruptcy filings are entered into under the federal government's guidelines known as Chapter 11. Under this provision, a company is granted time to reorganize its financial affairs and to develop a plan to satisfy both the creditors and the equity investors in the company. If you remember the discussion on raising capital, creditors have priority claims against company assets over equity investors. Hence, most Chapter 11 bankruptcy proceedings require a significant amount of input and involvement from the creditors in terms of managing the reorganization process.

The creditors have the majority of the rights and preferences in these proceedings to protect their financial interests first, and, as such, the investors are usually left "holding the bag." If the Chapter 11 reorganization plan is properly structured to satisfy all of the parties involved (to the fullest extent possible), the company's creditors and, to a lesser extent, its management team, in addition to the federal court, all approve the reorganization plan; the company then exits bankruptcy protection to operate as an independent business. We mention the management team only in the context that someone must be left to keep the business operating and going forward. Needless to say, neither the court nor the creditors have any interest in all the details of keeping the business going forward; therefore, it is necessary that a committed management team emerge from Chapter 11.

Under a Chapter 7 bankruptcy proceeding, the company's goal is not to reorganize but to liquidate all remaining assets to and pay off creditors to whatever extent possible (with the understanding that the legal entity will be formally terminated). Federal laws still govern this type of bankruptcy proceeding, but the focus turns from developing an ongoing viable economic business model toward liquidating remaining company assets as efficiently as possible. The remaining company's affairs are turned over to a court-appointed trustee, who is responsible for managing all of the necessary steps to formally terminate the business. This includes everything from liquidating remaining assets, to repayment of creditors (to whatever extent possible), to processing final paperwork, such as tax returns, legal notifications, and the like. Similar to a Chapter 11 bankruptcy, significant legal fees are usually incurred to support a Chapter 7 bankruptcy and are usually implemented by larger or more high-profile business operations.

Another type of termination proceeding available to companies in dire straits that warrants discussion is what's known as an Assignment for the Benefit of Creditors (or ABC). For lack of a better term, an ABC is nothing more than a poor man's version of a Chapter 7 bankruptcy proceeding. The same goals and objectives are present, in that a liquidation effort is undertaken to maximize the value of whatever company assets remain and to repay creditors and equity investors in the proper order. In addition, an independent trustee is required to manage the final termination affairs, but rather than being controlled under the laws of the federal court system, the process is left directly to the trustee to administer. This trustee is usually a law firm that specializes in these types of transactions or an independent consulting group with a niche expertise. Beyond the difference with how the trustee is secured, the cost of an ABC is usually far less than a Chapter 7 bankruptcy because the court process is bypassed (unless the ABC turns ugly).

Needless to say, most ABCs do not generate a return to the equity investors and usually produce far less cash than is needed to repay the creditors. ABCs are generally utilized (and represent a more efficient termination strategy) when the business entity is relatively small, legal squabbles are not anticipated, the different types of creditors and equity investors are limited, asset recovery potential is poor, and opportunities for fraud and/or other types of misconduct are not significant. ABCs also tend to follow a common path, in that the business owners clearly have come to

the conclusion that the end is at hand and have already communicated this to the creditors and the equity investors (without much resistance received).

In summary, the following key issues should be remembered when either bankruptcy proceedings or ABCs are implemented:

Key Issues to Keep in Mind When Considering Bankruptcy or Assignment for Benefit of Creditors (ABC)

+ Chapter 7 or 11 bankruptcy proceedings are generally very expensive and may take a relatively long time to complete. A business actually needs to be prepared to enter into bankruptcy with ample liquid financial resources just to get through the process.

+ Chapter 7 and 11 bankruptcy proceedings need to be supported by the proper legal and professional counsel because the issues involved can get highly technical.

+ Fighting, arguing, and bickering among the various creditors (as well as the investors) can get nasty, resulting in lengthy delays and increases in professional fees.

+ An ABC represents a viable option to a bankruptcy when the right conditions are met; the results are significant savings and the ability to streamline the process.

+ Investors' equity values usually get hammered under any of these proceedings. The risk/reward relationship definitely plays out here—with the highest appetite for risks comes either the highest returns or getting left holding the bag.

The Start of the End

The biggest stumbling block to terminating a business is often figuring out how to start. Well, when looking back at how the business was launched, a business plan was developed to guide the business during its formation and its growth years. Similarly, a *business termination plan* should be put together in order to guide the business through its final months. Although this plan will have a slightly different objective than that of the business plan, the basis remains the same—optimizing the business's remaining economic value and establishing a course of action to pursue. And just like the initial business plan identified the capital required to execute the strategy, so too must the termination plan ensure that the appropriate resources are available to properly end the business.

The business termination plan will most likely not be as formal, in terms of its presentation and data, as the initial business plan. Let's face it—when a business is shutting down, it's not attempting to impress potential capital sources. Rather its goal is to outline a termination strategy that maximizes asset values, repays creditors to the fullest extent possible, and provides a potential return to the equity investors, all within the most efficient means possible. The following list was prepared to highlight the macrolevel issues that need to be addressed in the plan:

Key Matters That Should Be Addressed in a Business Termination Plan

- A *simple executive summary* that outlines the events, market conditions, and so on, that lead to the business termination should be provided. While a number of parties will already have an understanding of the reasons, having proper documentation prepared and available will be extremely helpful to the slew of parties that are caught by surprise.

- The plan should include a *forecast for the time frame* in which the termination is expected to be carried out and the capital/cash needed to execute the plan. One of the biggest mistakes made when terminating a business is underestimating how much capital/cash is required to execute the plan correctly. Remember, nobody is going to extend credit to the business when it will soon be out of existence.

- A concise *summary of the company's remaining assets and liabilities* should be presented in the business plan. On the asset front, a detailed listing of all assets should be prepared with a marketing plan provided on how the assets will be disposed. For the liabilities, a listing of every liability by class (i.e., secured, unsecured, priority level, etc.) is essential to ensure that creditors are paid in the right order. *Note:* A summary of the equity investors by investment class should also be provided to identify potential liquidation preferences.

- A *summary of the internal* (i.e., remaining employees) *and external personnel resources* will need to be incorporated into the plan. Most business terminations require the support of external legal/professional counsel, and these resources (and their costs) need to be managed at the start of the process. There aren't too many professionals willing to extend payment terms in a business termination.

- Finally, an *overview of the various operating factors* should be provided, including insurance requirements, physical locations needed, outstanding operating leases and commitments, and similar business issues. Remember, at some point the lights will actually need to be turned off, and the postal service will need to know where the mail should be forwarded.

The business termination plan will be used not only as a "final road map" for the company's management, but also as a tool for presentation to the key parties responsible for approving the termination. The key parties will be either the board of directors and company officers still in control of the company or the creditors, who have effectively taken control of the company to protect their interests. Under either case, formal approval for the termination needs to be obtained from the responsible and authorized parties. Without formal approval, the company (and potentially the board members and officers) will expose itself to potential risks, acquisitions, and eventual legal action, which can create significant additional costs down the road. The company will want to make sure all relevant parties review the plan, agree that no other economically viable avenues exist, and formally approve the termination plan, which will include helping the officers and board members identify when to formally resign from their positions.

Company Assets—Tangible and Intangible

Liquidating the remaining assets of a company about to be shut down represents one of the most important components of the business termination plan. The cash raised is critical to getting creditors paid off. In addition, hidden values and potential risks are lurking behind the scenes. Table 12.1 presents an overview of the major asset types owned by a business and the hidden value and potential risk for each type. This overview is in no way meant to be all-inclusive; it is provided to highlight the various issues present when a termination effort is underway.

The examples provided in Table 12.1 only begin to scratch the surface. Many other issues (both positive and negative) surround each major asset type. And because each business is so unique, different issues will undoubtedly be present that offer additional value-enhancement opportunities while opening up the company to potential risks.

The following list summarizes several key recommendations to keep in mind when liquidating the assets of a business to be terminated.

Checklist for Asset Liquidations

♦ Ensure that the company has as complete and comprehensive an asset listing as possible. This will ensure that management has a solid starting point from which to manage the disposition of assets in terms of allocating resources to the most valuable assets (to increase values) and not wasting time on assets with little or no value.

♦ Remember that a number of intangible assets may be present, whether or not a cost is stated on the balance sheet. This may include customer lists, trade secrets, sales databases, a below-market transferable property lease, and even the company name or "Doing Business As" names (DBA). The potential to realize value from these assets should not be underestimated.

♦ The potential for fraud, theft, and/or misallocating assets is very high in a business termination. Certain items (e.g., a new computer) have a tendency to "walk away" when management is not paying attention. Proper safeguarding of assets with techniques as simple as making sure all items over $1,000 are locked in a separate area needs to be a priority.

♦ Ensure that all material transactions to liquidate assets are based on arm's-length transactions with fair market value received. Company insiders sometimes have a tendency to secure certain assets (with the idea of starting a new business) without really giving any consideration to the special legal and fairness requirements of the situation. You can be assured that if the dollar amounts are large enough, the creditors and the equity investors will pursue any transaction that smells of a related-party or insider deal.

♦ Take advantage of experts such as liquidators, commercial real estate brokers, or investment bankers (when feasible) to enhance the value of the assets being disposed. Even though added

TABLE 12.1—HIDDEN VALUES AND POTENTIAL RISKS IN ASSETS TO BE LIQUIDATED

Asset Type	Hidden Value	Potential Risks
Cash and Equivalents	Outstanding checks may remain that never cleared the bank, with the possibility that these checks could be recovered back into the company's bank accounts (subject to potential unclaimed poperty tax regulations).	Unprotected blank checks may be stolen, forged, and cashed. Protection of all bank documents and items is extremely important in a termination.
Accounts Receivable	An old account written off as worthless via the customer's bankruptcy may still have some value. Assigning this to a creditor in exchange for a cash payment may be possible. Perhaps a collection agent should be used.	The company's customers become aware of the termination and elect to string out payment in hopes of having to avoid making full payment. Who's going to collect the money if nobody's around?
Inventories	The shelf space the company's inventory occupies may have value to another business looking for additional exposure in a certain retail environment.	Disposing of old, worthless, and/or unwanted inventory may be costly and may contain potential hazardous-material problems.
Property, Plant, and Equipment (Fixed Assets)	Offering a package of fixed assets at a discount may provide the opportunity for the company to rid itself of an office lease with a personal guarantee; that is, the assets are sold below value, but a significant liability is also eliminated (not to mention that the company does not have to move the assets now).	Selling tangible property—desks, furniture, fixtures, computers, etc.—may trigger a sales tax obligation that needs to be remitted to the appropriate parties. Also note that property, plant, and equipment may have a secured lender attached, thus restricting the ability to liquidate these assets.
Intangible Assets	Customer lists, databases, and similar types of information may have significant value to certain third parties. Marketing of these intangible assets holds potential for raising additional cash.	Allowing management and/or insiders to acquire databases and other key information without consideration may trigger a potential claim of wrongdoing by creditors or equity investors.
Other Assets— Prepaids, Deposits, Loans Receivable, etc.	Prepayments for rent, insurance, advertising, and similar items offer an opportunity to recover cash for the unutilized time period.	Terminating insurance coverage too early may leave the company's assets exposed to potential third-party claims.

costs are present, the extra value obtained via their marketing knowledge and muscle may be more than enough to offset their costs.

◆ Document all asset sales transactions appropriately to ensure that future disclosures and accounting can be completed correctly. For example, if inventory is liquidated to a reseller, then no sales tax will be due (one business to another business). However, if inventory is sold at a bargain price to company employees (business to the end user), then sales tax will need to be collected.

◆ The ultimate value of an asset is really based in nothing more than its future cash flow (hmmm, haven't we discussed this issue before?). If other businesses are willing to buy a used computer for $250, then this is the value of the computer. If a patent generates a small royalty each month, then the future value of this royalty stream (discounted at the appropriate rate) represents its value. Similar to valuing and marketing a business for sale, anything that can be done to enhance an asset's future cash flow will increase its value today.

One key point not to forget is that the officers, executives, and/or parties retained to terminate the business have a fiduciary responsibility to the creditors and the equity investors to maximize the value of the assets being disposed. In today's business environment, one that is highly sensitive to fraud and corruption, creditors and investors are just looking for ways to recapture losses, even if it means piercing the corporate entity and pursuing key parties at the individual level.

The Pecking Order for Debt Repayment

Now that we've discussed the asset disposition side of a business termination, we turn to paying off its liabilities. Here, just like with the management of a business's assets, a complete and comprehensive listing of all liabilities must be prepared. This provides management with the necessary starting point to properly structure how the company's assets will be distributed (to its creditors), remembering the following extremely important liability pecking order:

General Payoff Order of Liabilities

• *Priority Creditors:* Certain liabilities represent priority obligations that will need to be addressed early in the process. These include wage and vacation obligations (within limits) to employees, unpaid payroll taxes, and sales/use taxes payable. Basically, the government does not want to see itself or the company's employees take a loss; and as such, these types of obligations can often pass through to the officers or the board of a company if they are not paid. Priority creditors, to a certain extent, have preference over almost all other types of creditors and need to be identified and managed first to avoid potential problems. Remember, a number of these items are considered to be held in trust for the recipient by the company's officers, board, and/or other key executives.

• *Secured Creditors:* These types of creditors are usually banks, credit unions, equipment financing groups, and the like. These creditors generally only lend on a secured basis with an underlying asset present to support the value of the loan extended. Hence, if the company ever gets into trouble, the value of the liquidated asset is (hopefully) adequate to cover the amount of the outstanding loan. These creditors have preference over the unsecured creditors of the company.

• *Unsecured Creditors:* These are typically your primary trade vendors of the company, including material suppliers (for inventory), utilities (e.g., phone, electric, water), professional service firms, and other general corporate vendors (e.g., office supplies, temporary staffing company). These creditors have a claim against the company but are generally not secured with a specific asset. Hence, these creditors generally take a beating when an involuntary company termination is undertaken because, normally, not enough funds are available to cover the outstanding debt obligations. Unsecured creditors may or may not have a preference over subordinated debt, depending on how the subordinated debt agreement is structured.

• *Subordinated Creditors:* The subordinated creditors of the company generally are in the last position in terms of receiving any repayment of debt before any payments can be made to the equity investors. As previously discussed, subordinated debt is often structured with some type of investment-return upside to compensate for the additional risks undertaken. This may be in the form of higher interest rates paid on the subordinated debt or a debt-to-equity conversion option, which allows the debt to be converted to equity if the company performs extremely well. Subordinated creditors may have a preference over unsecured creditors if a "second position" (i.e., the secured lender has the first position) is taken in various company assets.

Two items that warrant further discussions when dealing with the liabilities of the terminating company are (1) personal guarantees and (2) off-balance-sheet commitments, contingencies, and/or other contractual obligations. Vendors may demand a *personal guarantee* (PG) as a condition for extending credit when a company does not appear to be financially stable. The non-stable company may be a new company with limited credit history, or it could be a poorly performing company where the ability to continue as a going concern is in question. As the term suggests, a key founder, executive, or officer makes a personal guarantee, which allows the vendor to pursue personal assets of the individual if the company cannot cover the obligation.

Needless to say, PGs need to be well understood and entered into only when appropriate, as they can create significant financial distress on the individual(s) providing the PG. Also, PGs need to be identified when evaluating the liability repayment order, as a preference will be present to cover this type of debt first, versus obligations that do not have a PG attached (i.e., the individuals who provided the PGs certainly do not want their personal assets pursued to cover the obligation). But beware of a hidden trap: If an unsecured creditor with a PG is paid in full over an unsecured creditor paid at 50% on the dollar (without a PG), problems may arise as to the equitable distribution of cash.

It goes without saying that PGs can produce some of the worst migraine headaches and can expose the individuals providing the PGs to unforeseen risks and significant economic loss.

Businesses often enter into a variety of commitments, contingent obligations, and/or other contractual agreements that are not recorded as "traditional" liabilities on its balance sheet; yet these types of transactions represent real future monetary obligations. Operating leases or rental agreements for office space or equipment represent perfect examples of these types of commitments. A business could easily come to the conclusion that the office space or equipment can simply be returned to the rightful owner with no further rent or lease obligation present. However, if vendors are unable to realize appropriate value from the returned property to satisfy their loss, then these vendors may become unsecured creditors to the company for the losses incurred. For example, if office space is abandoned with 50 months left on the lease and the landlord is unable to release the space or must release it at a reduced rate, then an economic loss has occurred and an unsecured claim may be present.

To make matters worse, these types of contractual obligations may carry PGs for the future payment stream, which would allow the vendor to pursue the personal assets of the individual providing the PG in the case of a default. Countless other examples of off-balance-sheet obligations could be provided, as businesses operating in different industries execute different types of contracts (e.g., raw-material-price and volume-purchase commitments). The critical issue to remember with off-balance-sheet obligations is that every commitment, contingency, and/or contractual obligation executed by the terminating business needs to be accounted for and managed in a similar fashion to the stated or recorded liabilities (as previously discussed).

Finally, a quick review is warranted as to liquidation preferences for equity investors. Easily understood should be the concept of preferred equity over common equity. By its very nature, preferred equity provides these investors with a preference to any distribution of assets over common equity holders (assuming any assets are even available). The preferred stock agreements should spell out these preferences in terms of distributions to both common shareholders and other preferred shareholders. Companies will often issue different series of preferred stock with unique terms and conditions, including asset distribution preferences. Needless to say, the more complicated the equity ownership structure of a business, then the more likely you will have to call in a lawyer to sort things out for the distributions among the different classes of equity shareholders. A shrewd lawyer will be sure to get his or her distribution (fee) first, of course.

Operational Issues of Importance

The chapter to this point has focused on more of the technical, accounting, and financial issues surrounding a business termination. Clearly, these are important, but they do not address several operational areas that must be managed to avoid exposing the company to further risks and headaches. The remainder of this chapter will be focused on the plethora of operational-related issues that will need to be managed during the termination process.

Once a decision has been made to terminate the business, the majority of the company's employees will no longer be needed. Management will need to coordinate the termination of the nonessential employees, ensuring that ample warnings are provided, vacation and/or other accrued earnings are paid, employee benefit programs (e.g., 401k plans, medical/health, etc.) are properly transitioned or terminated, and other employee-related matters are properly managed. In certain cases, large employee reductions or reductions in force (RIF) may need to be disclosed to government agencies.

Also, special attention should be paid to the various employee benefit programs to ensure that the plan administrators and third parties (e.g., an external payroll service prepaid to process year-end W-2 forms) will be able to support the employee transitions. Although severance packages are usually not provided for in these types of situations, money should be set aside to ensure that the employees do not get stuck with direct costs from the various benefit plan administrators and third parties. Once again, the last thing the officers, directors, and so on of the terminating company want is a bunch of angry employees creating problems after the fact.

Next on the list is insurance. The importance of maintaining the proper types and amounts of insurance through the business termination process should not be underestimated. The business may have stopped selling products or offering services to the market, but this does not mean that insurance can be immediately terminated. Rather, focusing on risk-management issues, such as ensuring that the proper insurance is in force, is often more important than ever before. As such, the following forms of insurance will need to be managed during the termination process so the company is not caught short:

Insurance Coverage Checklist

- *Workers' Compensation:* As long as the company has employees, workers' compensation insurance will need to remain in force (as required by state laws). Generally, most companies will retain a few employees to close down the business and to manage the variety of administrative issues that come with the process.

- *Directors and Officers:* Directors and officers (D&O) insurance is designed to provide liability coverage to the directors and officers of the company for potential "wrongdoings." This has become an extremely hot issue over the past few years due to the high-profile fraud cases such as Enron and MCI/World-Com and has driven D&O insurance premiums very high. D&O insurance is often secured for trailing periods (which may be one, two, or three years after the company ceases active operations) to provide additional coverage for legal proceedings from investors, creditors, and/or other groups that finally get around to pursuing an issue.

♦ *General Liability:* As long as the doors are open, someone could get hurt on the company's property. For example, if an employee of a company that acquired fixed assets comes to your premise to pack and move the items and then slips and falls, your company may be on the hook. Keeping the general liability insurance in force until the last day of business is often a prudent business idea.

♦ *Property and Casualty:* Insuring your assets through their final disposition date provides the necessary coverage in case of theft, accident, damage, and/or other events that may impair the asset's value. Remember, safeguarding the company's assets represents a top priority during the termination process.

As we move forward, let's not forget how much fun we had digesting all of the business taxation and regulatory-mandated costs requirements present and how these can produce an almost unimaginable tax problem. First is the compliance element of business taxation and regulatory-mandated costs. It should go without saying that final returns for payroll, sales/use, property, income, benefit plans, etcetera, etcetera, should be filed for the terminating business. It helps to bring closure with all taxing authorities and governmental agencies that need to know that the business will no longer be operating and thus will not be required to file periodic returns. Although it may take a while for the authorities and agencies to actually acknowledge that the business

has terminated (translation—be prepared to follow up more than once to document the termination), it is important to notify all of the appropriate parties as to the legal status of the entity. This also holds true for all of the business licenses, fictitious name statements, certificates of authority to conduct business, etcetera etcetera, that the company has secured over the years.

Second is the planning and management element of business taxation and regulatory-mandated costs, which of course is where Uncle Sam gets the last laugh. The following two examples have been provided on tax-sensitive issues of which you should be aware when terminating a business and on the fact that nothing is final until the "fat bureaucrat sings."

Sales and Income Tax Issues

1. If the terminating company disposes of tangible business assets (furniture, computers, copiers, desks, and so on), a number of states will require that sales tax be collected on the sale of property to the end user. Just like a retail store selling used or secondhand furniture must collect sales tax, so must the terminating business. The danger here is that sales and use taxes are often held in trust for the taxing authority; and if the company can't pay, then somebody else will have to.

2. In most terminating business situations, not enough funds are available to repay the creditors in full. Okay, this sounds simple enough—the creditors get 35% on the dollar, with the rest written off. They can't pursue the company or its officers, board members, and so on, as no PGs are present and no assets remain. This is commonly referred to as debt forgiveness, which the IRS and numerous states view as income to the business. Yes, the terminating business can actually produce positive taxable income in its final year as a result of the amount of debt forgiveness realized. For a regular C corporation, where any income tax obligation either will be treated as an unsecured debt (and thus written off) or will be applied to a previous year's net operating loss, this shouldn't present too many problems. However, for pass-through taxable entities (S corporations, partnerships, and LLCs that elect to report taxable income on the accrual basis), the taxable income would be distributed to the individual owners who then must report their pro rata share of the income on their individual tax returns (thus triggering an additional income tax obligation at the personal level, without a distribution available from the company to cover the obligation).

Although other examples could be provided, the lesson with business taxation and regulatory-mandated costs within a terminating business is the same as for a new business or an ongoing operation: *Comply and Plan.*

Managing the Wide Range of Termination Logistical Items

1. All company records (accounting, human resources, corporate minutes, etc.) should be brought up to the most current status possible. This may be difficult to achieve due to the skeleton work staff remaining, but it can greatly assist with the actual termination in process, as well as with posttermination issues that may arise. A little extra effort put in up front can alleviate a number of problems down the road.

2. Certain critical company files, records, information, past transactions, and so on, will need to be stored in a secure location and in the proper format. The files will need to be boxed, indexed, properly packaged, marked, and moved to a physical location for storage over an appropriate period. This may range from one year to five (or more), depending on the termination environment present and the likelihood of posttermination legal action and/or other inquiries. Also, all of the company's electronic files, records, and information should be backed up and provided to appropriate parties for storage and future retrieval if needed.

Multiple backups may be needed, with one set kept by qualified and appropriate parties (trustee, officer, board member, etc.). Remaining company documents that are not vital or that are duplicates should be properly disposed of, which may include destroying information that is confidential. For example, copies of employee pay records should not be dumped in the local trash bin—this is just the type of confidential information that identity thieves are looking for.

3. A decision must be made regarding the most appropriate time to finalize the termination. Ideally, all termination issues would be resolved prior to the end of the company's annual fiscal year, as this would eliminate the added work and costs of keeping the business open into another fiscal year (e.g., processing another year of tax returns). Plenty of time should be provided to execute a termination with a keen eye kept on the company's annual fiscal year-end.

4. The pre- and post-termination management teams need to be identified and retained. Either internal remaining employees or external professionals can be used for this function, but they should be qualified, reliable, and prepared for the long haul. Setting aside money for these individuals is usually not a problem, as most trustees, courts, boards of directors, and so on, recognize the value these individuals bring and prioritize funds to be allocated for this use. Generally speaking, these individuals will need to be paid up front and to be offered some type of compensation incentive to properly tend to the buried business.

Capsule Summary

This chapter attempted to summarize, in the span of less than 20 pages, a business issue that few people will ever have to address in their life. Or to put it in a different perspective, let's remember what Captain James T. Kirk of *Star Trek* fame used to say at the beginning of each episode: "Space . . . the final Frontier. These are the voyages of the *Starship Enterprise*. Its five-year mission: To explore strange new worlds . . . to seek out new life and new civilizations . . . to boldly go where no man has gone before!"

It would be impossible to cover every potential element of a business termination because of the sheer volume of issues present and the diversity of companies and industries operating in today's economic environment. Rather, what we hoped to do was to provide a brief summary of the process and to remind the readers that planning for the death of a business is just as important as planning for its birth. As such, the following four macrolevel business termination attributes have been provided to summarize the process:

Final Overall Checklist for Business Terminations

1. The business termination will need to be appropriately planned for and managed, with the proper resources secured to complete the execution.

2. Retaining professional assistance to support the business termination process and to manage a number of highly technical issues associated with the termination is usually well worth the money.

3. All aspects of accounting and financial principles applied to birth and build a business are just as applicable to burying the business.

4. The business termination process should be marketed correctly and communicated efficiently to all of the employees, vendors, investors, and other parties tied to the company.

And if nothing else, the following thought should always be kept in mind: Although business terminations originate for a number of reasons and can proceed down various paths, one needs to remember that the termination process is far more than just business. It often involves the death of all of the effort, sweat, hard work, sleepless nights, and emotions put into the business, their child, by its founders.

ACCOUNTING AND FINANCIAL GLOSSARY

Note: This glossary includes some terms that are not discussed in the book but that are part of the lexicon or lingua franca used by business managers, lenders, and investors.

accelerated depreciation The term *accelerated* refers to two things: (1) the estimated useful life of the fixed asset being depreciated is shorter than a realistic forecast of its probable actual service life; and (2) most of the total cost of the fixed asset is allocated to the first half of its useful life and less to the second half (i.e., there is a front-end loading of depreciation expense).

accounting This is a broad, all-inclusive term that refers to the methods and procedures of financial record keeping by a business (or any entity); also refers to the main functions and purposes of record keeping, which are to assist in the operations of the entity, to provide necessary information for managers for making decisions and exercising control, to measure profit, to comply with income and other tax laws, and to prepare financial statements that are included in financial reports.

accounting equation This equation reflects the two-sided nature of a business entity: assets on one side, sources of assets on the other side: Assets = Liabilities + Owners' Equity. The assets of a business entity are subject to two types of claims that arise from its two basic sources of capital: liabilities and owners' equity. The accounting equation is the foundation for double-entry bookkeeping, which uses a scheme for recording changes in these basic types of accounts as either debits or credits such that the total of accounts with debit balances equals the total of accounts with credit balances. The accounting equation also serves as the framework for the statement of financial condition, or balance sheet, which is one of the three primary fundamental financial statements reported by a business. (The other two are the income statement and the statement of cash flows.)

accounts payable These are short-term, noninterest-bearing liabilities of a business that arise in the course of its activities and operations from purchases on credit. A business buys many things on credit; the purchase cost of goods and services are not paid for immediately. This liability account records the amounts owed for purchases on credit that will be paid in the short run, which generally means about one month. These are also referred to as *operating* liabilities.

accounts receivable These are short-term, noninterest-bearing debts owed to a business by its customers who bought goods and services from the business on credit. Generally, these debts should be collected within a month or so. In a balance sheet, this asset is listed immediately after cash. (Actually the amount of short-term marketable investments, if the business has any, is listed after cash and before accounts receivable.) Accounts receivable are viewed as a near-cash type of asset that will be turned into cash in the short run. A business may not be able to collect all of its accounts receivable. Uncollectible accounts receivable are called *bad debts*.

accounts receivable turnover ratio   This ratio is computed by dividing annual sales revenue by the year-end balance of accounts receivable. Technically speaking, to calculate this ratio, the amount of annual *credit* sales should be divided by the *average* accounts receivable balance; but this information is not readily available from external financial statements. For reporting internally to managers, this ratio should be refined and fine-tuned to be as accurate as possible.

accrual-basis accounting   Well, *accrual* is not the best descriptive term in the world. Perhaps the best way to begin is to mention that accrual-basis accounting is much more than cash-basis accounting. Recording only the cash receipts and cash disbursements of a business would be grossly inadequate. A business has many assets other than cash, as well as many liabilities, that must be recorded. Measuring profit for a period as the difference between cash inflows from sales and cash outflows for expenses would be wrong and, in fact, is not allowed by the income tax law for most businesses. For management, income tax, and financial reporting purposes, a business needs a comprehensive record keeping system—one that recognizes, records, and reports all the assets and liabilities of a business. This all-inclusive scope of financial record keeping is referred to as accrual-basis accounting. Accrual-basis accounting records revenue when sales are made (though cash is received before or after making sales) and records expenses when costs are incurred (though cash is paid before or after expenses are recorded). Established financial reporting standards are based on accrual-basis accounting. Even though accrual-basis accounting is required, a business also reports a financial statement that summarizes its cash sources and uses for the period.

accrued expenses (payable)   This account records the short-term, noninterest-bearing liabilities of a business that accumulate over time, such as vacation pay owed to employees. This liability is different than *accounts payable*, which is the liability account for bills that have been received by a business from purchases on credit.

accumulated depreciation   This is a contra, or offset, account; it is coupled with the property, plant, and equipment asset account in which the original costs of these long-term operating assets of a business are recorded. By the way, these resources of a business are also called *fixed assets*. The accumulated depreciation contra account accumulates the amount of depreciation expense that is recorded period by period. So, the balance in this account is the cumulative amount of depreciation that has been recorded since the assets were acquired. The balance in the accumulated depreciation account is deducted from the original cost of the assets recorded in the property, plant, and equipment asset account. The remainder, called the *book value* of the assets, is the amount included on the asset side of a business.

acid test ratio (also called the **quick ratio**)   The sum of cash, accounts receivable, and short-term marketable investments (if any) is divided by total current liabilities to compute this ratio. Suppose that all short-term creditors decided to stop extending credit to a business and that they all demanded payment when their debts come due. In this rather extreme scenario, the acid test ratio reveals whether the company's cash and near-cash assets would be enough to pay its short-term current liabilities—assuming that none of the liabilities could be renewed and rolled over. This ratio is an extreme test, which is not likely to be imposed on a business unless it is in financial straits. This ratio is quite relevant when a business is in a liquidation situation or is in bankruptcy proceedings.

amortization   Unfortunately, this term has two quite different meanings. First, the term refers to the allocation to expense each period of the total cost of an intangible asset (such as the cost of a patent purchased from the inventor or the cost of goodwill bought by the business) over the useful economic life of the intangible asset. In this sense, amortization is equivalent to depreciation, which allocates the cost of a tangible long-term operating asset (such as a machine) over its useful economic life. Second, amortization refers to the gradual pay down of the principal amount of a debt. *Principal* refers to the amount borrowed that has to be paid back to the lender, as opposed to interest that has to be paid on the principal. Each period, a business may pay interest and also make a payment on the principal of the loan, which reduces the principal amount of the loan, of course. In this situation, the loan is amortized, or gradually paid down.

asset turnover ratio   This broad-gauge ratio is computed by dividing annual sales revenue by total assets. It is a rough measure of the sales-generating power of a business's assets. The idea is that assets are used to make sales, and sales should lead to profit. The ultimate test is not sales revenue on assets, but the profit earned on assets that is measured by the *return on assets* (ROA) ratio.

bad debts   This term refers to accounts receivable from credit sales to customers that a business will not be able to collect (or not collect in full). In hindsight the business shouldn't have extended credit to these particular customers. The amounts owed to the business that will not be collected are written off and recorded to expense. The accounts receivable asset account is decreased by the estimated amount of uncollectible receivables, and the bad debts expense account is increased this amount. These write-offs can be done by the direct write-off method, which means that no expense is recorded until specific accounts receivable are identified as uncollectible, or by the allowance method, which is based on an estimated percent of bad debts from credit sales during the period. Under the allowance method, a contra asset account is created (called allowance for bad debts), and the balance of this account is deducted from the accounts receivable asset account.

balance sheet   This is the term often used instead of the more formal and correct term—*statement of financial condition*. This financial statement summarizes the assets, liabilities, and owners' equity sources of a business at a moment in time. It is prepared at the end of each profit period and whenever else it is needed. It is one of the three primary financial statements of a business, the other two being the income statement and the statement of cash flows. The values reported in the balance sheet are used to determine book value per share of capital stock. The book value of an asset is the amount, or balance, reported in a business's most recent balance sheet.

basic earnings per share (EPS)   This important ratio equals the net income for a period (usually one year) divided by the number of capital stock shares issued by a business corporation. Public companies must report EPS, but private companies are not required to report this ratio. EPS is so important for publicly owned business corporations that it is included in the daily stock trading tables published by the *Wall Street Journal*, the *New York Times*, and other major newspapers. Despite being a rather straightforward concept, several things complicate the calculation of EPS. As a result, a business may have to report its *basic* EPS, which uses the actual number of capital shares outstanding at the balance sheet date, and its *diluted* EPS, which includes additional shares of stock that may be issued when stock options are exercised, as well as any other shares that the business may be obligated to issue in the future. Also, a business may report not one but two net income figures—one before extraordinary gains and losses that were recorded in the period, and a second after deducting these nonrecurring gains and losses. To further complicate matters, some business corporations issue more than one class of capital stock, which makes the calculation of their EPS more technical.

big bath   This street-smart term refers to the practice of many businesses of recording very large lump-sum write-offs of certain assets or recording large amounts for pending liabilities. These unusual entries are triggered by business restructurings, massive employee layoffs, disposals of major segments of the business, and other traumas in the life of a business. Businesses have been known to use these occasions to record every conceivable asset write-off and/or liability write-up that they can think of—in order to clear the decks for the future. In this way, a business avoids recording expenses in the future, and its profits in the coming years will be higher. Investors don't seem to mind this accounting practice.

book value and **book value per share**   Generally speaking, these terms refer to the balance sheet value of an asset (or less often of a liability) or the balance sheet value of owners' equity per share. These terms are used to emphasize that the amount recorded in the accounts, or on the books, of a business is the value being used. The total of the accounts reported for owners' equity in its balance sheet is divided by the number of stock shares of a corporation to determine its book value per share of its capital stock.

bottom line   A commonly used term that refers to the net income (profit) reported by a business, which is the last, or bottom, line in its income statement. As you undoubtedly know, the term has taken on a much broader meaning in everyday use, which refers to the ultimate or most important effect or result of something. Not many accounting-based terms have found their way into everyday language, but *bottom line* is one that has.

breakeven point   The annual sales volume level at which total contribution margin equals total annual fixed expenses. The breakeven point is only a point of reference, not the goal of a business of course. It is computed by dividing total fixed expenses by unit margin. The breakeven point is quite useful in analyzing profit behavior. It provides managers a good point of reference for setting sales goals and for understanding the consequences of incurring fixed costs for a period.

capital   This is a very broad term with its roots in economic theory that refers to money and other assets that are invested in a business or other venture for the general purpose of earning a profit, or a return on the investment. Generally speaking, the sources of capital to a business are divided between debt and equity. *Debt*, as you probably know, is borrowed money on which interest is paid. *Equity* is the broad term for the ownership capital invested in a business, and most often is called owners' equity. Owners' equity arises from two quite different sources: money or other assets invested in the business by its owners, and profit earned by the business that is retained and not distributed to its owners (which is called retained earnings).

capital budgeting   This term refers generally to analysis procedures for comparing alternative investments given a limited amount of total capital that has to be allocated among the various capital investment opportunities of a business. The term sometimes is used interchangeably with the analysis techniques themselves, such as calculating present value, net present value, and the internal rate of return of investments.

capital expenditures   This term refers to investments by a business in long-term operating assets, including land and buildings, heavy machinery and equipment, vehicles, tools, and other economic resources used in the operations of a business. The term *capital* is used to emphasize that these are relatively large amounts and that a business has to raise capital for these expenditures from debt and equity sources.

capital investment analysis   This term refers to several techniques and methods for analyzing the future returns from an investment of capital in order to evaluate the periodic capital recovery and earnings from the investment. The two broad approaches for capital investment analysis are spreadsheet models and mathematical equations for calculating the *present value* and *internal rate of return* of an investment. Determining the present value of an investment is also referred to as the *discounted cash flow* technique.

capital stock   These are ownership shares issued by a business corporation. A business corporation may issue more than one class of capital stock shares. One class may have voting privileges in the election of the directors of the corporation, and the other class may not. One class (called preferred stock) may be entitled to a certain amount of dividends per share before cash dividends can be paid on the other class (usually called common stock). Stock shares may have a minimum amount for which they have to be issued (called the par value), or stock shares can be issued for any amount (called no par stock). Stock shares may be traded on public markets, such as the New York Stock Exchange, or through the Nasdaq network. There are about 10,000 stocks traded on public markets (although estimates vary for this number).

capital structure, or **capitalization**   These terms refer to the combination of capital sources that a business has tapped for the money to invest in its assets—in particular the mix of its interest-bearing debt and its owners' equity. In a more sweeping sense, the terms also include appendages and other features of the basic debt and equity instruments of a business. Such things as stock options, stock warrants, and convertible features of preferred stock and notes payable are included in the broader sense of the terms, as well as any debt-based and equity-based financial derivatives issued by the business.

capitalization of costs   When a cost is originally recorded as an increase in an asset account, it is said to be capitalized. This means that the outlay is treated as a capital expenditure, which becomes part of the total cost basis of the asset. The alternative is to immediately record the cost as an expense in the period the cost is incurred. Capitalized costs refer mainly to costs that are recorded in the long-term operating assets of a business, such as buildings, machines, equipment, tools, and vehicles.

cash burn rate   A relatively recent term that has come into use; it refers to how fast a business is using up its available cash, especially when its cash flow from operating activities is negative instead of positive. This term most often refers to a business struggling through its start-up or its early phases that has not yet generated enough cash inflow from sales to cover its cash outflow for expenses (and perhaps never will).

cash flow   This term is obvious but at the same time elusive. The term obviously refers to cash inflows and outflows during a period. But the specific sources and uses of cash flows are not clear in this general term. The statement of cash flows, which is one of the three primary financial statements of a business, classifies cash flows into three types: (1) from operating activities (sales and expenses, or profit-making operations), (2) from investing activities, and (3) from financing activities. Sometimes, the term *cash flow* is used as shorthand for *cash flow from profit* (i.e., cash flow from operating activities).

cash flow from operating activities   (also called **cash flow from profit** and **operating cash flow**). This equals the cash inflow from sales during the period minus the cash outflows for expenses during the period. According to generally accepted accounting principles (GAAP), a business must use accrual-basis accounting to measure its net income (i.e., to record its revenue and expenses). At the same time, a business is required by GAAP to present a statement of cash flows that includes the amount of cash flow from operating activities. Accountants don't like to admit it, but this cash flow amount equals what profit would be on the cash basis of accounting. So, you get both the accrual-basis profit number and the cash-basis profit number in a financial report. One impor-

tant reason that the accrual-basis number is more correct and realistic is because it deducts an expense for the depreciation of the company's fixed assets. You can't ignore the fact that a business's fixed assets wear out and lose their economic usefulness over time.

cash flows, statement of   This is one of the three primary financial statements that a business includes in the periodic financial reports to its outside shareowners and lenders. This financial statement summarizes the business's cash inflows and outflows for the period according to a threefold classification: (1) cash flow from operating (profit-making) activities; (2) cash flow from investing activities; and (3) cash flow from financing activities. *Warning:* The typical statement of cash flows is difficult to decipher; it includes too many lines of information and is overly technical compared with a typical balance sheet and income statement.

contribution margin   This is an intermediate measure of profit that is equal to sales revenue minus cost of goods sold expense and minus variable operating expenses—but before fixed operating expenses are deducted. Profit at this point contributes toward covering fixed operating expenses and toward interest and income tax expenses. The breakeven point is the sales volume at which contribution margin just equals total fixed expenses.

conversion cost   This term refers to the sum of direct labor and production overhead costs of manufacturing products. The cost of raw materials used to make products is not included in this definition. Generally speaking, this is a rough measure of the value added by the manufacturing process.

cost of capital   This refers to the interest cost of debt capital used by a business plus the amount of profit that the business should earn for its equity sources of capital to justify the use of the equity capital during the period. Interest is a contractual and definite amount for a period, whereas the profit that a business should earn on the equity capital employed during the period is not. A business should set a definite goal of earning at least a certain minimum return on equity (ROE) and should compare its actual performance for the period against this goal. The costs of debt and equity capital are combined, or weighted, into either a before-tax rate or an after-tax rate for capital investment analysis.

current assets   The term *current* refers to cash and those assets that will be turned into cash in the short run. Five types of assets are classified as current: cash, short-term marketable investments, accounts receivable, inventories, and prepaid expenses (and they are generally listed in this order in the balance sheet).

current liabilities   The term *current* refers to the liabilities that come due and will be paid in the near term, which generally means one year or less. In most cases these include accounts payable, accrued expenses payable, income tax payable, short-term notes payable, and the portion of long-term debt that will come due during the coming year. Keep in mind that a business may roll over its liabilities; the maturing liabilities are normally replaced in part or in whole by new liabilities that take the place of the old liabilities.

current ratio   This ratio is calculated to assess the short-term solvency, or debt-paying ability, of a business. It equals total current assets divided by total current liabilities. Some businesses remain solvent with a relatively low current ratio, and others could be in trouble with an apparently good current ratio. The general rule is that the current ratio should be 2:1 or higher, but current ratios vary widely from industry to industry.

debt-to-equity ratio   This is a widely used financial statement ratio to assess the overall debt load of a business and its capital structure. It equals total liabilities divided by total owners' equity. Both numbers for this ratio are taken from a business's latest balance sheet. There is no standard or generally agreed benchmark ratio, such as 1:1 or 2:1. Every industry is different in this regard. Some businesses, in particular banks and other financial institutions, have very high debt-to-equity ratios, whereas other businesses use very little debt relative to their owners' equity.

deferred maintenance   This term refers to decisions by managers to put off, or delay, making expenditures for the normal repair and maintenance of a company's assets, such as not painting a building or not servicing the company's boiler until the following year. The term implies that this is done to massage the numbers, that is, to avoid recording the expense this year in order to report a higher profit for the year.

depreciation   This term refers to the generally accepted accounting principle of allocating the cost of a long-term operating asset over the estimated useful life of the asset. Each year of use is allocated a fraction of the original cost of the asset. Generally speaking, either the accelerated method or the straight-line method of depreciation is used. (There are other methods, but they are not as common.) Useful-life estimates are heavily influenced by the schedules allowed in the federal income tax law. Depreciation is not a cash outlay in the period the expense is recorded—just the opposite. The cash inflow from sales revenue during the period includes an embedded amount that reimburses the business for the use of its fixed assets. In this respect, depreciation is a source of cash.

diluted earnings per share (EPS)   This measure of earnings per share recognizes that additional stock shares may be issued in the future for stock options and may be required by other contracts in which a business has entered, such as convertible features in its debt securities and preferred stock. Both basic earnings per share and, if applicable, diluted earnings per share are reported by publicly owned business corporations. Often the two EPS figures are not far apart; but in some cases the gap is significant. Privately owned businesses do not have to report earnings per share. *See also* **basic earnings per share**

discounted cash flow (DCF)   This term refers to a capital investment analysis technique that discounts, or scales-down, the future cash returns from an investment. The discount rate is based on the cost of capital for the business. In essence, each future return is downsized to take into account the cost of capital from the start of the investment until the future point in time when the return is received. *Present value* (PV) is the amount resulting from discounting the future returns. The entry cost is subtracted from present value of the investment to determine *net present value* (NPV). The net present value is positive if the present value is more than the entry cost, which signals that the investment would earn more than the cost of capital rate.

Conversely, if the entry cost is more than the present value, the net present value is negative, which means that the investment would earn less than the business's cost of capital rate.

dividend payout ratio   This ratio is computed by dividing total cash dividends for the year by the net income for the year. It's simply the percent of annual net income distributed as cash dividends for the year.

dividend yield ratio   This ratio equals the cash dividends per share paid by a business over the most recent 12 months (called the trailing 12 months) divided by the current market price per share of the stock. This ratio is reported in the daily stock trading tables in the *Wall Street Journal* and other major newspapers.

earnings before interest and income tax (EBIT)   This measure of profit equals sales revenue for the period minus cost of goods sold expense and all operating expenses—but before deducting interest and income tax expenses. It is a measure of the *operating* profit of a business before considering the cost of its debt capital and income tax.

earnings per share (EPS).   *See* **basic earnings per share; diluted earnings per share**

equity   This term refers to one of the two basic sources of capital to a business (the other being *debt* or borrowed money). Most often it is called *owners' equity* because it refers to the capital used by a business that "belongs" to the ownership interests in the business. Owners' equity arises from two quite distinct sources: capital invested by the owners in the business, and profit (net income) earned by the business that has not been distributed to its owners (which is called *retained earnings*). Owners' equity in our highly developed and sophisticated economic and legal system can be very complex—involving stock options, financial derivatives of all kinds, different classes of stock, convertible debt, and so on.

extraordinary gains and losses   No pun intended, but these gains and losses are extraordinarily important to understand. These are nonrecurring, one-time, unusual nonoperating gains or losses that are recorded by a business during the period. The amount of each of these gains or losses, net of the associated income tax effect, is reported separately in the income statement. Net income is reported before and after these gains and losses. These gains and losses should not be recorded very often; but, in fact, many businesses record them every other year or so, which causes much consternation to investors. In addition to evaluating the regular stream of sales and expenses that yield operating profit, investors also have to factor into their profit analysis these irregular gains and losses reported by a business.

financial condition, statement of.   *See* **balance sheet**

financial leverage   The equity (ownership) capital of a business serves as the basis for securing debt capital (borrowed money). In this way a business increases the total capital available to invest in assets and can make more sales and more profit. The strategy is to earn operating profit, or earnings before interest and income tax (EBIT), on the capital supplied from debt that is more than the interest paid on the debt capital. A financial leverage gain equals the EBIT earned on debt capital minus the interest on the debt. A financial leverage gain augments earnings on equity capital. A business must earn a rate of return on its assets (ROA) that is greater than the interest rate on its debt to make a financial leverage gain. If the spread between its ROA and interest rate is unfavorable, a business suffers a financial leverage loss.

financial reports and statements   *Financial* means having to do with money and economic wealth. *Statement* means a formal presentation. Financial reports are printed, and a copy is sent to each owner and to each major lender of the business (unless the lender doesn't want a copy). Today, public corporations make their financial reports available on a Web site, so all or part of the financial report can be downloaded by anyone. Businesses prepare three primary financial statements: (1) *the statement of financial condition*, or *balance sheet*; (2) the *statement of cash flows*; and (3) the *income statement*. The income statement is often called a *P&L* (profit and loss) report, especially inside a business. These three key financial statements constitute the core of the periodic financial reports that are distributed outside a business to its shareowners and lenders. Financial reports also include footnotes to the financial statements and much other information. Financial statements are prepared according to *generally accepted accounting principles* (GAAP), which are the authoritative rules that govern profit measurement and the reporting of profit-making activities, financial condition, and cash flows. Internal financial statements, although based on the same profit accounting methods, report more information to managers for their decision making and control. Sometimes, financial statements are called simply *financials*.

financing activities   This term refers to one of the three classes of cash flows reported in the statement of cash flows. This class includes borrowing money and paying debt, raising money from shareowners and the return of money to them, and dividends paid from profit.

first-in, first-out (FIFO)   This is one of the two popular accounting methods to measure cost of goods sold during a period and the cost of ending inventory. It is both an expense measurement and an asset-valuation method; you can't separate these two aspects. The first costs of purchasing or manufacturing products are the first costs charged out to record cost of goods sold expense. Thus, the most recent costs of acquisition remain in the inventories asset account (until the goods are sold sometime later). To offer a simple example, suppose a business bought two units of a new product during the year. The first unit cost $100 and the second unit, which was purchased sometime later, cost $105. The business sold one of the two units. FIFO assigns $100 to cost of goods sold expense and $105 to the cost of ending inventory. *See also* **last-in, first out** (LIFO—which uses the same facts but gives different results).

fixed assets   This is an informal term used to refer to the variety of long-term operating resources used by a business—real estate, machinery, equipment, tools, vehicles, office furniture, computers, and so on. In balance sheets, these assets are typically labeled *property, plant, and equipment*. The term *fixed assets* captures the idea that the assets are relatively fixed in place and are not held for sale in the normal course of business. The cost of fixed assets, except land, is depreciated, which means the cost is allocated to expenses over the estimated useful lives of the assets.

fixed expenses, or costs   These are expenses or costs that remain relatively constant in amount, or fixed, over the short run. These costs do not vary with changes in sales volume or sales revenue or other measures of business activity. Over the long run, however, these costs are raised or lowered as the business grows or declines. Fixed operating costs provide capacity to carry on operations and to make sales. Fixed manufacturing overhead costs provide production capacity. Fixed expenses are a pivot point for analyzing profit behavior, especially in determining the breakeven point and in analyzing strategies for improving profit performance.

free cash flow   Most often this term refers to cash flow from profit (cash flow from operating activities). The underlying idea is that a business is free to do what it wants with its cash flow from profit. However, a business usually has many ongoing commitments and demands on this cash flow, so it may not actually be free in deciding what do with this source of cash. *Caution:* This term is not officially defined anyplace, and different people use the term with different meanings. Pay particular attention to how an author or a speaker is using the term.

generally accepted accounting principles (GAAP)   This term refers to the body of authoritative rules and standards for measuring profit and preparing financial statements that are included in financial reports by a business to its outside shareowners and lenders. The development of these standards has been an ongoing, evolving process for more than 70 years. Congress passed a law in 1934 that bestowed primary jurisdiction over financial reporting by publicly owned businesses to the Securities and Exchange Commission (SEC). But the SEC has by and large left the development of GAAP to the private sector. Presently the Financial Accounting Standards Board (FASB) is the primary but not the only authoritative body that makes pronouncements on GAAP. *One caution:* GAAP are like a moveable feast. New rules are issued fairly frequently, old rules are amended from time to time, and some rules established years ago are discarded on occasion. Professional accountants have a heck of time keeping up with GAAP, that's for sure. New GAAP rules sometimes have the effect of closing the barn door after the horse has left. Accounting abuses occur, and then, after the damage has been done, new rules are issued to prevent such abuses in the future.

gross margin (also called **gross profit**) This first-line measure of profit equals sales revenue less cost of goods sold. This is profit before operating, interest, and income tax expenses are deducted. Financial reporting standards require that gross margin be reported in external income statements. Gross margin is a key variable in management profit reports for decision making and control. Gross margin doesn't apply to service businesses that don't sell products.

income statement This financial statement summarizes sales revenue and expenses for a period and reports one or more profit lines for the period. It also reports any other gains and losses for the period. It is one of the three primary financial statements of a business. The bottom-line profit figure is labeled *net income* or *net earnings* by most businesses. Externally reported income statements disclose less information than do internal management profit reports—but both are based on the same profit accounting principles and methods. Profit is not known until accountants complete the recording of sales revenue and expenses for the period (as well as determining whether any extraordinary gains and losses should be recorded). Profit measurement depends on the reliability of a business's accounting system, the choices of accounting methods by the business, and the end-of-period adjusting entries recorded by the business. *Caution:* A business may engage in certain accounting manipulations; managers may intervene in the normal course of operations for the purpose of improving the amount of profit recorded in the period, which is called *massaging the numbers, earnings management*, or *income smoothing*.

internal accounting controls This refers to forms and procedures established by a business (which go beyond what would be required for the record keeping function of accounting) that are designed to prevent accounting errors and fraud. Two common examples of internal controls are (1) requiring a second signature by someone higher in the organization to approve a transaction in excess of a certain dollar amount, and (2) giving customers printed receipts as proof of sale. Other examples of internal control procedures are restricting entry and exit routes of employees, requiring all employees to take their vacations and assigning another person to do their jobs while they are away, surveillance

cameras, surprise counts of cash and inventory, and rotation of duties. Internal controls should be cost-effective; the cost of a control should be less than the potential loss that is prevented. The guiding principle for designing internal accounting controls is to deter and detect errors and dishonesty. The best internal controls in the world cannot prevent most fraud by high-level managers who take advantage of their positions of trust and authority.

internal rate of return (IRR) This term refers to the precise discount rate that makes the present value (PV) of the future cash returns from a capital investment exactly equal to the initial amount of capital invested. If IRR is higher than the company's cost of capital rate, the investment is an attractive opportunity; if IRR is less, the investment is substandard from the cost of capital point of view.

inventory shrinkage This term refers to the loss due to customer shoplifting; employee theft; and damage, breakage, spoilage, and obsolescence of products while being handled, moved, or stored in a warehouse; it is also due to accounting errors in recording the purchase, manufacture, and sale of products. A business should make regular physical counts and inspections of its inventory to determine this loss.

inventory turnover ratio This ratio equals the cost of inventories divided into the cost of goods sold expense for a period (usually one year). The ratio depends on how long products are held in stock on average before they are sold. Managers should closely monitor this ratio to tell if products are being held too long before being sold.

inventory write-down This term refers to making an accounting entry, usually at the close of a period, to decrease the cost value of the business's inventory asset account in order to recognize loss of value due to products that cannot be sold at their normal mark-ups or that will be sold below cost. A business compares the recorded cost of products held in inventory against the sales value of the products. Based on the lower of cost or market rule, an entry is made to decrease inventory and to record an expense. (An inventory write-down entry is also recorded for inventory shrinkage.)

investing activities This term refers to one of the three classes of cash flows reported in the statement of cash flows. This class includes capital expenditures for replacing and expanding the fixed assets of a business, proceeds from disposals of its old fixed assets, and other long-term investment activities of a business.

last-in, first-out (LIFO) One of the two popular accounting methods to measure cost of goods sold during a period and the cost of ending inventory. It is both an expense measurement and an asset-valuation method; you can't separate these two aspects. The last, or most recent, costs of purchasing or manufacturing products are the first costs charged out to record cost of goods sold expense. Thus, the oldest costs of acquisition remain in the inventories asset account. To offer a simple example, suppose a business bought two units of a new product during the year. The first unit cost $100 and the second unit, which was purchased sometime later, cost $105. The business sold one of the two units. LIFO assigns $105 to cost of goods sold expense and $100 to the cost of ending inventory. *See also* **first-in, first-out** (FIFO—which uses the same facts but gives different results).

management control This term is difficult to define in a few words. The essence of management control is keeping a close watch on everything. Anything can go wrong and can get out of control. Management control can be thought of as the follow-through on strategy and policy decisions, to make sure that the actual outcomes are going according to the purposes and goals of the earlier decisions that set things in motion. Managers depend on feedback reports to know what's going on; and they compare actual outcomes against the plans, goals, and budgets for the period, which focus on major variances and deviations.

mark-to-market This term refers to the accounting method that actually records increases and decreases in assets based on changes in the assets' market values. For example, mutual funds revalue their securities portfolios every day based on closing prices on the New York Stock Exchange and the Nasdaq. Generally speaking, businesses do *not* use mark-to-market methods for their assets. A business, for instance, does not revalue its fixed assets (buildings, machines, equipment, etc.) at the end of each period—even though the replacement values of these assets fluctuate over time. Having made this general comment, we should mention that accounts receivable are written down to recognize bad debts, and a business's inventory asset account is written down to recognize stolen and damaged goods as well as products that will be sold below cost. If certain of a business's tangible and intangible long-term operating assets become impaired and will not have utility in the future consistent with their book values, then the assets are written down.

market capitalization, or **market cap** This amount equals the current market value per share of capital stock multiplied by the total number of capital stock shares outstanding of a publicly owned business. This value often differs widely from the book value of owners' equity reported in a business's balance sheet.

negative cash flow The cash flow from the operating activities of a business can be negative, which means that its cash balance decreased from its sales and expense activities during the period. When a business is operating at a loss instead of making a profit, its cash outflows for expenses could be more than its cash inflow from sales. Even when a business makes a profit for the period, its cash inflow from sales could be less than the sales revenue recorded for the period, thus causing a negative cash flow for the period. *Caution:* This term is also used for certain types of investments in which the net cash flow from all sources and uses is negative. For example, investors in rental real estate properties often use the term to mean that the cash inflow from rental income is less than all cash outflows during the period, including payments on the mortgage loan on the property.

net income (also called the **bottom line, net earnings, net operating earnings,** or just **earnings**) This key figure equals sales revenue for a period less all expenses for the period; any extraordinary gains and losses for the period are included in this final profit figure. Everything is taken into account to arrive at net income, which is popularly called the *bottom line*. Net income is clearly the single most important number in business financial reports.

net present value (NPV) This figure equals the present value (PV) of a capital investment minus the initial amount of capital that is invested, or the entry cost of the investment. A positive NPV signals an attractive capital investment opportunity; a negative NPV means that the investment is substandard from the cost of capital point of view.

net worth Generally, this term refers to the book value of owners' equity as reported in a business's latest balance sheet. If liabilities are subtracted from assets, the accounting equation becomes: Assets − Liabilities = Owners' Equity. In this version of the accounting equation, Owners' Equity equals net worth, or the amount of assets after deducting the liabilities of the business.

operating activities This term refers to the sales and the expense activities of a business, both those that sell products and those that sell services. The term is used to embrace all types of activities engaged in by profit-motivated entities toward the objective of earning profit. A bank, for instance, earns net income not from sales revenue but from loaning money on which it receives interest income. Making loans is the main revenue operating activity of banks.

operating cash flow. *See* **cash flow from operating activities**

operating liabilities These are the short-term liabilities generated by the operating (profit-making) activities of a business. Most businesses have three types of operating liabilities: (1) accounts payable from inventory purchases and from incurring expenses that are bought on credit; (2) accrued expenses payable for unpaid expenses; and (3) income tax payable. These short-term liabilities of a business are noninterest-bearing.

operating profit. *See* **earnings before interest and income tax (EBIT)**

overhead costs This term generally means indirect, in contrast to direct, costs. *Indirect* means that a cost cannot be matched or coupled in any obvious or objective manner with particular products, or specific revenue sources, or a particular organizational unit. Production overhead costs are the indirect costs of manufacturing products. The direct costs of manufacturing products are raw materials and production-line labor. Manufacturing overhead costs include variable costs (such as

electricity, gas, and water that vary with total production output) and fixed costs (that do not vary with increases or decreases in actual production output).

owners' equity This term refers to the capital invested in a business by its shareowners plus the profit earned by the business that has not been distributed to them, which is recorded in an account called *retained earnings*. Owners' equity is one of the two basic sources of capital to a business, the other being borrowed money, or debt. The book value, or value reported in a balance sheet for owners' equity, is not the market value of the business. Rather, the balance sheet value reflects the historical amounts of capital invested by the owners over the years in a business plus the accumulation of yearly profits that were not paid out to its owners.

present value (PV) This amount is calculated by discounting the future cash returns from a capital investment. The discount rate usually is the cost of capital rate for the business. If PV is more than the initial amount of capital that has to be invested, then the investment is attractive. If PV is less, then better investment alternatives should be looked for.

price/earnings (P/E) ratio This key ratio equals the current market price of a capital stock share divided by the earnings per share (EPS) for the stock. The EPS used in this ratio may be the *basic* EPS for the stock or its *diluted* EPS—you have to check to be sure about this. A low P/E may signal an undervalued stock or may reflect a pessimistic forecast by investors for the future earnings prospects of the business. A high P/E may reveal an overvalued stock or may reflect an optimistic forecast by investors. The average P/E ratio for the stock market as a whole varies considerably over time.

product cost This is a key factor in the profit model of a business. Product cost is purchase cost for a retailer or a wholesaler (distributor). A manufacturer has to accumulate three different types of production costs to determine product cost: direct materials, direct labor, and manufacturing overhead. The cost of products (goods) sold is deducted from sales revenue to determine gross margin (also called gross profit), which is the first profit line reported in an external income statement and in an internal profit report to managers.

profit   The general term *profit* is not precisely defined; it may refer to net gains over a period of time, or to cash inflows less cash outflows of an investment, or to earnings before or after certain costs and expenses are deducted from income or revenue. In the business world, profit is measured by the application of generally accepted accounting principles (GAAP). In the income statement, the final or bottom-line profit is generally labeled *net income* or *net earnings*. It equals revenue (plus any extraordinary gains) less all expenses (and less any extraordinary losses) for the period. Internal management profit reports may include several profit lines: gross margin, contribution margin, operating profit (earnings before interest and income tax), and earnings before income tax. External income statements report gross margin (also called gross profit) and often report one or more other profit lines, although practice varies from business to business in this regard.

profit-and-loss report (P&L)   This is an alternative moniker for an income statement or for an internal management profit report. Actually it's a misnomer because a business has either a profit *or* a loss for a period. It would be better called the profit *or* loss report, but the term has caught on and won't change.

profit ratios   These ratios are based on sales revenue for a period. A measure of profit is divided by sales revenue to compute a profit ratio. For example, gross margin is divided by sales revenue to compute the gross margin profit ratio. Dividing bottom-line profit (net income) by sales revenue gives the profit ratio that is generally called *return on sales*.

property, plant, and equipment   This title, or label, is generally used in financial reports for the long-term assets of a business, which include land, buildings, machinery, equipment, tools, vehicles, computers, furniture and fixtures, and other tangible long-lived resources that are not held for sale but are used in the operations of a business. The less formal name for these assets is *fixed assets*.

quick ratio.   *See* **acid test ratio.**

return on assets (ROA)   Although practice is not uniform for calculating this ratio, most often it equals operating profit (earnings before interest and income tax) for a year divided by the total assets that are used to generate the profit. ROA is the key ratio to test whether a business is earning enough on its assets to cover its cost of capital.

return on equity (ROE)   This key ratio equals net income for the year divided by owners' equity and is expressed as a percent. ROE should be higher than a business's interest rate on debt because the owners take more risk.

return on investment (ROI)   This very general concept refers to some measure of income, or earnings, or profit, or gain over a period of time divided by the amount of capital invested during the period. It is almost always expressed as a percent. For a business, an important ROI measure is its *return on equity* (ROE), which see.

return on sales   This ratio equals net income divided by sales revenue.

revenue-driven expenses   These are those operating expenses that vary with changes in total sales revenue (total dollars of sales). Examples are sales commissions based on sales revenue, credit card discount expenses, and rents and franchise fees based on sales revenue. These expenses are a key variable in a profit model. Segregating these expenses from other types of expenses that behave differently is essential for profit analysis. (These expenses are not disclosed separately in externally reported income statements.)

Securities and Exchange Commission (SEC)   This federal agency oversees the issuance of and trading in securities of public businesses. The SEC has broad powers and can suspend the trading in securities of a business. The SEC has supervisory responsibility for the recently established Public Company Accounting Oversight Board, created by the Sarbanes-Oxley Act of 2002. The SEC has the primary jurisdiction over making accounting and financial reporting rules, but over the years it has largely deferred to the private sector for the development of generally accepted accounting principles (GAAP).

solvency   This term refers to the ability of a business to pay its liabilities on time when they come due for payment. A business may be insolvent, which means that it is not able to pay its liabilities and debts on time. The current ratio and the acid test ratio are used to evaluate the short-term solvency prospects of a business. Also, the liabilities of a business can be compared with its cash flow from operating activities for a rough indication of its debt-paying ability.

stockholders' equity, statement of changes in   Although often referred to as a financial statement, this is more in the nature of a supporting schedule that summarizes in one place the various changes in the owners' equity accounts of a business during the period—including the issuance and retirement of capital stock shares, cash dividends, and other transactions affecting owners' equity. This statement (schedule) is very helpful when a business has more than one class of stock shares outstanding and when a variety of events occurred during the year that changed its owners' equity accounts. Also, generally accepted accounting principles allow that certain events that have a positive or a negative effect on owners' equity can bypass the income statement and be reported only in this statement.

straight-line depreciation   This depreciation method allocates a uniform amount of the total costs of long-lived operating assets (fixed assets) to each year of use. It is the alternative to *accelerated depreciation*. When using the straight-line method, a business may adopt a longer life estimate for depreciating a fixed asset as compared with the accelerated method (though not necessarily in every case). Both methods are allowed for income tax and under generally accepted accounting principles (GAAP).

sunk cost   This is a cost is that has been paid and cannot be undone or reversed. Once the cost has been paid, it is irretrievable, like water over the dam or spilt milk. Usually the term refers to the recorded value of an asset that has lost its value to a business. Examples are the costs of products in inventory that cannot be sold and fixed assets that are no longer usable. The book value of these assets should be written off to expense. Sunk costs are irrelevant and should be disregarded in making decisions about what to do with the assets (except that the income tax effects of disposing of the assets should be taken into account).

times interest earned   This is the ratio that tests the ability of a business to make interest payments on its debt. It is calculated by dividing annual earnings before interest and income tax by the interest expense for the year. There is no particular rule for this ratio, such as 3 or 4 times, but obviously the ratio should be higher than one.

variable expenses   These are operating expenses that vary with changes in either sales volume or sales revenue, in contrast with fixed expenses that remain the same over the short run, not fluctuating in response to changes in sales volume or sales revenue. *See* **revenue-driven expenses** and **volume-driven expenses**.

volume-driven expenses   Those expenses that vary with changes in total sales volume (total quantities, or units of sales). Examples of these types of expenses are delivery costs, packaging costs, and other costs that depend mainly on the number of products sold or the number of customers served. These expenses are a key factor in a model for profit behavior analysis. Segregating these expenses from other types of expenses that behave differently is very useful for management analysis and control. The cost of goods sold expense depends on sales volume and is a volume-driven expense. Product cost (i.e., the cost of goods sold) is such a dominant expense that it is treated separately from other volume-driven operating expenses.

weighted average cost of capital   *Weighted* means that the proportions of debt capital and equity capital of a business are used to calculate its average cost of capital. This key benchmark rate depends on the interest rate(s) on a business's debt and on the return on equity (ROE) goal established by a business. This is a return on capital rate and can be applied either on a before-tax basis or on an after-tax basis. A business should earn at least its weighted average rate on the capital invested in its assets. The weighted average cost of capital rate is used as the discount rate to calculate the present value (PV) of specific investments.

INDEX

Cybersecurity

by Joseph Steinberg

for
dummies®
A Wiley Brand

Cybersecurity For Dummies®

Published by: **John Wiley & Sons, Inc.,** 111 River Street, Hoboken, NJ 07030-5774, www.wiley.com

Copyright © 2020 by John Wiley & Sons, Inc., Hoboken, New Jersey

Published simultaneously in Canada

For general information on our other products and services, please contact our Customer Care Department within the U.S. at 877-762-2974, outside the U.S. at 317-572-3993, or fax 317-572-4002. For technical support, please visit https://hub.wiley.com/community/support/dummies.

Wiley publishes in a variety of print and electronic formats and by print-on-demand. Some material included with standard print versions of this book may not be included in e-books or in print-on-demand. If this book refers to media such as a CD or DVD that is not included in the version you purchased, you may download this material at http://booksupport.wiley.com. For more information about Wiley products, visit www.wiley.com.

Library of Congress Control Number: 2019948325

ISBN 978-1-119-56032-6 (pbk); ISBN 978-1-119-56035-7 (ePDF); ISBN 978-1-119-56034-0 (epub)

Manufactured in the United States of America

C10013871_091119

Contents at a Glance

Table of Contents

Introduction

I n the course of just a single generation, the world has undergone some of the greatest changes since the dawn of mankind. The availability of the Internet as a tool for consumers and businesses alike, coupled with the invention of mobile devices and wireless networking, have ushered in an Information Revolution that has impacted just about every aspect of human existence.

This reliance on technology, however, has also created enormous risks. It seems that not a day goes by without some new story emerging of a data breach, cyber-attack, or the like. Simultaneously, because humanity's reliance on technology increases on a daily basis, the potential adverse consequences of cyberattacks have grown exponentially to the point that people can now lose their fortunes, their reputations, their health, or even their lives, as the result of cyberattacks.

It is no wonder, therefore, that people living in the modern world understand the need to protect themselves from cyber-dangers. This book shows you how to do so.

About This Book

While many books have been written over the past couple decades on a wide variety of cybersecurity-related topics, most of them don't provide the general population with the information needed to properly protect themselves.

Many cybersecurity books are directed toward highly technical audiences and tend to overwhelm noncomputer scientists with extraneous information, creating severe challenges for readers seeking to translate the knowledge that they acquire from books into practical actions. On the flip side, various self-published introduction-to-cybersecurity books suffer from all sorts of serious deficiencies, including, in some cases, having been written by non-experts and presenting significant amounts of misinformation. Anyone interested in cybersecurity often shouldn't trust these materials. Likewise, many security tip sheets and the like simply relay oft-repeated clichés and outdated advice, sometimes causing people who follow the recommendations contained within such works to worsen their cybersecurity postures rather than improve them. Furthermore, the nearly constant repetition of various cybersecurity advice by media personalities after news stories about breaches ("Don't forget to reset all your passwords!"), coupled with the lack of consequences to most people after they do not comply with such directives, has led to *cybersecurity fatigue* — a condition in which folks simply don't act when they actually need to because they have heard the "boy cry wolf" one too many times.

I wrote *Cybersecurity For Dummies* to provide people who do not work as cybersecurity professionals with a foundational book that can teach them what they need to know about cybersecurity and explain why they need to know it. This book offers you practical, clear, and straightforward advice that you can easily translate into actions that can help keep you and your children, parents, and small businesses cybersecure.

Cybersecurity For Dummies is divided into several parts. Parts 1, 2, and 3 provide an overview of cybersecurity and give tips on protecting yourself and your loved ones from both external threats and from making dangerous (and potentially disastrous) mistakes. Topics such as how to secure your online accounts and how to select and protect passwords fall into these parts of the book.

Part 4 offers tips on securing small businesses, which may be especially pertinent for small business owners and employees. Part 4 then also discusses some of the unique security needs that face firms as they grow larger and touches on cybersecurity-in-government related matters.

Part 5 shows you how to identify security breaches. Part 6 covers the process of backing up, something that you should do proactively before the need to recover arises, as well as how to recover from security breaches.

Part 7 looks toward the future — both for those interested in potentially pursuing a cybersecurity-related career (or who have children or other relatives or friends considering doing so) as well as those interested in how emerging technologies are likely to impact their own personal cybersecurity.

Part 8 gives several lists of ten items that you may want to keep as tip sheets.

Please keep in mind that while internalizing all the information in this book, and putting it into practice, will likely dramatically improve your cybersecurity posture, reading this book will no more make you an expert in cybersecurity than reading a book on the workings of the human heart will quickly transform you into a competent cardiologist.

Cybersecurity is a complex, rapidly changing field whose professionals spend years, if not decades, studying and working full-time to develop, sharpen, and maintain the skills and expertise that they utilize on a constant basis. As such, please do not consider the advice within this book as a substitute for hiring a professional for any situation that reasonably warrants the latter.

Also, please keep in mind that technical products change quite often, so any screenshots included within the book may not be identical to the screens that you observe when you perform similar actions to those described in the text. Remember: Cybersecurity threats are constantly evolving, as are the technologies and approaches utilized to combat them.

Foolish Assumptions

In this book, I make some assumptions about your experience with technology:

>> You have experience with using a keyboard and pointer, such as a mouse, on either a Mac or Windows PC and have access to one of those machines.

>> You know how to use an Internet browser, such as Firefox, Chrome, Edge, Opera, or Safari.

>> You know how to install applications on your computer.

>> You know how to perform a Google search.

Conventions Used in This Book

As you explore each part of this book, keep the following points in mind:

>> Words that are being defined appear in *italic.*

>> Code and URLs (web addresses) are shown in monofont.

Icons Used in This Book

Throughout the margin of this book are small images, known as icons. These icons mark important tidbits of information:

TIP

The Tip icon identifies places where I offer additional tips for making this journey more interesting or clear. Tips cover some neat shortcuts that you may not have known about.

The Remember icon bookmarks important points that you'll want to keep in mind.

The Warning icon helps protect you from common errors and may even give you tips to undo your mistakes.

Beyond This Book

In addition to what you're reading right now, this product also comes with a free access-anywhere Cheat Sheet that covers important cybersecurity actions. To get this Cheat Sheet, simply go to www.dummies.com and search for *Cybersecurity For Dummies Cheat Sheet* in the Search box.

Where to Go from Here

Cybersecurity For Dummies is designed in such a fashion that you don't have to read the book in order or even read the entire book.

If you purchased this book because you suffered a cybersecurity breach of some sort, for example, you can skip to the Part 5 without reading the prior material (although reading it afterwards may be wise, as it may help you prevent yourself from becoming the victim of another cyberattack).

1
Getting Started with Cybersecurity

Discover what cybersecurity is and why defining it is more difficult than you might expect.

Find out why breaches seem to occur so often and why technology alone does not seem to stop them.

Explore various types of common cyberthreats and common cybersecurity tools.

Understand the who, how, and why of various types of attackers and threatening parties that aren't officially malicious.

Chapter **1**

What Exactly Is Cybersecurity?

To improve your ability to keep yourself and your loved ones cybersecure, you need to understand what cybersecure means, what your goals should be vis-à-vis cybersecurity, and what exactly you're securing against.

While the answers to these questions may initially seem simple and straightforward, they aren't. As you can see in this chapter, these answers can vary dramatically between people, company divisions, organizations, and even within the same entity at different times.

Cybersecurity Means Different Things to Different Folks

While *cybersecurity* may sound like a simple enough term to define, in actuality, from a practical standpoint, it means quite different things to different people in different situations, leading to extremely varied relevant policies, procedures, and practices. An individual who wants to protect her social media accounts from hacker takeovers, for example, is exceedingly unlikely to assume many of the approaches and technologies used by Pentagon workers to secure classified networks.

Typically, for example:

>> For **individuals,** *cybersecurity* means that their personal data is not accessible to anyone other than themselves and others whom they have so authorized, and that their computing devices work properly and are free from malware.

>> For **small business owners,** *cybersecurity* may include ensuring that credit card data is properly protected and that standards for data security are properly implemented at point-of-sale registers.

>> For **firms conducting online business,** *cybersecurity* may include protecting servers that untrusted outsiders regularly interact with.

>> For **shared service providers,** *cybersecurity* may entail protecting numerous data centers that house numerous servers that, in turn, host many virtual servers belonging to many different organizations.

>> For the **government,** *cybersecurity* may include establishing different classifications of data, each with its own set of related laws, policies, procedures, and technologies.

REMEMBER

The bottom line is that while the word cybersecurity is easy to define, the practical expectations that enters peoples' minds when they hear the word vary quite a bit.

Technically speaking, cybersecurity is the subset of information security that addresses information and information systems that store and process data in electronic form, whereas *information security* encompasses the security of all forms of data (for example, securing a paper file and a filing cabinet).

That said, today, many people colloquially interchange the terms, often referring to aspects of information security that are technically not part of cybersecurity as being part of the latter. Such usage also results from the blending of the two in many situations. Technically speaking, for example, if someone writes down a password on a piece of paper and leaves the paper on his desk where other people can see the password instead of placing the paper in a safe deposit box or safe, he has violated a principle of information security, not of cybersecurity, even though his actions may result in serious cybersecurity repercussions.

Cybersecurity Is a Constantly Moving Target

While the ultimate goal of cybersecurity may not change much over time, the policies, procedures, and technologies used to achieve it change dramatically as the years march on. Many approaches and technologies that were more than adequate to protect consumers' digital data in 1980, for example, are effectively worthless today, either because they're no longer practical to employ or because technological advances have rendered them obsolete or impotent.

While assembling a complete list of every advancement that the world has seen in recent decades and how such changes impact cybersecurity in effectively impossible, we can examine several key development area and their impacts on the ever-evolving nature of cybersecurity: technological changes, economic model shifts, and outsourcing.

Technological changes

Technological changes tremendously impact cybersecurity. New risks come along with the new capabilities and conveniences that new offerings deliver. As the pact of technological advancement continues to increase, therefore, so does the pace of new cybersecurity risks. While the number of such risks created over the past few decades as the result of new offerings is astounding, the areas described in the following sections have yielded a disproportionate impact on cybersecurity.

Digital data

The last few decades have witnessed dramatic changes in the technologies that exist, as well as vis-à-vis who use such technologies, how they do so, and for what purposes. All these factors impact cybersecurity.

Consider, for example, that when many of the people alive today were children, controlling access to data in a business environment simply meant that the data owner placed a physical file containing the information into a locked cabinet and gave the key to only people he recognized as being authorized personnel and only when they requested the key during business hours. For additional security, he may have located the cabinet in an office that was locked after business hours and which itself was in a building that was also locked and alarmed.

Today, with the digital storage of information, however, simple filing and protection schemes have been replaced with complex technologies that must automatically authenticate users who seek the data from potentially any location at potentially any time, determine whether the users are authorized to access a particular element or set of data, and securely deliver the proper data — all while preventing any attacks against the system servicing data requests, any attacks against the data in transit, and any of the security controls protecting the both of them.

Furthermore, the transition from written communication to email and chat has moved tremendous amounts of sensitive information to Internet-connected servers. Likewise, society's move from film to digital photography and videography has increased the stakes for cybersecurity. Nearly every photograph and video taken today is stored electronically rather than on film and negatives — a situation that has enabled criminals situated anywhere to either steal people's images and leak them, or to hold people's valuable images ransom with ransomware. The fact that movies and television shows are now stored and transmitted electronically has likewise allowed pirates to copy them and offer them to the masses — sometimes via malware-infested websites.

The Internet

The most significant technological advancement when it comes to cybersecurity impact has been the arrival of the Internet era. Just a few decades ago, it was unfathomable that hackers from across the globe could disrupt a business, manipulate an election, or steal a billion dollars. Today, no knowledgeable person would dismiss any such possibilities.

Prior to the Internet era, it was extremely difficult for the average hacker to financially profit by hacking. The arrival of online banking and commerce in the 1990s, however, meant that hackers could directly steal money or goods and services — which meant that not only could hackers quickly and easily monetize their efforts, but unethical people had strong incentives to enter the world of cybercrime.

Cryptocurrency

Compounding those incentives severalfold has been the arrival and proliferation of cryptocurrency over the past decade, along with innovation that has dramatically magnified the potential return-on-investment for criminals involved in cybercrime, simultaneously increasing their ability to earn money through cyber-crime and improving their ability to hide while doing so. Criminals historically faced a challenge when receiving payments since the account from which they ultimately withdrew the money could often be tied to them. Cryptocurrency effectively eliminated such risks.

Mobile workforces and ubiquitous access

Not that many years ago, in the pre-Internet era, it was impossible for hackers to access corporate systems remotely because corporate networks were not connected to any public networks, and often had no dial-in capabilities. Executives on the road would often call their assistants to check messages and obtain necessary data while they were remote.

Connectivity to the Internet created some risk, but initially firewalls did not allow people outside the organization to initiate communications — so, short of firewall misconfigurations and/or bugs, most internal systems remained relatively isolated. The dawn of e-commerce and e-banking, of course, meant that certain production systems had to be reachable and addressable from the outside world, but employee networks, for example, usually remained generally isolated.

The arrival of remote access technologies — starting with services like Outlook Web Access and pcAnywhere, and evolving to full VPN and VPN-like access — has totally changed the game.

Smart devices

Likewise, the arrival of smart devices and the *Internet of Things* (the universe of devices that are not traditional computers, but that are connected to the Internet) — whose proliferation and expansion are presently occurring at a startling rate — means that unhackable solid-state machines are being quickly replaced with devices that can potentially be controlled by hackers halfway around the world. The tremendous risks created by these devices are discussed more in Chapter 17.

Big data

While big data is helping facilitate the creation of many cybersecurity technologies, it also creates opportunities for attackers. By correlating large amounts of information about the people working for an organization, for example, a criminal can more easily than before identify ideal methods for social engineering his/her way into the organization or locate and exploit possible vulnerabilities in the organization's infrastructure. As a result, various organizations have been effectively forced to implement all sorts of controls to prevent the leaking of information.

Entire books have been written on the impact of technological advancement. The main point to understand is that technological advancement has had a significant impact on cybersecurity, making security harder to deliver and raising the stakes when parties fail to properly protect their assets.

Social shifts

Various changes in the ways that humans behave and interact with one another have also had a major impact on cybersecurity. The Internet, for example, allows people from all over the world to interact in real-time. Of course, this real-time interaction also enables criminals all over the world to commit crimes remotely. But it also allows citizens of repressive countries and free countries to communicate, creating opportunities for dispelling the perpetual propaganda utilized as excuses for the failure of totalitarianism to produce quality of lives on par with the democratic world. At the same time, it also delivers to the cyberwarriors of governments at odds with one another the ability to launch attacks via the same network.

The conversion of various information management systems from paper to computer, from isolated to Internet-connected, and from accessible-only-in-the-office to accessible from any smartphone or computer has dramatically changed the equation when it comes to what information hackers can steal. Furthermore, in many cases in which such conversions were, for security reasons, not initially done, the pressure emanating from the expectations of modern people that every piece of data be available to them at all times from anywhere has forced such conversions to occur, creating additional opportunities for criminals. To the delight of hackers, many organizations that, in the past, wisely protected sensitive information by keeping it offline have simply lost the ability to enjoy such protections if they want to stay in business.

Social media has also transformed the world of information — with people growing accustomed to sharing far more about themselves than ever before — often with audiences far larger than before as well. Today, due to the behavioral shift in this regard, it is trivial for evildoers from anywhere to assemble lists of a target's friends, professional colleagues, and relatives and to establish mechanisms for communication with all those people. Likewise, it is easier than ever before to find out what technologies a particular firm utilizes and for what purposes, discover people's travel schedules, and ascertain their opinions on various topics or their tastes in music and movies. The trend toward increased sharing continues. Most people remain blindly unaware of how much information about them lives on Internet-connected machines and how much other information about them can be extrapolated from the aforementioned data.

All these changes have translated into a scary reality: Due to societal shifts, an evildoer can easily launch a much larger, more sophisticated social engineering attack today than he or she could less than a decade ago.

Economic model shifts

Connecting nearly the entire world has allowed the Internet to facilitate other trends with tremendous cybersecurity ramifications. Operational models that were once unthinkable, such as that of an American company utilizing a call center in India and a software development shop in the Philippines, have become the mainstay of many corporations. These changes, however, create cybersecurity risks of all sorts.

The last 20 years have seen a tremendous growth in the outsourcing of various tasks from locations in which they're more expensive to carry out to regions in which they can be accomplished at much lower costs. The notion that a company in the United States could rely primarily on computer programmers in India or in the Philippines or that someone in New York seeking to have a logo made for her business could, shortly before going to bed, pay someone halfway around the globe $5.50 to create it and have the logo in her email inbox immediately upon waking up the next morning, would have sounded like economic science-fiction a generation ago. Today, it's not only common, but also in many cases, it is the more common than any other method of achieving similar results.

Of course, many cybersecurity ramifications result. Data being transmitted needs to be protected from destruction, modification, and theft, and greater assurance is needed that back doors are not intentionally or inadvertently inserted into code. Greater protections are needed to prevent the theft of intellectual property and other forms of corporate espionage. Hackers no longer necessarily need to directly breach the organizations that they seek to hack; they merely need to compromise one or more of its providers, which may be far less careful with their information security and personnel practices than the ultimate target.

Political shifts

As with advances in technology, political shifts have had tremendous cybersecurity repercussions, some of which seem to permanent fixtures of news headlines. The combination of government power and mighty technology has often proven to be a costly one for citizens. If current trends continue, the impact on cybersecurity of various political shifts will only continue to grow in the foreseeable future.

Data collection

The proliferation of information online and the ability to attack machines all over the world have meant that governments can spy on citizens of their own countries and on the residents of other nations to an extent never before possible.

Furthermore, as more and more business, personal, and societal activities leave behind digital footprints, governments have easy access to a much greater amount of information about their potential intelligence targets than they could acquire even at much higher costs just a few years ago. Coupled with the relatively low cost of digital storage, advancing big data technologies, and the expected eventual impotence of many of today's encryption technologies, and governments have a strong incentive to collect and store as much data as they can about as many people as they can, in case it is of use at some later date. There is little doubt that some governments are already doing exactly that.

The long-term consequences of this phenomenon are, obviously, as of yet unknown, but one thing is clear: If businesses do not properly protect data, less-than-friendly nations are likely to obtain it and store it for use in either the short term, the long term, or both.

Election interference

A generation ago, one nation interfering in the elections of another was no trivial matter. Of course, such interference existed — it has occurred as long as there have been elections — but carrying out significant interference campaigns was expensive, resource-intensive, and risky.

To spread misinformation and other propaganda, materials had to be printed and physically distributed or recorded and transmitted via radio, meaning that individual campaigns were likely to reach only small audiences. As such, the efficacy effects of such efforts were often quite low, and the risk of the party running the campaign being exposed was relatively high.

Manipulating voter registration databases to prevent legitimate voters from voting and/or to allow bogus voters to vote was extremely difficult and entailed tremendous risks; someone "working on the inside" would likely have had to be a traitor. In a country such as the United States, in which voter registration databases are decentralized and managed on a county level, recruiting sufficient saboteurs to truly impact a major election would likely have been impossible, and the odds of getting caught while attempting to do so were likely extremely high. Likewise, in the era of paper ballots and manual counting, for a foreign power to manipulate actual vote counts on any large scale was practically impossible.

Today, however, the game has changed. A government can easily spread misinformation through social media at an extremely low cost. If it crafts a well-thought-out campaign, it can rely on other people to spread the misinformation — something that people could not do en masse in the era of radio recordings and printed pamphlets. The ability to reach many more people, at a much lower cost than ever before, has meant that more parties are able to interfere in political campaigns and can do so with more efficacy than in the past. Similarly, governments can spread misinformation to stir up civil discontent within their adversaries nations and to spread hostility between ethnic and religious groups living in foreign lands.

With voter registration databases stored electronically and sometimes on servers that are at least indirectly connected to the Internet, records may be able to be added, modified, or deleted from halfway across the globe without detection. Even if such hacking is, in reality, impossible, the fact that many citizens today believe that it may be possible has led to an undermining of faith in elections, a phenomenon that we have witnessed in recent years and that has permeated throughout all levels of society. Even Jimmy Carter, a former president of the United States, has expressed that he believes that full investigation into the 2016 presidential election would show that Donald Trump lost the election — despite there being absolutely no evidence whatsoever to support such a conclusion, even after a thorough FBI investigation into the matter.

It is also not hard to imagine that if online voting were ever to arrive, the potential for vote manipulation by foreign governments, criminals, and even political parties within the nation voting — and for removing the ballot auditability that exists today — would grow astronomically.

Less than a decade ago, the United States did not consider election-related computer systems to be critical infrastructure and did not directly provide federal funding to secure such systems. Today, most people understand that the need for cybersecurity in such areas is of paramount importance, and the policies and behavior of just a few years ago seems nothing short of crazy.

Hacktavism

Likewise, the spread of democracy since the collapse of the Soviet Union a generation ago, coupled with Internet-based interaction between people all over the globe, has ushered in the era of hacktivism. People are aware of the goings-on in more places than in the past. Hackers angry about some government policy or activity in some location may target that government or the citizens of the country over which it rules from places far away.

Greater freedom

At the same time, repressed people are now more aware of the lifestyles of people in freer and more prosperous countries, a phenomenon that has both forced some governments to liberalize, and motivated others to implement cybersecurity-type controls to prevent using various Internet-based services.

Sanctions

Another political ramification of cybersecurity has been vis-à-vis international sanctions: Rogue states subject to such sanctions have been able to use cybercrime of various forms to circumvent the sanctions.

For example, North Korea is believed to have spread malware that mines cryptocurrency for the totalitarian state to computers all over the world, thereby allowing the country to circumvent sanctions by obtaining liquid money that can easily be spent anywhere.

In 2019, the failure by individuals to adequately secure their personal computers can directly impact political negotiations.

Creating a new balance of power

While the militaries of certain nations have long since grown more powerful than those of their adversaries — both the quality and quantity of weapons vary greatly between nations — when it comes to cybersecurity the balance of power is totally different.

While the quality of cyberweapons may vary between countries, the fact that launching cyberattacks costs little means that all militaries have an effectively unlimited supply of whatever weapons they use. In fact, in most cases, launching millions of cyberattacks costs little more than launching just one.

Also, unlike in the physical world in which any nation that bombed civilian homes in the territory of its adversary may face a severe reprisal, rogue governments regularly hack with impunity people in other countries. Victims often are totally unaware that they have been compromised, rarely report such incidents to law enforcement, and certainly don't know whom to blame.

Even when a victim realizes that a breach has occurred and even when technical experts point to the attackers as the culprits, the states behind such attacks often enjoy plausible deniability, preventing any government from publicly retaliating. In fact, the difficulty of ascertaining the source of cyberattacks coupled with the element of plausible deniability is a strong incentive for governments to use cyberattacks as a mechanism of proactively attacking an adversary, wreaking various forms of havoc without fear of significant reprisals.

Furthermore, the world of cybersecurity created a tremendous imbalance between attackers and defenders that works to the advantage of less powerful nations.

Governments that could never afford to launch huge barrages against an adversary in the physical world can easily do so in the world of cyber, where launching each attack costs next to nothing. As a result, attackers can afford to keep attacking until they succeed — and they need to breach systems only once to "succeed" — creating a tremendous problem for defenders who must shield their assets against every single attack. This imbalance has translated into a major advantage for attackers over defenders and has meant that even minor powers can successfully breach systems belonging to superpowers.

In fact, this imbalance contributes to the reason why cybersecurity breaches seem to occur so often, as many hackers simply keep attacking until they succeed. If an organization successfully defends against 10 million attacks but fails to stop the 10,000,001, it may suffer a severe breach and make the news. Reports of the breach likely won't even mention the fact that it has a 99.999999 percent success rate in protecting its data and that it successfully stopped attackers one million times in a row. Likewise, if a business installed 99.999 percent of the patches that it should have but neglected to fix a single known vulnerability, it's likely to suffer a breach due to the number of exploits available to criminals. Media outlets will point out the organization's failure to properly patch, overlooking its near perfect record in that area.

As such, the era of cyber has also changed the balance of power between criminals and law enforcement.

Criminals know that the odds of being caught and successfully prosecuted for a cybercrime are dramatically smaller than those for most other crimes, and that repeated failed attempts to carry out a cybercrime are not a recipe for certain arrest as they are for most other crimes. They are also aware that law enforcement agencies lack the resources to pursue the vast majority of cyber criminals. Tracking down, taking into custody, and successfully prosecuting someone stealing data from halfway across the world via numerous hops in many countries and a network of computers commandeered from law-abiding folks, for example, requires gathering and dedicating significantly more resources than does catching a thief who was recorded on camera while holding up in a store in a local police precinct.

With the low cost of launching repeated attacks, the odds of eventual success in their favor, the odds of getting caught and punished miniscule, and the potential rewards growing with increased digitalization, criminals know that cybercrime pays, underscoring the reason that you need to protect yourself.

Looking at the Risks That Cybersecurity Mitigates

People sometimes explain the reason that cybersecurity is important as being "because it prevent hackers from breaking into systems and stealing data and money." But such a description dramatically understates the role that cybersecurity plays in keeping the modern home, business, or even world running.

In fact, the role of cybersecurity can be looked at from a variety of different vantage points, with each presenting a different set of goals. Of course the following lists aren't complete, but they should provide food for thought and underscore the importance of understanding how to cybersecure yourself and your loved ones.

The goal of cybersecurity: The CIA triad

Cybersecurity professionals often explain that the goal of cybersecurity is to ensure the Confidentiality, Integrity, and Availability (CIA) of data, sometimes referred to as the CIA Triad, with the pun lovingly intended:

WARNING

» **Confidentiality** refers to ensuring that information isn't disclosed or in any other way made available to unauthorized entities (including people, organizations, or computer processes).

   Don't confuse confidentiality with privacy: Confidentiality is a subset of the realm of privacy. It deals specifically with protecting data from unauthorized viewers, whereas privacy in general encompasses much more.

   Hackers that steal data undermine confidentiality.

» **Integrity** refers to ensuring that data is both accurate and complete.

   Accurate means, for example, that the data is never modified in any way by any unauthorized party or by a technical glitch. *Complete* refers to, for example, data that has had no portion of itself removed by any unauthorized party or technical glitch.

   Integrity also includes ensuring *nonrepudiation,* meaning that data is created and handled in such a fashion that nobody can reasonably argue that the data is not authentic or is inaccurate.

   Cyberattacks that intercept data and modify it before relaying it to its destination — sometimes known as *man-in-the-middle attacks* — undermine integrity.

>> **Availability** refers to ensuring that information, the systems used to store and process it, the communication mechanisms used to access and relay it, and all associated security controls function correctly to meet some specific benchmark (for example, 99.99 percent uptime). People outside of the cybersecurity field sometimes think of availability as a secondary aspect of information security after confidentiality and integrity. In fact, ensuring availability is an integral part of cybersecurity. Doing so, though, is sometimes more difficult than ensuring confidentiality or integrity. One reason that this is true is that maintaining availability often requires involving many more noncybersecurity professionals, leading to a "too many cooks in the kitchen" type challenge, especially in larger organizations. Distributed denial-of-service attacks attempt to undermine availability. Also, consider that attacks often use large numbers of stolen computer power and bandwidth to launch DDoS attacks, but responders who seek to ensure availability can only leverage the relatively small amount of resources that they can afford.

From a human perspective

The risks that cybersecurity addresses can also be thought of in terms better reflecting the human experience:

>> **Privacy risks:** Risks emanating from the potential loss of adequate control over, or misuse of, personal or other confidential information.

>> **Financial risks:** Risks of financial losses due to hacking. Financial losses can include both those that are direct — for example, the theft of money from someone's bank account by a hacker who hacked into the account — and those that are indirect, such as the loss of customers who no longer trust a small business after the latter suffers a security breach.

>> **Professional risks:** Risks to one's professional career that stem from breaches. Obviously, cybersecurity professionals are at risk for career damage if a breach occurs under their watch and is determined to have happened due to negligence, but other types of professionals can suffer career harm due to a breach as well. C-level executives can be fired, Board members can be sued, and so on. Professional damage can also occur if hackers release private communications or data that shows someone in a bad light — for example, records that a person was disciplined for some inappropriate action, sent an email containing objectionable material, and so on.

» **Business risks:** Risks to a business similar to the professional risks to an individual. Internal documents leaked after breach of Sony Pictures painted various the firm in a negative light vis-à-vis some of its compensation practices.

» **Personal risks:** Many people store private information on their electronic devices, from explicit photos to records of participation in activities that may not be deemed respectable by members of their respective social circles. Such data can sometimes cause significant harm to personal relationships if it leaks. Likewise, stolen personal data can help criminals steal people's identities, which can result in all sorts of personal problems.

Chapter **2**

Getting to Know Common Cyberattacks

Many different types of cyberattacks exist — so many that I could write an entire series of books about them. In this book, however, I do not cover all types of threats in detail because the reality is, that you're likely reading this book to learn about how to keep yourself cybersecure, not to learn about matters that have no impact on you, such as forms of attacks that are normally directed at espionage agencies, industrial equipment, or military armaments.

In this chapter, you find out about the different types of problems that cyberattackers can create through the use of attacks that commonly impact individuals and small businesses.

Attacks That Inflict Damage

Attackers launch some forms of cyberattacks with the intent to inflict damage to victims. The threat posed by such attacks is not that a criminal will directly steal your money or data, but that the attackers will inflict harm to you in some other specific manner — a manner that may ultimately translate into financial, military, political, or other benefit to the attacker and (potentially) damage of some sort to the victim.

Types of attacks that inflict damage include

>> Denial-of-service (DoS) attacks

>> Distributed denial-of-service (DDoS) attacks

>> Botnets and zombies

>> Data destruction attacks

Denial-of-service (DoS) attacks

A *denial-of-service attack* is one in which an attacker intentionally attempts to paralyze a computer or computer network by flooding it with large amounts of requests or data, which overload the target and make it incapable of responding properly to legitimate requests.

In many cases, the requests sent by the attacker are each, on their own, legitimate — for example, a normal request to load a web page.

In other cases, the requests aren't normal requests. Instead, they leverage knowledge of various protocols to send requests that optimize, or even magnify, the effect of the attack.

In any case, denial-of-service attacks work by overwhelming computer systems' Central Processing Units (CPU)s and/or memory, utilizing all the available network communications bandwidth, and/or exhausting networking infrastructure resources such as routers.

Distributed denial-of-service (DDoS) attacks

A *Distributed DoS attack* is a DoS attack in which many individual computers or other connected devices across disparate regions simultaneously flood the target with requests. In recent years, nearly all major denial-of-service attacks have been distributed in nature — and some have involved the use of Internet-connected cameras and other devices as attack vehicles, rather than classic computers. Figure 2-1 illustrates the anatomy of a simple DDoS attack.

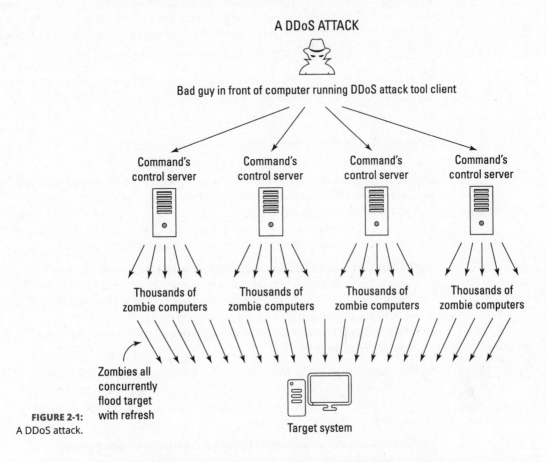

FIGURE 2-1:
A DDoS attack.

The goal of a DDoS attack is to knock the victim offline, and the motivation for doing so varies.

Sometimes the goal is financial: Imagine, for example, the damage that may result to an online retailer's business if an unscrupulous competitor knocked the former's site offline during Black Friday weekend. Imagine a crook who shorts the stock of a major retailer of toys right before launching a DDoS attack against the retailer two weeks before Christmas.

DDoS attacks remain a serious and growing threat. Criminal enterprises even offer DDoS for hire services, which are advertised on the dark web as offering, for a fee, to "take your competitor's websites offline in a cost-effective manner."

In some cases, DDoS launchers may have political, rather than financial, motives. For example, a corrupt politician may seek to have his or her opponent's website taken down during an election season, thereby reducing the competitor's ability to spread messages and receive online campaign contributions. Hacktivists may also launch DDoS attacks in order to take down sites in the name of "justice" — for example, targeting law enforcement sites after an unarmed person is killed during an altercation with police.

In fact, according to a 2017 study by Kaspersky Lab and B2B International, almost half of companies worldwide that experienced a DDoS attack suspect that their competitors may have been involved.

DDoS attacks can impact individuals in three significant ways:

>> **A DDoS attack on a local network can significantly slow down all Internet access from that network.** Sometimes these attacks make connectivity so slow that connections to sites fail due to *session timeout* settings, meaning that the systems terminate the connections after seeing requests take longer to elicit responses than some maximum permissible threshold.

>> **A DDoS attack can render inaccessible a site that a person plans on using.** On October 21, 2016, for example, many users were unable to reach several high-profile sites, including Twitter, PayPal, CNN, HBO Now, The Guardian, and dozens of other popular sites, due to a massive DDoS attack launched against a third party providing various technical services for these sites and many more.

TIP

The possibility of DDoS attacks is one of the reasons that you should never wait until the last minute to perform an online banking transaction — the site that you need to utilize may be inaccessible for a number of reasons, one of which is an ongoing DDoS attack.

>> **A DDoS attack can lead users to obtain information from one site instead of another.** By making one site unavailable, Internet users looking for specific information are likely to obtain it from another site — a phenomenon that allows attackers to either spread misinformation or prevent people from hearing certain information or vantage points on important issues. As such, DDoS attacks can be used as an effective mechanism — at least over the short term — for censoring opposing points of view.

Botnets and zombies

Often, DDoS attacks use what are known as *botnets*. Botnets are a collection of compromised computers that belong to other parties, but that a hacker remotely controls and uses to perform tasks without the legitimate owners' knowledge.

Criminals who successfully infect one million computers with malware can, for example, potentially use those machines, known as *zombies,* to simultaneously make many requests from a single server or server farm in an attempt to overload the target with traffic.

Data destruction attacks

Sometimes attackers want to do more than take a party temporarily offline by overwhelming it with requests — they may want to damage the victim by destroying or corrupting the target's information and/or information systems. A criminal may seek to destroy a user's data through a *data destruction attack* — for example, if the user refuses to pay a ransomware ransom that the crook demands.

Of course, all the reasons for launching DDoS attacks (see preceding section) are also reasons that a hacker may attempt to destroy someone's data as well.

Wiper attacks are advanced data destruction attacks in which a criminal uses malware to wipe the data on a victim's hard drive or SSD, in such a fashion that the data is difficult or impossible to recover.

To put it simply, unless the victim has backups, someone whose computer is wiped by a wiper is likely to lose access to all the data and software that was previously stored on the attacked device.

Impersonation

One of the great dangers that the Internet creates is the ease with which mischievous parties can impersonate others. Prior to the Internet era, for example, criminals could not easily impersonate a bank or a store and convince people to hand over their money in exchange for some promised rate of interest or goods. Physically mailed letters and later telephone calls became the tools of scammers, but none of those earlier communication techniques ever came close to the power of the Internet to aid criminals attempting to impersonate law-abiding parties.

Creating a website that mimics the website of a bank, store, or government agency is quite simple and can sometimes be done within minutes. Criminals can find a near-endless supply of domain names that are close enough to those of legitimate parties to trick some folks into believing that a site that they are seeing is the real deal when it's not, giving crooks the typical first ingredient in the recipe for online impersonation.

Sending an email that appears to have come from someone else is simple and allows criminals to perpetrate all sorts of crimes online. I myself demonstrated over 20 years ago how I could defeat various defenses and send an email that was delivered to recipients on a secure system — the message appeared to readers to have been sent from god@heaven.sky. Figure 2-2 shows another email message that may have been faked.

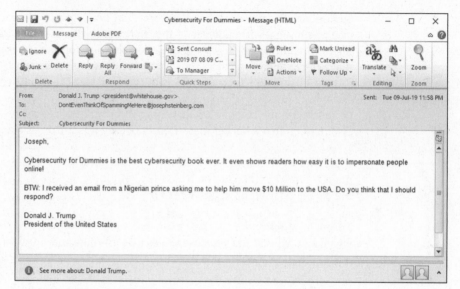

FIGURE 2-2:
An impersonation message.

Phishing

Phishing refers to an attempt to convince a person to take some action by impersonating a trustworthy party that reasonably may legitimately ask the user to take such action.

For example, a criminal may send an email that appears to have been sent by a major bank and that asks the recipient to click on a link in order to reset his or her password due to a possible data breach. When the user clicks the link, he or she is directed to a website that appears to belong to the bank, but is actually a replica run by the criminal. As such, the criminal uses the fraudulent website to collect usernames and passwords to the banking site.

Spear phishing

Spear phishing refers to phishing attacks that are designed and sent to target a specific person, business, or organization. If a criminal seeks to obtain credentials into a specific company's email system, for example, he or she may send emails crafted specifically for particular targeted individuals within the organization. Often, criminals who spear phish research their targets online and leverage overshared information on social media in order to craft especially legitimate-sounding emails.

For example, the following type of email is typically a lot more convincing than "Please login to the mail server and reset your password.":

"Hi, I am going to be getting on my flight in ten minutes. Can you please login to the Exchange server and check when my meeting is? For some reason, I cannot get in. You can try to call me by phone first for security reasons, but, if you miss me, just go ahead, check the information, and email it to me — as you know that I am getting on a flight that is about to take off."

CEO fraud

CEO fraud is similar to spear phishing (see preceding section) in that it involves a criminal impersonating the CEO or other senior executive of a particular business, but the instructions provided by "the CEO" may be to take an action directly, not to log in to a system, and the goal may not be to capture usernames and passwords or the like.

The crook, for example, may send an email to the firm's CFO instructing her or him to issue a wire payment to a particular new vendor or to send all the organization's W2 forms for the year to a particular email address belonging to the firm's accountant. See Figure 2-3.

CEO fraud often nets significant returns for criminals and makes employees who fall for the scams appear incompetent. As a result, people who fall prey to such scams are often fired from their jobs.

Smishing

Smishing refers to cases of phishing in which the attackers deliver their messages via text messages (SMS) rather than email. The goal may be to capture usernames and passwords or to trick the user into installing malware.

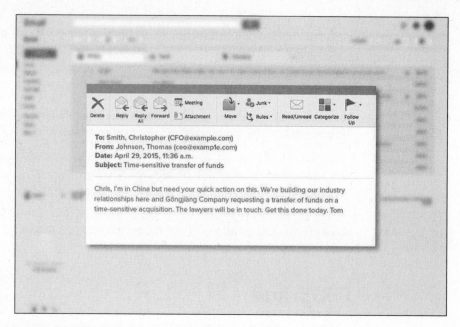

To: Smith, Christopher (CFO@example.com)
From: Johnson, Thomas (ceo@example.com)
Date: April 29, 2015, 11:36 a.m.
Subject: Time-sensitive transfer of funds

Chris, I'm in China but need your quick action on this. We're building our industry relationships here and Gōngjiàng Company requesting a transfer of funds on a time-sensitive acquisition. The lawyers will be in touch. Get this done today. Tom

FIGURE 2-3:
A fraudulent
email.

Vishing

Vishing, or voice-based phishing, is phishing via POTS — that stands for "plain old telephone service." Yes, criminals use old, time-tested methods for scamming people. Today, most such calls are transmitted by Voice Over IP systems, but, in the end, the scammers are calling people on regular telephones much the same way that scammers have been doing for decades.

Whaling

Whaling refers to spear phishing that targets high-profile business executives or government officials. For more on spear phishing, see the section earlier in this chapter.

Tampering

Sometimes attackers don't want to disrupt an organization's normal activities, but instead seek to exploit those activities for financial gain. Often, crooks achieve such objectives by manipulating data in transit or as it resides on systems of their targets in a process known as *tampering.*

In a basic case of tampering with data in transit, for example, imagine that a user of online banking has instructed his bank to wire money to a particular account, but somehow a criminal intercepted the request and changed the relevant routing and account number to his own.

A criminal may also hack into a system and manipulate information for similar purposes. Using the previous example, imagine if a criminal changed the payment address associated with a particular payee so that when the Accounts Payable department makes an online payment, the funds are sent to the wrong destination (well, at least it is wrong in the eyes of the payer).

Interception

Interception occurs when attackers capture information in transit between computers. If the data isn't properly encrypted, the party intercepting it may be able to misuse it.

One special type of interception is known as a *man-in-the-middle attack*. In this type of an attack, the interceptor proxies the data between the sender and recipient in an attempt to disguise the fact that the data is being intercepted. *Proxying* in such a case refers to the man-in-the-middle intercepting requests and then transmitting them (either in modified form or unmodified) to their original intended destinations and then receiving the responses from those destination and transmitting them (in modified form or unmodified) back to the sender. By employing proxying, the man-in-the-middle makes it difficult for the sender to know that his communications are being intercepted because when he communicates with a server, he receives the responses that he expects.

For example, a criminal may set up a bogus bank site (see the earlier "Phishing" section) and relay any information that anyone enters on the bogus site to the actual bank site so that the criminal can respond with the same information that the legitimate bank would have sent. Proxying of this sort not only helps the criminal avoid detection — a user who provides the crook with his or her password and then performs his or her normal online banking tasks may have no idea that anything abnormal occurred during the online banking session — but, also helps the criminal ensure that he or she captures the right password. If a user enters an incorrect password, the criminal will know to prompt for the correct one.

Figure 2-4 shows the anatomy of a man-in-the-middle intercepting and relaying communications.

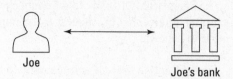

Man-in-the-middle attack
Joe wants to communicate with his bank

Joe

Joe's bank

But Bob's evil server is acting as a man-in-the-middle

FIGURE 2-4:
A man-in-the-middle interception.

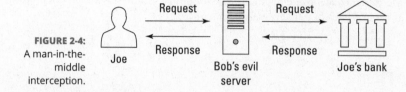

Joe

Request

Response

Bob's evil server

Request

Response

Joe's bank

Data Theft

Many cyberattacks involve stealing the victim's data. An attacker may want to steal data belonging to individuals, businesses, or a government agency for one or more of many possible reasons.

People, businesses, nonprofits, and governments are all vulnerable to data theft.

Personal data theft

Criminals often try to steal people's data in the hope of finding items that they can monetize, including:

>> Data that can be used for identity theft or sold to identity thieves

>> Compromising photos or health-related data that may be sellable or used as part of blackmail schemes

>> Information that is stolen and then erased from the user's machine that can be ransomed to the user

>> Password lists that can be used for breaching other systems

>> Confidential information about work-related matters that may be used to make illegal stock trades based on insider information

>> Information about upcoming travel plans that may be used to plan robberies of the victim's home

Business data theft

Criminals can use data stolen from businesses for a number of nefarious purposes:

>> **Making stock trades:** Having advance knowledge of how a quarter is going to turn out gives a criminal insider information on which he or she can illegally trade stocks or options and potentially make a significant profit.

>> **Selling data to unscrupulous competitors:** Criminals who steal sales pipeline information, documents containing details of future products, or other sensitive information can sell that data to unscrupulous competitors or to unscrupulous employees working at competitors whose management may never find out how such employees suddenly improved their performance.

>> **Leaking data to the media:** Sensitive data can embarrass the victim and cause its stock to decline (perhaps after selling short some shares).

>> **Leaking data covered by privacy regulations:** The victim may be potentially fined.

>> **Recruiting employees:** By recruiting employees or selling the information to other firms looking to hire employees with similar skills or with knowledge of competitions' systems, criminals who steal emails and discover communication between employees that indicates that one or more employees are unhappy in their current positions can sell that information to parties looking to hire.

>> **Stealing and using intellectual property:** Parties that steal the source code for computer software may be able to avoid paying licensing fees to the software's rightful owner. Parties that steal design documents created by others after extensive research and development can easily save millions of dollars — and, sometimes, even billions of dollars — in research and development costs. For more on the effects of this type of theft, see the nearby sidebar "How a cyberbreach cost one company $1 billion without 1 cent being stolen."

Malware

Malware, or malicious software, is an all-encompassing term for software that intentionally inflicts damage on its users who typically have no idea that they are running it.

Malware includes computer viruses, worms, Trojans, ransomware, scareware, spyware, cryptocurrency miners, adware, and other programs intended to exploit computer resources for nefarious purposes.

Viruses

Computer viruses are instances of malware that, when executed, replicate by inserting their own code into computer systems. Typically, the insertion is in data files (for example, as rogue macros within a Word document), the special portion of hard drives or solid state drives that contain the code and data used to boot a computer or disk (also known as *boot sectors*), or other computer programs.

Like biological viruses, computer viruses can't spread without having hosts to infect. Some computer viruses significantly impact the performance of their hosts, while others are, at least at times, hardly noticeable.

While computer viruses still inflict tremendous damage worldwide, the majority of serious malware threats today arrive in the form of worms and Trojans.

Worms

Computer worms are stand-alone pieces of malware that replicate themselves without the need for hosts in order to spread. Worms often propagate over connections by exploiting security vulnerabilities on target computers and networks.

Because they normally consume network bandwidth, worms can inflict harm even without modifying systems or stealing data. They can slow down network connections — and few people, if any, like to see their internal and Internet connections slow down.

Trojans

Trojans (appropriately named after the historical Trojan horse) is malware that is either disguised as nonmalicious software or hidden within a legitimate, nonmalicious application or piece of digital data.

Trojans are most often spread by some form of social engineering — for example, by tricking people into clicking on a link, installing an app, or running some email attachment. Unlike viruses and worms, Trojans typically don't self-propagate using technology — instead, they rely on the effort (or more accurately, the mistakes) of humans.

Ransomware

Ransomware is malware that demands that a ransom be paid to some criminal in exchange for the infected party not suffering some harm.

Ransomware often encrypts user files and threatens to delete the encryption key if a ransom isn't paid within some relatively short period of time, but other forms of ransomware involve a criminal actually stealing user data and threatening to publish it online if a ransom is not paid.

Some ransomware actually steals the files from users' computers, rather than simply encrypting data, so as to ensure that the user has no possible way to recover his or her data (for example, using an anti-ransomware utility) without paying the ransom.

Ransomware is most often delivered to victims as a Trojan or a virus, but has also been successfully spread by criminals who packaged it in a worm. In recent years sophisticated criminals have even crafted targeted ransomware campaigns that leverage knowledge about what data is most valuable to a particular target and how much that target can afford to pay in ransoms.

Figure 2-5 shows the ransom demand screen of WannaCry — a flavor of ransomware that inflicted at least hundreds of millions of dollars in damage (if not billions), after initially spreading in May 2017. Many security experts believe that the North Korean government or others working for it created WannaCry, which, within four days, infected hundreds of thousands of computers in about 150 countries.

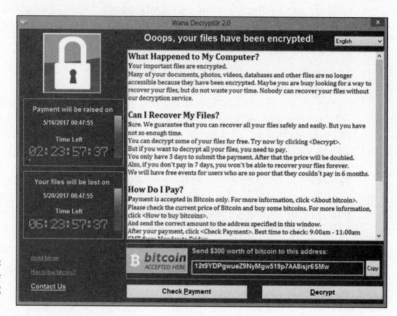

FIGURE 2-5:
Ransomware
demanding
ransom.

Scareware

Scareware is malware that scares people into taking some action. One common example is malware that scares people into buying security software. A message appears on a device that the device is infected with some virus that only a particular security package can remove, with a link to purchase that "security software."

Spyware

Spyware is software that surreptitiously, and without permission, collects information from a device. Spyware may capture a user's keystrokes (in which case it is called a *keylogger*), video from a video camera, audio from a microphone, screen images, and so on.

It is important to understand the difference between spyware and invasive programs. Some technologies that may technically be considered spyware if users had not been told that they were being tracked online are in use by legitimate businesses; they may be invasive, but they are not malware. These types of *nonspyware that also spies* includes beacons that check whether a user loaded a particular web page and tracking cookies installed by websites or apps. Some experts have argued that any software that tracks a smartphone's location while the app is not being actively used by the device's user also falls into the category of *nonspyware that also spies* — a definition that would include popular apps, such as Uber.

Cryptocurrency miners

Cryptocurrency miners are malware that, without any permission from devices' owners, commandeers infected devices' brainpower (its CPU cycles) to generate new units of a particular cryptocurrency (which the malware gives to the criminals operating the malware) by completing complex math problems that require significant processing power to solve.

The proliferation of cryptocurrency miners exploded in 2017 with the rise of cryptocurrency values. Even after price levels subsequently dropped, the miners are still ubiquitous as once criminals have invested in creating the miners, there is little cost in continuing to deploy them. Not surprisingly, as cryptocurrency prices began to rise again in 2019, new strains of cryptominers began to appear as well — some of which specifically target Android smartphones.

Many low-end cybercriminals favor using cryptominers. Even if each miner, on its own, pays the attacker very little, miners are easy to obtain and directly monetize cyberattacks without the need for extra steps (such as collecting a ransom) or the need for sophisticated command and control systems.

Adware

Adware is software that generates revenue for the party operating it by displaying online advertisements on a device. Adware may be malware — that is, installed and run without the permission of a device's owner — or it may be a legitimate component of software (for example, installed knowingly by users as part of some free, ad-supported package).

TIP

Some security professionals refer to the former as *adware malware*, and the latter as adware. Because no consensus exists, it's best to clarify which of the two is being discussed when you hear someone mention just the generic term adware.

Blended malware

Blended malware is malware that utilizes multiple types of malware technology as part of an attack — for example, combining features of Trojans, worms, and viruses.

Blended malware can be quite sophisticated and often stems from skilled attackers.

Zero day malware

Zero day malware is any malware that exploits a vulnerability not previously known to the public or to the vendor of the technology containing the vulnerability, and is, as such, often extremely potent.

Regularly creating zero day malware requires significant resource and development. It's quite expensive and is often crafted by the cyber armies of nation states rather than by other hackers.

Commercial purveyors of zero day malware have been known to charge over $1 million for a single exploit.

Poisoned Web Service Attacks

Many different types of attacks leverage vulnerabilities in servers, and new weaknesses are constantly discovered, which is why cybersecurity professionals have full-time jobs keeping servers safe. Entire books — or even several series of books — can be written on such a topic, which is, obviously, beyond the scope of this work.

That said, it is important for you to understand the basic concepts of server-based attacks because some such attacks can directly impact you.

One such form of attack is a *poisoned web service attack*, or a *poisoned web page attack*. In this type of attack, an attacker hacks into a web server and inserts code onto it that causes it to attack users when they access a page or set of pages that the server is serving.

For example, a hacker may compromise the web server serving www.abc123.com and modify the home page that is served to users accessing the site so that the home page contains malware.

But, a hacker does not even need to necessarily breach a system in order to poison web pages!

If a site that allows users to comment on posts isn't properly secured, for example, it may allow a user to add the text of various commands within a comment — commands that, if crafted properly, may be executed by users' browsers any time they load the page that displays the comment. A criminal can insert a command to run a script on the criminal's website, which can receive the authentication credentials of the user to the original site because it is called within the context of one of that site's web pages. Such an attack is known as *cross site scripting*, and it continues to be a problem even after over a decade of being addressed.

Network Infrastructure Poisoning

As with web servers, many different types of attacks leverage vulnerabilities in network infrastructure, and new weaknesses are constantly discovered. The vast majority of this topic is beyond the scope of this book. That said, as is the case with poisoned web servers, you need to understand the basic concepts of server-based attacks because some such attacks can directly impact you.

For example, criminals may exploit various weaknesses in order to add corrupt domain name system (DNS) data into a DNS server.

DNS is the directory of the Internet that translates human readable addresses into their numeric, computer-usable equivalents (IP addresses). For example, if you type `https://JosephSteinberg.com` into your web browser, DNS directs your connection to an address of 104.18.45.53.

By inserting incorrect information into DNS tables, a criminal can cause a DNS server to return an incorrect IP address to a user's computer. Such an attack can easily result in a user's traffic being diverted to a computer of the attacker's choice instead of the user's intended destination. If the criminal sets up a phony bank site on the server to which traffic is being diverted, for example, and impersonates on that server a bank that the user was trying to reach, even a user who enters the bank URL into his or her browser (as opposed to just clicking on a link) may fall prey after being diverted to the bogus site. (This type of attack is known as *DNS poisoning* or *pharming*.)

Network infrastructure attacks take many forms. Some seek to route people to the wrong destinations. Others seek to capture data, while others seek to effectuate denial-of-service conditions. The main point to understand is that the piping of the Internet is quite complex was not initially designed with security in mind, and is vulnerable to many forms of misuse.

Malvertising

Malvertising is an abbreviation of the words malicious advertising and refers to the use of online advertising as a vehicle to spread malware or to launch some other form of a cyberattack.

Because many websites display ads that are served and managed by third-party networks and that contain links to various other third parties, online advertisements are a great vehicle for attackers. Even companies that adequately secure their websites may not take proper precautions to ensure that they do not deliver problematic advertisements created by, and managed by, someone else.

As such, malvertising sometimes allows criminals to insert their content into reputable and high-profile websites with large numbers of visitors (something that would be difficult for crooks to achieve otherwise), many of whom may be security conscious and who would not have been exposed to the criminal's content had it been posted on a less reputable site.

Furthermore, because websites often earn money for their owners based on the number of people who click on various ads, website owners generally place ads on their sites in a manner that will attract users to the ads.

As such, malvertising allows criminals to reach large audiences via a trusted site without having to hack anything.

Some malvertising requires users to click on the ads in order to become infected with malware; others do not require any user participation — users' devices are infected the moment that the ad displays.

Drive-by downloads

Drive-by downloads is somewhat of a euphemism that refers to software that a user downloads without understanding what he or she is doing. A drive-by download may occur, for example, if a user downloads malware by going to a poisoned website that automatically sends the malware to the user's device when he or she opens the site.

Drive-by downloads also include cases in which a user knows that he or she is downloading software, but is not aware of the full consequences of doing so. For example, if a user is presented with a web page that says that a security vulnerability is present on his or her computer and that tells the user to click on a button that says Download to install a security patch, the user has provided authorization for the (malicious) download — but only because he or she was tricked into believing that the nature of the download was far different than it truly is.

Stealing passwords

Criminals can steal passwords many different ways. Two common methods include

» **Thefts of password databases:** If a criminal steals a password database from an online store, anyone whose password appears in the database is at risk of having his or her password compromised. (If the store properly encrypted its passwords, it may take time for the criminal to perform what is known as a *hash attack,* but nonetheless, passwords — especially those that are likely to be tested early on — may still be at risk. To date, stealing passwords is the most common way that passwords are undermined.

» **Social engineering attacks:** *Social engineering attacks* are attacks in which a criminal tricks someone into doing something that he would not have done had he realized that the person making the request was tricking him in some way. One example of stealing a password via social engineering is when a criminal pretends to be a member of the tech support department of his target's employer and tells his target that the target must reset a particular password to a particular value to have the associated account tested as is needed after the recovery from some breach, and the target obeys. (For more information, see the earlier section on phishing.)

» **Credential attacks:** Credential attacks are attacks that seek to gain entry into a system by entering, without authorization, a valid username and password combination (or other authentication information as needed). These attacks fall into four primary categories:

  - *Brute force:* Criminals use automated tools that try all possible passwords until they hit the correct one.

  - *Dictionary attacks:* Criminals use automated tools to feed every word in the dictionary to a site until they hit the correct one.

  - *Calculated attacks:* Criminals leverage information about a target to guess his or her password. Criminals may, for example, try someone's mother's maiden name because they can easily garner it for many people by looking at the most common last names of their Facebook friends or from posts on social media. (A Facebook post of "Happy Mother's Day to my wonderful mother!" that includes a user tag to a woman with a different last name than the user himself/herself is a good giveaway.)

  - *Blended attacks:* Some attacks leverage a mix of the preceding techniques — for example, utilizing a list of common last names, or performing a brute force attack technology that dramatically improves its efficiency by leveraging knowledge about how users often form passwords.

>> **Malware:** If crooks manage to get malware onto someone's device, it may capture passwords. (For more details, see the section on malware, earlier in this chapter.)

>> **Network sniffing:** If someone transmits his or her password to a site without proper encryption while using a public Wi-Fi network, a criminal using the same network may be able to see that password in transit — as can potentially other criminals connected to networks along the path from the user to the site in question.

>> **Credential stuffing:** In credential stuffing, someone attempts to log in to one site using usernames and passwords combinations stolen from another site.

You can utilize passwords and a password strategy that can help defeat all these techniques —see Chapter 7.

REMEMBER

Exploiting Maintenance Difficulties

Maintaining computer systems is no trivial matter. Software vendors often release updates, many of which may impact other programs running on a machine. Yet, some patches are absolutely critical to be installed in a timely fashion because they fix bugs in software — bugs that may introduce exploitable security vulnerabilities. The conflict between security and following proper maintenance procedures is a never-ending battle — and security doesn't often win.

As a result, the vast majority of computers aren't kept up to date. Even people who do enable automatic updates on their devices may not be up to date — both because checks for updates are done periodically, not every second of every day, and because not all software offers automatic updating. Furthermore, sometimes updates to one piece of software introduce vulnerabilities into another piece of software running on the same device.

Advanced Attacks

If you listen to the news during a report of a major cyberbreach, you'll frequently hear commentators referring to advanced attacks. While some cyberattacks are clearly more complex than others and require greater technical prowess to launch, no specific, objective definition of an advanced attack exists. That said, from a subjective perspective, you may consider any attack that requires a significant investment in research and development to be successfully executed to be advanced. Of course, the definition of significant investment is also subjective. In some cases, R&D expenditures are so high and attacks are so sophisticated that there is near universal agreement that an attack was advanced. Some experts consider any zero-day attack to be advanced, but others disagree.

Advanced attacks may be opportunistic, targeted, or a combination of both.

Opportunistic attacks are attacks aimed at as many possible targets as possible in order to find some that are susceptible to the attack that was launched. The attacker doesn't have a list of predefined targets — his targets are effectively any and all reachable systems that are vulnerable to the attack that he is launching. These attacks are similar to someone firing a massive shotgun in an area with many targets in the hope that one or more pellets will hit a target that it can penetrate.

Targeted attacks are attacks that target a specific party and typically involve utilizing a series of attack techniques until one eventually succeeds in penetrating into the target. Additional attacks may be launched subsequently in order to move around within the target's systems.

Opportunistic attacks

The goal of most opportunistic attacks is usually to make money — which is why the attackers don't care whose systems they breach; money is the same regardless of whose systems are breached in order to make it.

Furthermore, in many cases, opportunistic attackers may not care about hiding the fact that a breach occurred — especially after they've had time to monetize the breach, for example, by selling lists of passwords or credit card numbers that they stole.

While not all opportunistic attacks are advanced, some certainly are.

Opportunistic attacks are quite different than targeted attacks.

Targeted attacks

When it comes to targeted attacks, successfully breaching any systems not on the target list isn't considered even a minor success.

For example, if a Russian operative is assigned the mission to hack into the Democratic and Republican parties' email systems and steal copies of all the email on the parties' email servers, his or her mission is going to be deemed a success only if he achieves those exact aims. If he manages to steal $1 million from an online bank using the same hacking techniques that he is directing at his targets, it will not change a failure to breach the intended targets into even a small success. Likewise, if the goal of an attacker launching a targeted attack is to take down the website of a former employer that fired him, taking down other websites doesn't accomplish anything in the attacker's mind.

Because such attackers need to breach their targets no matter how well defended those parties may be, targeted attacks often utilize advanced attack methods — for example, exploiting vulnerabilities not known to the public or to the vendors who would need to fix them.

As you may surmise, advanced targeted attacks are typically carried out by parties with much greater technical prowess than those who carry out opportunistic attacks. Often, but not always, the goal of targeted attacks is to steal data undetected or to inflict serious damage — not to make money. After all, if one's goal is to make money, why expend resources targeting a well-defended site? Take an opportunistic approach and go after the most poorly defended, relevant sites.

Some advanced threats that are used in targeted attacks are described as *advanced persistent threats* (APTs):

>> **Advanced:** Uses advanced hacking techniques, likely with a major budget to support R&D

>> **Persistent:** Keeps trying different techniques to breach a targeted system and won't move on to target some other system just because the initial target is well protected

>> **Threat:** Has the potential to inflict serious damage

Blended (opportunistic and targeted) attacks

Another type of advanced attack is the opportunistic, semi-targeted attack.

If a criminal wants to steal credit card numbers, for example, he may not care whether he successfully steals an equivalent number of active numbers from Best Buy, Walmart, or Barnes & Noble. All that he or she likely cares about is obtaining credit card numbers — from whom the numbers are pilfered isn't relevant.

At the same time, launching attacks against sites that don't have credit card data is a waste of the attacker's time and resources.

Chapter **3**

Bad Guys and Accidental Bad Guys: The Folks You Must Defend Against

Many centuries ago, the Chinese military strategist and philosopher, Sun Tzu, wrote

If you know the enemy and know yourself, you need not fear the result of a hundred battles.

If you know yourself but not the enemy, for every victory gained you will also suffer a defeat.

If you know neither the enemy nor yourself, you will succumb in every battle.

As has been the case since ancient times, knowing your enemy is critical for your own defense.

Such wisdom remains true in the age of digital security. While Chapter 2 covers many of the threats posed by cyber-enemies, this chapter covers the enemies themselves:

>> Who are they?

>> Why do they launch attacks?

>> How do they profit from attacks?

You also find out about nonmalicious attackers — both people and inanimate parties who can inflict serious damage even without any intent to do harm.

Bad Guys and Good Guys Are Relative Terms

Albert Einstein famously said that "Everything is relative," and that concept certainly holds true when it comes to understanding who the "good" guys and "bad" guys are online.

As someone seeking to defend himself or herself against cyberattacks, for example, you may view Russian hackers seeking to compromise your computer in order to use it to hack U.S. government sites as bad guys, but to patriotic Russian citizens, they may be heroes.

Likewise, if you live in the West, you may view the creators of *Stuxnet* — a piece of malware that destroyed Iranian centrifuges used for enriching uranium for potential use in nuclear weapons — as heroes. If you're a member of the Iranian military's cyber-defense team, however, your feelings are likely quite different. (For more on Stuxnet, see the nearby sidebar.)

If you're an American enjoying free speech online and make posts promoting atheism, Christianity, Buddhism, or Judaism and an Iranian hacker hacks your computer, you'll likely consider him to be a bad guy, but various members of the Iranian government and other fundamentalist Islamic groups may consider the hacker's actions to be a heroic attempt to stop the spread of blasphemous heresy.

In many cases, determining who is good and who is bad may be even more complicated and create deep divides between members of a single culture.

STUXNET

Stuxnet is a computer worm that was first discovered in 2010 and is believed to have inflicted, at least temporarily, serious damage to Iran's nuclear program. To date, nobody has claimed responsibility for creating Stuxnet, but the general consensus in the information security industry is that it was built as a collaborative effort by American and Israeli cyberwarriors.

Stuxnet targets programmable logic controllers (PLCs) that manage the automated control of industrial machinery, including centrifuges used to separate heavier and lighter atoms of radioactive elements. Stuxnet is believed to have compromised PLCs at an Iranian uranium-enrichment facility by programming centrifuges to spin out of control and effectively self-destruct, all while reporting that everything was functioning properly.

Stuxnet exploited four zero-day vulnerabilities that were unknown to the public and to the vendors involved at the time that Stuxnet was discovered. The worm was designed to propagate across networks — and spread like wildfire — but to go dormant if it didn't detect the relevant PLC and Siemens' software used at the Iranian facility.

For example, how would you view someone who breaks the law and infringes on the free speech of neo-Nazis by launching a crippling cyberattack against a neo-Nazi website that preaches hate against African Americans, Jews, and gays? Or someone outside of law enforcement who illegally launches attacks against sites spreading child pornography, malware, or jihadist material that encourages people to kill Americans? Do you think that everyone you know would agree with you? Would U.S. courts agree?

Before answering, please consider that in the 1977 case *National Socialist Party of America v. Village of Skokie,* the U.S. Supreme Court ruled that freedom of speech goes so far as to allow Nazis brandishing swastikas to march freely in a neighborhood in which many survivors of the Nazi Holocaust lived. Clearly, in the world of cyber, only the eye of the beholder can measure good and bad.

For the purposes of this book, therefore, you need to define who the good and bad guys are, and, as such, you should assume that the language in the book operates from your perspective as you seek to defend yourself digitally. Anyone seeking to harm your interests, for whatever reason, and regardless of what you perceive your interests to be, is, for the purposes of this book, bad.

Bad Guys Up to No Good

A group of potential attackers that is likely well-known to most people are the bad guys who are up to no good. This group consists of multiple types of attackers, with a diverse set of motivations and attack capabilities, who share one goal in common: They all seek to benefit themselves at the expense of others, including, potentially, you.

Bad guys up to no good include

>> Script kiddies

>> Kids who are not kiddies

>> Nations and states

>> Corporate spies

>> Criminals

>> Hacktivists

Script kiddies

The term *script kiddies* (sometimes shortened to skids or just kiddies) refers to people — often young — who hack, but who are able to do so only because they know how to utilize scripts and/or programs developed by others to attack computer systems. These folks lack the technological sophistication needed in order to create their own tools or to hack without the assistance of others.

Kids who are not kiddies

While script kiddies are technologically unsophisticated (see preceding section), plenty of other kids are not.

For many years, the caricature of a hacker has been a young, nerdy male, interested in computers, who hacks from his parents' home or from a dorm room at college.

In fact, the first crop of hackers targeting civilian systems included many technologically sophisticated kids interested in exploring or carrying out various mischievous tasks for bragging rights or due to curiosity.

While such attackers still exist, the percentage of attacks emanating from these attackers has dropped dramatically from a huge portion to a minute fraction of a percentage of all attacks.

Simply put, teenage hackers similar to those depicted in movies from the 1980s and 1990s may have been a significant force in the precommercial-Internet-era, but once hacking could deliver real money, expensive goods, and valuable, monetizable data, criminals seeking to profit joined the fray en masse. Furthermore, as the world grew increasingly reliant on data and more government and industrial systems were connected to the Internet, nation and states began to dramatically increase the resources that they allocated to cyber-operations from both espionage and military standpoints, further diluting the classic teenage hacker to a minute portion of today's cyberattackers.

Nations and states

Hacking by nations and states has received significant press coverage in recent years. The alleged hackings of the Democratic party email systems by Russian agents during the 2016 Presidential election campaign and the Republican party email system during the 2018 midterm elections are high profiles examples of nation state hacking.

Likewise, the Stuxnet malware is an example of nation or state-sponsored malware. (For more on Stuxnet, see the sidebar earlier in this chapter.)

That said, most nation and state cyberattacks are not nearly as high profile as those examples, do not receive media coverage, and do not target high profile targets. Often, they're not even discovered or known to anyone but the attackers!

Furthermore, in some countries, it is difficult, if not impossible, to distinguish between nation or state hacking and commercial espionage. Consider countries in which major companies are owned and operated by the government, for example. Are hackers from such companies nation or state hackers? Are such companies legitimate government targets, or is hacking them an example of corporate espionage?

Of course, nation and states that hack may also be seeking to impact public sentiment, policy decisions, and elections in other nations. Discussions of this topic have been aired via major media outlets on a regular basis since the 2016 presidential election.

Corporate spies

Unscrupulous companies sometimes utilize hacking as a way to gain competitive advantages or steal valuable intellectual property. The United States government, for example, has repetitively accused Chinese corporations of stealing the intellectual property of American businesses, costing Americans billions of dollars per year. Sometimes the process of stealing intellectual property involves hacking the home computers of employees at targeted companies with the hope that those employees will use their personal devices to connect to their employers' networks.

Criminals

Criminals have numerous reasons for launching various forms of cyberattacks:

>> **Stealing money directly:** Attacking to gain access to someone's online banking account and issue a wire transfer of money to themselves.

>> **Stealing credit card numbers, software, video, music files, and other goods:** Attacking to purchase goods or add bogus shipping instructions into a corporate system leading to products being shipped without payment ever being received by the shipper, and so on.

>> **Stealing corporate and individual data:** Attacking to obtain information that criminals can monetize in multiple ways (see the section "Monetizing Their Actions," later in this chapter).

Over the years, the type of criminals who commit online crimes has evolved from being strictly solo actors to a mix of amateurs and organized crime.

CHINESE FIRMS STEAL AMERICAN IP: UNIT 61398

In May 2014, United States federal prosecutors charged five members of the People's Liberation Army (PLA) of China with hacking four U.S. businesses and one labor union as part of their service in Unit 61398, China's cyber-warrior unit. The allegedly hacked parties included Alcoa, Allegheny Technologies, SolarWorld, and Westinghouse, all of which are major suppliers of goods to utilities, and the United Steel Workers labor union.

While the full extent of the damage to American businesses caused by the hacking remains unknown to this day, SolarWorld claimed that as a result of confidential information stolen by the hackers, a Chinese competitor appeared to have gained access to SolarWorld's proprietary technology for making solar cells more efficient. This particular case illustrates the blurred lines between nation and state and corporate espionage when it comes to Communist nations and also highlights the difficulty in bringing hackers who participate in such attacks to justice; none of the indicted parties were ever tried, because none have left China to any jurisdiction that would extradite them to the United States.

Hacktivists

Hacktivists are activists who use hacking to spread the message of their "cause" and to deliver justice to parties whom they feel aren't being otherwise punished for infractions that the activists view as crimes. Hacktivists include terrorists and rogue insiders.

Terrorists

Terrorists may hack for various purposes, including to

>> Directly inflict damage (for example, by hacking a utility and shutting off power)

>> Obtain information to use in plotting terrorist attacks (for example, hacking to find out when weapons are being transported between facilities and can be stolen)

>> Finance terrorist operations (see the earlier section on criminals)

Rogue insiders

Disgruntled employees, rogue contractors, and employees who have been financially incentivized by an unscrupulous party pose serious threats to businesses and their employees alike.

WARNING

Insiders intent on stealing data or inflicting harm are normally considered to be the most dangerous group of cyberattackers. They typically know far more than do any outsiders about what data and computer systems a company possesses, where those systems are located, how they are protected, and other information pertinent to the target systems and their potential vulnerabilities. Rogue insiders may target a businesses for one or more reasons:

>> They may seek to disrupt operations in order to lighten their own personal workloads or to help a competitor.

>> They may seek revenge for not receiving a promotion or bonus.

>> They may want to make another employee, or team of employees, look bad.

>> They may want to cause their employer financial harm.

>> They may plan on leaving and want to steal data that will be valuable in their next job or in their future endeavors.

Cyberattackers and Their Colored Hats

Cyberattackers are typically grouped based on their goals:

» **Black hat hackers** have evil intent and hack in order to steal, manipulate, and/or destroy. When the typical person thinks of a hacker, he or she is thinking of a black hat hacker.

» **White hat hackers** are ethical hackers who hack in order to test, repair, and enhance the security of systems and networks. These folks are typically computer security experts who specialize in penetration testing, and who are hired by businesses and governments to find vulnerabilities in their IT systems. A hacker is considered to be a white hat hacker only if he or she has explicit permission to hack from the owner of the systems that he or she is hacking.

» **Grey hat hackers** are hackers who do not have the malicious intent of black hat hackers, but who, at least at times, act unethically or otherwise violate anti-hacking laws. A hacker who attempts to find vulnerabilities in a system without the permission of the system's owner and who reports his or her findings to the owner without inflicting any damage to any systems that he or she scans is acting as a grey hat hacker. Grey hat hackers sometimes act as such to make money. For example, when they report vulnerabilities to system owners, they may offer to fix the problems if the owner pays them some consulting fees. Some of the hackers who many people consider to be black hat hackers are actually grey hats.

» **Green hat hackers** are novices who seek to become experts. Where a green hat falls within the white-grey-black spectrum may evolve over time, as does his or her level of experience.

» **Blue hat hackers** are paid to test software for exploitable bugs before the software is released into the market.

For the purposes of this book, black and gray hat hackers are the hackers that should primarily concern you as you seek to cyberprotect yourself and your loved ones.

Monetizing Their Actions

Many, but not all, cyberattackers seek to profit financially from their crimes. Cyberattackers can make money through cyberattacks in several ways:

>> Direct financial fraud

>> Indirect financial fraud

>> Ransomware

>> Cryptominers

Direct financial fraud

Hackers may seek to steal money directly through attacks. For example, hackers may install malware on people's computers to capture victims' online banking sessions and instruct the online banking server to send money to the criminals' accounts. Of course, criminals know that bank systems are often well-protected against such forms of fraud, so many have migrated to target less well-defended systems. For example, some criminals now focus more on capturing login credentials (usernames and passwords) to systems that store credits — for example, coffee shop apps that allow users to store prepaid card values — and steal the money effectively banked in such accounts by using it elsewhere in order to purchase goods and services. Furthermore, if criminals compromise accounts of users that have auto-refill capabilities configured, criminals can repetitively steal the value after each auto-reload. Likewise, criminals may seek to compromise people's frequent traveler accounts and transfer the points to other accounts, purchase goods, or obtain plane tickets and hotel rooms that they sell to other people for cash. Criminals can also steal credit card numbers and either use them or quickly sell them to other crooks who then use them to commit fraud.

REMEMBER

Direct is not a black-and-white concept; there are many shades of grey.

Indirect financial fraud

Sophisticated cybercriminals often avoid cybercrimes that entail direct financial fraud because these schemes often deliver relatively small dollar amounts, can be undermined by the compromised parties even after the fact (for example, by reversing fraudulent transactions or invalidating an order for goods made with stolen information), and create relatively significant risks of getting caught. Instead, they may seek to obtain data that they can monetize for indirect fraud. Several examples of such crimes include

>> Profiting off illegal trading of securities

>> Stealing credit card information

>> Stealing goods

>> Stealing data

Profiting off illegal trading of securities

Cybercriminals can make fortunes through illegal trading of securities, such as stocks, bonds, and options, in several ways:

>> **Pump and dump:** Criminals hack a company and steal data, short the company's stock, and then leak the company's data online to cause the company's stock price to drop, at which point they buy the stock (to cover the short sale) at a lower price than they previously sold it.

>> **Bogus press releases and social media posts:** Criminals either buy or sell a company's stock and then release a bogus press release or otherwise spread fake news about a company by hacking into the company's marketing systems or social media accounts and issuing false bad or good news via the company's official channels.

>> **Insider information:** A criminal may seek to steal drafts of press releases from a public company's PR department in order to see whether any surprising quarterly earnings announcements will occur. If the crook finds that a company is going to announce much better numbers than expected by Wall Street, he or she may purchase *call options* (options that give the crook the right to purchase the stock of the company at a certain price), which can skyrocket in value after such an announcement. Likewise, if a company is about to announce some bad news, the crook may short the company's stock or purchase *put options* (options that give the crook the right to sell the stock of the company at a certain price), which, for obvious reasons, can skyrocket in value if the market price of the associated stock drops.

Discussions of indirect financial fraud of the aforementioned types is not theoretical or the result of paranoid or conspiracy theories; criminals have already been caught engaging in precisely such behavior. These types of scams are often also less risky to criminals than directly stealing money, as it is difficult for regulators to detect such crimes as they happen, and it is nearly impossible for anyone to reverse any relevant transactions. For sophisticated cybercriminals, the lower risks of getting caught coupled with the relatively high chances of success translate into a potential gold mine.

Stealing credit card information

As often appears in news reports, many criminals seek to steal credit card numbers. Thieves can use these numbers to purchase goods or services without paying. Some criminals tend to purchase electronic gift cards, software serial numbers, or other semi-liquid or liquid assets that they then resell for cash to unsuspecting people, while others purchase actual hard goods and services that they may have delivered to locations such as empty houses, where they can easily pick up the items.

Other criminals don't use the credit cards that they steal. Instead, they sell the numbers on the dark web (that is, portions of the Internet that can be accessed only when using technology that grants anonymity to those using it) to criminals who have the infrastructure to maximally exploit the credit cards quickly before people report fraud on the accounts and the cards are blocked.

Stealing goods

Besides the forms of theft of goods described in the preceding section, some criminals seek to find information about orders of high-value, small, liquid items, such as jewelry. In some cases, their goal is to steal the items when the items are delivered to the recipients rather than to create fraudulent transactions.

Stealing data

Some criminals steal data so they can use it to commit various financial crimes. Other criminals steal data to sell it to others or leak it to the public. Stolen data from a business, for example, may be extremely valuable to an unscrupulous competitor.

Ransomware

Ransomware is computer malware that prevents users from accessing their files until they pay a ransom to some criminal enterprise. This type of cyberattack alone has already netted criminals billions of dollars (yes, that is billions with a *b*) and endangered many lives as infected hospital computer systems became inaccessible to doctors. Ransomware remains a growing threat, with criminals constantly improving the technical capabilities and earning potential of their cyberweapons. Criminals are, for example, crafting ransomware that, in an effort to obtain larger returns on investment, infects a computer and attempts to search through connected networks and devices to find the most sensitive systems and data. Then, instead of kidnapping the data that it first encountered, the ransomware activates and prevents access to the most valuable information.

REMEMBER

Criminals understand that the more important the information is to its owner, the greater the likelihood that a victim will be willing to pay a ransom, and the higher the maximum ransom that will be willingly paid is likely to be.

Ransomware is growing increasingly stealthy and often avoids detection by antivirus software. Furthermore, the criminals who use ransomware are often launching targeted attacks against parties that they know have the ability to pay decent ransoms. Criminals know, for example, that the average American is far more likely to pay $200 for a ransom than the average person living in China. Likewise, they often target environments in which going offline has serious consequences — a hospital, for example, can't afford to be without its patient records system for any significant period of time.

Cryptominers

A *cryptominer*, in the context of malware, refers to software that usurps some of an infected computer's resources in order to use them to perform the complex mathematical calculations needed to create new units of cryptocurrency. The currency that is created is transferred to the criminal operating the cryptominer. Many modern day cryptominer malware variants utilize groups of infected machines working in concert to do the mining.

Because cryptominers create money for criminals without the need for any involvement by their human victims, cybercriminals, especially those who lack the sophistication to launch high-stakes targeted ransomware attacks, have increasingly gravitated to cryptominers as a quick way to monetize cyberattacks.

While the value of cryptocurrencies fluctuates wildly (at least as of the time of the writing of this chapter), some relatively unsophisticated cryptocurrency mining networks are believed to net their operators more than $30,000 per month.

Dealing with Nonmalicious Threats

While some potential attackers are intent on benefiting at your expense, others have no intentions of inflicting harm. However, these parties can innocently inflict dangers that can be even greater than those posed by hostile actors.

Human error

Perhaps the greatest cybersecurity danger of all — whether for an individual, business, or government entity — is the possibility of human error. Nearly all major breaches covered in the media over the past decade were made possible, at least in part, because of some element of human error. In fact, human error is often necessary for the hostile actors to succeed with their attacks — a phenomenon about which they're well aware.

Humans: The Achilles' heel of cybersecurity

Why are humans so often the weak point in the cybersecurity chain — making the mistakes that enable massive breaches? The answer is quite simple.

Consider how much technology has advanced in recent years. Electronic devices that are ubiquitous today were the stuff of science-fiction books and movies just one or two generations ago. In many cases, technology has even surpassed predictions about the future — today's phones are much more powerful and convenient than Maxwell Smart's shoe-phone, and Dick Tracy's watch would not even be perceived as advanced enough to be a modern day toy when compared with devices that today cost under $100.

Security technology has also advanced dramatically over time. Every year multiple new products are launched, and many new, improved versions of existing technologies appear on the market. The intrusion detection technology of today, for example, is so much better than that of even one decade ago that even classifying them into the same category of product offering is questionable.

On the flip side, however, consider the human brain. It took tens of thousands of years for human brains to evolve from that of earlier species — no fundamental improvement takes place during a human lifetime, or even within centuries of generations coming and going. As such, security technology advances far more rapidly than the human mind.

Furthermore, advances in technology often translate into humans needing to interact with, and understand how to properly utilize a growing number of increasingly complex devices, systems, and software. Given human limitations, the chances of people making significant mistakes keep going up over time.

The increasing demand for brainpower that advancing technology places on people is observable even at a most basic level. How many passwords did your grandparents need to know when they were your age? How many did your parents need? How many do you need? And, how easily could remote hackers crack passwords and exploit them for gain in the era of your grandparents? Your parents? Yourself?

Most of your grandparents likely had no more than one or two passwords when they were your age — if not zero. And, none of these passwords were hackable by any remote computers — meaning that both selecting and remembering passwords was trivial, and did not expose them to risk. Today, however, you're likely to have many dozens of passwords, most of which can be hacked remotely using automated tools, dramatically increasing the relevant risk.

TIP

The bottom line: You must internalize that human error poses a great risk to your cybersecurity — and act accordingly.

Social engineering

In the context of information security, *social engineering* refers to the psychological manipulation of human beings into performing actions that they otherwise would not perform and which are usually detrimental to their interests.

Examples of social engineering include

>> Calling someone on the telephone and tricking that person into believing that the caller is a member of the IT department and requesting that the person reset his email password

>> Sending phishing emails (see Chapter 2)

>> Sending CEO fraud emails (see Chapter 2)

While the criminals launching social engineering attacks may be malicious in intent, the actual parties that create the vulnerability or inflict the damage typically do so without any intent to harm the target. In the first example, the user who resets his or her password believes that he or she is doing so to help the IT department repair email problems, not that he or she is allowing hackers into the mail system. Likewise, someone who falls prey to a phishing or CEO fraud scam is obviously not seeking to help the hacker who is attacking him or her.

Other forms of human error that undermine cybersecurity include people accidentally deleting information, accidentally misconfiguring systems, inadvertently infecting a computer with malware, mistakenly disabling security technologies, and other innocent errors that enable criminals to commit all sorts of mischievous acts.

WARNING

The bottom line is never to underestimate both the inevitability of, and power of, human mistakes — including your own. You will make mistakes, and so will I — everyone does. So, on important matters, always double-check to make sure that everything is the way it should be.

External disasters

As described in Chapter 2, cybersecurity includes maintaining your data's confidentiality, integrity, and availability. One of the greatest risks to availability — which also creates secondhand risks to its confidentiality and integrity — is external disasters. These disasters fall into two categories: naturally occurring and man-made.

Natural disasters

A large number of people live in areas prone to some degree to various forms of natural disasters. From hurricanes to tornados to floods to fires, nature can be brutal — and can corrupt, or even destroy, computers and the data that the machines house.

Continuity planning and disaster recovery are, therefore, taught as part of the certification process for cybersecurity professionals. The reality is that, statistically speaking, most people will encounter and experience at least one form of natural disaster at some point in their lives. As such, if you want to protect your systems and data, you must plan accordingly for such an eventuality.

A strategy of storing backups on hard drives at two different sites may be a poor strategy, for example, if both sites consist of basements located in homes within flood zones.

Man-made environmental problems

Of course, nature is not the only party creating external problems. Humans can cause floods and fires, and man-made disasters can sometimes be worse than those that occur naturally. Furthermore, power outages and power spikes, protests and riots, strikes, terrorist attacks, and Internet failures and telecom disruptions can also impact the availability of data and systems.

Businesses that backed up their data from systems located in New York's World Trade Center to systems in the nearby World Financial Center learned the hard way after 9/11 the importance of keeping backups outside the vicinity of the corresponding systems, as the World Financial Center remained inaccessible for quite some time after the World Trade Center was destroyed.

Risks posed by governments and businesses Some cybersecurity risks — including, one might reasonably argue, the most dangerous ones to individuals' privacy — are not created by criminals, but, rather, by businesses and government entities, even in Western democracies.

Cyberwarriors and cyberspies

Modern-day governments often have tremendous armies of cyberwarriors at their disposal.

Such teams often attempt to discover vulnerabilities in software products and systems to use them to attack and spy on adversaries, as well as to use as a law enforcement tool.

Doing so, however, creates risks for individuals and businesses. Instead of reporting vulnerabilities to the relevant vendors, various government agencies often seek to keep the vulnerabilities secret — meaning that they leave their citizens, enterprises, and other government entities vulnerable to attack by adversaries who may discover the same vulnerability.

Additionally, governments may use their teams of hackers to help fight crime — or, in some cases, abuse their cyber-resources to retain control over their citizens and preserve the ruling party's hold on power. Even in the United States, in the aftermath of 9/11, the government implemented various programs of mass data collection that impacted law-abiding U.S. citizens. If any of the databases that were assembled had been pilfered by foreign powers, U.S. citizens may have been put at risk of all sorts of cyberproblems.

The dangers of governments creating troves of data exploits are not theoretical. In recent years, several powerful cyberweapons believed to have been created by a U.S. government intelligence agency surfaced online, clearly having been stolen by someone whose interests were not aligned with those of the agency. To this day, it remains unclear whether those weapons were used against American interests by whoever stole them.

The impotent Fair Credit Reporting Act

Many Americans are familiar with the Fair Credit Reporting Act (FCRA), a set of laws initially passed nearly half a century ago and updated on multiple occasions. The FCRA regulates the collection and management of credit reports and the data used therein. The FCRA was established to ensure that people are treated fairly, and that credit-related information remains both accurate and private.

According to the Fair Credit Reporting Act, credit reporting bureaus must remove various forms of adverse information from people's credit reports after specific time frames elapse. If you don't pay a credit card bill on time while you're in college, for example, it's against the law for the late payment to be listed on your report and factored against you into your credit score when you apply for a mortgage two decades later. The law even allows people who declare bankruptcy in order to start over to have records of their bankruptcy removed. After all, what good would starting over be if a bankruptcy forever prevented someone from having a clean slate?

Today, however, various technology companies undermine the protections of the FCRA. How hard is it for a bank's loan officer to find online databases of court filings related to bankruptcies by doing a simple Google search and then looking into such databases for information relevant to a prospective borrower? Or to see whether any foreclosure records from any time are associated with a name matching that of someone seeking a loan? Doing either takes just seconds, and no laws prohibit such databases from including records old enough to be gone from credit reports, and, at least in the United States, none prohibit Google from showing links to such databases when someone searches on the name of someone involved with such activities decades earlier.

Expunged records are no longer really expunged

The justice system has various laws that, in many cases, allow young people to keep minor offenses off of their permanent criminal records and affords judges the ability to seal certain files and to expunge other forms of information from people's records. These laws help people start over, and many wonderful, productive members of society may not have turned out as they did without these protections.

But what good are such laws if a prospective employer can find the supposedly purged information within seconds by doing a Google search on a candidate's name? Google returns results from local police blotters and court logs published in local newspapers that are now archived online. Someone who was cited for a minor offense and then had all the charges against him or her dropped can still suffer professional and personal repercussions decades later — even though he or she was never indicted, tried, or found guilty of any offense.

Social Security numbers

A generation ago, it was common to use Social Security numbers as college ID numbers. The world was so different back then that for privacy reasons, many schools even posted people's grades using Social Security numbers rather than using students' names! Yes, seriously.

Should all students who went to college in the 1970s, 1980s, or early 1990s really have their Social Security numbers exposed to the public because college materials that were created in the pre-web world have now been archived online and are indexed in some search engines? To make matters worse, some parties authenticate users by asking for the last four digits of people's phone numbers, which can often be found in a fraction of a second via a cleverly crafted Google or Bing search. If it is common knowledge that such information has been rendered insecure by previously acceptable behaviors, why does the government still utilize Social Security numbers and treat them as if they were still private?

Likewise, online archives of church, synagogue, and other community newsletters often contain birth announcements listing not only the name of the baby and his or her parents, but the hospital in which the child was born, the date of birth, and the grandparents' names. How many security questions for a particular user of a computer system can be undermined by a crook finding just one such announcement? All of these examples show how advances in technology can undermine our privacy and cybersecurity — even legally undermining laws that have been established to protect us.

THE RIGHT TO BE FORGOTTEN

The *right to be forgotten* refers to the right of people to either have certain adverse data about them blocked from being Internet accessible or to have entries removed from search engine results on their names if the information in those entries is outdated or irrelevant. Today, residents of the European Union enjoy the latter of these two rights; Americans enjoy neither.

The rationale behind the right to be forgotten is that it is clearly in society's interest that people not be forever negatively judged, stigmatized, and/or punished as a consequence of some long-ago minor infraction that doesn't represent the nature of their present self. For example, if a 45-year-old professional with a stellar professional and personal history and no criminal record applies for a job, it's unfair to him or her, and detrimental to society as a whole, if he or she would lose that opportunity because search engine results seen by a potential employer show that he or she was charged with disorderly conduct at age 18 for a nonviolent and non-damaging noisy prank carried out when he or she was an immature high school senior nearly three decades prior.

Various nations outside of the EU are also adopting various forms of the right to be forgotten: A court in India — a country that, technically speaking, has no laws on the books guaranteeing anyone the right to be forgotten — has ruled in favor of a plaintiff seeking the removal of accurate information that would reasonably have impacted her reputation, apparently adopting a position that people have an inherent right to prevent the spread of adverse information that may not be outdated, but that is likely to inflict harm on them while providing little benefit to anyone else.

Adopting some form of a right to be forgotten can help reduce some of the cybersecurity and privacy risks discussed in this chapter, by making it more difficult for criminals to obtain the answers to challenge questions, to launch social engineering attacks, and so on. It would also restore some of the protections offered by laws, such as the FCRA, that have been rendered impotent by technology.

Social media platforms

One group of technology businesses that generate serious risks to cybersecurity are social media platforms.

Cybercriminals increasingly scan social media — sometimes with automated tools — to find information that they can use against companies and their employees. Attackers then leverage the information that they find to craft all sorts of attacks, such as one involving the delivery of ransomware. (For more on ransomware, see the relevant section earlier in this chapter.) For example, they may craft highly effective spear-phishing emails credible enough to trick employees into clicking on URLs to ransomware-delivering websites or into opening ransomware-infected attachments.

The number of virtual kidnapping scams — in which criminals contact the family of a person who is off the grid due to being on a flight or the like and demand a ransom in exchange for releasing the person they claim to have kidnapped — has skyrocketed in the era of social media, as criminals often can discern from looking at users' social media posts both when to act and whom to contact.

Google's all-knowing computers

One of the ways that computer systems verify that a person is who he or she claims to be is by asking questions to which few people other than the legitimate party would know the correct answers. In many cases, someone who can successfully answer "How much is your current mortgage payment?" and "Who was your seventh grade science teacher?" is more likely to be the authentic party than an impersonator.

MOTHER'S MAIDEN NAME

How many times have you been asked your mother's maiden name as a security question in order to prove your identity?

Besides the fact that guessing any common English name will provide a criminal with some hits if he or she is attempting to impersonate people living in the United States, social media has truly undermined this form of challenge question. Cyberattackers can obtain this information from social media in many ways, even if people don't list their relatives in their profiles on any platform — for example, by trying the last names most commonly found among someone's Facebook friends. For many folks, one of those names will be their mother's maiden name.

But the all-knowing Google engine undermines such authentication. Many pieces of information that were difficult to obtain quickly just a few year ago can now be obtained almost instantaneously via a Google search. In many cases, the answers to security questions used by various websites to help authenticate users are, for criminals, "just one click away."

While more advanced sites may consider the answer to security questions to be wrong if entered more than a few seconds after the question is posed, most sites impose no such restrictions — meaning that anyone who knows how to use Google can undermine many modern authentication systems.

Mobile device location tracking

Likewise, Google itself can correlate all sorts of data that it obtains from phones running Android or its Maps and Waze applications — which likely means from the majority of people in the Western World. Of course, the providers of other apps that run on millions of phones and that have permission to access location data can do the same as well. Any party that tracks where a person is and for how long he or she is there may have created a database that can be used for all sorts of nefarious purposes — including undermining knowledge-based authentication, facilitating social engineering attacks, undermining the confidentiality of secret projects, and so on. Even if the firm that creates the database has no malicious intent, rogue employees or hackers who gain access to, or steal, the database pose serious threats.

Such tracking also undermines privacy. Google knows, for example, who is regularly going into a chemotherapy facility, where people sleep (for most people, the time that they are asleep is the only time that their phones do not move at all for many hours), and various other information from which all sorts of sensitive extrapolations can be made.

Defending against These Attackers

REMEMBER

It is important to understand that there is no such thing as 100 percent cybersecurity. Rather, adequate cybersecurity is defined by understanding what risks exist, which ones are adequately mitigated, and which ones persist.

Defenses that are adequate to shield against some risks and attackers are inadequate to protect against others. What may suffice for reasonably protecting a home computer, for example, may be wildly inadequate to shield an online banking server. The same is true of risks that are based on who uses a system:

A cellphone used by the President of the United States for speaking with his or her advisors, for example, obviously requires better security than the cellphone used by the average sixth grader.

Addressing Risks through Various Methods

Not all risks require attention, and not all risks that do require attention require addressing in the same manner. You may decide, for example, that buying insurance is sufficient protection against a particular risk or that the risk is so unlikely and/or de minimis so as to be not worth the likely cost of addressing it.

On the other hand, sometimes risks are so great that a person or business may decide to abandon a particular effort altogether in order to avoid the associated risk. For example, if the cost of adequately securing a small business would consistently be more than the profit that the business would have made without the security, it may be unwise to open up shop in the first place.

2

Improving Your Own Personal Security

Understand why you may be less cybersecure than you think.

Find out how to protect against various cyberdangers.

Learn about physical security as it relates to cybersecurity.

Chapter **4**

Evaluating Your Current Cybersecurity Posture

The first step in improving your protection against cyberthreats is to understand exactly what it is that you need to protect. Only after you have a good grasp on that information can you evaluate what is actually needed to deliver adequate security and determine whether you have any gaps to address.

You must consider what data you have, from whom you must protect it, and how sensitive it is to you. What would happen if, for example, it were publicized on the Internet for the world to see? Then you can evaluate how much you're willing to spend — timewise and moneywise — on protecting it.

Identifying Ways You May Be Less than Secure

You need to understand the various areas in which your current cybersecurity posture may suffer so that you can figure out how to address the issues and ensure that you're adequately protected. You must inventory all items that could contain sensitive data, become launching pads for attacks, and so on.

Your home computer(s)

Your home computers may suffer from one or major types of potential problems relevant to cybersecurity:

>> **Breached:** A hacker may have penetrated your home computer and be able to use it much as you can — view its contents, use it to contact other machines, leverage it as a staging ground from which to attack other machines and penetrate them, mine cryptocurrency, view data on your network, and so on.

>> **Malware:** Similar to the dangers created by human invaders, a computer-based attacker — that is *malware* — may be present on your home computer, enabling a criminal to use the computer much as you can — view the computer's contents, contact other machines, mine cryptocurrency, and so on — as well as read data from your network traffic and to infect other computers on your network and outside of it.

>> **Shared computers:** When you share a computer with other people — including your significant other and your children — you expose your device to the risk that the other folks using it won't practice proper cyber-hygiene to the same level that you do and, as a result, expose the device to infection by malware or a breach by some hacker or unintentionally inflict self-damage.

>> **Connections to other networks and storage applications:** If you connect your computer via a virtual private network (VPN) to other networks, such as the network at your place of employment, network-borne malware on those remote networks or hackers lurking on devices connected to those networks can potentially attack your network and local devices as well. In some cases, similar risks may exist if you run applications that connect your computer to remote services, such as remote storage systems.

>> **Physical security risks:** As discussed in detail in Chapter 5, the physical location of your computer may endanger it and its contents.

Your mobile devices

From an information security standpoint, mobile devices are inherently risky because they

>> Are constantly connected to the insecure Internet

>> Often have confidential information stored on them

>> Are used to communicate with many people and systems, both of which are groups that include parties who aren't always trustworthy, via the Internet (which is also inherently not trustworthy)

>> Can receive inbound messages from parties with which you have never interacted prior to receiving the messages in question

>> Often don't run full-blown security software due to resource limitations

>> Can easily be lost, stolen, or accidentally damaged or destroyed

>> Connect to insecure and untrusted Wi-Fi networks

Your gaming systems

Gaming systems are computers and, as computers, can sometimes be exploited for various nefarious purposes in addition to game-specific mischief. If the devices contain software vulnerabilities, for example, they may be able to be hacked and commandeered, and software other than the gaming system can potentially be run on them.

Your Internet of Things (IoT) devices

As discussed in detail in Chapter 17, the world of the connected computing has changed dramatically in recent years. Not that long ago, the only devices that were connected to the Internet were classic computers — desktops, laptops, and servers that could be used for many different computing purposes. Today, however, we live in a different world.

From smartphones to security cameras, refrigerators to cars, and coffeemakers to exercise equipment, electronic devices of all types now have computers embedded within them, and many of these computers are perpetually connected to the Internet.

The Internet of Things (IoT), as the ecosystem of connected devices is commonly known, has been growing exponentially over the past few years, yet the security of such devices is often inadequate.

Many IoT devices do not contain adequate security technology to secure themselves against breaches. Even those that do are often not properly configured to be secure. Hackers can exploit IoT devices to spy on you, steal your data, hack or launch denial-of-service attacks against other devices, and inflict various other forms of damage.

Your networking equipment

Networking equipment can be hacked to route traffic to bogus sites, capture data, launch attacks, block Internet access, and so on.

Your work environment

You may have sensitive data in your work environment — and you can be put at risk by colleagues at work as well.

For example, if you bring any electronic devices to work, connect them to a network at work, and then bring those devices home and connect them to your home network, malware and other problems can potentially spread to your device from a device belonging to your employer or to any one or more of your colleagues using the same infrastructure and then later spread from your device to other machines on your home network.

Social engineering

Every person in your family and social circle poses risks to you as a source of information about you that can potentially be exploited for social engineering purposes. I discuss social engineering in detail in Chapter 8.

Identifying Risks

To secure anything, you must know what it is that you're securing; securing an environment is difficult, if not impossible, to do if you do not know what is in that environment.

To secure yourself, therefore, you must understanding what assets — both those that are in digital formats and those in related physical formats — you have, and what it is that you seek to protect. You must also understand what risks you face to those assets.

TIP

Inventorying such assets is usually pretty simple for individuals: Make a written list of all devices that you attach to your network. You can often get a list by logging into your router and looking at the Connected devices section. Of course, you may have some devices that you connect to your network only occasionally or that must be secured even though they do not attach to your network, so be sure to include those on your list as well.

Add to that list — in a separate section — all storage devices that you use, including external hard drives, flash drives, and memory cards.

Write or print the list; forgetting even a single device can lead to problems.

Protecting against Risks

After you identify what you must protect (see preceding section), you must develop and implement appropriate safeguards for those items to keep them as secure as appropriate and limit the impact of a potential breach.

In the context of home users, protecting includes providing barriers to anyone seeking to access your digital and physical assets without proper authorization to do so, establishing (even informal) processes and procedures to protect your sensitive data, and creating backups of all configurations and basic system restore points.

Basic elements of protection for most individuals include

>> Perimeter defense

>> Firewall/router

>> Security software

>> Your physical computer(s)

>> Backup

Perimeter defense

Defending your cyber-perimeter is essentially the digital equivalent of building a moat around a castle — attempting to stop anyone from entering except through authorized pathways while under the watchful eyes of guards.

You can build that digital moat by never connecting any computer directly to your Internet modem. Instead connect a firewall/router to the modem and connect computers to the firewall/router. (If your modem contains a firewall/router, then it serves both purposes; if your connection is to the firewall/router portion, not to the modem itself, that is okay.) Normally, the connections between firewalls and modems are wired — that is, are achieved using a physical network cable.

Firewall/router

Modern routers used in home environments include firewalling capabilities that block most forms of inbound traffic when such traffic isn't generated as the result of activities initiated by devices protected by the firewall. That is, a firewall will block outsiders from trying to contact a computer inside your home, but it will not block a web server from responding if a computer inside your home requests a web page from the server. Routers use multiple technologies to achieve such protection.

One important technology of note is Network Address Translation, which allows computers on your home network to use Internet Protocol (IP) addresses that are invalid for use on the Internet and can be used only on private networks. To the Internet, all the devices appear to use one address, which is that of the firewall.

The following recommendations help your router/firewall protect you:

REMEMBER

>> **Keep your router up to date.** Make sure to install all updates before initially putting your router into use and regularly check for new updates (unless your router has an auto-update feature, in which case you should leverage that feature).

An unpatched vulnerability in your router can allow outsiders to enter your network.

>> **Change the default administrative password on your firewall/router to a strong password that only you know.** Write it down and put the paper in a safe or safe deposit box. Practice logging into the router — and continue doing so on a regular basis so that you do not forget the password.

>> **Don't use the default name provided by your router for your Wi-Fi network name (its SSID).** Create a new name.

>> **Configure your Wi-Fi network to use encryption of at least the WPA2 standard.** This is the current standard at the time of the writing of this book.

>> **Establish a password that any device is required to know to join your Wi-Fi network.** Make that password a strong one. For information on creating strong passwords that you can easily remember, see Chapter 7.

>> **If all your wireless devices know how to use the modern 802.11ac and 802.11n wireless networking protocols, disable older Wi-Fi protocols that your router supports** — for example, 802.11b and 802.11g.

>> **Enable MAC address filtering or make sure that all members of your household know that nobody is to connect anything to the wired network without your permission.** At least in theory, MAC address filtering prevents any device from connecting to the network if you do not previously

configure the router to allow it to connect — do not allow people to connect insecure devices to the network without first securing them.

>> **Locate your wireless router centrally within your home.** Doing so will provide better signal for you and will also reduce the strength of the signal that you provide to people outside your home who may be seeking to piggyback onto your network.

>> **Do not enable remote access to your router.** You want the router to be manageable only via connections from devices that it is protecting, not from the outside world. The convenience of remote management of a home firewall is rarely worth the increase in security risk created by enabling such a feature.

>> **Maintain a current list of devices connected to your network.** Also include devices that you allow to connect to your network.

>> **For any guests for whom you want to give network access, turn on the guest network capability of the router and, as with the private network, activate encryption and require strong password.** Give guests access to that guest network and not to your primary network. The same applies for anyone else to whom you must give Internet access but whose security you do not fully trust, including family members, such as children.

>> **If you're sufficiently technically knowledgeable to turn off DHCP and change the default IP address range used by the router for the internal network, do so.** Doing so interferes with some automated hacking tools and provides other security benefits. If you're not familiar with such concepts or don't have a clue what the aforementioned sentence means, simply ignore this paragraph. In this case, the security benefits of the recommendation are likely going to be outweighed by the problems that you may encounter due to the additional technical complexity that turning off DHCP and changing the default IP address range can create.

Security software

How should you use security software to protect yourself?

>> Use security software on all your computers and mobile devices. The software should contain at least antivirus and personal device firewall capabilities.

>> Use antispam software on any device on which you read email.

>> Enable remote wipe on any and every mobile device.

>> Require a strong password to log in to any computer and mobile device.

>> Enable auto-updates whenever possible and keep your devices updated.

Your physical computer(s)

To physically secure your computers:

>> **Control physical access to your computer and keep it in a safe location.** If anyone entering your home can get to a machine, for example, that device can be relatively easily stolen, used, or damaged without your knowledge.

>> **If possible, do not share your computer with family members.** If you must share your computer, create separate accounts for each family member and do not give any other users of the device administrative privileges on it.

>> **Do not rely on deleting data before throwing out, recycling, donating, or selling an old device.** Use a multiwipe erasure system for all hard drives and solid state drives. Ideally, remove the storage media from the computer before getting rid of the device — and physically destroy the storage media.

Backup

Back up regularly. For more on backups, see Chapter 13.

Detecting

Detecting refers to implementing mechanisms by which you can detect cybersecurity events as quickly as possible after they commence. While most home users do not have the budget to purchase specialized products for the purpose of detection, that does not mean that the detection phase of security should be ignored.

Today, most personal computer security software has detection capabilities of various types. Make sure that every device that you manage has security software on it that looks for possible intrusions, for example, and see Chapter 11 for more details on detecting possible breaches.

Responding

Responding refers to acting in response to a cybersecurity incident. Most security software will automatically prompt users to act if they detect potential problems.

For more on responding, see Chapter 12.

Recovering

Recovering refers to restoring an impacted computer, network, or device — and all of its relevant capabilities — to its fully functioning, proper state after a cybersecurity event occurs. See Chapters 12, 14, and 15 for more on recovering.

REMEMBER

Ideally, a formal, prioritized plan for how to recover should be documented before it is needed. Most home users do not actually create one, but doing so can be extremely beneficial. In most home cases, such a plan will be less than one page long.

Improving

Shame on anyone who does not learn from his or her own mistakes. Every cybersecurity incident offers lessons learned that can be put into action to reduce risk in the future. For examples of learning from mistakes, see Chapter 19.

Evaluating Your Current Security Measures

After you know what you need to protect and how to protect such items, you can determine the difference between what you need and what you currently have in place.

The following sections cover some things to consider. Not all of the following apply in every case:

Software

When it comes to software and cybersecurity, think about the following questions for each device:

>> Are all the software packages (including the operating system itself) on your computer legally obtained — and known to be legitimate versions?

>> Are all the software packages (including the operating system itself) currently supported by their respective vendors?

>> Are all the software packages (including the operating system itself) up-to-date?

>> Are all the software packages (including the operating system itself) set to automatically update?

>> Is security software on the device?

- » Is the security software configured to auto-update?

- » Is the security software up-to-date?

- » Does the security software include antimalware technology — and is that capability fully enabled?

- » Are virus scans configured to run after every update is applied?

- » Does the software include firewall technology — and is that capability fully enabled?

- » Does the software include antispam technology — and is that capability fully enabled? If not, is other antispam software present, and is it running?

- » Does the software include remote lock and/or remote wipe technology — and is that capability fully enabled? If not, is other remote lock/remote wipe software present, and is it running?

- » Are all other aspects of the software enabled? If not, what is not?

- » Is backup software running that will back up the device as part of a backup strategy?

- » Is encryption enabled for at least all sensitive data stored on the device?

- » Are permissions properly set for the software — locking out people who may have access to the device, but who should not have access to the software?

- » Have permissions been set to prevent software from making changes to the computer that you may not want done (for example, is any software running with administrator privileges when it should not be)?

Of course, all these questions refer to software on a device that you use, but that you don't expose to use by untrusted, remote outsiders. If you have devices that are used as in the latter case — for example, a web server — you must address many other security issues, which are beyond the scope of this book.

Hardware

For all your hardware devices, consider the following questions:

- » Was the hardware obtained from a trusted party? (If you bought an IP-based camera directly from China via some online retailer than you never of heard of prior to making the purchase, for example, the answer to this question may not be yes.)

- » Is all your hardware adequately protected from theft and damage (rain, electrical spikes, and so on) as it resides in its home location?

>> What protects your hardware when it travels?

>> Do you have an uninterruptible power supply or built-in battery protecting the device from a hard, sudden shut-off if power fails even momentarily?

>> Is all your hardware running the latest firmware — and did you download that firmware from a reliable source, such as the vendor's website or via an update initiated from within the device's configuration tool?

>> For routers (and firewalls), does your device meet the criteria listed as recommendations in the "Firewall/router" section earlier in this chapter?

>> Do you have a BIOS password, locking a device from use until a password is entered?

>> Have you disabled all wireless protocols that you do not need? If you're not using Bluetooth on a laptop, for example, turn off the Bluetooth radio, which not only improves security, but also helps your battery last longer.

Insurance

While cybersecurity insurance is often overlooked, especially by smaller businesses and individuals, it is a viable way of mitigating some cyber-risks. Depending on the particulars of your situation, purchasing a policy protecting against specific risks may make sense.

If you own a small business that may go bankrupt if a breach occurs, you will, of course, want to implement strong security. But, as no security is 100 percent perfect and foolproof, purchasing a policy to cover catastrophic situations may be wise.

Education

A little bit of education can go a long way in helping to prevent the people in your household from becoming the Achilles' heels of your cybersecurity. The following list covers some things to think about and discuss:

>> Do all you family members know what their rights and responsibilities are regarding vis-à-vis technology in the house, vis-à-vis connecting devices to the home network, and vis-à-vis allowing guest to connect to the home network (or the guest network)?

>> Have you taught your family members about the risks they need to be aware — for example, phishing emails. Do you have confidence that they "get it"?

>> Have you ensured that everyone in the family who uses devices knows about cybersecurity hygiene (for example, not clicking on links in emails)?

>> Have you ensured that everyone in the family who uses devices knows about password selection and protection?

>> Have you ensured that everyone in the family who uses social media knows about what can and can't be safely shared?

>> Have you ensured that everyone in the family understand the concept on thinking before acting?

Privacy 101

Technology threatens personal privacy in many ways: Ubiquitous cameras watch you on a regular basis, technology companies track your online behaviors via all sorts of technical methods, and mobile devices track your location.

While technology has certainly made the task of maintaining privacy far more challenging than doing so was just a few years ago, privacy is not dead. You can do many things to improve your level of privacy, even in the modern, connected era.

Think before you share

People often willingly overshare information when asked for it. Consider the paperwork that the typical doctor's office, which you have likely been asked to complete at more than one facility at your initial appointment with the doctor in question. While the answers to many of the questions are relevant and may contain information that is valuable for the doctor to know to properly evaluate and treat you, other portions are probably not. Many (if not most) such forms ask patients for their Social Security numbers. Such information was needed decades ago when medical insurance companies typically used Social Security numbers as insurance ID numbers, but that practice has long since ended. Perhaps some facilities use the Social Security number to report your account to credit bureaus if you don't pay your bills, but, in most cases, the reality is that the question is a vestige of the past, and you can leave the field blank.

REMEMBER

Even if you don't believe that a party asking you for personal data would ever abuse the information that it collected about you, as the number of parties that have private information about you increases, and as the quantity and quality of that data grows, the odds that you will suffer a privacy violation due to a data breach go up.

If you want to improve your privacy, the first thing to do is to consider what information you may be disclosing about yourself and your loved ones before you disclose it. This is true when interacting with government agencies, corporations, medical facilities, and other individuals. If you do not need to provide private information, don't.

Think before you post

Consider the implications of any social media post before making it — there could be adverse consequences of many sorts, including effectively compromising the privacy of information. For example, criminals can leverage shared information about a person's family relationships, place of employment, and interests as part of identity theft and to social engineer their way into your accounts.

WARNING

If, by choice or due to the negligent policies of a provider, you use your mother's maiden name as a de facto password, make sure that you do not make it easy for criminals to find out that name by listing your mother as your mother on Facebook or by being friends on Facebook with many cousins whose last name is the same as your mother's maiden name. Often, people can obtain someone's mother's maiden name simply by selecting from another person's Facebook friends list the most common last name that is not the same as the account holder's name.

Sharing information about a person's children and their schedules may help facilitate all sorts of problems — including potentially kidnapping, break-ins into the person's home while he is carpooling to work, or other harmful actions.

Sharing information related to medical activities may lead to disclosure of sensitive and private information. For example, photographs or location data placing a person at a particular medical facility may divulge that the person suffers from a condition that the facility is known to specialize in treating.

Sharing various types of information or images may impact a user's personal relationships and leak private information about such.

Sharing information or images may leak private information about potentially controversial activities in which a person has engaged — for example, consuming alcohol or using recreational drugs, using various weapons, participating in certain controversial organizations, and so on. Even disclosing that one was at a particular location at a certain time may inadvertently compromise the privacy of sensitive information.

REMEMBER

Also, keep in mind that the problem of oversharing is not limited to social networks. Oversharing information via chat, email, group chats, and so on is a serious modern day problem as well. Sometimes people do not realize that they are oversharing, and sometimes they accidentally paste the wrong data into emails or attach the wrong files to emails.

General privacy tips

In addition to thinking before you share, you can do a few other things to reduce your exposure to risks of oversharing:

» **Use social media privacy settings.** In addition to not sharing private information (see preceding section), make sure that your privacy settings on social media are set to protect your data from viewing by members of the public — unless the post in question is intended for public consumption.

» **But do not rely on them.** Nonetheless, never rely on social media security settings to ensure the privacy of information. Significant vulnerabilities that undermine the effectiveness of various platforms' security controls have been repetitively discovered.

» **Keep private data out of the cloud unless you encrypt the data.** Never store private information in the cloud unless you encrypt it. Do not rely on the encryption provided by the cloud provider to ensure your privacy. If the provider is breached, in some cases the encryption can be undermined as well.

» **Do not store private information in cloud applications designed for sharing and collaboration.** For example, do not store a list of your passwords, photos of your driver's license or passport, or confidential medical information in a Google doc. This may seem obvious, but many people do so anyway.

» **Leverage the privacy settings of a browser — or better yet, use Tor.** If you're using the a web browser to access material that you don't want associated with you, at a minimum, turn on Private/Incognito Mode (which offers only partial protection), or, if possible, use a web browser like the Tor Browser Bundle (which contains obfuscated routing, default strong privacy settings, and various, preconfigured, privacy add-ons).

   If you do not take precautions when using a browser, you may be tracked. If you search for detailed information on a medical condition in a normal browser window, various parties will likely capitalize on that data. You have probably seen the effects of such tracking — for example, when ads appear on one web page related to something that you searched for on another.

» **Do not publicize your real cellphone number.** Get a forwarding number from a service like Google Voice and, in general, give out that number rather than your actual cellphone number. Doing so helps protect against many risks — SIM swapping, spam, and so on.

» **Store private materials offline.** Ideally, store highly sensitive materials offline, such as in a fireproof safe or in a bank safe deposit box. If you must store them electronically, store them on a computer with no network connection.

>> **Encrypt all private information,** such as documents, images, videos, and so on. If you're not sure if something should be encrypted, it probably should.

>> **If you use online chat, use end-to-end encryption.** Assume that all your text messages sent via regular cellphone service (SMS messages) can potentially be read by outsiders. Ideally, do not share sensitive information in writing. If you must share some sensitive item in writing, encrypt the data.

TIP

The simplest way to encrypt data is to use a chat application that offers end-to-end encryption. *End-to-end* means that the messages are encrypted on your device and decrypted on the recipient's device and vice versa — with the provider effectively unable to decrypt the messages; as such, it takes far more effort by hackers who breach the provider's servers to read your messages if end-to-end encryption is utilized. (Sometimes, providers claim that hackers can't read such messages altogether, which isn't correct. for two reasons: 1. Hackers may be able to see the metadata — for example, with whom you chatted and when you did so, and 2. If hackers breach enough internal servers, they may be able to upload to the app store a poisoned version of the app containing a backdoor of some sort.) WhatsApp is probably the most popular chat application that uses end-to-end encryption.

>> **Practice proper cyberhygiene.** Because so much of the information that you want to keep private is stored in electronic form, practicing proper cyber-hygiene is critical to preserving privacy. See the tips in Chapter 18.

TURNING ON PRIVACY MODE

To turn on privacy mode:

- **Google Chrome:** Control + Shift-N or choose New incognito window from the menu
- **Firefox:** Control + Shift + P or choose New private window from the menu
- **Opera:** Control + Shift + N or choose New private window from the menu
- **Microsoft Edge:** Control + Shift + P or choose New inprivate window from the menu
- **Vivaldi:** Control + Shift + N or choose New private window from the menu
- **Safari:** Command + Shift + N or choose New private window from the File menu

Banking Online Safely

Eschewing online banking due to the security concerns that it creates is simply not practical for most people living in the modern age. Fortunately, you don't have to give up the relevant conveniences to stay secure. In fact, I'm keenly aware of the risks involved because I have been banking online since online banking was first offered by several major financial institutions in the mid-1990s as a replacement for direct-dial-up banking services. Here are some suggestions of what you can do to improve your security as you bank online:

>> **Your online banking password should be strong, unique, and committed to memory** — not stored in a database, password manager, or anywhere else electronic. (If you want to write it down and keep the paper in a safe deposit box, that is okay — but rarely necessary.)

>> **Choose a random Personal Identification Number (PIN) for your ATM card and/or phone identification.** The PIN should be unrelated to any information that you know. Don't use a PIN that you have used for some other purpose and don't establish any PINs or passwords based on the one you chose for your ATM card. Never write down your PIN. Never add it to any computer file. Never tell your PIN to anyone, including bank employees.

>> **Consider asking your bank for an ATM card that can't be used as a debit card.** While such cards may lack the ability to be used to buy goods and services, if you make your purchases using credit cards, you don't need the purchase feature on your ATM card. By preventing the card from being used as a debit card, you make it more likely that only someone who knows your PIN number can take money out of your account. Perhaps equally as important is that "crippled" ATM cards can also not be used by crooks to make fraudulent purchases.

REMEMBER

If your debit card is used fraudulently, you're out money and need to get it back. If your credit card is used fraudulently, you're not out any money unless an investigation reveals that you were the one doing the defrauding.

>> **Log in to online banking only from trusted devices that you control, that have security software on them, and that are kept up to date.**

>> **Log in to online banking only from secure networks that you trust.** If you're on the road, use your cellular provider's connection, not public Wi-Fi.

>> **Log in to online banking using a web browser or the official app of the bank.** Never log in from a third-party app or an app obtained from anywhere other than the official app store for your device's platform.

>> **Sign up for alerts from your bank.** You should configure to be alerted by text message and/or email any time a new payee is added, a withdrawal is made, and so on.

>> **Use multifactor authentication and protect any device used for such authentication.** If you generate one-time passwords on your phone, for example, and your phone is stolen, your second factor becomes (at least temporarily) usable by the crook and not by you.

>> **Do not allow your browser to store your online banking password.** Your online banking password should not be written down anywhere — certainly not in a system that will enter it on behalf of someone using a web browser.

>> **Enter the URL of your bank every time you visit the bank on the web.** Never click links to it.

>> **Ideally, use a separate computer for online banking than you use for online shopping, email access, and social media.** If that isn't possible or practical, use a different web browser — and be sure to keep that browser up to date.

TIP

As an extra precaution, you can configure your browser to remember the wrong password to a site so that if someone ever does get into your laptop or phone, he or she will be less likely to successfully log into that site using your credentials.

>> **Make sure to secure any devices from which you bank online.** That includes physically securing them (don't leave them on a table in a restaurant while going to the restroom), requiring a password to unlock them, and enabling remote wipe.

>> **Monitor your account for unauthorized activity.**

Safely Using Smart Devices

As I discuss in detail in Chapter 17, smart devices and the so-called Internet of Things create all sorts of cybersecurity risks. Here are some recommendations as to how to improve your security as you use such devices:

>> **Make sure that none of your IoT devices create security risks in the event of a failure.** Never create a situation in which a smart lock prevents you from leaving a room during a fire, for example, or lets robbers into your house during a power outage or network failure.

- >> **If possible, run your IoT devices on a separate network than your computers.** The IoT network should have a firewall protecting it.

- >> **Keep all IoT devices up to date.** Hackers have exploited vulnerabilities in IoT devices to commandeer the devices and use them to carry out major attacks. If a device has a firmware auto-update capability, consider enabling it.

- >> **Keep a full, current list of all devices connected to your network.** Also keep a list of all devices that are not currently connected but that are authorized to connect and sometimes do connect.

- >> **If possible, disconnect devices when you're not using them.** If a device is offline, it is obviously not hackable by anyone not physically present at the device.

- >> **Password-protect all devices.** Never maintain the default passwords that come with the devices. Each device should have a unique login and password.

- >> **Check your devices' settings.** Many devices come with default setting values that are terrible from a security perspective.

- >> **Keep your smartphone physically and digitally secure.** It likely runs apps with access to some or all of your devices,

- >> **If possible, disable device features that you do not need.** Doing so reduces the relevant attack surface — that is, it reduces the number of potential points at which an unauthorized user can attempt to hack into the device — and simultaneously lowers the chances of the device exposing an exploitable software vulnerability.

  Universal Plug and Play simplifies device setup, but it also makes it easier for hackers to discover devices and attack them for many reasons, including that many implementations of UPnP contain vulnerabilities, UPnP can sometimes allow malware to bypass firewall security routines, and UPnP can sometimes be exploited by hackers to run commands on routers.

- >> **Do not connect your IoT devices to untrusted networks.**

Chapter **5**

Enhancing Physical Security

Y ou may be tempted to skip this chapter — after all, you are reading this book to learn about cybersecurity, not physical security.

But, don't.

Certain aspects of physical security are essential ingredients of any cybersecurity program, whether formal or informal. In fact, just a few decades ago, the teams responsible for protecting computers and the data housed within them focused specifically on physical security. Locking a computer in a secured area accessible by only authorized personnel was often sufficient to protect it and its contents. Of course, the dawn of networks and the Internet era, coupled with the mass proliferation of computing devices, totally transformed the risks. Today, even computers locked in a physical location can still be accessed electronically by billions of people around the world. That said, the need for physical security is as important as ever.

This chapter covers elements of physical security that are necessary in order to implement and deliver proper cybersecurity. I cover the "what and why" that you need to know about physical security in order to keep yourself cyber-secure. Ignoring the concepts discussed in this chapter may put you at risk of a data breach equivalent to, or even worse than, one carried out by hackers.

Understanding Why Physical Security Matters

Physical security means protecting something from unauthorized physical access, whether by man or nature. Keeping a computer locked in an office server closet, for example, to prevent people from tampering with it is an example of physical security.

SECRETARY OF STATE HILLARY CLINTON'S EMAIL PROBLEM

Whenever politicians or journalists attack former U.S. Secretary of State Hillary Clinton for storing sensitive information on a server located inside a spare closet in her home in Chappaqua, New York, they're effectively accusing her of endangering national security by placing sensitive digital data in an insufficiently secure physical location. After all, as far as the risks of Internet-based hackers are concerned, digital security is what matters; to hackers from China and Russia, for example, whether her server was located in her spare closet or in a data center protected by armed guards is irrelevant.

The security experts who devised our national security procedures for the handling of classified information understood the necessity of keeping such data physically secure — it is, generally speaking, against the law to remove classified information from the secure locations in which it's intended to be handled. While many modern-day workers may telecommute and bring work home with them at times, folks who handle classified information can be sentenced to serve time in prison for even attempting to do the same with classified data.

The laws governing the protection of classified information prohibit removing it from classified networks, which are never supposed to be connected to the Internet. All people who handle classified information are required to obtain clearances and be trained on the handling of sensitive information; they are required by federal law to understand, and to adhere to, strict rules. As such, Sec. Clinton should have never removed classified information from classified networks and should never have brought it home or accessed it via a server in her home.

In fact, people can be charged with a crime for mishandling classified information — even if they do so inadvertently, which is a point that the Republicans mentioned repetitively during the 2016 Presidential election.

The goal of physical security is to provide a safe environment for the people and assets of a person, family, or organization. Within the context of cybersecurity, the goal of physical security is to ensure that digital systems and data are not placed at risk because of the manner in which they're physically housed.

REMEMBER

Classified information contains secrets whose compromise can endanger American intelligence agents and operations, undermine diplomatic and military operations, and harm national security.

I hope that you're not storing highly sensitive classified files in your home. If you are, you had better know a lot more about information security than is taught in this book; because removing classified information from its proper storage location is often a serious crime, I suggest that you get yourself a good lawyer. (See the nearby sidebar "Secretary of State Hillary Clinton's email problem.")

Nonetheless, I do assume that you do have data that you want to remain confidential, available, and free from corruption. It may not be classified in the government sense, but, to you, its privacy may be of vital importance.

Taking Inventory

Before you implement a physical security plan, you need to understand what it is that you have to secure. You likely possess more than one type of electronic device and have data that varies quite a bit in terms of the level of secrecy and sensitivity that you attach to it. Step 1 in implementing proper physical security is to understand what data and systems you have and determine what type of security level each one demands.

In all likelihood, your computer devices fall into two categories:

>> **Stationary devices,** such as a desktop computer sitting in your family room on which your teenagers play video games

>> **Mobile devices,** such as laptops, tablets, and cellphones

REMEMBER

Don't forget to inventory the equipment to which your devices are connected. When you inventory your devices, pay attention to networks and networking equipment. To what networks are stationary devices attached? How many networks are in place? Where do they connect to the outside world? Where is the relevant network equipment located? What mobile devices connect to wirelessly?

Stationary devices

Stationary devices, such as desktop computers, networking equipment, and many Internet-of-Things devices (IoT), such as wired cameras, are devices that don't move from location to location on a regular basis.

These devices can, of course, still be stolen, damaged, or misused, and, therefore, must be adequately protected. Damage need not be intentionally inflicted — early in my career I helped troubleshoot a server problem that began when a nighttime custodian unplugged an improperly secured server from its uninterruptible power supply in order to plug in a vacuum cleaner. Yes, seriously. As it is imperative to secure stationary devices in the locations in which they "live," you must inventory all such devices. Securing something that you do not know that you possess is difficult, if not impossible.

REMEMBER

In many cases, anyone who can physically access a computer or other electronic device can access all the data and programs on that device, regardless of security systems in place. The only question is how long it will take that party to gain the unauthorized access that it desires. Never mind that anyone who can access a device can physically damage it — whether by physically striking it, sending into it a huge power surge, dumping water on it, or setting it ablaze. In case you think that these scenarios are far-fetched, know that I have seen all four of these options utilized by people intent on damaging computers.

Mobile devices

Mobile devices are computerized devices that are frequently moved. Laptops, tablets, and smartphones are all mobile devices.

In some ways mobile devices are inherently more secure than stationary devices — you likely always have your cellphone with you, so it's not sitting at home unwatched for long periods of time as a computer may be.

That said, in reality, experience shows that portability dramatically increases the chances of a device being lost or stolen. In fact, in some ways, mobile devices are the stuff of security professionals' nightmares. The "smartphone" in your pocket is constantly connected to an insecure network (the Internet), contains highly sensitive data, has access tokens to your email, social media, and a whole host of other important accounts, likely lacks security software of the sophistication that is on desktop computers, is frequently in locations in which it is likely to be stolen, is often out of sight, is taken on trips that cause you to deviate from your normal routine, and so on.

SMARTPHONES ARE A LOT MORE THAN SMART PHONES

The term *smartphone* is extremely misleading — the device in your pocket is a full-blown computer with more processing power than all the computers used to first put a man on the moon combined. It is only a smartphone in the same way that a Ferrari is a fast, horseless carriage — a technically correct description, but one that is highly misleading. Why do you call these devices smartphones — well, think of where you encountered your first smartphone.

Most people's first experience with a smartphone was when they upgraded from a regular cellphone — and they obtained the new devices from cellphone providers who (likely correctly) reasoned that people would be more likely to upgrade their cellphone to "smartphones" than to replace their cellphones with "pocket computers that have a phone app."

Properly inventorying every mobile device so that you can properly secure all such devices is critical.

Locating Your Vulnerable Data

Review what data your devices house. Think of the worst-case consequences if an unauthorized person obtained your data or it leaked to the public on the Internet.

No list of items to search for can possibly cover all possible scenarios, but here are some things to think about. Do you have

» Private photos and videos

» Recordings of your voice

» Images of your handwriting (especially of your signature)

» Financial records

» Medical records

» School-related documents

» Password lists

- » Repositories of digital keys

- » Documents containing:

  - Credit card numbers

  - SSNs/EINs/taxpayer identification numbers

  - Maiden names

  - Codes to physical locks or other passcodes

  - Correspondence with the IRS and state tax authorities

  - Lawsuit-related information

  - Employment-related information

  - Mother's maiden name

  - Birth dates

  - Passport numbers

  - Driver's license numbers

  - Information about your vehicles

  - Information about your former addresses

  - Biometric data (fingerprints, retina scan, facial geometry, keyboard dynamics, and so on)

These items will need to be protected against cyberthreats, as described in multiple later chapters. But, the data stores in which they reside also need to be protected physically, as described in the next section.

Creating and Executing a Physical Security Plan

In order to adequately physically protect your technology and data, you should not attempt to simply deploy various security controls on an ad hoc basis. Rather, it is far better to develop and implement a physical security plan — doing so, will help you avoid making costly mistakes.

In most cases, physically securing computing systems relies on applying a well-known established principal of crime prevention, known as Crime Prevention Through Environmental Design (CPTD), that states that you can reduce the likelihood of certain crimes being committed if you create a physical environment that allows legitimate users to feel secure, but makes ill-doers unconformable with actually carrying out any planned problematic activities.

Understanding this high-level concept can help you think about ways to keep your own systems and data safe.

Three components of Crime Prevention Through Design as they apply in general to preventing crime include access control, surveillance, and marking:

>> **Access control:** Limiting access to authorized parties, by using fences, monitored entrances and exits, proper landscaping, and so on makes it harder for criminals to penetrate a building or other facility, and increases the risk to crooks that they will be noticed, thus discouraging potential criminals from actually carrying out crimes.

>> **Surveillance:** Criminals often avoid committing crimes that are likely to be seen and recorded; as such, they gravitate away from environments that they know are well-watched. Cameras, guards, and motion-sensitive-lighting all discourage crime.

>> **Marking:** Criminals tend to avoid areas that are clearly marked as belonging to someone else — for example, through the use of fences and signs — as they do not want to stand out and be easily noticeable when committing crimes. Likewise, they avoid environments in which authorized parties are marked. Consider, for example, that an unauthorized person not wearing a post office uniform while walking around in an area marked "US Postal Service Employees Only" is far more likely to be noticed and stopped than someone else walking in a similar unmarked environment belonging to a business that does not require uniforms.

TIP

You can apply these same principles in your home — for example, placing a computer in a parent's home office sends a message to children, babysitters, and guests that the device is off limits, far stronger than the message would be delivered if the same machine were located in a family room or den. Likewise, a curious babysitter or houseguest is far less likely to go into one's private home office without permission after being told not to if he/she is aware that the area is monitored with cameras.

You know your own environment. By applying these concepts you can improve the likelihood that unauthorized parties will not attempt to gain unauthorized access to your computers and data.

Implementing Physical Security

You can use many techniques and technologies to help secure an object or facility.

How much physical security you implement for a device depends heavily on the purpose for which it is being used and what types of information it houses. (For more information on inventorying your devices, see the section "Taking Inventory," earlier in this chapter.)

Here are some examples of methods of securing devices — based on your tolerance level for risk and your budget, you may choose variants of all, some, or none of these techniques:

>> **Locks:** For example, store devices in a locked room, with access to the room provided to only those people who need to use the device. In some environments, you may be able to record or monitor all entrances and exits from the room. Another popular variant is to store laptops in a safe located in one's master bedroom or home office when the computers are not in use.

>> **Video cameras:** For example, consider having a video camera focused on the devices to see who accesses them and when they do so.

>> **Security guards:** Obviously, security guards are not a practical solution in most home environments, but human defenders do have a time and place. For example, consider posting guards inside the room where the device is located, outside the room, in halls around the entrance to the room, outside the building, and outside the perimeter fence.

>> **Alarms:** Alarms not only serve as a reactive force that scare away criminals who actually attempt to enter a home or office, they also serve as a strong deterrent, pushing many opportunistic evildoers to "look elsewhere" and target someone else.

>> **Perimeter security:** Traffic posts prevent people from crashing cars into a facility, and proper fences and walls prevent people from approaching a home or office building. You should note that most experts believe that a fence under 8 feet tall does not provide any significant security value when it comes to potential human intruders.

>> **Lighting:** Criminals tend to avoid well-lit places. Motion-triggered lighting is even more of a deterrent than static lighting. When lights go on suddenly, people in the area are more likely to turn and look at what just happened — and see the criminal just as he or she is illuminated.

>> **Environmental risk mitigation:** If you're in an area that is likely to be hit by floods, for example, ensure that computing resources are stationed somewhere not likely to flood. If such advice seems obvious, consider that residents

of northern New Jersey lost telephone service after a storm in the late 1990s when telephone switching equipment flooded — because it was situated in the basement of a building standing next to a river. Having proper defenses against fires is another critical element of environmental risk mitigation.

>> **Backup power and contingencies for power failures:** Power failures impact not only your computers, but, many security systems as well.

>> **Contingencies during renovations and other construction, and so forth:** The risks to data and computers during home renovations are often over-looked. Leaving your cellphone unattended when workers are routinely entering and exiting your home, for example, can be a recipe for a stolen device and/or the compromise of data on the device.

>> **Risks from backups:** Remember to protect backups of data with the same security precautions as you do the original copies of the data. Spending time and money protecting a computer with a safe and cameras because of the data on its hard drive, for example, is silly if you leave backups of that same data on portable hard drives stored on a family room shelf in plain sight of anyone visiting your home.

Of course, you should not consider the preceding list to be comprehensive. But, if you think about how you can apply each of these items to help keep your devices safe within the context of a CPTD approach, you will likely benefit from much greater odds against an "unfortunate incident" occurring than if you do not. (For more on CPTD, see the earlier section "Creating and Executing a Physical Security Plan.")

Security for Mobile Devices

TIP

Of course, mobile devices — that is, computers, tablets, smartphones, and other electronic devices that are moved from location to location on a regular basis — pose additional risks because these devices can be easily lost or stolen. As such, when it comes to mobile devices, one simple, yet critically important, physical security principle should be added: Keep your devices in sight or locked up.

Such advice may sound obvious; sadly, however, a tremendous number of devices are stolen each year when left unattended, so you can be sure that the advice is either not obvious or not followed — and, in either case, you want to internalize it and follow it.

In addition to watching over your phone, tablet, or laptop, you should enable location broadcasting, remotely triggerable alarms, and remote wipe — all of which can be invaluable at quickly reducing the risk posed if the device is lost or stolen. Some devices even offer a feature to photograph or video record anyone using a mobile device after the user flags it as stolen — which can not only help you locate the device, but also catch any thieves involved in stealing it.

Realizing That Insiders Pose the Greatest Risks

According to most experts, the majority of information-security incidents involve insider threats — meaning that the biggest risk to businesses are their employees. Likewise, if you share a home computer with family members who are less cyber-aware, they may pose the greatest risk to your cybersecurity. You may take great care of your machine, but if your teen downloads malware-infected software onto the device, you may be in for a nasty surprise.

One critical rule from "the old days" that rings true today — even though it is often dismissed as outdated due to the use of technologies such as encryption — is that anyone who can physically access a computer may be able to access the data on that computer. This rule is true even if encryption is utilized, for at least two reasons: Someone who accesses your device may not be able to access your data, but he or she can certainly destroy it and may even be able to access it due to one or more of the following reasons:

>> You may not have set up the encryption properly.

>> Your machine may have an exploitable vulnerability.

>> The encryption software may have a bug in it that undermines its ability to properly protect your secrets.

>> Someone may have obtained the password to decrypt.

>> Someone may be willing to copy your data and wait until computers are powerful enough to break your encryption.

WARNING

Here is the bottom line: If you do not want people to access data, not only should you secure it logically (for example, with encryption), you should also secure it physically in order to prevent them from obtaining a copy of the data, even in encrypted form.

On that note, if your computer contains files that you do not want your children to have access to, do not share your computer with your children.

HUMANS ALWAYS COME FIRST

As you ponder how to physically secure your data, keep in mind one cardinal rule when it comes to safety and security: Humans always come first — with no exceptions.

If a fire occurs in a home, for example, saving the residents is the top priority with no close second. You should never enter a dangerous environment in order to retrieve computers or backup drives. Make sure to store some backups offsite and/or keep some in a fire- and water-resistant safe. You need to assume that in many environmental disasters, your systems and data may need to be "sheltered in place" until after the disaster passes.

Do not rely solely on digital security. Utilize a physical defense. While it is true that crafty, skilled children may be able to hack your computer across your LAN, the risks of such an attack occurring are miniscule compared with the temptation of a curious child who is actually using your computer. That said, ideally you should keep your most sensitive data and machines on a network physically isolated from the one that your children use.

3
Protecting Yourself from Yourself

Chapter 6

Securing Your Accounts

The weakest link in the cybersecurity chain is almost always people, and the greatest threat to your own cybersecurity is likely yourself and the members of your family.

As such, all the technology and technical knowledge in the world won't deliver much value if you don't also address various human shortcomings.

Realizing That You're a Target

Perhaps the most significant first step in securing yourself digitally is to understand that you're a target and that nefarious parties have the desire to breach your computer systems, electronically accessible accounts, and anything else they can get their hands on.

Even if you already realize that you're a target, make sure to fully internalize such a notion. People who truly believe that criminals want to breach their computers and phones act differently than people who do not fully appreciate this reality and whose lack of skepticism sometimes leads them into trouble.

WARNING

Because your family members can also impact your digital security, they also need to be aware that they are a potential targets. If your children take unwise risks online, they may inadvertently inflict harm not only on themselves, but upon you and other members of the family as well. In some cases, attackers have managed to attack people's employers via remote connections that were compromised because children misused computers on the same networks as computers that the employees were using for working remotely.

The threat posed by such attacks is usually not that a criminal will directly steal someone's money or data, but rather that some party will seek to harm the target in some other manner — a manner that may ultimately translate into some form of financial, military, political, or other benefit to the attacker and (potentially) damage of some sort to the victim.

Securing Your External Accounts

Chapter 4 discusses how you can acquire your own technology products. But using these products isn't enough to keep you cybersecure as you, no doubt, have digital data of significant value that is stored outside of your own physical possession — that is, outside of data systems and data stores under your control.

In fact, data about every person living in the western world today is likely stored on computer systems belonging to many businesses, organizations, and governmental agencies. Sometimes those systems reside within the facilities of the organizations to which they belong, sometimes they're located at shared data centers, and, sometimes the systems themselves are virtual machines rented from a third-party provider. Additionally, some such data may reside in cloud-based systems offered by a third party.

Such data can be broken down and divided into many different categories, depending on which aspects of it a person is interested in. One way of examining the data for the purposes of discovering how to secure it, for example, is to group it according to the following scheme:

>> Accounts, and the data within them, that a user established and controls

>> Data belonging to organizations that a user has willingly and knowingly interacted with, but the user has no control over the data

>> Data in the possession of organizations that the user has never knowingly established a relationship with

Addressing the risks of each type of data requires a different strategy.

Securing Data Associated with User Accounts

When you bank online, shop online, or even browse the web, you provide all sorts of data to the parties that you interact with.

When you establish and maintain an account with a bank, store, social media provider, or other online party, you gain control over significant amounts of data related to yourself that the party maintains on your behalf. Obviously, you can't fully control the security of that data because the data is not in your possession. That said, you obviously also have a strong interest in protecting that data — and, in not undermining the protections for the data that the party hosting the account has established.

While every situation and account has its unique attributes, certain strategies can help keep your data secure at third parties. Obviously, not all the ideas in the following sections apply to every situation, but applying the appropriate items from the menu to your various accounts and online behavior can dramatically improve your odds of remaining cybersecure.

Conduct business with reputable parties

There is nothing wrong with supporting small businesses — in fact, doing so is quite admirable. (It is also true that many large firms have suffered serious security breaches.) But if you search for the latest electronic gizmo, for example, and one store that you have never heard of is offering it at a substantial discount from the prices offered at all well-known stores, be wary. There may be a legitimate reason for the discount — or there may be a scam in the works.

WARNING

Always check the websites of stores that you're conducting business with to see whether something looks off — and beware if it does.

Use official apps and websites

Clones of official apps have been found in various app stores. If you install a banking, credit card, or shopping app for a particular company, make sure that you install the official app and not some malicious impersonator. Install apps only from reputable app stores, such as Google Play, Amazon AppStore, and Apple App Store.

Don't install software from untrusted parties

Malware that infects a computer can capture sensitive information from both other programs and web sessions running on the device. If a website is offering free copies of movies, software, or other items that normally cost money, not only may the offerings be stolen copies, but ask yourself how the operator is making money — it may be by distributing malware.

Don't root your phone

You may be tempted to *root your phone* — a process that allows you greater control over your device — but doing so undermines various security capabilities of the device and may allow malware to capture sensitive information from other apps on the device, leading to account compromises.

Don't provide unnecessary sensitive information

Don't provide private information to anyone who doesn't need that data. For example, don't give your Social Security number to any online stores or doctors because they have no need for it.

REMEMBER

Keep in mind that the less information about you that a specific party has, the less data that can be compromised, and correlated, in case of a breach.

Use payment services that eliminate the need to share credit card numbers with vendors

Services like PayPal, Samsung Pay, Apple Pay, and so on let you make online payments without having to give vendors your actual credit card number. If a vendor is breached, the information about your account that is likely to be stolen is significantly less likely to lead to fraud (and, perhaps, even various forms of identity theft) than if actual credit card data were stored at the vendor. Moreover, major payment sites have armies of skilled information security professionals working to keep them safe that vendors accepting such payments can rarely, if ever, match.

Use one-time, virtual credit card numbers when appropriate

Some financial institutions allow you to use an app (or website) to create disposable, one-time *virtual credit card numbers* that allow you to make a charge to a real credit card account (associated with the virtual number) without having to give the respective merchant your real credit card number. As seen in Figure 6-1, some virtual credit card systems also allow you to specify the maximum allowable charge size on a particular virtual card number at a figure much lower than it would be on the real corresponding card.

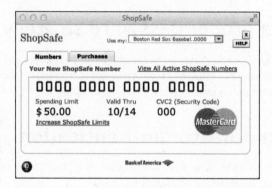

FIGURE 6-1:
A (slightly edited image of) a one-time credit card number generator.

While creating one-time numbers takes time and effort and may be overkill when doing repeat deals with a reputable vendor in whose information-security practices you have confidence, virtual credit card numbers do offer benefits for defending against potential fraud and may be appropriately used when dealing with less familiar parties.

Besides minimizing the risk to yourself if a vendor turns out to be corrupt, virtual credit card numbers offer other security benefits. If criminals hack a vendor and steal your virtual credit card number that was previously used, not only can they not make charges with it, their attempts to do so may even help law enforcement track them down, as well as help forensics teams identify the source of the credit card number data leak.

Monitor your accounts

Regularly checking for any unrecognized activities on your payment, banking, and shopping accounts is a good idea.

TIP

Ideally, do this check by not only looking at online transaction logs, but also by checking relevant monthly statements (no matter the delivery method) for anything that does not belong.

Report suspicious activity ASAP

REMEMBER

The faster a potential fraud is reported to the parties responsible for addressing it, the greater the chance of reversing it and preventing further abuse of whatever materials were abused in order to commit the first act of fraud. Also, the sooner the fraud is reported, the greater the chance of catching the parties committing it.

Employ a proper password strategy

While conventional wisdom may be to require complex passwords for all systems, such a password strategy fails in practice. Be sure to implement a proper password strategy. For more on choosing passwords, see Chapter 7.

Utilize multifactor authentication

Multifactor authentication means authentication that requires a user to authenticate using two or more of the following methods:

>> Something that the user knows, such as a password

>> Something that the user is, such as a fingerprint

>> Something that the user has, such as a hardware token

For extremely sensitive systems, you should use forms of authentication that are stronger than passwords alone. The following forms of authentication all have their places:

>> **Biometrics,** which means using measurements of various human characteristics to identify people. Fingerprints, voiceprints, iris scans, the speed at which people type different characters on a keyboard, and the like are all examples of biometrics.

>> **Digital certificates,** which effectively prove to a system that a particular public key represents the presenter of the certificate. If the presenter of the certificate is able to decrypt messages encrypted with the public key in the certificate, it means that the presenter possesses the corresponding private key, which only the legitimate owner should have.

>> **One-time passwords,** or one-time tokens, generated by apps or sent via SMS to your cellphone.

>> **Hardware tokens,** which are typically small electronic devices that either plug into a USB port, display a number that changes every minute or so, or allow users to enter a challenge number and receive a corresponding response number back. Today, smartphone apps perform such functions, allowing, at least theoretically, the smartphone to assume the role of a hardware token. Figure 6-2 shows you an example of using such an app to generate a one-time code for logging into Snapchat. (Note that smartphones can suffer from all sorts of security vulnerabilities that hardware tokens can't suffer from, so hardware tokens are still likely more appropriate for certain high-risk situations.)

Snapchat: john

SNAPCHAT TOKEN IS:

538 144

YOUR TOKEN EXPIRES IN (28)

FIGURE 6-2:
One-time password for Snapchat generated by the app Authy — an example of an app-generated multifactor authentication token.

TIP

>> **Knowledge-based authentication,** which is based on real knowledge, not simply answering questions with small numbers of possible answers that are often guessable like "What color was your first car?" Note that technically speaking, adding knowledge-based authentication questions to password authentication doesn't create multifactor authentication since both the password and the knowledge-based answer are examples of things that a user knows. However, doing so certainly does improve security when the questions are chosen properly.

Most financial institutions, social media companies, and major online retailers offer multifactor authentication — use it.

Also, note that while sending one-time passwords to users' smartphones via text messages theoretically verifies that a person logging in possesses the smartphone that the user is supposed to possess (something that the user has), various vulnerabilities undermine that supposition. It is possible, for example, for a criminal to intercept text messages even without possessing the phone.

Log out when you're finished

Don't rely on automatic timeouts, closing the browser, or shutting down a computer to log you out of accounts. Log out every time you're finished.

Don't leave yourself logged in between sessions unless you're on a device that you know with — as close as possible to — certainty will remain secure.

Use your own computer or phone

You don't know how well someone else has secured his or her device — it may have malware on it that can capture your passwords and other sensitive information or hijack sessions and perform all sorts of nefarious activities.

Furthermore, despite the fact that doing so is severely problematic, some applications and websites — to this day — cache data on endpoints that are used for accessing them. You don't want to leave other people souvenirs of your sensitive sessions.

Lock your computer

Lock any computer that you use for accessing sensitive accounts and keep it physically secure as well.

Use a separate, dedicated computer for sensitive tasks

Consider purchasing a special computer that you use for online banking and other sensitive tasks. For many people, a second computer isn't practical, but if it is, having such a machine — on which you never read email, access social media, browse the web, and so on — offers security benefits.

Use a separate, dedicated browser for sensitive web-based tasks

If you can't obtain a separate computer, at least use a separate browser for sensitive tasks. Don't use the same browser that you use for reading the news, checking out blog posts, and most other activities.

Secure your access devices

Every phone, laptop, tablet, and desktop used for accessing secure systems should have security software on it, and that security software should be configured to regularly scan applications when they're added, as well as to run periodic general scans (see Figure 6-3). Also, make sure to keep that software up to date — most antivirus technology products perform far better against newer strains of malware when they're kept up to date than when they're not.

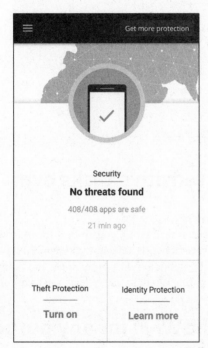

FIGURE 6-3:
The results of a periodic scan of a phone's installed apps for malware.

Keep your devices up to date

Besides keeping your security software up to date, be sure to install operating system and program updates to reduce your exposure to vulnerabilities. Windows

AutoUpdate and its equivalent on other platforms can simplify this task for you, as shown in Figure 6-4.

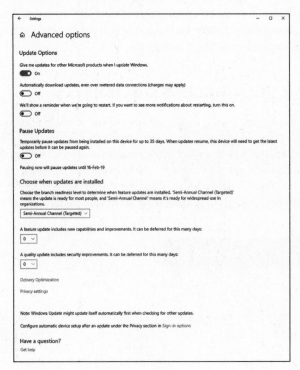

FIGURE 6-4:
The AutoUpdate
settings page in
Windows 10.

Don't perform sensitive tasks over public Wi-Fi

If you must perform a sensitive task while you're in a location where you don't have access to a secure, private network, do what you need to do over the cellular system, not over public Wi-Fi. Public Wi-Fi simply poses too many risks. (To find out more about how to use public Wi-Fi safely, please see Chapter 20.)

Never use public Wi-Fi for any purpose in high-risky places

Don't connect any device from which you plan to perform sensitive tasks to a Wi-Fi network in areas that are prone to *digital poisoning* — that is, to the hacking of, or distribution of malware, to devices that connect to a network.

Hacker conferences and certain countries, such as China, that are known for performing cyberespionage are examples of areas that are likely to experience digital poisoning. Many cybersecurity professionals recommend keeping your primary computer and phone off and using a separate computer and phone when working in such environments.

Access your accounts only when you're in a safe location

Even if you're using a private network, don't type passwords to sensitive systems or perform other sensitive tasks while in a location where people can easily watch what you type and see your screen.

Set appropriate limits

Various online venues let you set limits — for example, how much money can be transferred out of a bank account, the largest charge that can be made on a credit card with the card not physically present (as in the case of online purchases), or the maximum amount of goods that you can purchase in one day.

TIP

Set these limits. Not only will they limit the damage if a criminal does breach your account, but in some cases, they may trigger fraud alerts and prevent theft altogether.

Use alerts

If your bank, credit card provider, or a store that you frequent offers the ability to set up text or email alerts, you should seriously consider taking advantage of those services.

Theoretically, it is ideal to have the issuer send you an alert every time activity occurs on your account. From a practical standpoint, however, if doing so would overwhelm you and cause you to ignore all the messages (as is the case for most people), consider asking to be notified when transactions are made over a certain dollar amount (which may be able to be set to different thresholds for different stores or accounts) or otherwise appear to the issuer to be potentially fraudulent.

Periodically check access device lists

Some websites and apps — especially those of financial institutions — allow you to check the list of devices that have accessed your account. Checking this list each time that you log in can help you identify potential security problems quickly.

Check last login info

After you log in to some websites and via some apps — especially those of financial institutions — you may be shown information as to when and from where you last successfully logged in prior to the current session. Whenever any entity shows you such information, take a quick glance. If something is amiss and a criminal recently logged in while pretending to be you, it may stand out like a sore thumb.

Respond appropriately to any fraud alerts

If you receive a phone call from a bank, credit card company, or store about potential fraud on your account, respond quickly. But do not do so by speaking with the party who called you. Instead, contact the outlet at a known valid number that is advertised on its website.

Never send any sensitive information over an unencrypted connection

When you access websites, look for the padlock icon (see Figure 6-5), indicating that encrypted HTTPS is being used. Today, HTTPS is ubiquitous; even many websites that do not ask users to submit sensitive data utilize it.

FIGURE 6-5:
A secure website.

If you don't see the icon, unencrypted HTTP is being used. In such a case, don't provide sensitive information or log in.

The lack of a padlock on a site that is prompting for a login and password or handling financial transactions is a huge red flag that something is seriously amiss. However, contrary to what you've likely heard in the past, the presence of the lock doesn't necessarily mean that the site is safe.

Beware of social engineering attacks

In the context of cybersecurity, social engineering refers to the psychological manipulation by cyberattackers of their intended victims into performing actions that without such manipulation the targets would not perform or into divulging confidential information that they otherwise would not divulge.

To help prevent yourself from falling prey to social engineering attacks, consider any and all emails, text messages, phone calls, or social media communications from all banks, credit card companies, healthcare providers, stores, and so on to be potentially fraudulent.

Never click on links in any such correspondence. Always connect with such parties by entering the URL in the URL bar of the web browser.

For more on social engineering attack prevention, see Chapter 8.

Establish voice login passwords

Online access isn't the only path that a criminal can use to breach your accounts. Many crooks do reconnaissance online and subsequently social engineer their ways into people's accounts using old-fashioned phone calls to the relevant customer service departments at the target organizations.

To protect yourself and your accounts, establish voice login passwords for your accounts whenever possible — that is, set up passwords that must be given to customer service personnel in order for them to be able to provide any information from your accounts or to make changes to them. Many companies offer this capability, but relatively few people actually use it.

Protect your cellphone number

If you use strong authentication via text messages, ideally set up a forwarding phone number to your cellphone and use that number when giving out your cell number. Doing so reduces the chances that criminals will be able to intercept one-time passwords that are sent to your phone and also diminishes the chances of various other attacks succeeding.

For example, Google Voice, shown in Figure 6-6, allows you to establish a new phone number that forwards to your cellphone so that you can give out a number other than your real cellphone number and reserve the real number for use within the authentication process.

FIGURE 6-6:
The Google Voice app as made available in the Google Play Store.

Don't click on links in emails or text messages

Clicking on links is one of the primary ways that people get diverted to fraudulent websites.

For example, I recently received an email message that contained a link. If I had clicked the link in the message shown in Figure 6-7, I would have been brought to a phony LinkedIn login page that collects LinkedIn username and password combinations and provides them to criminals.

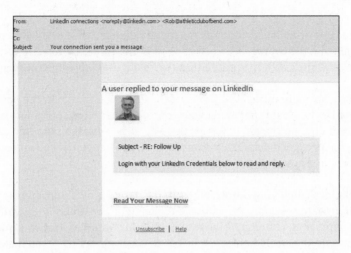

From: LinkedIn connections <noreply@linkedin.com> <Rob@athleticclubofbend.com>
To:
Cc:
Subject: Your connection sent you a message

A user replied to your message on LinkedIn

Subject - RE: Follow Up

Login with your LinkedIn Credentials below to read and reply.

Read Your Message Now

Unsubscribe | Help

FIGURE 6-7:
Email with a link
to a phony page.

Don't overshare on social media

You don't want to provide criminals with the answers to challenge questions that are being used to protect your account or offer them information that they can use to social engineer their way into your accounts. See Chapter 8 for more on preventing social engineering.

Pay attention to privacy policies

Understand what a site means if it says that it is going to share your data with third parties or sell your data to others.

Securing Data with Parties That You've Interacted With

When you interact online with a party, not all the data is under your control. If you browse a website with typical web browser settings, that site may track your activity. Because many sites syndicate content from third parties — for example from advertising networks — sites may even be able to track your behavior on other sites.

If you have an account on any sites that do such tracking and log in, all the sites utilizing the syndicated content may know your true identity and plenty of information about you — even though you never told them anything about yourself. Even if you don't have such an account or don't log in, profiles of your behavior may be established and used for marketing purposes, even without knowing who you are. (Of course, if you ever log in in the future to any site using the network, all the sites with the profiles may correlate them to your true identity.)

It is far more difficult to protect data about you that is in the possession of third parties but that is not under your control than it is to protect data in your accounts. That does not mean, however, that you're powerless. (Ironically, and sadly, most owners of such data likely do a better job protecting data about people than do the people themselves.)

TIP

Besides employing the strategies in the previous section, you may want to browse in private sessions. For example, by using a Tor browser — which, as shown in Figure 6-8, automatically routes all your Internet traffic through computers around the world before sending it to its destination — you make it difficult for third parties to track you. As discussed in Chapter 4, the Tor browser bundle is free and comes with all sorts of privacy-related features enabled, including blocking cookies and canvas fingerprinting, an advanced form of tracking devices.

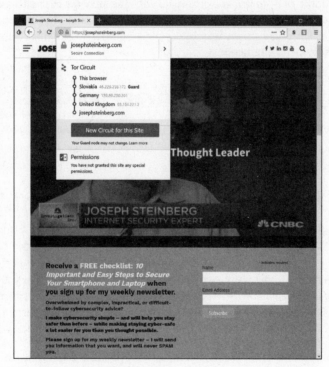

FIGURE 6-8: The author's website as seen in a Tor browse, with the Tor circuit information button clicked so as to show how Tor is hiding the user's point of origin. The image was generated with the Tor browser running on a computer in New Jersey, but, because of Tor's security features, appears to the web server as if it is in the United Kingdom.

If Tor seems complicated, you can also utilize a reputable VPN service for similar purposes.

By using browsing technology that makes it harder for sites to track you, they are less likely to establish as detailed profiles about you — and the less data about you that they have, the less data about you that can be stolen. Besides, you may not want those parties to build profiles about you in the first place.

WARNING

One technology that, despite its name, does not prevent tracking at anywhere near the level that do Tor or VPNs is the private mode offered by most web browsers. Unfortunately, despite its name, the private mode suffers from multiple serious weaknesses in this regard and does not come close to ensuring privacy.

Securing Data at Parties That You Haven't Interacted With

Numerous entities likely maintain significant amounts of data about you, despite the fact that you've never knowingly interacted with them or otherwise authorized them to maintain such information.

For example, at least one major social media service builds de facto profiles for people who don't have accounts with the service, but who have been mentioned by others or who have interacted with sites that utilize various social widgets or other related technologies. The service can then use these profiles for marketing purposes — even, in some cases, without knowing the person's true identity.

Furthermore, various information services that collect information from numerous public databases establish profiles based on such data — containing details that you may not even realize was available to the public.

Some genealogy sites utilize all sorts of public records and also allow people to update the information about other people. This ability can lead to situations in which all sorts of nonpublic information about you may be available to subscribers to the site (or people with free trial subscriptions) without your knowledge or consent. Such sites make finding people's mothers' maiden names easy, which undermines the authentication scheme used by many organizations.

Besides family tree sites, various professional sites maintain information about folks' professional histories, publications, and so on. And, of course, credit bureaus maintain all sorts of information about your behavior with credit — such information is submitted to them by financial institutions, collection agencies, and so on.

While the Fair Credit Reporting Act may help you manage the information that the bureaus have about you, it can't help you remove negative information that appears in other venues, such as in old newspaper articles that are online. Besides the privacy implications of such, if any information in those articles provides the answer to challenge questions used for authentication, it can create security risks. In such cases, you may want to reach out to the provider of the data, explain the situation, and ask it to remove the data. In some cases, they will cooperate.

In addition, some businesses, such as insurance companies and pharmacies, maintain medical information about people. Typically, individuals have little control over such data.

Of course, this type of data, which isn't under your complete control, can impact you. The bottom line is that many entities likely maintain significant amounts of data about you, even though you have never directly interacted with them.

It is the duty of such organizations to protect their data stores, but, they do not always properly do so. As the Federal Trade Commission notes on its website, a data breach at the credit bureau Equifax, discovered in 2017, exposed the sensitive personal information of 143 million Americans.

And, the reality is, that other than in the cases in which you can manually update records or request that they be updated, you can do little to protect the data in such scenarios.

» Discovering how often you need to change passwords — or not

» Storing passwords

» Finding alternatives to passwords

Chapter **7**

Passwords

Most people alive today are familiar with the concept of passwords and with their use in the realm of cybersecurity. Yet, there are so many misconceptions about passwords, and misinformation about them has spread like wildfire, often leading to people undermining their own security with poor password practices.

In this chapter, you discover some best practices vis-à-vis passwords. These practices should help you both maximize your own security and maintain reasonable ease of use.

Passwords: The Primary Form of Authentication

Password authentication refers to the process of verifying the identity of a user (whether human or computer process) by asking that user to supply a password — that is, a previously-agreed-upon secret piece of information — that ostensibly the party authenticating would only know if he or she were truly the party who it claimed to be. While the term password implies that the information consists of a single word, today's passwords can include combinations of characters that don't form words in any spoken or written language.

Despite the availability for decades of many other authentication approaches and technologies — many of which offer significant advantages over passwords — passwords remain de facto worldwide standard for authenticating people online. Repeated predictions of the demise of passwords have been proven untrue, and the number of passwords in use grows every day.

Because password authentication is so common and because so many data breaches have resulted in the compromise of password databases, the topic has received significant media attention, with reports often spreading various misleading information. Gaining a proper understanding of the realm of passwords is important if you want to be cybersecure.

Avoiding Simplistic Passwords

Passwords only secure systems if unauthorized parties can't easily guess them.

Criminals often guess passwords by

>> **Guessing common passwords:** It's not a secret that 123456 and password are common passwords — data from recent breaches reveals that they are, in fact, among the most common passwords used on many systems (see the nearby sidebar)! Criminals exploit such sad reality and often attempt to breach accounts by using automated tools that feed systems passwords one at a time from lists of common passwords — and record when they have a hit. Sadly, those hits are often quite numerous.

>> **Launching dictionary attacks:** Because many people choose to use actual English words as passwords, some automated hacker tools simply feed all the words in the dictionary to a system one at a time. As with lists of common passwords, such attacks often achieve numerous hits.

>> **Credential stuffing:** *Credential stuffing* refers to when attackers take lists of usernames and passwords from one site — for example, from a site that was breached and whose username password database was subsequently posted online — and feed its entries to another system one at a time in order to see whether any of the login credentials from the first system work on the second.

Because many people reuse username and password combinations between systems, credential stuffing is, generally speaking, quite effective.

THE MOST COMMON PASSWORDS OF 2018

Since 2011, password manager app vendor SplashData has released a list of the 25 most common passwords that it assembles from various sources. Here is the list from 2018:

123456	password	123456789	12345678	12345
111111	1234567	sunshine	qwerty	iloveyou
princess	admin	welcome	666666	abc123
football	123123	monkey	654321	!@#$%^&*
Charlie	aa123456	donald	password1	qwerty123

As you can see, criminals benefit from the fact that many people use weak, easily guessable passwords.

Password Considerations

When you create passwords, keep in mind that more complex isn't always better, and that the password strength that you choose should depend on how sensitive the data and system are that the password protects. The following sections discuss easily guessable passwords, complicated passwords, sensitive passwords, and password managers.

Easily guessable personal passwords

Criminals know that many people use the name or birth date of their significant other or pet as a password, so crooks often look at social media profiles and do Google searches in order to find likely passwords. They also use automated tools to feed lists of common names to targeted systems one by one, while watching to see whether the system being attacked accepts any of the names as a correct password.

Criminals who launch targeted attacks can exploit the vulnerability created by such personalized, yet easily guessable, passwords. However, the problem is much larger: Sometimes, reconnaissance is done through automated means — so, even opportunistic attackers can leverage such an approach.

Furthermore, because, by definition, a significant percentage of people have common names, the automated feeders of common names often achieve a significant number of hits.

Complicated passwords aren't always better

To address the problems inherent in weak passwords, many experts recommend using long, complex passwords — for example, containing both uppercase and lowercase letters, as well as numbers and special characters.

Using such passwords makes sense in theory, and if such a scheme is utilized to secure access to a small number of sensitive systems, it can work quite well. However, employing such a model for a larger number of passwords is likely to lead to problems that can undermine security:

» Inappropriately reusing passwords

» Writing down passwords in insecure locations

» Selecting passwords with poor randomization and formatted using predictable patterns, such as using a capital for the first letter of a complicated password, followed by all lowercase characters, and then a number

Hence, in the real world, from a practical perspective, because the human mind can't remember many complex passwords, using significant numbers of complex passwords can create serious security risks.

According to *The Wall Street Journal*, Bill Burr, the author of NIST Special Publication 800-63 Appendix A (which discusses password complexity requirements), recently admitted that password complexity has failed in practice. He now recommends using passphrases, and not complex passwords, for authentication.

Passphrases are passwords consisting of entire phrases or phrase-length strings of characters, rather than of simply a word or a word-length group of characters. Sometimes passphrases even consist of complete sentences. Think of passphrases as long (usually at least 25 characters) but relatively easy to remember passwords.

Different levels of sensitivity

Not all types of data require the same level of password protection. For example, the government doesn't protect its unclassified systems the same way that it secures its top-secret information and infrastructure.

In your mind or on paper, classify the systems for which you need secure access.

Then informally classify the systems that you access and establish your own informal password policies accordingly.

On the basis of risk levels, feel free to employ different password strategies. Random passwords, passwords composed of multiple words possibly separated with numbers, passphrases, and even simple passwords each have their appropriate uses. Of course, multifactor authentication can, and should, help augment security when it's both appropriate and available.

TIP

Establishing a stronger password for online banking than for commenting on a blog on which you plan to comment only once in a blue moon makes sense. Likewise, your password to the blog should probably be stronger than the one used to access a free news site that requires you to log in but on which you never post anything and at which, if your account were compromised, the breach would have zero impact upon you.

Your most sensitive passwords may not be the ones that you think

When classifying your passwords, keep in mind that while people often believe that their online banking and other financial system passwords are their most sensitive passwords, that is not always the case. Because many modern online systems allow people to reset their passwords after validating their identities through email messages sent to their previously known email addresses, a criminal who gains access to someone's email account may be able to do a lot more than just read email without authorization: He or she may be able to reset that user's passwords to many systems, including to some financial institutions.

Likewise, many sites leverage social-media-based authentication capabilities — especially those provided by Facebook and Twitter — so a compromised password on a social media platform can lead to unauthorized parties gaining access to other systems as well, some of which may be quite a bit more sensitive in nature than a site on which you just share pictures.

You can reuse passwords — sometimes

You may be surprised to read this statement in an information security book: You don't need to use strong passwords for accounts that you create solely because a website requires a login, but that does not, from your perspective, protect anything of value. If you create an account in order to access free resources, for example, and you have nothing whatsoever of value stored within the account, and you don't mind getting a new account the next time you log in, you can even use a weak password — and use it again for other similar sites.

TIP

Essentially, think about it like this: If the requirement to register and log in is solely for the benefit of the site owner — to track users, market to them, and so on — and it doesn't matter one iota to you whether a criminal obtained the access credentials to your account and changed them, use a simple password. Doing so will preserve your memory for sites where password strength matters. Of course, if you use a password manager, you can use a stronger password for such sites.

Consider using a password manager

Alternatively, you can use a password manager tool, shown in Figure 7-1, to securely store your passwords. Password managers are software that help people manage passwords by generating, storing, and retrieving complex passwords. Password managers typically store all their data in encrypted formats and provide access to users only after authenticating them with either a strong password or multifactor authentication.

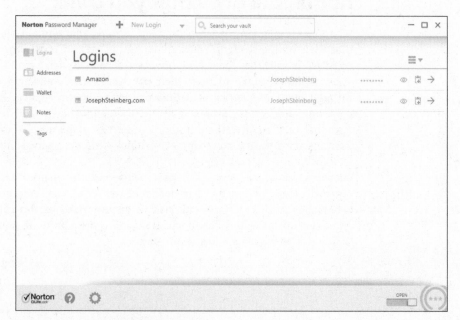

FIGURE 7-1:
A password
manager.

Such technology is appropriate for general passwords, but not for the most sensitive ones. Various password managers have been hacked, and if something does go wrong when all your eggs are in one basket, you may have a nightmare on your hands.

Of course, be sure to properly secure any device that you use to access your password manager.

Many password managers are on the market. While all utilize encryption to protect the sensitive data that they store, some store passwords locally (for example, in a database on your phone), while others store them in the cloud.

Many modern smartphones come equipped with a so-called *secure area* — a private, encrypted space that is *sandboxed,* or separated, into its own running environment. Ideally, any password information stored on a mobile device is stored protected in the secure area (see Figure 7-2).

Data that is stored in the secure area can't be accessed unless a user enters the secure area, usually by running a secure area app and entering a special password. Devices also typically display some special symbol somewhere on the screen when a user is working with data or an app located in the secure area.

FIGURE 7-2:
Secure Folder, the secure area app provided by Samsung for its Android series of phones, as seen in the Google Play Store.

Creating Memorable, Strong Passwords

The following list offers suggestions that may help you create strong passwords that are, for most people, far easier to remember than a seemingly random, unintelligible mix of letters, numbers, and symbols:

>> **Combine three or more unrelated words and proper nouns, with numbers separating them.** For example, laptop2william7cows is far easier to remember than 6ytBgv%j8P. In general, the longer the words you use within the password, the stronger the resulting password will be.

>> **If you must use a special character, add a special character before each number; you can even use the same character for all your passwords.** (If you use the same passwords as in the previous example and follow this advice, the passwords is laptop%2william%7cows.) In theory, reusing the same character may not be the best way to do things from a security standpoint, but, doing so makes memorization much easier, and the security should still be good enough for purposes for which a password is suitable on its own anyway.

>> **Ideally, use at least one non-English word or proper name.** Choose a word or name that is familiar to you but that others are unlikely to guess. Don't use the name of your significant other, best friend, or pet.

>> **If you must use both capital and lowercase letters (or want to make your password even stronger), use capitals that always appear in a particular location throughout all your strong passwords.** Make sure, though, that you don't put them at the start of words because that location is where most people put them. For example, if you know that you always capitalize the second and third letter of the last word, then laptop2william7kALb isn't harder to remember than laptop2william7kalb.

Knowing When to Change Your Password

Conventional wisdom — as you have likely heard many times — is that it is ideal to change your password quite frequently. The American Association of Retired Persons (AARP), for example, recommends on its website that people (including the disproportionately older folks who comprise its membership) "change critical passwords frequently, possibly every other week."

Theoretically, such an approach is correct — frequent changes reduce risks in several ways — but, in reality, it's bad advice that you shouldn't follow.

If you have a bank account, mortgage, a couple credit cards, a phone bill, high speed Internet bill, utility bills, social media accounts, email accounts, and so on, you may easily be talking about a dozen or so critical passwords. Changing them every two weeks would mean 312 new critical passwords to remember within the span of every year — and you likely have many more passwords on top of that figure. For many people, changing important passwords every two weeks may mean learning a hundred new passwords every month.

Unless you have a phenomenal, photographic memory, how likely is it that you'll remember all such passwords? Or will you simply make your passwords weaker in order to facilitate remembering them after frequent changes?

The bottom line is that changing passwords often makes remembering them far more difficult, increasing the odds that you'll write them down and store them insecurely, select weaker passwords, and/or set your new passwords to be the same as old passwords with minute changes (for example, password2 to replace password1).

REMEMBER

So, here is the reality: If you select strong, unique passwords to begin with and the sites where you've used them aren't believed to have been compromised, the cons of frequently changing the passwords outweigh the pros. Changing such passwords every few years may be a good idea. In reality, if a system alerts you of multiple failed attempts to log in to your account and you're not alerted of such activity, you can likely go for many years with no changes without exposing yourself to significant risk.

Of course, if you use a password manager that can reset passwords, you can configure it to reset them often. In fact, I've worked with a commercial password-management system used for protecting system administration access to sensitive financial systems that automatically reset administrators' passwords every time they logged on.

Changing Passwords after a Breach

If you receive notification from a business, organization, or government entity that it has suffered a security breach and that you should change your password, follow these tips:

> >> Don't click any links in the message because most such messages are scams.

>> Visit the organization's website and official social media accounts to verify that such an announcement was actually made.

>> Pay attention to news stories to see whether reliable, mainstream media is reporting such a breach.

>> If the story checks out, go to the organization's website and make the change.

TIP

Do not change all your passwords after every breach. Ignore experts who cry wolf and tell you to do so after every single breach as a matter of extra caution. Doing so isn't necessary, uses up your brainpower, time, and energy, and dissuades you from changing passwords when you actually need to do so. After all, if you do make such password changes and then find out that your friends who fared no worse than you after a breach, you may grow weary and ignore future warnings to change your password when doing so is actually necessary.

If you reuse passwords on sites where the passwords matter — which you should not be doing — and a password that is compromised somewhere is also used on other sites, be sure to change it at the other sites as well. In such a case, also take the opportunity when resetting passwords to switch to unique passwords for each of the sites.

Providing Passwords to Humans

On its website, the United States Federal Trade Commission (FTC) recommends the following:

Don't share passwords on the phone, in texts, or by email. Legitimate companies will not send you messages asking for your password.

That sounds like good advice, and it would be, if it were not for one important fact: Legitimate businesses do ask you for passwords over the phone!

So, how do you know when it is safe to provide your password and when it is not?

Should you just check your caller ID?

No. The sad reality is that crooks spoof caller IDs on a regular basis.

What you should do is never provide any sensitive information — including passwords, of course — over the phone unless you initiated the call with the party requesting the password and are sure that you called the legitimate party. It is far less risky, for example, to provide an account's phone-access password to a customer service representative who asks for it during a conversation initiated by you calling to the bank using the number printed on your ATM card than if someone calls you claiming to be from your bank and requests the same private information in order to "verify your identity."

Storing Passwords

Ideally, don't write down your passwords to sensitive systems or store them anywhere other than in your brain.

For less sensitive passwords, use a password manager or store them in an encrypted form on a strongly-secured computer or device. If you store your passwords on a phone, use the secure area. (For more on password managers and your phone's secure area, see the section "Consider using a password manager," earlier in this chapter.)

Transmitting Passwords

Theoretically, you should never email or text someone a password. So, what should you do if your child texts you from school saying that he or she forgot the password to his or her email, or the like?

TIP

Ideally, if you need to give someone a password, call him or her and don't provide the password until you identify the other party by voice. If, for some reason, you must send a password in writing, choose to use an encrypted connection, which is offered by various chat tools. If no such tool is available, consider splitting the password and sending some via email and some via text.

Obviously, none of these methods are ideal ways to transmit passwords, but they certainly are better options than what so many people do, which is to simply text or email people passwords in clear text.

Discovering Alternatives to Passwords

On some occasions, you should take advantage of alternatives to password authentication. While there are many ways to authenticate people, a modern user is likely to encounter certain types:

>> Biometric authentication

>> SMS-based authentication

>> App-based one-time passwords

>> Hardware token authentication

>> USB-based authentication

Biometric authentication

Biometric authentication refers to authenticating using some unique identifier of your physical person — for example, your fingerprint.

Using biometrics — especially in combination with a password — can be a strong method of authentication, and it certainly has its place. Two popular forms used in the consumer market are fingerprints and iris-based authentication.

In many cases, though, you may be better off using a strong password. Before using biometric authentication, consider the following points:

>> **Your fingerprints are likely all over your phone.** You hold your phone with your fingers. How hard would it be for criminals who steal the phone to lift your prints and unlock the phone if you enable fingerprint based authentication using a phone's built-in fingerprint reader (see Figure 7-3)? If anything sensitive is on the device, it may be at risk. No, the average crook looking to make a quick buck selling your phone is unlikely to spend the time to unlock it — he or she will more than likely just wipe it — but if someone wants the data on your phone for whatever reason, and you used fingerprints to secure your device, you may have a serious problem on your hands (pun intended).

>> **If your biometric information is captured, you can't reset it as you can a password.** Do you fully trust the parties to whom you're giving this information to properly protect it?

>> **If your biometric information is on your phone or computer, what happens if malware somehow infects your device?** What happens if a server where you stored the same information is breached? Are you positive that all the data is properly encrypted and that the software on your device fully defended your biometric data from capture?

>> **Cold weather creates problems.** Fingerprints can't be read even through smartphone-compatible gloves.

>> **Glasses, as worn by millions of people, pose challenges to iris scanners.** Some iris readers require a user to take off his or her glasses in order to authenticate. If you use such authentication to secure a phone, you may have difficulty unlocking your phone when you're outdoors on a sunny day.

HACKERS VERSUS SENSOR

How long did it take hackers to defeat a new fingerprint sensor? Less than 24 hours.

Within 24 hours of the release of the first iPhone with a fingerprint reader, hackers claimed to have defeated it. Furthermore, several years ago, the Discovery Channel television show *Myth Busters* demonstrated how simple it can be for someone to defeat a fingerprint authentication system. Technology has improved since then — but so have criminals' capabilities.

>> **Biometrics can undermine your rights.** If, for some reason, law enforcement wants to access the data on your biometric-protected phone or other computer system, it may be able to force you to provide your biometric authentication, even in countries like the United States where you have the right to remain silent and not provide a password. Likewise, the government may be able to obtain a warrant to collect your biometric data, which, unlike a password, you can't reset. Even if the data proves you innocent of whatever the government suspects you have done wrong, do you trust the government to properly secure the data over the long term?

>> **Impersonation is possible.** Some quasi-biometric authentication, such as the face recognition on some devices, can be tricked into believing that a person is present by playing to them a high-definition video of that person.

>> **Voice-based authentication is useful for voice phone calls.** This type of authentication is especially useful when used in combination with other forms of authentication, such as a password. Many organizations use it to authenticate customers who call in — sometimes without even telling customers. That said, voice authentication can't be used for online sessions without inconveniencing users.

As such, biometrics have their place. Using a fingerprint to unlock features on your phone is certainly convenient but think before you proceed. Be certain that in your case the benefits outweigh the drawbacks.

SMS-based authentication

In *SMS (text message)-based authentication*, a code is sent to your cellphone. You then enter that code into a web or app to prove your identity. This type of authentication is, in itself, not considered secure enough for authentication when true multifactor authentication in required. Sophisticated criminals have ways of intercepting such passwords, and social engineering of phone companies in order to take over people's phone numbers remains a problem.

That said, SMS one-time passwords used in combination with a strong password are a step above just using the password.

WARNING

Keep in mind, however, that, in most cases, one-time passwords are worthless as a security measure if you send them to a criminal's phishing website instead of a legitimate site. The criminal can replay them to the real site in real time.

App-based one-time passwords

One-time passwords generated with an app running on a phone or computer are a good addition to strong passwords, but they should not be used on their own. App-based one-time passwords are likely a more secure way to authenticate than SMS-based one-time passwords (see preceding section), but they can be inconvenient; if you get a new phone, for example, you may need to reconfigure information at every one of the sites where you're using one-time passwords created by the generator app running on your smartphone.

As with SMS-based one-time passwords, if you send an app-generated one-time password to a criminal's phishing website instead of a legitimate site, the criminal can replay it to the corresponding real site in real time, undermining the security benefits of the one-time password in their entirety.

Hardware token authentication

Hardware tokens (see Figure 7-4) that generate new one-time passwords every x seconds are similar to the apps described in the preceding section with the major difference being that you need to carry a specialized device that generates the one-time codes. Some tokens can also function in other modes — for example, allowing for challenge-response types of authentication in which the site being logged into displays a challenge number that the user enters into the token in order to retrieve a corresponding response number that the user enters into the site in order to authenticate.

FIGURE 7-4:
An RSA SecureID brand one-time password generator hardware token.

Although hardware token devices normally are more secure than one-time generator apps in that the former don't run on devices that can be infected by malware or taken over by criminals remotely, they can be inconvenient. They are also prone to getting lost and are not always waterproof — and sometimes get destroyed when people do their laundry after leaving the devices in their pants pockets.

USB-based authentication

USB devices that contain authentication information — for example, digital certificates — can strengthen authentication. Care must be exercised, however, to use such devices only in combination with trusted machines — you don't want the device infected or destroyed by some device, and you want to be sure that the machine obtaining the certificate, for example, doesn't transmit it to an unauthorized party.

Many modern USB-based devices offer all sorts of defenses against such attacks. Of course, you can connect USB devices only to devices and apps that support USB-based authentication. You also must carry the device with you and ensure that it doesn't get lost or damaged.

Chapter **8**

Preventing Social Engineering

Most, if not all, major breaches that have occurred in recent years have involved some element of social engineering. Do not let devious criminals trick you or your loved ones. In this chapter, you find out how to protect yourself

Don't Trust Technology More than You Would People

Would you give your online banking password to a random stranger who asked for it after walking up to you in the street and telling you that he worked for your bank?

If the answer is no — which it certainly should be — you need to exercise the same lack of trust when it comes to technology. The fact that your computer shows you an email sent by some party that claims to be your bank instead of a random person approaching you on the street and making a similar claim is no reason to give that email your trust any more than you would give the stranger.

In short, you don't give offers from strangers approaching you on the street the benefit of the doubt, so don't do so for offers communicated electronically — they may be even more risky.

Types of Social Engineering Attacks

Phishing attacks are one of the most common forms of social engineering attacks. (For more on phishing and social engineering, see Chapter 2.) Figure 8-1 shows you an example of a phishing email.

Phishing attacks sometimes utilize a technique called *pretexting* in which the criminal sending the phishing email fabricates a situation that both gains trust from targets as well as underscores the supposed need for the intended victims to act quickly. In the phishing email shown in Figure 8-1, note that the sender, impersonating Wells Fargo bank, included a link to the real Wells Fargo within the email, but failed to properly disguise the sending address.

Chapter 2 discusses common forms of social engineering attacks, including spear phishing emails, smishing, spear smishing, vishing, spear vishing, and CEO fraud. Additional types of social engineering attacks are popular as well:

>> **Baiting:** An attacker sends an email or chat message — or even makes a social media post that promises someone a reward in exchange for taking some action — for example, telling a target that if she completes a survey, she will receive a free item (see Figure 8-2). Sometimes such promises are real, but often they're not and are simply ways of incentivizing someone to take a specific action that she would not take otherwise. Sometimes such scammers seek payment of a small shipping fee for the prize, sometimes they distribute malware, and sometimes they collect sensitive information. There is even malware that baits.

WARNING

Don't confuse baiting with *scambaiting*. The latter refers to a form of vigilantism in which people pretend to be gullible, would-be victims, and waste scammers' time and resources through repeated interactions, as well as (sometimes) collect intelligence about the scammer that can be turned over to law enforcement or published on the Internet to warn others of the scammer.

FIGURE 8-1:
A phishing email.

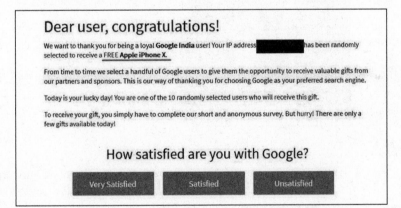

FIGURE 8-2:
Example of a baiting message.

>> **Quid pro quo:** The attacker states that he needs the person to take an action in order to render a service for the intended victim. For example, an attacker may pretend to be an IT support manager offering assistance to an employee in installing a new security software update. If the employee cooperates, the criminal walks him through the process of installing malware.

>> **Social media impersonation:** Some attackers impersonate people on social media in order to establish social media connections with their victims. The parties being impersonated may be real people or nonexistent entities.

The scammers behind the impersonation shown in Figure 8-3 and many other such accounts frequently contact the people who follow the accounts, pretending to be the author, and request that the followers make various "investments." (To find out how you can protect yourself from social media impersonation, see the section "General Cyberhygiene Can Help Prevent Social Engineering," later in this chapter.)

FIGURE 8-3:
An example of an Instagram account impersonating the author, using his name, bio, and primarily photos lifted from his real Instagram account.

>> **Tantalizing emails:** These emails attempt to trick people into running malware or clicking on poisoned links by exploiting their curiosity, sexual desires, and other characteristics.

>> **Tailgating:** *Tailgating* is a physical form of social engineering attack in which the attacker accompanies authorized personnel as they approach a doorway that they, but not the attacker, are authorized to pass and tricks them into letting him pass with the authorized personnel. The attacker may pretend to be searching through a purse for an access card, claim to have forgotten his card, or may simply act social and follow the authorized party in.

>> **False alarms:** Raising false alarms can also social engineer people into allowing unauthorized people to do things that they should not be allowed to. Consider the case in which an attacker pulls the fire alarm inside a building

and manages to enter normally secured areas through an emergency door that someone else used to quickly exit due to the so-called emergency.

>> **Water holing:** Water holing combines hacking and social engineering by exploiting the fact that people trust certain parties, so, for example, they may click on links when viewing that party's website even if they'd never click on links in an email or text message. Criminals may launch a watering hole attack by breaching the relevant site and inserting the poisoned links on it (or even depositing malware directly onto it).

>> **Virus hoaxes:** Criminals exploit the fact that people are concerned about cybersecurity, and likely pay undeserved attention to messages that they receive warning about a cyberdanger. Virus hoax emails may contain poisoned links, direct a user to download software, or instruct a user to contact IT support via some email address or web page. These attacks come in many flavors — some attacks distribute them as mass emails, while others send them in a highly targeted fashion.

Some people consider scareware that scares users into believing that they need to purchase some particular security software (as described in Chapter 2) to be a form of virus hoax. Others do not because scareware's "scaring" is done by malware that is already installed, not by a hoax message that pretends that malware is already installed.

>> **Technical failures:** Criminals can easily exploit humans' annoyance with technology problems to undermine various security technologies.

For example, if a criminal impersonating a website that normally displays a security image in a particular area places a "broken image symbol" in the same area of the clone website, many users will not perceive danger, as they are accustomed to seeing broken-image symbols and associate them with technical failures rather than security risks.

Six Principles Social Engineers Exploit

Social psychologist Robert Beno Cialdini, in his 1984 work published by Harper-Collins, *Influence: The Psychology of Persuasion*, explains six important, basic concepts that people seeking to influence others often leverage. Social engineers seeking to trick people often exploit these same six principles, so I provide a quick overview of them in the context of information security.

The following list helps you understand and internalize the methods crooks are likely to use to try to gain your trust:

>> **Social proof:** People tend to do things that they see other people doing.

>> **Reciprocity:** People, in general, often believe that if someone did something nice for them, they owe it to that person to do something nice back.

>> **Authority:** People tend to obey authority figures, even when they disagree with the authority figures and even when they think what they're being asked to do is objectionable.

>> **Likeability:** People are, generally speaking, more easily persuaded by people who they like than by others.

>> **Consistency and commitment:** If people make a commitment to accomplish some goal and internalize that commitment, it becomes part of their self-image, and they're likely to attempt to pursue the goal even if the original reason for pursuing the goal is no longer at all relevant.

>> **Scarcity:** If people think that a particular resource is scarce, regardless of whether it actually is scarce, they will want it, even if they don't need it.

Don't Overshare on Social Media

Oversharing information on social media arms criminals with material that they can use to social engineer you, your family members, your colleagues at work, and your friends.

If, for example your privacy settings allow anyone with access to the social media platform to see your posted media, your risk increases. Many times, people accidentally share posts with the whole world that they intended for only a small group of people.

Furthermore, in multiple situations, bugs in social media platform software have created vulnerabilities that allowed unauthorized parties to view media and posts that had privacy settings set to disallow such access.

Also, consider your privacy settings. Family-related material with privacy settings set to allow nonfamily members to view it may result in all sorts of privacy-related issues and leak the answers to various popular challenge questions used for authenticating users, such as "Where does your oldest sibling live?" or "What is your mother's maiden name?"

WARNING

Don't rely on social media privacy settings to protect truly confidential data. Some social media platforms allow for granular protection of posted items, while others do not.

Certain items, if shared, may help criminals social engineer you or someone you know. This list isn't meant to be comprehensive. Rather, it's meant to illustrate examples to stimulate your thinking about the potential risks of what you intend to post on social media before you go ahead and post it.

The following sections describes information you should be cautious of sharing on social media.

REMEMBER

Numerous other types of social media posts than the ones I list in the following sections can help criminals orchestrate social engineering attacks. Think about potential consequences before you post and set your posts' privacy settings accordingly.

SOCIAL MEDIA WARNING SYSTEMS

Tools are available to warn people if they are oversharing on social media, including one which the author helped design. A snippet of a configuration screen appears in the figure

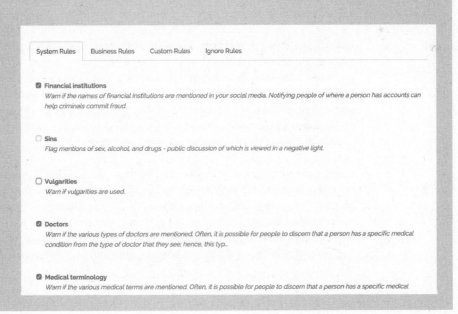

Your schedule and travel plans

Details of your schedule or someone else's schedule may provide criminals with information that may help them set up an attack. For example, if you post that you'll be attending an upcoming event, such as a wedding, you may provide criminals with the ability to *virtually kidnap* you or other attendees — never mind incentivizing others to target your home with a break-in attempt when the home is likely to be empty. (*Virtual kidnapping* refers to a criminal making a ransom demand in exchange for the same return of someone who the criminal claims to have kidnapped, but who in fact, the criminal has not kidnapped.)

Likewise, revealing that you'll be flying on a particular flight may provide criminals with the ability to virtually kidnap you or attempt CEO-type fraud against your colleagues. They may impersonate you and send an email saying that you're flying and may not be reachable by phone for confirmation of the instructions so just go ahead and follow them anyway.

Also, avoid posting about a family member's vacation or trip, which may increase risks of virtual kidnapping (and of real physical dangers to that person or his belongings).

Financial information

Sharing a credit card number may lead to fraudulent charges, while posting a bank account number can lead to fraudulent bank activity.

In addition, don't reveal that you visited or interacted with a particular financial institution or the locations where you store your money — banks, crypto-exchange accounts, brokerages, and so forth. Doing so can increase the odds that criminals will attempt to social engineer their way into your accounts at the relevant financial institution(s). As such, such sharing may expose you to attempts to breach your accounts, as well as targeted phishing, vishing, and smishing attacks and all sorts of other social engineering scams.

Posting about potential investments, such as stocks, bonds, precious metals, or cryptocurrencies, can expose you to cyberattacks because criminals may assume that you have significant money to steal. (If you encourage people to invest or make various other forms of posts, you may also run afoul of SEC, CFTC, or other regulations.) You may also open the door to criminals who impersonate regulators and contact you to pay a fine for posting information inappropriately.

Personal information

For starters, avoid listing your family members in your Facebook profile's About section. That About section links to their Facebook profiles and explains to viewers the nature of the relevant family relationship with each party listed. By listing these relationships, you may leak all sorts of information that may be valuable for criminals. Not only will you possibly reveal your mother's maiden name (challenge question answer!), you may also provide clues about where you grew up. The information found in your profile also provides criminals with a list of people to social engineer or contact as part of a virtual kidnapping scam.

Also you should avoid sharing the following information on social media, as doing so can undermine your authentication questions and help criminals social engineer you or your family:

>> Your father's middle name

>> Your mother's birthday

>> Where you met your significant other

>> Your favorite vacation spot

>> The name of the first school that you attended

>> The street on which you grew up

>> The type, make, model, and/or color of your first car or someone else's

>> Your or others' favorite food or drink

Likewise, never share your Social Security number as doing so may lead to identity theft.

Information about your children

WARNING

Sharing information about your children can not only set you up for attacks, but put your children at great risk of physical danger. For example, photos of your children may assist a kidnapper. The problem may be exacerbated if the images contain a timestamp and/or *geotagging* — that is, information about the location at which a photograph was taken.

Timestamps and geotagging do not need to be done per some technical specification to create risks. If it is clear from the images where your kids go to school, attend after-school activities, and so on, you may expose them to danger.

In addition, referring to the names of schools, camps, day care facilities, or other youth programs that your children or their friends attend may increase the risk of a pedophile, kidnapper, or other malevolent party targeting them. Such a post may also expose you to potential burglars because they'll know when you're likely not to be home. The risk can be made much worse if a clear pattern regarding your schedule and/or your children's schedule can be extrapolated from such posts.

Also avoid posting about a child's school or camp trip.

Information about your pets

As with your mother's maiden name, sharing your current pet's name or your first pet's name can set you or others who you know up for social engineering attacks because such information is often used as an answer to authentication questions.

Work information

Details about with which technologies you work with at your present job (or a previous job) may help criminals both scan for vulnerabilities in your employers' systems and social engineer your colleagues.

Many virus hoaxes and scams have gone viral — and inflicted far more damage than they should have — because criminals exploit people's fear of cyberattacks and leverage the likelihood that many people will share posts about cyber-risks, often without verifying the authenticity of such posts.

Information about a moving violation or parking ticket that you received not only presents yourself in a less-than-the-best light, but can inadvertently provide prosecutors with the material that they need to convict you of the relevant offense. You may also give crooks the ability to social engineer you or others — they may pretending to be law enforcement, a court, or an attorney contacting you about the matter — perhaps even demanding that a fine be paid immediately in order to avoid an arrest.

In addition to helping criminals social engineer you in a fashion similar to the moving violation case, information about a crime that you or a loved one committed may harm you professionally and personally.

Medical or legal advice

If you offer medical or legal advice, people may be able to extrapolate that you or a loved one has a particular medical condition, or involved in a particular legal situation.

Your location

Your location or *check-in* on social media may not only increase the risk to yourself and your loved ones of physical danger, but may help criminals launch virtual kidnapping attacks and other social engineering scams.

A happy birthday message to anyone may reveal the person's birthday. Folks who use fake birthdays on social media for security reasons have seen their precautions undermined in such a fashion by would be well-wishers. Anything that is "sin-like" may lead not only to professional or personal harm, but to blackmail-like attempts as well as social engineering of yourself or others depicted in such posts or media.

In addition, an image of you in a place frequented by people of certain religious, sexual, political, cultural, or other affiliations can lead to criminals extrapolating information about you that may lead to all sorts of social engineering. Criminals are known, for example, to have virtually kidnapped a person who was in synagogue and unreachable on the Jewish holiday of Yom Kippur. They knew when and where he would be walking on his way to the temple, and called family members (at a time that they knew he would be impossible to reach) claiming to have kidnapped the person. The family members fell for the virtual kidnapping scam because the details were right and they were unable to reach the "victim" by telephone in the middle of a synagogue service.

Leaking Data by Sharing Information as Part of Viral Trends

From time to time, a *viral trend* occurs, in which many people share similar content. Posts about the ice bucket challenge, your favorite concerts, and something about you today and ten years ago are all examples of viral trends. Of course, future viral trends may have nothing to do with prior ones. Any type of post that spreads quickly to large numbers of people is said to have "gone viral."

WARNING

While participating may seem fun — and "what everyone else is doing" — be sure that you understand the potential consequences of doing so. For example, sharing information about the concerts that you attended and that you consider to be your favorites can reveal a lot about you — especially in combination with other profile data — and can expose you to all sorts of social engineering risks.

Identifying Fake Social Media Connections

Social media delivers many professional and personal benefits to its users, but it also creates amazing opportunities for criminals — many people have an innate desire to connect with others and are overly trusting of social media platforms. They assume that if, for example, Facebook sends a message that Joseph Steinberg has requested to become a friend, that the real "Joseph Steinberg" has requested as such — when, often, that is not the case.

Criminals know, for example, that by connecting with you on social media, they can gain access to all sorts of information about you, your family members, and your work colleagues — information that they can often exploit in order to impersonate you, a relative, or a colleague as part of criminal efforts to social engineer a path into business systems, steal money, or commit other crimes.

One technique that criminals often use to gain access to people's "private" Facebook, Instagram, or LinkedIn information is to create fake profiles — profiles of nonexistent people — and request to connect with real people, many of whom are likely to accept the relevant connection requests. Alternatively, scammers may set up accounts that impersonate real people — and which have profile photos and other materials lifted from the impersonated party's legitimate social media accounts.

How can you protect yourself from such scams? The following sections offer advice on how to quickly spot fake accounts — and how to avoid the possible repercussions of accepting connections from them.

REMEMBER

Keep in mind that none of the clues in the following sections operates in a vacuum or is absolute. The fact that a profile fails when tested against a particular rule, for example, doesn't automatically mean that it is bogus. But applying smart concepts such as the ones I list in the following sections should help you identify a significant percentage of fake accounts and save yourself from the problems that can ultimately result from accepting connection requests from them.

Photo

Many fake accounts use photos of attractive models, sometimes targeting men who have accounts that show photos of women and women whose accounts have photos of men. The pictures often appear to be stock photos, but sometimes are stolen from real users.

While it may be true that most fake accounts don't have Premium status, some crooks do invest in obtaining Premium status in order to make their accounts seem more real. In some cases, they are paying with stolen credit cards, so it doesn't cost them anything anyway. So, remain vigilant even if an account is showing the Premium icon.

LinkedIn endorsements

Fake people are not going to be endorsed by many real people. And the endorsers of fake accounts may be other fake accounts that seem suspicious as well.

Group activity

Fake profiles are less likely than real people to be members of closed groups that verify members when they join and are less likely to participate in meaningful discussions in both closed and open groups on Facebook or LinkedIn. If they are members of closed groups, those groups may have been created and managed by scammers and contain other fake profiles as well.

Fake folks may be members of many open groups — groups that were joined in order to access member lists and connect with other participants with "I see we are members of the same group, so let's connect" type messages.

WARNING

In any case, keep in mind that on any social platform that has groups, being members of the same group as someone else is not, in any way, a reason to accept a connection from that person.

Appropriate levels of relative usage

Real people who use LinkedIn or Facebook heavily enough to have joined many groups are more likely to have filled out all their profile information. A connection request from a person who is a member of many groups but has little profile information is suspicious.

Likewise, an Instagram account with 20,000 followers but only two posted photos that seeks to follow your private account is suspicious for the same reason.

Human activities

Many fake accounts seem to list cliché-sounding information in their profiles, interests, and work experience sections, but contain few other details that seem to convey a true, real-life human experience.

WARNING

If you receive a social media connection request from someone who you don't remember ever meeting and the picture is of this type, beware. If you're in doubt, you can load the image into Google's reverse image search and see where else it appears.

You can also search on the person's name (and, if appropriate, on LinkedIn) or title to see whether any other similar photos appear online. However, a crafty impersonator may upload images to several sites.

Obviously, any profile without a photo of the account holder should raise red flags. Keep in mind, though, that some people do use emojis, caricatures, and so on as profile photos, especially on nonprofessional-oriented social media networks.

Verification

If an account appears to represent a public figure who you suspect is likely to be verified (meaning it has a blue check mark next to the user's account name to indicate that the account is the legitimate account of a public figure), but it is not verified, that is a likely sign that something is amiss.

Likewise, it is unlikely that a verified account on a major social media platform is fake. However, there have been occasions on which verified accounts of such nature have been taken over temporarily by hackers.

Friends or connections in common

Fake people are unlikely to have many friends or connections in common with you, and fake folks usually will not even have many secondary connections (Friends of Friends, LinkedIn second level connections, and so on) in common with you either.

WARNING

Don't assume that an account is legitimate just because it has one or two connections in common with you; some of your connections may have fallen for a scam and connected with a fake person, and your contact's connecting with the fake account may be how the criminal found out about you in the first place. Even in such a scenario, the number of shared connections is likely to be relatively small as compared with a real, mutual connection, and the human relationship between the friends who did connect with the crook's profile may seem difficult to piece together.

You know your connections better than anyone else — exercise caution when someone's connection patterns don't make sense. You may want to think twice, for example, if someone trying to connect with you seems to know nobody in the industry in which she works, but knows three of your most gullible friends who live in three different countries and who do not know one another.

Relevant posts

Another huge red flag is when an account is not sharing material that it should be sharing based on the alleged identity of the account holder. If someone claims to be a columnist who currently writes for *Forbes*, for example, and attempts to but has never shared any posts of any articles that he or she wrote for *Forbes*, something is likely amiss.

Number of connections

A senior-level person, with many years of work experience, is likely to have many professional connections, especially on LinkedIn. The fewer connections that an account ostensibly belonging to a senior level person has on LinkedIn (the further it is from 500 or more), the more suspicious you should be.

Of course, every LinkedIn profile started with zero connections — so legitimate, new LinkedIn accounts may seems suspicious when they truly are not — but practical reality comes into play: How many of the real, senior-level people who are now contacting you didn't establish their LinkedIn accounts until recently? Of course, a small number of connections and a new LinkedIn account isn't abnormal for a person who just started his first job or for people working in certain industries, in certain roles, and/or at certain companies — CIA secret agents don't post their career progress in their LinkedIn profiles — but if you work in those industries, you're likely aware of this fact already.

Contrast the number of connection with the age of an account and the number of posts it has interacted with or has shared — a person who has been on Facebook for a decade and who posts on a regular basis, for example, should have more than one or two Friends.

Industry and location

Common sense applies vis-à-vis accounts purporting to represent people living in certain locations or working in certain industries. If, for example, you work in technology and have no pets and receive a LinkedIn connection request from a veterinarian living halfway across the world whom you have never met, something may be amiss.

Likewise, if you receive a Facebook friend request from someone with who have nothing in common, beware.

Don't assume that any claims made in a profile are necessarily accurate an if you share a lot in common, the sender is definitely safe. Someone targetin may have discerned your interests from information about you that is pu available online.

Similar people

If you receive multiple requests from people with similar titles or who clai work for the same company and you don't know the people and aren't acti doing some sort of deal with that company, beware. If those folks don't seei be connected to anyone else at the company who you know actually works th consider that a potential red flag as well.

You can always call, text, or email a real contact and ask whether she sees t person listed in a staff directory.

Duplicate contact

If you receive a Facebook friend request from a person who is already your Fac book friend, verify with that party that she is switching accounts. In many case such requests come from scammers.

Contact details

Make sure the contact details make sense. Fake people are far less likely than rea people to have email addresses at real businesses and rarely have email addresses at major corporations. They're unlikely to have physical addresses that show where they live and work, and, if such addresses are listed, they rarely correspond with actual property records or phone directory information that can easily be checked online.

LinkedIn Premium status

Because LinkedIn charges for its Premium service, some experts have suggested that Premium status is a good indicator that an account is real because a criminal is unlikely to pay for an account.

Here are a few signs that things may not be what they seem:

» On LinkedIn, the Recommendations, Volunteering Experience, and Education sections of a fake person may seem off.

» On Facebook, a fake profile may seem to be cookie cutter and the posts generic enough in nature that millions of people could have made the same post.

» On Twitter, they may be retweeting posts from others and never share their own opinions, comments, or other original material.

» On Instagram the photos may be lifted from other accounts or appear to be stock photos — sometimes none of which include an image of the actual person who allegedly owns the accounts.

TIP

The content within a user's social media profile may provide terms and phrases that you can search for in Google along with the person's name to help you verify whether the account truly belongs to a human being whose identity the profile alleges to represent.

Likewise, if you perform a Google image search on someone's Instagram images and see that they belong to other people, something is amiss.

Cliché names

Some fake profiles seem to use common, flowing American names, such as Sally Smith, that both sound overly American and make performing a Google search for a particular person far more difficult than doing so would be for someone with an uncommon name.

TIP

More often than occurs in real life, but certainly not always, bogus profiles seem to use first and last names that start with the same letter. Perhaps, scammers just like the names or, for some reason, find them funny.

Poor contact information

If a social media profile contains absolutely no contact information that can be used to contact the person behind the profile via email, telephone, or on another social platform, beware.

Skill sets

If skill sets don't match someone's work or life experience, beware. Something may seem off when it comes to fake accounts. For example, if someone claims to have graduated with a degree in English from an Ivy League university, but makes serious grammatical errors throughout his profile, something may be amiss.

Likewise, if someone claims to have two PhDs in mathematics, but claims to be working as a gym teacher, beware.

Spelling

Spelling errors are common on social media. However, something may be amiss if someone misspells her own name or the name of an employer, or makes errors of this nature on LinkedIn (a professionally oriented network).

Suspicious career or life path

People who seem to have been promoted too often and too fast or who have held too many disparate senior positions, such as VP of Sales, then CTO, and then General Counsel, may be too good to be true.

Of course, real people have moved up the ladder quickly and some folks (including myself) have held a variety of different positions throughout the course of their careers, but scammers often overdo it when crafting the career progression or role diversity data of a bogus profile. People may shift from technical to managerial roles, for example, but it is extremely uncommon for someone to serve as a company's VP of Sales, then as its CTO, and then as its General Counsel — roles that require different skill sets, educational backgrounds, and potentially, different certifications and licenses.

TIP

If you find yourself saying to yourself "no way" when looking at someone's career path, you may be right.

Level or celebrity status

LinkedIn requests from people at far more senior professional levels than yourself can be a sign that something is amiss, as can Facebook requests from celebrities and others about whose connection request you're flattered to have received.

It is certainly tempting to want to accept such connections (which is, of course, why the people who create fake accounts often create such fake accounts), but think about it: If you just landed your first job out of college, do you really think the CEO of a major bank is suddenly interested in connecting with you out of the blue? Do you really think that Ms. Universe, whom you have never met, suddenly wants to be your friend?

In the case of Facebook, Instagram, and Twitter, be aware that most celebrity accounts are verified. If a request comes in from a celebrity, you should be able to quickly discern if the account sending it is the real deal.

Using Bogus Information

Some experts have suggested that you use bogus information as answers to common challenge questions. Someone — especially someone whose mother has a common last name as her maiden name — may establish a new mother's maiden name to be used for all sites that ask for such information as part of an authentication process. There is truth to the fact that such an approach somewhat helps reduce the risk of social engineering.

What it does even stronger, though, is reveal how poor challenge questions are as a means of authenticating people. Asking one's mother's maiden name is effectively asking for a password while providing a hint that the password is a last name!

Likewise, because in the era of social media and online public records, finding out someone's birthday is relatively simple, some security experts recommend creating a second fake birthday for use online. Some even recommend using a phony birthday on social media, both to help prevent social engineering and make it harder for organizations and individuals to correlate one's social media profile and various public records.

While all these recommendations do carry weight, keep in mind that, in theory, there is no end to such logic — establishing a different phony birthday for every site with which one interacts offers stronger privacy protections than establishing just one phony birthday, for example.

In general, however, having one fake birthday, one fake mother's maiden name, and so on is probably worthwhile and doesn't require much additional brainpower and mindshare over using just the real one. Be sure, however, not to mislead any sites where providing accurate information is required by law (for example, when opening a credit card account).

Using Security Software

Besides providing the value of protecting your computer and your phone from hacking, various security software may reduce your exposure to social engineering attacks. Some software, for example, filters out many phishing attacks, while other software blocks many spam phone calls. While using such software is wise, don't rely on it. There is a danger that if few social engineering attacks make it through your technological defenses, you may be less vigilant when one does reach you — don't let that happen.

While smartphone providers have historically charged for some security features, over time they have seen the value to themselves of keeping their customers secure. Today, basic versions of security software, including technology to reduce spam calls, are often provided at no charge along with smartphone cellular-data service.

General Cyberhygiene Can Help Prevent Social Engineering

Practicing good cyberhygiene in general can also help reduce your exposure to social engineering. If your children, for example, have access to your computer but you encrypt all your data, have a separate login, and don't provide them with administrator access, your data on the machine may remain safe even if a criminal social engineers his way into your child's account.

Likewise, not responding to suspicious emails or providing information to potential scammers who solicit it can help prevent all sorts of social engineering and technical attacks.

If you receive a social media connection request from someone who you don't remember ever meeting and the picture is of this type, beware. If you're in doubt, you can load the image into Google's reverse image search and see where else it appears.

You can also search on the person's name (and, if appropriate, on LinkedIn) or title to see whether any other similar photos appear online. However, a crafty impersonator may upload images to several sites.

Obviously, any profile without a photo of the account holder should raise red flags. Keep in mind, though, that some people do use emojis, caricatures, and so on as profile photos, especially on nonprofessional-oriented social media networks.

Verification

If an account appears to represent a public figure who you suspect is likely to be verified (meaning it has a blue check mark next to the user's account name to indicate that the account is the legitimate account of a public figure), but it is not verified, that is a likely sign that something is amiss.

Likewise, it is unlikely that a verified account on a major social media platform is fake. However, there have been occasions on which verified accounts of such nature have been taken over temporarily by hackers.

Friends or connections in common

Fake people are unlikely to have many friends or connections in common with you, and fake folks usually will not even have many secondary connections (Friends of Friends, LinkedIn second level connections, and so on) in common with you either.

Don't assume that an account is legitimate just because it has one or two connections in common with you; some of your connections may have fallen for a scam and connected with a fake person, and your contact's connecting with the fake account may be how the criminal found out about you in the first place. Even in such a scenario, the number of shared connections is likely to be relatively small as compared with a real, mutual connection, and the human relationship between the friends who did connect with the crook's profile may seem difficult to piece together.

You know your connections better than anyone else — exercise caution when someone's connection patterns don't make sense. You may want to think twice, for example, if someone trying to connect with you seems to know nobody in the industry in which she works, but knows three of your most gullible friends who live in three different countries and who do not know one another.

Relevant posts

Another huge red flag is when an account is not sharing material that it should be sharing based on the alleged identity of the account holder. If someone claims to be a columnist who currently writes for *Forbes*, for example, and attempts to but has never shared any posts of any articles that he or she wrote for *Forbes*, something is likely amiss.

Number of connections

A senior-level person, with many years of work experience, is likely to have many professional connections, especially on LinkedIn. The fewer connections that an account ostensibly belonging to a senior level person has on LinkedIn (the further it is from 500 or more), the more suspicious you should be.

Of course, every LinkedIn profile started with zero connections — so legitimate, new LinkedIn accounts may seems suspicious when they truly are not — but practical reality comes into play: How many of the real, senior-level people who are now contacting you didn't establish their LinkedIn accounts until recently? Of course, a small number of connections and a new LinkedIn account isn't abnormal for a person who just started his first job or for people working in certain industries, in certain roles, and/or at certain companies — CIA secret agents don't post their career progress in their LinkedIn profiles — but if you work in those industries, you're likely aware of this fact already.

Contrast the number of connection with the age of an account and the number of posts it has interacted with or has shared — a person who has been on Facebook for a decade and who posts on a regular basis, for example, should have more than one or two Friends.

Industry and location

Common sense applies vis-à-vis accounts purporting to represent people living in certain locations or working in certain industries. If, for example, you work in technology and have no pets and receive a LinkedIn connection request from a veterinarian living halfway across the world whom you have never met, something may be amiss.

Likewise, if you receive a Facebook friend request from someone with whom you have nothing in common, beware.

WARNING

Don't assume that any claims made in a profile are necessarily accurate and that if you share a lot in common, the sender is definitely safe. Someone targeting you may have discerned your interests from information about you that is publicly available online.

Similar people

If you receive multiple requests from people with similar titles or who claim to work for the same company and you don't know the people and aren't actively doing some sort of deal with that company, beware. If those folks don't seem to be connected to anyone else at the company who you know actually works there, consider that a potential red flag as well.

REMEMBER

You can always call, text, or email a real contact and ask whether she sees that person listed in a staff directory.

Duplicate contact

If you receive a Facebook friend request from a person who is already your Facebook friend, verify with that party that she is switching accounts. In many cases, such requests come from scammers.

Contact details

Make sure the contact details make sense. Fake people are far less likely than real people to have email addresses at real businesses and rarely have email addresses at major corporations. They're unlikely to have physical addresses that show where they live and work, and, if such addresses are listed, they rarely correspond with actual property records or phone directory information that can easily be checked online.

LinkedIn Premium status

Because LinkedIn charges for its Premium service, some experts have suggested that Premium status is a good indicator that an account is real because a criminal is unlikely to pay for an account.

While it may be true that most fake accounts don't have Premium status, some crooks do invest in obtaining Premium status in order to make their accounts seem more real. In some cases, they are paying with stolen credit cards, so it doesn't cost them anything anyway. So, remain vigilant even if an account is showing the Premium icon.

LinkedIn endorsements

Fake people are not going to be endorsed by many real people. And the endorsers of fake accounts may be other fake accounts that seem suspicious as well.

Group activity

Fake profiles are less likely than real people to be members of closed groups that verify members when they join and are less likely to participate in meaningful discussions in both closed and open groups on Facebook or LinkedIn. If they are members of closed groups, those groups may have been created and managed by scammers and contain other fake profiles as well.

Fake folks may be members of many open groups — groups that were joined in order to access member lists and connect with other participants with "I see we are members of the same group, so let's connect" type messages.

WARNING

In any case, keep in mind that on any social platform that has groups, being members of the same group as someone else is not, in any way, a reason to accept a connection from that person.

Appropriate levels of relative usage

Real people who use LinkedIn or Facebook heavily enough to have joined many groups are more likely to have filled out all their profile information. A connection request from a person who is a member of many groups but has little profile information is suspicious.

Likewise, an Instagram account with 20,000 followers but only two posted photos that seeks to follow your private account is suspicious for the same reason.

Human activities

Many fake accounts seem to list cliché-sounding information in their profiles, interests, and work experience sections, but contain few other details that seem to convey a true, real-life human experience.

Here are a few signs that things may not be what they seem:

» On LinkedIn, the Recommendations, Volunteering Experience, and Education sections of a fake person may seem off.

» On Facebook, a fake profile may seem to be cookie cutter and the posts generic enough in nature that millions of people could have made the same post.

» On Twitter, they may be retweeting posts from others and never share their own opinions, comments, or other original material.

» On Instagram the photos may be lifted from other accounts or appear to be stock photos — sometimes none of which include an image of the actual person who allegedly owns the accounts.

TIP

The content within a user's social media profile may provide terms and phrases that you can search for in Google along with the person's name to help you verify whether the account truly belongs to a human being whose identity the profile alleges to represent.

Likewise, if you perform a Google image search on someone's Instagram images and see that they belong to other people, something is amiss.

Cliché names

Some fake profiles seem to use common, flowing American names, such as Sally Smith, that both sound overly American and make performing a Google search for a particular person far more difficult than doing so would be for someone with an uncommon name.

TIP

More often than occurs in real life, but certainly not always, bogus profiles seem to use first and last names that start with the same letter. Perhaps, scammers just like the names or, for some reason, find them funny.

Poor contact information

If a social media profile contains absolutely no contact information that can be used to contact the person behind the profile via email, telephone, or on another social platform, beware.

Skill sets

If skill sets don't match someone's work or life experience, beware. Something may seem off when it comes to fake accounts. For example, if someone claims to have graduated with a degree in English from an Ivy League university, but makes serious grammatical errors throughout his profile, something may be amiss.

Likewise, if someone claims to have two PhDs in mathematics, but claims to be working as a gym teacher, beware.

Spelling

Spelling errors are common on social media. However, something may be amiss if someone misspells her own name or the name of an employer, or makes errors of this nature on LinkedIn (a professionally oriented network).

Suspicious career or life path

People who seem to have been promoted too often and too fast or who have held too many disparate senior positions, such as VP of Sales, then CTO, and then General Counsel, may be too good to be true.

Of course, real people have moved up the ladder quickly and some folks (including myself) have held a variety of different positions throughout the course of their careers, but scammers often overdo it when crafting the career progression or role diversity data of a bogus profile. People may shift from technical to managerial roles, for example, but it is extremely uncommon for someone to serve as a company's VP of Sales, then as its CTO, and then as its General Counsel — roles that require different skill sets, educational backgrounds, and potentially, different certifications and licenses.

TIP

If you find yourself saying to yourself "no way" when looking at someone's career path, you may be right.

Level or celebrity status

LinkedIn requests from people at far more senior professional levels than yourself can be a sign that something is amiss, as can Facebook requests from celebrities and others about whose connection request you're flattered to have received.

It is certainly tempting to want to accept such connections (which is, of course, why the people who create fake accounts often create such fake accounts), but think about it: If you just landed your first job out of college, do you really think the CEO of a major bank is suddenly interested in connecting with you out of the blue? Do you really think that Ms. Universe, whom you have never met, suddenly wants to be your friend?

In the case of Facebook, Instagram, and Twitter, be aware that most celebrity accounts are verified. If a request comes in from a celebrity, you should be able to quickly discern if the account sending it is the real deal.

Using Bogus Information

Some experts have suggested that you use bogus information as answers to common challenge questions. Someone — especially someone whose mother has a common last name as her maiden name — may establish a new mother's maiden name to be used for all sites that ask for such information as part of an authentication process. There is truth to the fact that such an approach somewhat helps reduce the risk of social engineering.

What it does even stronger, though, is reveal how poor challenge questions are as a means of authenticating people. Asking one's mother's maiden name is effectively asking for a password while providing a hint that the password is a last name!

Likewise, because in the era of social media and online public records, finding out someone's birthday is relatively simple, some security experts recommend creating a second fake birthday for use online. Some even recommend using a phony birthday on social media, both to help prevent social engineering and make it harder for organizations and individuals to correlate one's social media profile and various public records.

While all these recommendations do carry weight, keep in mind that, in theory, there is no end to such logic — establishing a different phony birthday for every site with which one interacts offers stronger privacy protections than establishing just one phony birthday, for example.

In general, however, having one fake birthday, one fake mother's maiden name, and so on is probably worthwhile and doesn't require much additional brainpower and mindshare over using just the real one. Be sure, however, not to mislead any sites where providing accurate information is required by law (for example, when opening a credit card account).

Using Security Software

Besides providing the value of protecting your computer and your phone from hacking, various security software may reduce your exposure to social engineering attacks. Some software, for example, filters out many phishing attacks, while other software blocks many spam phone calls. While using such software is wise, don't rely on it. There is a danger that if few social engineering attacks make it through your technological defenses, you may be less vigilant when one does reach you — don't let that happen.

While smartphone providers have historically charged for some security features, over time they have seen the value to themselves of keeping their customers secure. Today, basic versions of security software, including technology to reduce spam calls, are often provided at no charge along with smartphone cellular-data service.

General Cyberhygiene Can Help Prevent Social Engineering

Practicing good cyberhygiene in general can also help reduce your exposure to social engineering. If your children, for example, have access to your computer but you encrypt all your data, have a separate login, and don't provide them with administrator access, your data on the machine may remain safe even if a criminal social engineers his way into your child's account.

Likewise, not responding to suspicious emails or providing information to potential scammers who solicit it can help prevent all sorts of social engineering and technical attacks.

4

Cybersecurity for Businesses and Organizations

Chapter **9**

Securing Your Small Business

Nearly everything I discuss in this book applies to both individuals and businesses. Small business owners and workers should be aware of some other points that may not necessarily be important for individuals. This chapter discusses some of these cybersecurity issues. I could write an entire series of books about improving the cybersecurity of small businesses. As such, this chapter isn't a comprehensive list of everything that every small business needs to know. Rather, it provides food for thought for those running small businesses.

Making Sure Someone Is in Charge

Individuals at home are responsible for the security of their computers, but what happens when you have a network and multiple users? Somebody within the business needs to ultimately "own" responsibility for information security. That person may be you, the business owner, or someone else. But whoever is in charge must clearly understand that he or she is responsible.

In many cases of small businesses, the person in charge of information security will outsource some of the day-to-day activities. Even so, that person is ultimately responsible for ensuring that necessary activities, such as installing security patches, happen — and happen on time. If a breach occurs, "I thought so-and-so was taking care of that security function" is not an excuse that will carry a lot of weight.

Watching Out for Employees

Employees, and the many cybersecurity risks that they create, can become major headaches for small businesses. Human errors are the No. 1 catalyst for data breaches. Even if you're reading this book and seeking to improve your cybersecurity knowledge and posture, your employees and coworkers may not have the same level of commitment as you do when it comes to protecting data and systems.

As such, one of the most important things that a small business owner can do is to educate his or her employees. Education consists of essentially three necessary components:

>> **Awareness of threats:** You must ensure that every employee working for the business understands that he or she, and the business as a whole, are targets. People who believe that criminals want to breach their computers, phones, and databases act differently than people who have not internalized this reality. While formal, regular training is ideal, even a single, short conversation conducted when workers start, and refreshed with periodic reminders, can deliver significant value in this regard.

>> **Basic information-security training:** All employees should understand certain basics of information security. They should, for example, know to avoid cyber-risky behavior, such as opening attachments and clicking on links found in unexpected email messages, downloading music or videos from questionable sources, inappropriately using public Wi-Fi for sensitive tasks, or buying products from unknown stores with too-good-to-be-true" prices and no publicly known physical address. (See Chapter 20 for tips on how to safely use public Wi-Fi.)

Numerous related training materials (often free) are available online. That said, never rely on training in itself to serve as the sole line of defense against any substantial human risk. Many people do stupid things even after receiving clear training to the contrary. Furthermore, training does nothing to address rogue employees who intentionally sabotage information security.

>> **Practice:** Information security training should not be theoretical. Employees should be given the opportunity to practice what they have learned — for example, by identifying and deleting/reporting a test phishing email.

Incentivize employees

Just as you should hold employees accountable for their actions if things go amiss, you should also reward employees for performing their jobs in a cyber-secure fashion and acting with proper cyberhygiene. Positive reinforcement can go a long way and is almost always better received than negative reinforcement.

Furthermore, many organizations have successfully implemented reporting systems that allow employees to anonymously notify the relevant powers within the business of suspicious insider activities that may indicate a threat, as well as potential bugs in systems, that could lead to vulnerabilities. Such programs are common among larger businesses, but can be of benefit to many small companies as well.

Avoid giving out the keys to the castle

There are countless stories of employees making mistakes that open the organizational door to hackers and of disgruntled employees stealing data and/or sabotaging systems. The damage from such incidents can be catastrophic to a small business. Protect yourself and your business from these types of risks by setting up your information infrastructure to contain the damage if something does go amiss.

TIP

How can you do this? Give workers access to all the computer systems and data that they need in order to do their jobs with maximum performance, but do not give them access to anything else of a sensitive nature. Programmers shouldn't be able to access a business's payroll system, for example, and a comptroller doesn't need access to the version control system housing the source code of a company's proprietary software.

Limiting access can make a world of difference in terms of the scope of a data leak if an employee goes rogue. Many businesses have learned this lesson the hard way. Don't become one of them.

Give everyone his or her own credentials

Every employee accessing each and every system in use by the organization should have his or her own login credentials to that system. Do not share credentials!

Implementing such a scheme improves the ability to audit people's activities (which may be necessary if a data breach or other cybersecurity event happens) and also encourages people to better protect their passwords because they know that if the account is misused, management will address the matter with them personally rather than with a team. The knowledge that a person is going to be held accountable for his or her behavior for maintaining or compromising security can work wonders in a proactive sense.

Likewise, every person should have his or her own multifactor authentication capabilities — whether that be a physical token, a code generated on his/her smartphone, and so on.

Restrict administrators

System administrators typically have superuser privileges — meaning that they may be able to access, read, delete, and modify other people's data. It is essential, therefore, that if you — the business owner — are not the only superuser, that you implement controls to monitor what an administrator does. For example, you can log administrator actions on a separate machine that the administrator does not have access to.

Allowing access from only a specific machine in a specific location — which is sometimes not possible due to business needs — is another approach, as it allows a camera to be aimed toward that machine to record everything that the administrator does.

Limit access to corporate accounts

Your business itself may have several of its own accounts. For example, it may have social media accounts — a Facebook page, Instagram account, and a Twitter account — customer support, email accounts, phone accounts, and other utility accounts.

REMEMBER

Grant access only to the people who absolutely need access to those accounts (see preceding section). Ideally, every one of the folks to whom you do give access should have *auditable access* — that is, it should be easy to determine who did what with the account.

Basic control and audibility are simple to achieve when it comes to Facebook Pages, for example, as you can own the Facebook Page for the business, while providing other people the ability to write to the page. In some other environments, however, granular controls aren't available and you will need to decide between providing multiple people logins to a social media account or having them submit content to a single person (perhaps, even you) who makes the relevant posts.

The challenge of providing every authorized user of corporate social media accounts with his or her own account to achieve both control and audibility is exacerbated by the fact that all sensitive accounts should be protected with multifactor authentication. (See Chapter 6 for more on multifactor authentication.)

Some systems offer multifactor authentication capabilities that account for the fact that multiple independent users may need to be given auditable access to a single account. In some cases, however, systems that offer multifactor authentication capabilities do not blend well with multi-person environments. They may, for example, allow for only one cellphone number to which one-time passwords are sent via SMS. In such scenarios, you will need to decide whether to

>> Use the multifactor authentication, but with a work-around — for example, by using a VOIP number to receive the texts and configuring the VOIP number to forward the messages on to multiple parties via email (as is offered at no cost, for example, by Google Voice).

>> Use the multifactor authentication with no work-around — and configure the authorized users' devices not to need multifactor authentication for the activities that they perform.

>> Not use the multifactor authentication, but instead rely solely on strong passwords (not recommended).

>> Find another work-around by modifying your processes, procedures, or technologies used to access such systems.

>> Utilize third-party products that overlay systems (often the best option when available).

TIP

The last option is often the best option. Various content management systems, for example, allow themselves to be configured for multiple users, each with his or her own independent, strong authentication capabilities, and all such users have auditable access to a single social media account.

While larger enterprises almost always follow some variant of the last approach — both for management and security reasons — many small businesses tend to take the easy way out and simply not use strong authentication in such cases. The cost of implementing proper security — both in terms of dollars and time — is usually quite low, so exploring third-party products should definitely be done before deciding to take another approach.

REMEMBER

The value of having proper security with auditability will become immediately clear if you ever have a disgruntled employee who had access to the company's social media accounts or if a happy and satisfied employee with such access is hacked.

Implementing employee policies

Businesses of all sizes that have employees need an employee handbook that includes specific rules regarding employee usage of business technology systems and data.

It is beyond the scope of this book to cover all elements of employee handbooks, but the following are examples of rules that businesses can implement to govern the use of company technology resources:

>> Company's employees are expected to use technology responsibly, appropriately, and productively, as necessary to perform their professional responsibilities.

>> The use of company devices, as well as company Internet access and email, as provided to employee by company, are for job-related activities. Minimal personal use is acceptable provided that the employee's using it as such does not violate any other rules described in this document and does not interfere with his or her work.

>> Each employee is responsible for any computer hardware and software provided to him or her by the company, including for the safeguarding of such items from theft, loss, or damage.

>> Each employee is responsible for his or her accounts provided by the company, including the safeguarding of access to the accounts.

>> Employees are strictly prohibited from sharing any company-provided items used for authentication (passwords, hardware authentication devices, PINs, and so on) and are responsible for safeguarding such items.

>> Employees are strictly prohibited from connecting any networking devices, such as routers, access points, range extenders, and so on, to company networks unless explicitly authorized to do so by the company's CEO. Likewise, employees are strictly prohibited from connecting any personal computers or electronic devices — including any Internet of Things (IoT) devices — to company networks other than to the Guest network, under the conditions stated explicitly in the Bring Your Own Device (BYOD) policy. (See the section on BYOD, later in this chapter.)

>> Employees are responsible to make sure that security software is running on all company-provided devices. Company will provide such software, but it is beyond company's ability to check that such systems are always functioning as expected. Employees may not deactivate or otherwise cripple such security systems, and must promptly notify company's IT department if they suspect that any portion of the security systems may be compromised, nonfunctioning, or malfunctioning.

>> Employees are responsible to make sure that security software is kept up to date. All company-issued devices come equipped with Auto-Update enabled; employees must not disable this feature.

>> Likewise, employees are responsible for keeping their devices up to date with the latest operating system, driver, and application patches when vendors issue such patches. All company-issued devices come equipped with Auto-Update enabled; employees must not disable this feature.

>> Performing any illegal activity — whether or not the act involved is a felony, a misdemeanor, or a violation of civil law — is strictly prohibited. This rule applies to federal law, state law, and local law in any area and at any time in which the employee is subject to such laws.

>> Copyrighted materials belonging to any party other than the company or employee may not be stored or transmitted by the employee on company equipment without explicit written permission of the copyright holder. Material that the company has licensed may be transmitted as permitted by the relevant licenses.

>> Sending mass unsolicited emails (spamming) is prohibited.

>> The use of company resources to perform any task that is inconsistent with company's mission — even if such task is not technically illegal — is prohibited. This includes, but is not limited to, the accessing or transmitting sexually explicit material, vulgarities, hate speech, defamatory materials, discriminatory materials, images or description of violence, threats, cyberbullying, hacking-related material, stolen material, and so on.

>> The previous rule shall not apply to employees whose job entails working with such material, only to the extent that is reasonably needed for them to perform the duties of their jobs. For example, personnel responsible for configuring the company's email filter may, without violating the preceding rule, email one another about adding to the filter configuration various terms related to hate speech and vulgarities.

>> No company devices equipped with Wi-Fi or cellular communication capabilities may be turned on in China or Russia without explicit written permission from the company's CEO. Loaner devices will be made available for employees making trips to those regions. Any personal device turned on in those regions may not be connected to the Guest network (or any other company network).

>> All use of public Wi-Fi with corporate devices must comply with the company's Public Wi-Fi policies.

>> Employees must backup their computers by using the company's backup system as discussed in the company's backup policy.

>> Employees may not copy or otherwise back up data from company devices to their personal computers and/or storage devices.

>> Any and all passwords for any and all systems used as part of an employees' job must be unique and not reused on any other systems. All such passwords must consist of three or more words, at least one of which is not found in the English dictionary, joined together with numbers or special characters or meet all the following conditions:

  - Contain eight characters or more with at least one uppercase character

  - Contain at least one lowercase character

  - Contain at least one number

  - Not contain any words that can be found in an English dictionary

  - In either case, names of relatives, friends, or colleagues may not be used as part of any password.

>> Data may be taken out of the office for business purposes only and must be encrypted prior to removal. This rule applies whether the data is on hard drive, SSD, CD/DVD, USB drive, or on any other media or is transmitted over the Internet. Any and all such data must be returned to the office (or at company's sole discretion, destroyed,) immediately after its remote use is complete or upon employee's termination of employment, whichever is sooner.

>> In the event of a breach or other cybersecurity event or of any natural or man-made disaster, no employees other than the company's officially designated spokesperson may speak to the media on behalf of the company.

>> No devices from any manufacturer that the FBI or other United States federal law enforcement and intelligence agencies have warned that they believe foreign governments are using to spy on Americans may be connected to any company network (including the guest network) or brought into the physical offices of the company.

Enforcing social media policies

Devising, implementing, and enforcing social media policies is important because inappropriate social media posts made by your employees (or yourself) can inflict all sorts of damage. They can leak sensitive information, violate compliance rules, and assist criminals to social engineer and attack your organization, expose your business to boycotts and/or lawsuits, and so on.

You want to make clear to all employees what is and is not acceptable use of social media. As part of the process of crafting the policies, consider consulting an attorney to make sure that you do not violate anyone's freedom of speech. You may also want to implement technology to ensure social media does not transform from a marketing platform into a nightmare.

Monitoring employees

Regardless of whether or not they plan to actually monitor employees' usage of technology, companies should inform users that they have a right to do so. If an employee were to go rogue and steal data, for example, you do not want to have the admissibility of evidence challenged on the grounds that you had no right to monitor the employee. Furthermore, telling employees that they may be monitored reduces the likelihood of employees doing things that they are not supposed to do because they know that they may be monitored while doing such things.

Here is an example of text that you can provide to employees as part of an employee handbook or the like when they begin work:

Company, at its sole discretion, and without any further notice to employee, reserves the right to monitor, examine, review, record, collect, store, copy, transmit to others, and control any and all email and other electronic communications, files, and any and all other content, network activity including Internet use, transmitted by or through its technology systems or stored in its technology systems or systems, whether onsite or offsite. Such systems shall include systems that it owns and operates and systems that it leases, licenses, or to which it otherwise has any usage rights.

Furthermore, whether sent to an internal party, external party, or both, any and all email, text and/or other instant messages, voicemail, and/or any and all other electronic communications are considered to be Company's business records, and may be subject to discovery in the event of litigation and/or to disclosure based on warrants served upon company or requests from regulators and other parties.

Considering Cyber Insurance

While cybersecurity insurance may be overkill for most small businesses, if you believe that your business could suffer a catastrophic loss or even fail altogether if it were to be breached, you may want to consider buying insurance. If you do pursue this route, keep in mind that nearly all cybersecurity insurance policies have *carve outs*, or exclusions — so make sure that you understand exactly what is covered and what is not and for what amount of damage you are actually covered. If your business fails because you were breached, a policy that pays only to have an expert spend two hours restoring your data is not going to be worth much.

REMEMBER

Cybersecurity insurance is never a replacement for proper cybersecurity. In fact, insurers normally require that a business meet a certain standard of cybersecurity to purchase and maintain coverage. In some cases, the insurer may even refuse to pay a claim if it finds that the insured party was breached at least in part due to negligence on the insured's part or due to the failure of the breached party to adhere to certain standards or practices mandated by the relevant insurance policy.

Complying with Regulations and Compliance

Businesses may be bound by various laws, contractual obligations, and industry standards when it comes to cybersecurity. Your local Small Business Administration office may be able to provide you with guidance as to what regulations potentially impact you. Remember, though, that there is no substitute for hiring a properly trained lawyer experienced with this area of law to provide professional advice optimized for your particular situation.

The following sections provide examples of several such regulations, standards, and so on that often impact small businesses.

Protecting employee data

You're responsible for protecting sensitive information about your employees. For physical files, you should, in general, protect records with at least *double-locking* — storing the paper files in a locked cabinet within a locked room (and not using the same key for both). For electronic files, the files should be stored encrypted within a password-protected folder, drive, or virtual drive. Such standards, however, may not be adequate in every particular situation, which is why you should check with an attorney.

REMEMBER

Keep in mind that failure to adequately protect employee information can have severe effects: If your business is breached and a criminal obtains private information about employees, the impacted employees and former employees can potentially sue you, and the government may fine you as well. Remediation costs may also be much higher than the costs of proactive prevention would have been. And, of course, the impact of bad publicity on the business's sales may also be catastrophic.

Remember, employee personnel records, W2 forms, Social Security numbers, I9 employment eligibility forms, home addresses and phone numbers, medical information, vacation records, family leave records, and so on are all potentially considered private.

TIP

In general, if you're unsure as to whether some information may be considered private, err on the side of caution and treat it as if it is private.

PCI DSS

Payment Card Industry Data Security Standard (PCI DSS) is an information security standard for organizations that handle major credit cards and their associated information.

While all companies of all sizes that are subject to the PCI DSS standard must be compliant with it, PCI does take into effect the different levels of resources available to different sized businesses. PCI Compliance has effectively four different levels. To what level an organization must comply is normally based primarily on how many credit card transactions it processes per year. Other factors, such as how risky the payments are that the company receives, also weigh in. The different levels are

>> **PCI Level 4:** Standards for businesses that process fewer than 20,000 credit card transactions per year

>> **PCI Level 3:** Standards for businesses that process between 20,000 and 1,000,000 credit card transactions per year

>> **PCI Level 2:** Standards for businesses that process between 1,000,000 and 6,000,000 credit card transactions per year

>> **PCI Level 1:** Standards for businesses that process more than 6,000,000 credit card transactions per year

Exploring PCI in detail is beyond the scope of this book. Multiple, entire books have been written on the topic. If you operate a small business and process credit card payments or store credit card data for any other reason, be sure to engage someone knowledgeable in PCI to help guide you. In many cases, your credit card processors will be able to recommend a proper consultant or guide you themselves.

Breach disclosure laws

In recent years, various jurisdictions have enacted so-called *breach disclosure laws*, which require businesses to disclose to the public if they suspect that a breach may have endangered certain types of stored information. Breach disclosure laws vary quite a bit from jurisdiction to jurisdiction, but, in some cases, they may apply even to the smallest of businesses.

REMEMBER

Be sure that you are aware of the laws that apply to your business. If, for some reason, you do suffer a breach, the last thing that you want is the government punishing you for not handling the breach properly. Remember: Many small businesses fail as the result of a breach; the government entering the fray only worsens your business's odds of surviving.

The laws that apply to your business may include not only those of the jurisdiction within which you're physically located but the jurisdictions of the people you're handling information for.

GDPR

The *General Data Protection Regulation* (GDPR) is a European privacy regulation that went into effect in 2018 and applies to all businesses handling the consumer data of residents of the European Union, no matter the size, industry, or country of origin of the business and no matter whether the EU resident is physically located within the EU. It provides for stiff fines for businesses that do not properly protect private information belonging to EU residents. This regulation means that a small business in New York that sells an item to an EU resident located in New York may be subject to GDPR for information about the purchaser and, can, in theory, face stiff penalties if it fails to properly protect that person's data. For example, in July 2019, the United Kingdom's Information Commissioner's Office (ICO) announced that it intended to fine British Airways about $230 million and Marriott about $123 million for GDPR-related violations stemming from data breaches.

GDPR is complex. If you think that your business may be subject to GDPR, speak with an attorney who handles such matters.

TIP

Do not panic about GDPR. Even if a small business in the United States is technically subject to GDPR, it is unlikely that the EU will attempt to fine small American businesses that do not operate in Europe anytime soon; it has much bigger fish to fry. That said, do not ignore GDPR because eventually American small businesses may become targets for enforcement actions.

HIPAA

Federal law throughout the United States of America requires parties that house healthcare-related information to protect it in order to maintain the privacy of the individuals whose medical information appears in the data. The *Health Insurance Portability and Accountability Act* (HIPAA), which went into effect in 1996, provides for stiff penalties for improperly defending such information. Be sure to learn whether HIPAA applies to your business and, if so, ensure that you are properly protecting the data to which it applies according to industry standards or better.

Biometric data

If you utilize any forms of biometric authentication or for any other reason store biometric data, you may be subject to various privacy and security laws governing that data. Multiple states have already enacted laws in this regard, and others are likely to follow.

Handling Internet Access

Small businesses face significant challenges related to Internet access and information systems that individuals rarely must think about, and must take various actions to prevent the emergence of various dangers. The following sections cover a few examples.

Segregate Internet access for personal devices

If you provide Internet access for visitors to your place of business, and/or for your employees to use with their personal smartphones and tablets while at work, implement this Internet access on a separate network from the network(s) used to run your business (see Figure 9-1). Most modern routers offer such a capability, which is usually found somewhere in the configuration with a name like Guest network.

Bring your own device (BYOD)

If you allow employees to perform business activities on their own personal laptops or mobile devices, you need to create policies regarding such activity and implement technology to protect your data in such an environment.

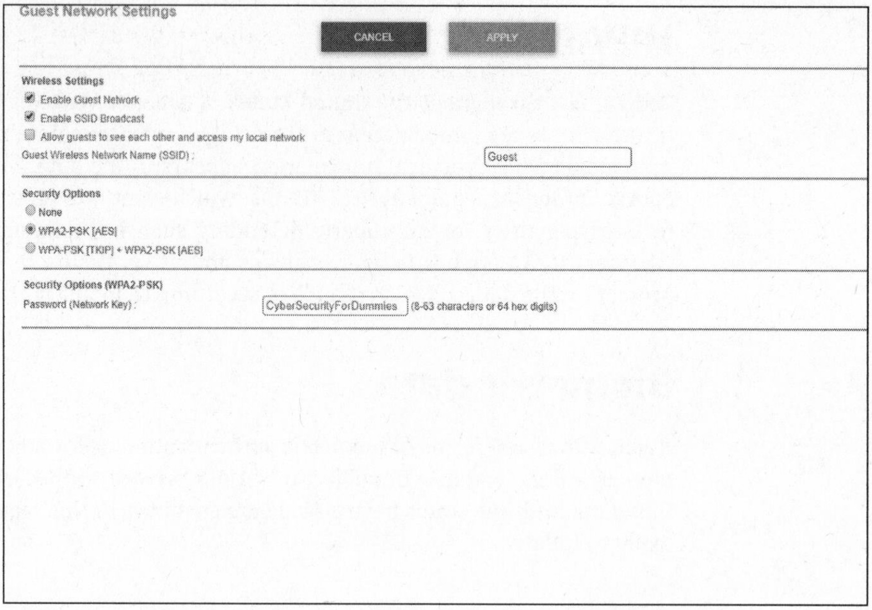

Guest Network Settings

CANCEL   APPLY

Wireless Settings

☑ Enable Guest Network
☑ Enable SSID Broadcast
☐ Allow guests to see each other and access my local network

Guest Wireless Network Name (SSID) : | Guest |

Security Options

○ None
● WPA2-PSK [AES]
○ WPA-PSK [TKIP] + WPA2-PSK [AES]

Security Options (WPA2-PSK)

Password (Network Key) : | CyberSecurityForDummies | (8-63 characters or 64 hex digits)

FIGURE 9-1:
Configuring a guest network for connecting nonbusiness machines to the Internet.

WARNING

Don't rely on policies. If you don't enforce policies with technology, you could suffer a catastrophic theft of data if an employee goes rogue or makes a mistake.

In general, small businesses should not allow bring your own device (BYOD) — even if doing so is tempting. In the vast majority of cases when small businesses do allow employees to use their own devices for work-related activities, data remains improperly protected, and problems develop if an employee leaves the organization (especially if he or she leaves under less than optimal circumstances).

TIP

Many Android keyboards "learn" about a user's activities as he or she types. While such learning helps improve spelling correction and word prediction, it also means that in many cases, sensitive corporate information may be learned on a personal device and remain as suggested content when a user types on it even after he leaves his or her employer.

If you do allow BYOD, be sure to set proper policies and procedures — both for usage and for decommissioning any company technology on such devices, as well as for removing any company data when an employee leaves. Develop a full mobile device security plan that includes remote wipe capabilities, enforces protection of passwords and other sensitive data, processes work-related data in an isolated area of the device that other apps can't access (a process known as *sandboxing*), installs, runs, and updates mobile-optimized security software, prohibits staff from using public Wi-Fi for sensitive work-related tasks, prohibits certain activities from the devices while corporate data is on them, and so on.

Handling inbound access

One of the biggest differences between individuals and businesses using the Internet is often the need of the business to provide inbound access for untrusted parties. Unknown parties must be able to initiate communications that result in communications with internal servers within your business.

For example, if a business offers products for sale online, it must allow untrusted parties to access its website to make purchases (see Figure 9-2). Those parties connect to the website, which must connect to payment systems and internal order tracking systems, even though they are untrusted. (Individuals typically do not have to allow any such inbound access to their computers.)

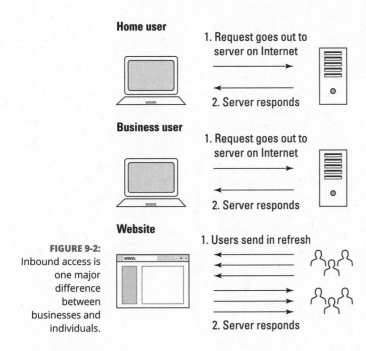

Home user

1. Request goes out to server on Internet

2. Server responds

Business user

1. Request goes out to server on Internet

2. Server responds

Website

1. Users send in refresh

2. Server responds

FIGURE 9-2: Inbound access is one major difference between businesses and individuals.

While small businesses can theoretically properly secure web servers, email servers, and so on, the reality is that few, if any, small businesses have the resources to adequately do so, unless they're in the cybersecurity business to begin with. As such, it is wise for small businesses to consider using third-party software and infrastructure, set up by an expert, and managed by experts, to host any systems used for inbound access. To do so, a business may assume any one or more of several approaches:

>> **Utilize a major retailer's website.** If you're selling items online, and sell only through the websites of major retailers, such as Amazon, Rakuten, and/or eBay, those sites serve as a major buffer between your business's systems and the outside world. The security armies at those companies defend their customer-facing systems from attacks. In many cases, such systems don't require small businesses to receive inbound communications, and when they do, the communications emanate from those retailers' systems, not from the public. Of course, many factors go into deciding whether to sell via a major retailer — online markets do take hefty commissions, for example. When you weigh the factors in making such a decision, keep the security advantages in mind.

>> **Utilize a third-party hosted retail platform.** In such a case, the third party manages most of the infrastructure and security for you, but you customize and manage the actual online store. Such a model does not offer quite the same level of isolation from outside users as does the preceding model, but it does offer much greater buffering against attacks than if you operate your own platform by yourself. Shopify is an example of a popular third-party platform.

>> **Operate your own platform, hosted by a third party that is also responsible for security.** This approach offers better protection than managing the security yourself, but it does not isolate your code from outsiders trying to find vulnerabilities and attack. It also places responsibility for the upkeep and security of the platform on you.

>> **Operate your own system hosted either internally or externally and use a managed services provider to manage your security.** In such a case, you're fully responsible for the security of the platform and infrastructure, but you're outsourcing much of the actual work required to satisfy that responsibility to a third party.

Other models and many variants of the models I list exist as well.

While the models may step from easier to secure to harder to secure, they also step from less customizable to more customizable. In addition, while the earlier models may cost less for smaller businesses, the expense of the earlier models typically grows much faster than do the later ones as a business grows.

TIP

While using third-party providers does add some risks; the risk that a small business will be unable to properly implement and perpetually manage security is likely much greater than any security risk created by using a reliable third party. Of course, outsourcing anything to an unknown third party that you have done no due diligence on is extremely risky and is not recommended.

Protecting against denial-of-service attacks

If you operate any Internet-facing sites as part of your business, make sure that you have security technology implemented to protect against denial-of-service type attacks. If you're selling via retailers, they likely have it already. If you're using a third-party cloud platform, the provider may supply it as well. If you're running the site on your own, you should obtain protection to ensure that someone can't easily take your site — and your business — offline.

Use https for your website

If your business operates a website, be sure to install a valid TLS/SSL certificate so that users can communicate with it over a secure connection and know that the site actually belongs to your business.

TIP

Some security systems that protect against denial-of-service attacks include a certificate as part of the package.

Providing remote access to systems

If you intend on providing employees remote access to corporate systems, consider using a Virtual Private Network (VPN) and multifactor authentication. In the case of remote access, the VPN should create an encrypted tunnel between your remote users and your business, not between users and a VPN provider. The tunnel both protects against people snooping on the communications between remote users and the business and also allows remote users to function as if they were in the company's offices, and utilize various business resources available only to insiders. Multifactor authentication is discussed in detail in Chapter 6.

Of course, if you use third-party, cloud-based systems, the relevant providers should already have security capabilities deployed that you can leverage — do so.

Running penetration tests

Individuals rarely run tests to see whether hackers can penetrate into their systems, and neither do most small businesses. Doing so, however, can be valuable — especially if you are deploying a new system of some sort or upgrading network infrastructure. See Chapter 16 for more on penetration testing.

Being careful with IoT devices

Many businesses today utilize connected cameras, alarms, and so on. Be sure that someone is responsible for overseeing the security of these devices, which should be run on separate networks (or virtual segments) than any computers used to operate the business. Control access to these devices and do not allow employees to connect any unauthorized IoT devices to the business's networks. For more on IoT devices, see Chapter 17.

Using multiple network segments

Depending on the size and nature of your business, isolating various computers onto different network segments may be wise. A software development company, for example, should not have developers coding on the same network that the operations folks use to manage payroll and accounts payable.

Being careful with payment cards

If you accept credit and/or debit cards — and are not selling via a major retailer's website — make sure to speak with your processor about various anti-fraud technology options that may be available to you.

Managing Power Issues

Use an uninterruptable power supply on all systems that you can't afford to have go down even momentarily. Also, make sure the power supplies can keep the systems up and running for longer than any expected outage. If you're selling various goods and services via online retail, for example, you may lose current sales and future sales, as well as suffer reputational harm, if your ability to sell goes offline even for a short period of time.

LOCKING ALL NETWORKING EQUIPMENT AND SERVERS IN A VENTILATED CLOSET

You must control physical access to your systems and data if you want to protect them from unauthorized access. While individuals typically store computers in the open in their homes, businesses usually keep servers in locked racks or closets. You need to be sure, though, that any such rack or closet where you locate computer equipment is well ventilated, or your equipment may overheat and die. You may even need to install a small air conditioner in the closet if ventilation on its own does not sufficiently get rid of the heat generated by the equipment.

WARNING

Never let cleaning personnel enter the server closet unaccompanied — even for a moment. The author personally witnessed a case in which a server used by dozens of people went down because an administrator allowed cleaning personnel to enter a server room unaccompanied only to find later that someone unplugged a server from an uninterruptible power supply (UPS) — a device that serves as both the entry point for power into the system as well as a battery backup — to plug in a vacuum cleaner.

Chapter **10**

Cybersecurity and Big Businesses

M any of the information security challenges facing large enterprises and small business are the same. In fact, over the past decade, cloud-based offerings have brought to small businesses many well-protected systems with enterprise-class technologies, reducing some of the historical differences between the firms of different sizes as far as the architecture of some systems is concerned.

Of course, many security risks scale with enterprise size, but don't qualitatively differ based on the number of employees, partners, and customers that a business has or the size of its information technology budget.

At the same time, however, bigger companies often face significant additional complications — sometimes involving orders of magnitude more complexity than the cybersecurity challenges facing small businesses. A large number of diverse systems, often spread across geographies, with custom code and so on, often make securing a large enterprise quite difficult and complex.

Thankfully, however, larger firms tend to have significantly larger budgets to acquire defenses and defenders. Furthermore, despite the fact that all companies should, in theory, have formal information security programs, small business tend not to, while large businesses almost always do.

This chapter explores some areas that disproportionately impact large companies.

Utilizing Technological Complexity

Large enterprises often have multiple offices and lines of business, many different information systems, complex business arrangements with partners and suppliers, and so on — all of which are reflected in much more complicated information infrastructure than typically exists in the case of smaller businesses. As such, large companies have a much larger *attack surface* — that is, they have many more potential points of attack than do small businesses — and the varied systems mean that no individual, or even small number of people, can possibly be experts on addressing all of them. Large firms use a blend of cloud and local systems, of commercial-off-the-shelf and custom-built systems, a blend of technologies, complex network architectures, and so on — and their security teams must make sure that all of these work together in a secure fashion.

Managing Custom Systems

Large enterprises almost always have significant amounts of custom-built technology systems that are managed in-house. Depending on how they are deployed and utilized, these systems may require the same level of security patching that off-the-shelf software requires — which means that internal folks need to maintain the code from a security perspective, push out patches, and so on.

Furthermore, security teams must be involved with internal systems throughout the systems' entire life cycle — including phases such as initial investigation, analysis and requirements definition, design, development, integration and testing, acceptance and deployment, ongoing operations, and maintenance, evaluation, and disposal.

Security as an element of software development is a complicated matter. Entire books are written about delivering security during the software development life cycle, and professional certifications are awarded specifically in this area as well.

Continuity Planning and Disaster Recovery

While small businesses should have business continuity and disaster recovery plans (sometimes known as BCPs and DRPs) and should regularly test those plans as well, they typically have, at least from a formal perspective, rudimentary plans — at best. Large businesses typically have much more formal plans — including detailed arrangements for resumption of work in case a facility becomes unavailable and so on. Entire books cover disaster recovery and continuity planning — testaments to the complexity and robustness of the relevant processes.

Looking at Regulations

Large enterprises are often subject to many more regulations, laws, guidance, and industry standards than are small businesses. Besides all the issues that are described in the chapter on securing small businesses, for example, the following sections cover some other ones that may impact large enterprises.

Sarbanes Oxley

The Sarbanes Oxley Act of 2002, technically known as either the Public Company Accounting Reform and Investor Protection Act or the Corporate and Auditing Accountability, Responsibility, and Transparency Act, established many rules intended to help protect investors in public companies. Many of its mandates, for example, are intended to improve the accuracy, objectivity, and reliability of corporate statements and disclosures and to create formal systems of internal checks and balances within companies. SOX, as it is often known, mandated stronger corporate governance rules, closed various accounting loopholes, strengthened protections for whistle-blowers, and created substantial penalties (including jail time) for corporate and executive malfeasance.

As its name implies, all publicly held American companies are subject to SOX, as are companies outside of the United States that have registered any equity or debt securities with the United States Securities and Exchange Commission (SEC).

Additionally, any third party, such as an accounting firm, that provides accounting or other financial services to companies regulated by SOX, is itself mandated to comply with SOX, regardless of its location.

SOX has many implications on information security — both directly and indirectly. Two sections of SOX effectively mandate that companies implement various information security protections:

>> **Section 302** of SOX addresses the corporate responsibility to utilize controls to ensure that the firm produces accurate financial reports and requires companies to implement systems to prevent any unauthorized tampering with corporate data used to create such reports — whether the tampering is done by employees or external folks.

>> **Section 404** is perhaps the most controversial portion of SOX and certainly, for many businesses, the most expensive with which to comply. This section makes corporate managers responsible to ensure that the company has adequate and effective internal control structures and requires that any relevant shortcomings be reported to the public. Section 404 makes management responsible to ensure that the corporation can properly protect its data processing systems and their contents and mandates that the firm must make all relevant data available to auditors, including information about any potential security breaches.

In addition to these two areas in which SOX plays a role, information security professionals are likely to deal with many other systems that companies have implemented in order to comply with other SOX requirements. Such systems need protection as well as they themselves must adhere to SOX, too.

SOX is complicated — and public companies normally employ people who are experts in the relevant requirements. Information security professionals are likely to interface with such folks.

Stricter PCI requirements

The PCI DSS standards for protecting credit card information (see Chapter 9) include stricter mandates for larger companies (for example, those processing more credit card transactions) than for smaller firms. Also, keep in mind that from a practical perspective, larger firms are likely to have more processing terminals and more credit card data, as well as more diverse technology involved in their credit card processing processes — raising the stakes when it comes to PCI. Larger firms also face a greater risk of reputational damage: A violation of PCI DSS standards by a larger firm is far more likely to make the national news than if the same violation were made by a mom-and-pop shop.

Public company data disclosure rules

Public companies — that is, businesses owned by the public via their shares being listed on a stock exchange (or on various other public trading platforms) — are subject to numerous rules and regulations intended to protect the integrity of the markets.

One such requirement is that the company must release to the entire world at the same time various types of information that may impact the value of the company's shares. The firm can't, for example, provide such information to investment banks before disclosing it to the media. In fact, anyone to whom the firm does release the information prior to the disclosure to the public — for example, the public company's accounting or law firms — is strictly prohibited from trading shares or any derivative based on them based on that data.

As such, large corporations often have all sorts of policies, procedures, and technologies in place to protect any data subject to such regulations — and to address situations in which some such data was inadvertently released.

Breach disclosures

Some breach disclosure rules exempt smaller businesses, but all require disclosures from large enterprises. Furthermore, large enterprises often have multiple departments that must interact and coordinate in order to release information about a breach — sometimes also involving external parties. Representatives of the marketing, investor relations, information technology, security, legal, and other departments, for example, may need to work together to coordinate the text of any release and may need to involve a third-party public relations firm and external counsel as well. Large enterprises also tend to have official spokespeople and media departments to which the press can address any questions.

Industry-specific regulators and rules

Various industry-specific rules and regulations tend to apply to larger firms more often than to small businesses.

For example, the Nuclear Regulatory Commission (NRC), which is an independent federal agency that regulates nuclear power companies in the United States, regulates some major utilities, but few, if any, mom-and-pop shops will ever be subject to its regulations. Hence, only larger firms dedicate significant resources to ensuring compliance with its rules. In the world of NRC regulations, cybersecurity is an important element in governing various Supervisory Control and Data Acquisition systems (SCADA), which are computer-based control and management systems that speak to the controllers in components of a plant.

Likewise, with the exception of certain hedge funds and other financial operations, few small businesses are required to monitor and record all the social media interactions of their employees, the way major banks must do for certain workers.

As a result of industry specific regulations, many large businesses have various processes, policies, and technologies in place that yield data and systems requiring all sorts of information security involvement.

Fiduciary responsibilities

While many small businesses don't have external shareholders to whom management or a board of directors may be fiduciarily responsible, most large corporations do have investors who may sue either or both parties if a cybersecurity breach harms the firm's value. Various laws require management and boards to ensure that systems are appropriately secured. In some cases, folks may even be able to be criminally charged if they were negligent. Even if senior executives are not charged after a breach, they may still suffer severe career and reputational damage for their failure to prevent it.

Deep pockets

Because large enterprises have much deeper pockets than small businesses — in other words, they have a lot more money at their disposal — and because targeting mom-and-pop shops isn't usually as politically advantageous as targeting a large firm that exhibited some bad behavior, regulators tend to pursue compliance cases against large enterprises suspected of violations with much more gusto than they do against small businesses.

Deeper Pockets — and Insured

Because larger organizations are more likely to have large amounts of cash and assets than small businesses, they make better targets for class action and various other forms of lawsuits than do mom-and-pop shops. Lawyers don't want to expend large amounts of time fighting a case if their target has no money with which to settle or may go bankrupt (and therefore not pay) in the case of a judgment.

As a result, the odds that a larger enterprise will be targeted with a lawsuit if data leaks from it as a result of a breach are relatively high when compared with the odds that the same would happen to a much smaller business suffering a similar breach.

Considering Employees, Consultants, and Partners

Employees are often the weakest link in a business's security chain. Far more complex employment arrangements utilized by large enterprises — often involving unionized employees, non-unionized employees, directly hired contractors, contractors hired through firms, subcontractors, and so on — threaten to make the problem even worse for larger business.

Complexity of any sort increases the odds of people making mistakes. With human errors being the No. 1 catalyst for data breaches, large enterprises must go beyond the human management processes and procedures of small businesses. They must, for example, have streamlined processes for deciding who gets to access what and who can give authorization for what. They must establish simple processes for revoking permissions from diverse systems when employees leave, contractors complete their assignments, and so on.

Revoking access from departing parties is not as simple as many people might imagine. An employee of a large corporation might, for example, have access to multiple, unconnected data systems located in many different locations around the globe and that are managed by different teams from different departments. Identity and access management systems that centralize parts of the authentication and authorization processes can help, but many large enterprises still lack the totally comprehensive centralization necessary to make revoking access a single-step process.

Dealing with internal politics

While all businesses with more than one employee have some element of politics, large businesses can suffer from conflicts between people and groups that are literally incentivized to perform in direct opposition to one another. For example, a business team may be rewarded if it delivers new product features earlier than a certain date — which it can do more easily if it skimps on security — while the information security team may be incentivized to delay the product release because it's incentivized to ensure that there are no security problems and not to get the product to market quickly.

Offering information security training

All employees should understand certain basics of information security. They should, for example, know to avoid cyber-risky behavior, such as opening attachments and clicking on links found in unexpected email messages, downloading music or videos from questionable sources, inappropriately using public Wi-Fi for sensitive tasks, or buying products from unknown stores with "too good to be true" prices and no publicly known physical address.

In large firms, however, most employees do not personally know most other employees. Such a situation opens the door for all sorts of social engineering attacks — bogus requests from management to send W2s, bogus requests from the IT department to reset passwords, and so on. Training and practice to make sure that such attacks cannot successfully achieve their aims are critical.

Replicated environments

Larger businesses often replicate environments not only in order to protect against outages, but also for maintenance purposes. As such, they often have three replicas for every major system in place: the production system (which may be replicated itself for redundancy purposes), a development environment, and a staging environment for running tests of code and patches.

Looking at the Chief Information Security Officer's Role

While all businesses need someone within them to ultimately own responsibility for information security, larger enterprises often have large teams involved with information security and need someone who can oversee all the various aspects of information security management, as well as manage all the personnel involved in doing so. This person also represents the information security function to senior management — and sometimes to the board. Typically that person is the chief information security officer (CISO).

While the exact responsibilities of CISOs vary by industry, geography, company size, corporate structure, and pertinent regulations, most CISO roles share basic commonalities.

In general, the CISO's role includes overseeing and assuming responsibility for all areas of information security. The following sections describe those areas.

Overall security program management

The CISO is responsible to oversee the company's security program from A to Z. This role includes not only establishing the information security policies for the enterprise, but everything needed to ensure that business objectives can be achieved with the desired level of risk management — something that requires performing risk assessments, for example, on a regular basis.

While, in theory, small businesses also have someone responsible for their entire security programs, in the case of large enterprises, the programs are usually much more formal, with orders of magnitude more moving parts. Such programs are also forever ongoing.

Test and measurement of the security program

The CISO is responsible to establish proper testing procedures and success metrics against which to measure the effectiveness of the information security plan and to make adjustments accordingly. Establishing proper security metrics is often far more complicated than one might initially assume, as defining "successful performance" when it comes to information security is not a straightforward matter.

Human risk management

The CISO is responsible for addressing various human risks as well. Screening employees before hiring them, defining roles and responsibilities, training employees, providing employees with appropriate user manuals and employee guides, providing employees with information security breach simulations and feedback, creating incentive programs, and so on all often involve the participation of the CISO's organization.

Information asset classification and control

This function of the CISO includes performing an inventory of informational assets, devising an appropriate classification system, classifying the assets, and then deciding what types of controls (at a business level) need to be in place to adequately secure the various classes and assets. Auditing and accountability should be included in the controls as well.

Security operations

Security operations means exactly what it sounds like. It is the business function that includes the real-time management of security, including the analysis of threats, and the monitoring of a company's technology assets (systems, networks, databases, and so on) and information security countermeasures, such as firewalls, whether hosted internally or externally, for anything that may be amiss. Operations personnel are also the folks who initially respond if they do find that something has potentially gone wrong.

Information security strategy

This role includes devising the forward-looking security strategy of the company to keep the firm secure as it heads into the future. Proactive planning and action is a lot more comforting to shareholders than reacting to attacks.

Identity and access management

This role deals with controlling access to informational assets based on business requirements, and includes identity management, authentication, authorization, and related monitoring. It includes all aspects of the company's password management policies and technologies, any and all multifactor authentication policies and systems, and any directory systems that store lists of people and groups and their permissions.

The CISO's identity and access management teams are responsible to give workers access to the systems needed to perform the workers' jobs and to revoke all such access when a worker leaves. Likewise, they manage partner access and all other external access.

Major corporations almost always utilize formal directory services type systems — Active Directory, for example, is quite popular.

Data loss prevention

Data loss prevention includes policies, procedures, and technologies that prevent proprietary information from leaking. Leaks can happen accidentally — for example, a user may accidentally attach the wrong document to an email before sending the message — or through malice (for example, a disgruntled employee steals valuable intellectual property by copying it to a USB drive and taking the drive home just before resigning).

In recent years, some social media management functions have been moved into the data loss prevention group. After all, oversharing on social media often includes the de facto sharing by employees of information that businesses do not want going out onto publicly accessible social networks.

Fraud prevention

Some forms of fraud prevention often fall in the CISO's domain. For example, if a company operates consumer-facing websites that sell products, it is often part of the CISO's responsibility to minimize the number of fraudulent transactions that are made on the sites. Even when such responsibility doesn't fall within the purview of the CISO, the CISO is likely to be involved in the process, as anti-fraud systems and information security systems often mutually benefit from sharing information about suspicious users.

Besides dealing with combatting fraudulent transactions, the CISO may be responsible for implementing technologies to prevent rogue employees from stealing money from the company via one or more of many types of schemes — with the CISO usually focusing primarily on means involving computers.

Incident response plan

The CISO is responsible to develop and maintain the company's incident response plan. The plan should include not only the technical steps described in Chapters 11 and 12, but also detail who speaks to the media, who clears messages with the media, who informs the public, who informs regulators, who consults with law enforcement, and so on. It should also detail the identities (specified by job description) and roles of all other decision-makers within the incident response process.

Disaster recovery and business continuity planning

This function includes managing disruptions of normal operations through contingency planning and the testing of all such plans.

While large businesses often have a separate DR and BCP team, the CISO almost always plays a major role in these functions — if not owns them outright —for multiple reasons:

>> **Keeping systems and data available is part of the CISO's responsibility.** As such, there is little difference from a practical perspective if a system goes

down because a DR and BC plan is ineffective or because a DDoS attack hit — if systems and data are not available, it is the CISO's problem.

>> **CISOs need to make sure that BCP and DR plans provide for recovery in such a manner that security is preserved.** This is especially true because it is often obvious from major media news stories when major corporations may need to activate their continuity plans, and hackers know that companies in recovery mode make ideal targets.

Compliance

The CISO is responsible to ensure that the company complies with all with legal and regulatory requirements, contractual obligations, and best practices accepted by the company as related to information security. Of course, compliance experts and attorneys may advise the CISO regarding such matters, but ultimately, it is the CISO's responsibility to ensure that all requirements are met.

Investigations

If (and when) an information security incident occurs, the folks working for the CISO in this capacity investigate what happened. In many cases, they'll be the folks who coordinate investigations with law enforcement agencies, consulting firms, regulators, or third-party security companies. These teams must be skilled in forensics and in preserving evidence. It does little good to know that some rogue employee stole money or data if, as a result of mishandling digital evidence, you can't prove in a court of law that that is the case.

Physical security

Ensuring that corporate informational assets are physically secure is part of the CISO's job. This includes not only systems and networking equipment, but the transport and storage of backups, disposal of decommissioned computers, and so on.

In some organizations, the CISO is also responsible for the physical security of buildings housing technology and for the people within them. Regardless of whether this is the case, the CISO is always responsible to work with those responsible to ensure that information systems and data stores are protected with properly secured facilities sporting adequate security perimeters and with appropriate access controls to sensitive areas on a need-to-access basis.

Security architecture

The CISO and his or her team are responsible to design and oversee the building and maintenance of the company's security architecture. Sometimes, of course, CISOs inherit pieces of the infrastructure, so the extent to which they get to design and build may vary. The CISO effectively decides what, where, how, and why various countermeasures are used, how to design network topology, DMZs, and segments, and so on.

Ensuring auditability of system administrators

It is the CISO's responsibility to ensure that all system administrators have their actions logged in such a fashion that their actions are auditable, and attributable to the parties who took them.

Cyber-insurance compliance

Most large companies have cybersecurity insurance. It is the CISO's job to make sure that the company meets all security requirements for coverage under the policies that are in effect, so that if something does go amiss and a claim is made, the firm will be covered.

5

Handling a Security Incident (This Is a When, Not an If)

Chapter **11**

Identifying a Security Breach

Despite valiant efforts to protect your computer systems and data, you may suffer some sort of breach. In fact, the odds that your data will — at some point — be breached are close to 100 percent. The only real question is whether the breach will take place on your system or on someone else's.

Because you're ultimately responsible for maintaining your own computer systems, you need to be able to recognize the signs of a potential breach of your equipment. If a hacker does manage to penetrate your systems, you need to terminate his or her access as quickly as possible. If your data has been manipulated or destroyed, you need to restore an accurate copy. If systems are malfunctioning, you need to get them back on track.

In this chapter, you discover the symptoms of a breach. Armed with this knowledge, you can hopefully recognize if something is amiss and know the corrective actions to take.

If you've already receive notification from a third-party-provider where you store data that your data has been compromised or may have been compromised, refer to Chapter 13.

Identifying Overt Breaches

The easiest breaches to identify are those in which the attacker announces to you that you've been breached and provides proof of that accomplishment.

Three of the most common overt breaches are those involving ransomware, defacement, and claimed destruction.

Ransomware

Ransomware is a form of malware that encrypts or steals data on a user's device and demands a ransom in order to restore the data to the user's control (see Figure 11-1). Typically, ransomware includes an expiration date with a warning to the tune of "pay within *x* hours or the data will be destroyed forever!" (See Chapter 2 for more on ransomware.)

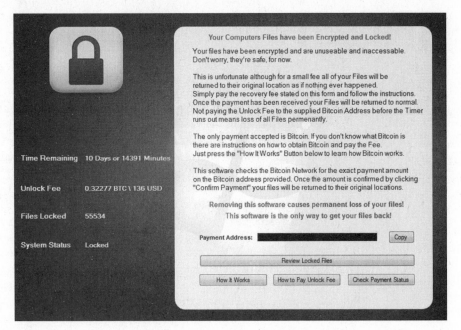

Your Computers Files have been Encrypted and Locked!

Your files have been encrypted and are unuseable and inaccessable. Don't worry, they're safe, for now.

This is unfortunate although for a small fee all of your Files will be returned to their original location as if nothing ever happened. Simply pay the recovery fee stated on this form and follow the instructions. Once the payment has been received your Files will be returned to normal. Not paying the Unlock Fee to the supplied Bitcoin Address before the Timer runs out means loss of all Files permenantly.

The only payment accepted is Bitcoin. If you don't know what Bitcoin is there are instructions on how to obtain Bitcoin and pay the Fee. Just press the "How It Works" Button below to learn how Bitcoin works.

This software checks the Bitcoin Network for the exact payment amount on the Bitcoin address provided. Once the amount is confirmed by clicking "Confirm Payment" your files will be returned to their original locations.

Removing this software causes permanent loss of your files!
This software is the only way to get your files back!

Payment Address: [   ] Copy

Review Locked Files

How It Works | How to Pay Unlock Fee | Check Payment Status

Time Remaining 10 Days or 14391 Minutes

Unlock Fee 0.32277 BTC \ 136 USD

Files Locked 55534

System Status Locked

FIGURE 11-1: A ransomware screen from an overt infection.

Obviously, if your device presents you with such a demand and important files that should be accessible to you aren't available because they're missing or encrypted, you can be reasonably sure that you need to take corrective action.

One note: Some strains of bogus smartphone ransomware — yes, that is a real thing — display such messages but do not actually encrypt, destroy, or pilfer data. Before taking any corrective action, always check that ransomware is real.

Defacement

Defacement refers to breaches in which the attacker defaces the systems of the victim — for example, changing the target's website to display a message that the hacker hacked it (in an almost "virtual subway graffiti"-like sense) or a message of support for some cause, as is often the case with hacktivists (see Figure 11-2).

FIGURE 11-2: A defaced website (ostensibly by the hacker group known as the Syrian Electronic Army).

If you have a personal website and it's defaced or if you boot up your computer and it displays a `hacked by <some hacker>` message, you can be reasonably certain that you were breached and that you need to take corrective action. Of course, the breach may have occurred at the site hosting your site, and not on your local computer — a matter that I discuss in Chapter 12.

Claimed destruction

Hackers can destroy data or programs, but so can technical failures or human errors. The fact that data has been deleted, therefore, doesn't mean that a system was breached. However, if some party claims responsibility, the odds that the problems are the result of a breach can skyrocket.

If someone contacts you, for example, and claims to have deleted a specific file or set of files that only a party with access to the system would know about, and those are the only files gone, you can be reasonably certain that the issue with which you are dealing is not a failure of hard disk sectors or solid-state disk chips.

Detecting Covert Breaches

While some breaches are obviously discernable to be breaches, most breaches are actually quite hard to detect. In fact, breaches are sometimes so hard to notice that various enterprises that spend millions of dollars a year on systems that try to identify breaches have had breaches go undetected for significant periods of time — sometimes for years!

The following sections describe some symptoms that may indicate that your computer, tablet, or smartphone has been breached.

Please keep in mind that none of the following clues exists in a vacuum, nor does the presence of any individual symptom, on its own, provide a guarantee that something is amiss. Multiple reasons other than the occurrence of a breach may cause devices to act abnormally and to exhibit one or more of the ailments described in the following sections.

However, if a device suddenly seems to suffer from multiple suspicious behaviors or if the relevant issues develop just after you clicked on a link in an email or text message, downloaded and ran some software provided by a source with potentially deficient security practices, opened some questionable attachment, or did something else about which wisdom you now question, you may want to take corrective action, as described Chapter 12.

When considering the likelihood that a system was breached, keep in mind relevant circumstances. If problems start occurring after an operating system auto-update, for example, the likely risk level is much lower than if the same symptoms start showing up right after you click on a link in a suspicious email message offering you $1,000,000 if you process a payment being sent from a Nigerian prince to someone in the United States. Maintain a proper perspective and do not panic. If something did go amiss, you can still take action to minimize the damage — see Chapter 12.

Your device seems slower than before

Malware running on a computer, tablet, or smartphone often impacts the performance of the device in a noticeable fashion. Malware that transmits data can also sometimes slow down a device's connection to the Internet or even to internal networks.

REMEMBER

Keep in mind, however, that updates to a device's operating system or to various software packages can also adversely impact the device's performance, so don't panic if you notice that performance seems to be somewhat degraded just after you updated your operating system or installed a software upgrade from a trusted source. Likewise, if you fill up the memory on your device or install many processor and bandwidth intensive apps, performance is likely to suffer even without the presence of malware.

You can see what is running on a Windows PC by pressing Ctrl + Shift + Esc and checking out the Task Manager window that pops up. On a Mac, use the Activity Monitor, which you can access by clicking the magnifying glass on the right side of the menu bar on the top of the screen and starting to type Activity Monitor. After you type the first few characters, the name of the tool should display, at which point you can press Enter to run it.

Your Task Manager doesn't run

If you try to run Task Manager on Windows (see Figure 11-3) or Activity Monitor on a Mac (see preceding section) and the tool does not run, your computer may be infected with malware. Various strains of malware are known to impact the ability of these programs to operate.

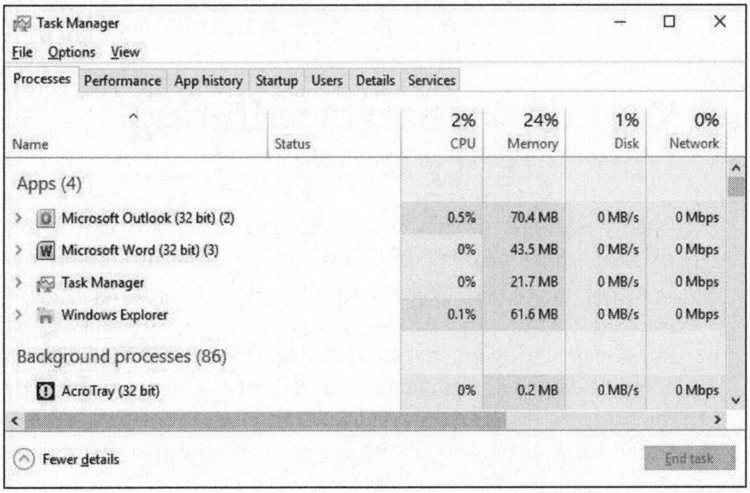

Task Manager				− □ ×

File Options View

Processes Performance App history Startup Users Details Services

Name	Status	2% CPU	24% Memory	1% Disk	0% Network
Apps (4)					
> [O] Microsoft Outlook (32 bit) (2)		0.5%	70.4 MB	0 MB/s	0 Mbps
> [W] Microsoft Word (32 bit) (3)		0%	43.5 MB	0 MB/s	0 Mbps
> [⊞] Task Manager		0%	21.7 MB	0 MB/s	0 Mbps
> [⊞] Windows Explorer		0.1%	61.6 MB	0 MB/s	0 Mbps
Background processes (86)					
[!] AcroTray (32 bit)		0%	0.2 MB	0 MB/s	0 Mbps

⊙ Fewer details   End task

FIGURE 11-3:
The Microsoft Windows Task Manager.

Your Registry Editor doesn't run

If you try to run Registry Editor, shown in Figure 11-4, on Windows (for example, by typing **regedit** at the Run prompt) and it does not run, your computer may be infected with malware. Various strains of malware are known to impact the ability of the Registry Editor to execute.

FIGURE 11-4:
The Microsoft
Windows Registry
Editor.

WARNING

Note that you may receive a warning when running Registry Editor that it requires Administrator permissions. That warning is normal and not the sign of a problem. It also should remind you of the potentially serious consequences of making registry edits: Don't make any if you're not sure what you are doing.

Your device starts suffering from latency issues

Latency refers to the time it takes for data to begin to travel after the instruction is issued to make it travel. If you're noticing delays that were not present before — especially if the delays seem significant — something may be amiss. Of course, your Internet provider or someone else may be experiencing problems, and everything may be fine on your local device. However, if the latency issues appear from only one device or a particular set of devices and not from all devices connected to the same network and if rebooting the impacted device/s does not ameliorate the situation, your device/s may have been compromised.

TIP

If the device is using a wired network connection, be sure to test it with a new cable. If the problem goes away, the cause was likely a defective or damaged physical connection.

Your device starts suffering from communication and buffering issues

One highly visual symptom of communication-performance problems that can easily be discerned without much technical knowledge is if streaming videos seem to freeze while preloading future frames, or *buffering*, far more often than they did in the past (see Figure 11-5). While buffering is an annoyance that happens to most folks from time to time, if it is happening regularly on a connection that previously did not suffer on a regular basis from such an ailment or it's happening from only one or more particular devices using the connection but not on others, it may be indicative of a compromised system.

FIGURE 11-5: An example of communication problems while streaming video. Note the viewable portion of the rotating circle in the middle of the video image.

If the device is using a wired network connection, be sure to check any physical cables that may be causing network issues.

REMEMBER

Note that communication performance problems can also be a sign that someone is *piggy-backing* on your Internet connection, which is also a type of breach.

Your device's settings have changed

If you notice that some of your device's settings have changed — and you're certain that you did not make the change — that may be a sign of problems. Of course, some software makes setting changes, too (especially on classic computers, as opposed to smartphones), so changes may have a legitimate source as well. Most software, however, does not make major changes without notifying you. If you see dramatic settings changes, beware.

Your device is sending or receiving strange email messages

If your friends or colleagues report receiving emails from you that you did not send to them, something is likely amiss — this is especially true if the messages appear to be spam. Likewise, if you're receiving emails that appear to be from people who claim to have never sent the relevant messages, you may have suffered a breach.

REMEMBER

Keep in mind, however, that many other reasons (including other kinds of attacks on systems other than your own devices and accounts) can lead to spam appearing to have emanated from you.

Your device is sending or receiving strange text messages

If your friends or colleagues report receiving text messages or other smartphone-type communications from you that you did not send to them, your smartphone may have been breached. Likewise, if you're receiving messages that appear to be from people who claim to have never sent the relevant messages, you may have suffered a breach.

New software (including apps) is installed on your device — and you didn't install it

If new programs or apps suddenly appear on your device and you did not install them, something may be amiss. While, in the case of some portable devices, the manufacturer or relevant service provider may occasionally install certain types of apps without your knowledge, if new apps suddenly appear, you should always look into the matter. Do a Google search on the apps and see what reliable tech sites say about them. If the apps are not showing up on other people's devices, you may have a serious issue on your hands.

REMEMBER

Keep in mind, however, that sometimes the installation routines of one program install other applications as well. It is relatively common, for example, for various programs that are offered for free to users in a limited-feature version to also install other programs that are comarketed alongside them. Normally, such installation programs ask for permission to install the additional programs, but such transparency is not mandated by law, and some applications do not afford users such choices.

Also, remember that if you let someone else your computer, he or she may have installed something (legitimate or illegitimate).

Your device's battery seems to drain more quickly than before

Malware running in the background uses battery power and can help drain the battery of laptops, smartphones, and tablets.

Your device seems to run hotter than before

Malware running the background uses CPU cycles and can cause a device to run physically hotter than before. You may hear internal cooling fans going on louder or more often than you usually do, or you may feel that the device is physically hotter to the touch.

File contents have been changed

If the contents of files have changed without you changing them and without you running any software that you expect would change them, something may be seriously amiss.

Of course, if you let someone else use your computers and gave him or her access to the files in question, before blaming malware or a hacker, be sure to check with the person you let use the computer whether he or she made any changes.

Files are missing

If files seem to have disappeared without you deleting them and without you running any software that you expect might delete them, something may be seriously amiss.

Of course, technical failures and human mistakes can also cause files to disappear — and, if you let someone else use your computer, he or she may be the culprit.

Websites appear somewhat different than before

If someone has installed malware that is *proxying* on your device — that is, sitting between your browser and the Internet and relaying the communications between them (while reading all the contents of the communications and, perhaps, inserting various instructions of its own) — it may affect how some sites display.

Your Internet settings show a proxy, and you never set one up

If someone has configured your device to use his/her server as a proxy, that party may be attempting to read data sent to and from your device and may try to modify the contents of your session or even seek to hijack it altogether.

Some legitimate programs do configure Internet proxies — but, such proxy information should show up when the software is installed and initially run, not suddenly after you click on a questionable link or download a program from a less-than-trustworthy source. (See Figure 11-6.)

Some programs (or apps) stop working properly

If apps that you know used to work properly on your device suddenly stop functioning as expected, you may be experiencing a symptom of either proxying or malware interfering with the apps' functionality.

TIP

Of course, if such a problem develops immediately after you perform an operating system update, the update is a far more likely source of the issue than is something more sinister.

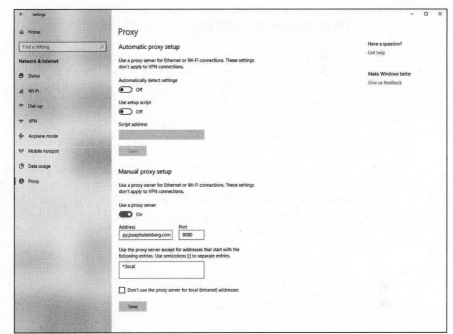

FIGURE 11-6:
Internet connections configured to use a proxy. If you do not use a proxy and suddenly one appears listed in your Internet settings, something is likely amiss.

Security programs have turned off

If the security software that you normally run on your device has suddenly been disabled, removed, or configured to ignore certain problems, it may be a sign that a hacker has penetrated your device and has turned off its defenses to prevent both his or her efforts from being blocked as well as to ensure that you do not receive warnings as he or she carries out various additional nefarious activities.

An increased use of data or text messaging (SMS)

If you monitor your smartphone's data or SMS usage and see greater usage figures than you expect, especially if that increase begins right after some suspicious event, it may be a sign that malware is transmitting data from your device to other parties. You can even check your data usage per app — if one of them looks like it is using way too much data for the functionality that it provides, something may be amiss.

WARNING

If you installed the app from a third-party app store, you can try deleting the app and reinstalling it from a more trusted source. Keep in mind, however, that if malware is on your device, reinstalling the app may not always fix the problem, even if the app was the original source of the infection.

Increased network traffic

If you monitor your device's Wi-Fi or wired network usage and see greater levels of activity than you expect, especially if that increase begins right after some suspicious event, it may be a sign that malware is transmitting data from your device to other parties.

TIP

On some systems, you can even check your data usage per app — if one or more apps look like they are using way too much data for the functionality that they provide, something may be amiss. If you installed the app in question from a less-than-reliable source, you can try deleting the app and reinstalling it from a more trusted source — but if malware is present on your device, reinstalling the app that it brought to the device may not always fix the problem, even if the app was, in fact, the original source of the infection.

You can check how much data your computer is using — and even how much each program is using — by installing a bandwidth monitor program on the device in question.

Unusual open ports

Computers and other Internet-connected devices communicate using virtual ports. Communications for different applications typically enter the device via different ports. Ports are numbered, and most port numbers should always be *closed* — that is, not configured to allow communications in.

TIP

If ports that are not normally open on your computer are suddenly open and you did not just install software that could be using such ports, it is usually indicative of a problem. If you use Windows — especially if you understand a little about networking — you can use the built-in `netstat` command to determine which ports are open and what is connecting to your device.

Your device starts crashing

If your computer, tablet, or smartphone suddenly starts to crash on a much more frequent basis than in the past, malware may be running on it. Of course, if you just upgraded your operating system, that is the likely source for the problem.

WARNING

If you are regularly seeing screens like the Blue Screen of Death (see Figure 11-7) — or other screens indicating that your computer suffered a fatal error and must be restarted, you have a problem. It may be technical, or it may be due to corruption from malware or a hacker.

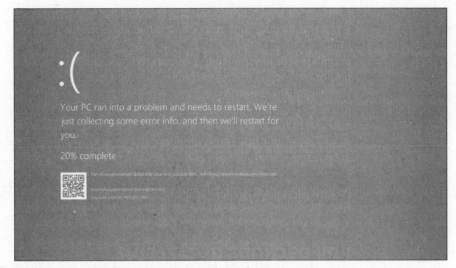

FIGURE 11-7: The modern version of the notorious Blue Screen of Death that appears after a severe crash of a computer running Microsoft Windows 10.

Your cellphone bill shows unexpected charges

Criminals are known to have exploited compromised smartphones in order to make expensive overseas phone calls on behalf of a remote party proxying through the device. Likewise, they can use a breached device to send SMS messages to international numbers and can ring up various other phone charges in other ways.

Unknown programs request access

Most security software for computers warns users when a program first attempts to access the Internet. If you receive such warnings and you don't recognize the program that is seeking access, or you recognize the program but can't understand why it would need to access the Internet (for example, Windows Calculator or Notepad), something may be amiss.

External devices power on unexpectedly

If one or more of your external input devices (including devices such as cameras, scanners, and microphones) seem to power on at unexpected times (for example, when you're not using them), it may indicate that malware or a hacker is communicating with them or otherwise using them.

There are attacks that are known to have involved criminals remotely turning on people's cameras and spying on them.

Your device acts as if someone else were using it

Malicious actors sometimes take over computers and use them via remote access almost as if they were sitting in front of the device's keyboard. If you see your device acting as if someone else is in control — for example, you see the mouse pointer moving or keystrokes being entered while you're not using your mouse or keyboard — it may be a sign that someone else is actually controlling the machine.

New browser search engine default

As part of several attack techniques, hackers are known to change the default search engine used by people browsing the web. If your own browser's default search engine changed and you did not change it, something may be amiss. (To check if you're search engine change, see the list of default applications, as shown in Figure 11-8.)

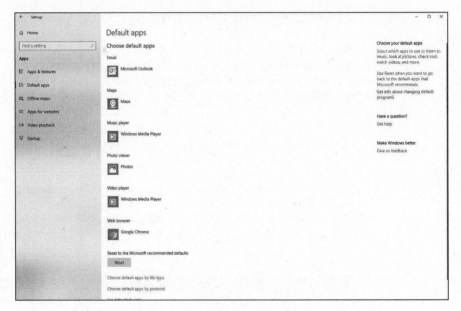

FIGURE 11-8:
The Windows 10 Default apps configuration screen.

Your device password has changed

If the password to your phone, tablet, or computer changed without you changing it, something is wrong, and the cause is likely something serious.

Pop-ups start appearing

WARNING

Various strains of malware produce pop-up windows asking the user to perform various actions (see Figure 11-9). If you're seeing pop-ups, beware. Such malware is common on laptops, but it exists for some smartphones as well.

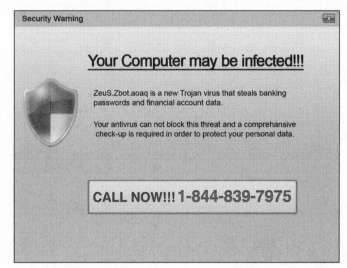

FIGURE 11-9:
This pop-up window from adware malware attempts to scare people into purchasing bogus security software.

Keep in mind that pop-ups that appear when you're not using a web browser are a big red flag, as are pop-ups advising you to download and install "security software" or to visit websites of questionable repute.

New browser add-ons appear

You should be prompted before any browser add-on is installed (see Figure 11-10). If a new add-on is installed without your knowledge, it likely indicates a problem. Some malware is delivered in poisoned versions of various browser toolbars.

New browser home page

As part of several attack techniques, hackers are known to change the home page of users' browsers. If your own browser's home page changed and you did not change it, something may be amiss.

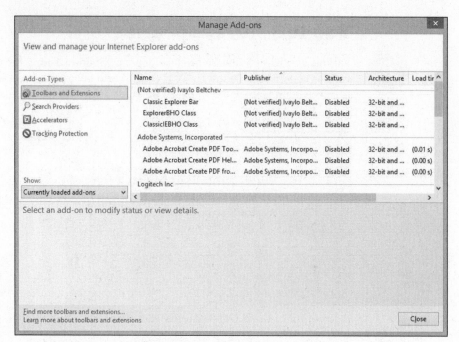

FIGURE 11-10:
The Manage
Add-ons window
in Internet
Explorer.

Your email from the device is getting blocked by spam filters

If email that you send from the device in question used to be able to reach intended recipients with no problem, but is suddenly getting blocked by spam filters, it may be a sign that someone or something altered your email configuration in order to relay your messages through some server that is allowing him or her to read, block, or even modify, your messages, and which other security systems are flagging as problematic.

Your device is attempting to access "bad" sites

If you use your computer, tablet, or smartphone on a network that blocks access to known problematic sites and networks (many businesses, organizations, and government entities have such technology on both their internal and bring-your-own-device [BYOD] networks) and you find out that your device was trying to access such sites without your knowledge, your device is likely compromised.

You're experiencing unusual service disruptions

If your smartphone seems to be suddenly dropping calls, or you find it unable to make calls at times when you appear to have good signal strength, or you hear strange noises during your phone conversations, something may be amiss.

Keep in mind that in most cases, these symptoms are those of technical issues unrelated to a breach. However, in some cases, a breach is the reason for such ailments. So, if you noticed the relevant symptoms shortly after you took some action that you now question or regret, you may want to consider whether you need to take corrective action (see Chapter 12).

Your device's language settings changed

People rarely change the language settings on their computers after performing the initial setup procedure, and few software packages do so either. So, if your computer is suddenly displaying menus and/or prompts in a foreign language or even has a language installed that you never installed, something is likely wrong.

You see unexplained activity on the device

If, on your device, you see emails in your Sent folder that you did not send, your device or email account was likely compromised.

Likewise, if files that you're certain that you never downloaded appear in your Downloads folder, someone else may have downloaded them to your device.

You see unexplained online activity

If your social media account has social media posts that you're certain that neither you nor any app that you have authorized made, something is clearly amiss. It may be that your account was breached, and your devices are all secure, or it may be that one of your devices with access to the account was breached and became the conduit for the unauthorized access to your account.

The same is true if you see videos that you never ordered appearing in your previous rentals of a video streaming service, purchases that you never made appearing in your order history at an online retailer, and so on.

Your device suddenly restarts

While restarts are an integral part of many operating system updates, they should not happen suddenly outside the context of such updates. If your device is regularly rebooting without your approval, something is wrong. The only question is whether the problem emanates from a security breach or from some other issue.

You see signs of data breaches and/or leaks

Of course, if you know that some of your data has leaked, you should try to determine the source of the problem — and the process of checking obviously includes examining for signs of problems on all your smartphones, tablets, and computers.

You are routed to the wrong website

If you're sure that you typed in a correct URL, but were still routed to the wrong website, something is amiss. The problem may reflect a security breach elsewhere, but it could indicate that someone has compromised your device as well.

If the misrouting happens from only one or more particular devices, but not from others on the same network, the odds are that the devices in question were compromised. In any case, never perform any sensitive task (such as logging into a website) from a device that is routing you incorrectly.

Your hard drive light never seems to turn off

If your hard drive light remains on constantly, or near constantly, malware may be doing something to the drive. Of course, hard drive lights come on for legitimate reasons when you are not actively using a computer — and, sometimes, a legitimate reason will entail the light being on for quite some time — so don't panic if it's the only sign that something is amiss.

Other abnormal things happen

It is impossible to list all the possible symptoms that malware can cause a device to exhibit. So, if you keep in mind that parties are seeking to hack into your systems, and that anomalous behavior by your device may be a sign of problems, you increase your odds of noticing when something seems off — and, of properly responding to a breach if one does, in fact, occur.

Chapter **12**

Recovering from a Security Breach

You've discovered that you've suffered a data breach. Now what? Read this chapter, which covers how to respond in these types of situations.

An Ounce of Prevention Is Worth Many Tons of Response

REMEMBER

When it comes to recovering from a security breach, there simply is no substitute for adequate preparation. No amount of post-breach expert actions will ever deliver the same level of protection as proper pre-breach prevention.

If you follow the various techniques described throughout this book about how to protect your electronic assets, you're likely to be in far better shape to recover from a breach than if you did not. Preparation not only helps you recover, but also helps ensure that you can detect a breach. Without proper preparation, you may not even be able to determine that a breach occurred, never mind contain the attack and stop it. (If you're unsure whether you've suffered a breach, see Chapter 11.)

Stay Calm and Act Now with Wisdom

A normal human reaction to a cyber breach is to feel outraged, violated, and upset and/or to panic, but to properly respond to a breach, you need to think logically and clearly and act in an orderly fashion. Spend a moment to tell yourself that everything will be all right and that the type of attack with which you are dealing is one that most successful people and businesses will likely have to deal with at some point (or at many points).

WARNING

Likewise, don't act irrationally. Do not attempt to fix your problem by doing a Google search for advice. Plenty of people online provide bad advice. Even worse, plenty of rogue websites with advice on removing malware and stopping attacks deposit malware on computers accessing them! Obviously, do not download security software or anything else from questionable sites.

Also, keep in mind that you need to act ASAP. Stop whatever else you're doing and focus on fixing the problem. Shut down any programs that you're using, save (and back up onto media that you will scan for malware before you reuse) any open documents and so on, and get to work on recovering from the breach.

REMEMBER

When a breach occurs, time works against you. The sooner that you stop someone from stealing your files, corrupting your data, or attacking additional devices on your network, the better off you will be.

Bring in a Pro

Ideally, you should bring in a cybersecurity professional to help you recover. While this book gives you good guidance, when it comes to technical skills, there is simply no substitute for the years of experience that a good pro has.

TIP

You should apply the same logic and seek professional help when faced with a serious computer and data crisis as you would if any of the following were true:

>> If you were seriously ill, you'd go to the doctor or hospital.

>> If you were arrested and charged with a crime, you'd hire a lawyer.

>> If the IRS sent you a letter that you're being audited, you'd hire an accountant.

Recovering from a Breach without a Pro's Help

TIP

If you do not have the ability to bring in a pro, the following steps are those that you should follow. These steps are essentially the ones most professionals follow:

1. **Figure out what happened (or is happening).**
2. **Contain the attack.**
3. **Terminate and eliminate the attack.**

Step 1: Figure out what happened or is happening

If possible, you want to figure out as much about the attack as possible so that you can respond accordingly. If an attacker is transferring files from your computer to another device, for example, you want to disconnect your device from the Internet ASAP.

That said, most home users do not have the technical skills to properly analyze and understand exactly what the nature of a particular attack may be — unless, of course, the attack is overt in nature (see Chapter 11).

Gather as much information as you can about

>> What happened

>> What information systems and databases were hit

>> What could a criminal or other mischievous party do with the stolen material

>> What data and programs have been affected

>> Who, besides yourself, may face risks because of the breach (this includes any potential implications for your employer)

REMEMBER

Do not spend a lot of time on this step — you need to take action, not just document — but the more information that you do have, the greater the chances that you will be able to prevent another similar attack in the future.

Step 2: Contain the attack

Cut off the attacker by isolating him or her from the compromised devices. Containing may entail:

>> **Terminating all network connectivity ASAP:** To terminate network connectivity for all devices on a network, turn off your router by unplugging it. (*Note:* If you're in a business setting, this step is usually not possible.)

>> **Unplugging any Ethernet cables:** Understand, however, that a network-borne attack may have already spread to other devices on the network. If so, disconnect the network from the Internet and disconnect each device from your network until it is scanned for security problems.

>> **Turning off Wi-Fi on the infected device:** Again, a network-borne attack may have already spread to other devices on the network. If so, disconnect the network from the Internet and disconnect each device from your network by turning off Wi-Fi at the router and any access points, not just on the infected computer.

>> **Turning off cellular data:** In other words, put your device into airplane mode.

>> **Turning off Bluetooth and NFC:** Bluetooth and NFC are both wireless communication technologies that work with devices that are in close physical proximity to one another. All such communications should be blocked if there is a possibility of infections spreading or hackers jumping from device to device.

>> **Unplugging USB drives and other removable drives from the system:** *Note:* The drives may contain malware, so do not attach them to any other systems.

>> **Revoking any access rights that the attacker is exploiting:** If you have a shared device and the attacker is using an account other than yours to which he or she somehow gained authorized access, temporarily set that account to have no rights to do anything.

TIP

If, for some reason, you need Internet access from your device in order to get help cleaning it up, turn off all other devices on your network, to prevent any attacks from spreading over the network to your device. Keep in mind that such a scenario is far from ideal. You want to cut off the infected device from the rest of the world, not just sever the connections between it and your other devices.

Step 3: Terminate and eliminate the attack

Containing an attack (see preceding section) is not the same thing as terminating and eliminating an attack. Malware that was present on the infected device is still present after disconnecting the device from the Internet, for example, as are any vulnerabilities that a remote hacker or malware may have exploited in order to take control of your device. So, after containing the attack, it is important to clean up the system.

The following sections describe some steps to follow at this point:

Boot the computer from a security software boot disk

If you have a security software boot disk, boot from it. Most modern users will not have such a disk. If you do not, skip to the next section.

1. Remove all USB drives, DVDs, CDs, floppies (yes, some people still have them), and any other external drives from your computer.

2. Insert the boot disk into the CD/DVD drive.

3. Shut down your computer.

4. Wait ten seconds and push the power button to start your computer.

5. **If you are using a Windows computer and it does not boot from the CD, turn the machine off, wait ten seconds, and restart it while pressing the BIOS-boot button (different computers use different buttons, but most use some F-key, such as F1 or F2) to go into the BIOS settings and set it to boot from the CD if a CD is present, before trying to boot from the hard drive.**

6. **Exit the BIOS and Reboot.**

If you're using a Windows PC, boot the computer in Safe Mode. Safe Mode is a special mode of windows that allows only essential system services and programs to run when the system starts up. To do this, follow these steps:

1. **Remove all USB drives, DVDs, CDs, floppies (yes, some people still have them), and any other external drives from your computer.**

2. **Shut down your computer.**

3. **Wait ten seconds and push the power button to start your computer.**

4. **While your computer is starting, press the F8 key repeatedly to display the Boot Options menu.**

5. **When the Boot Options menu appears, select the option to boot in Safe Mode.**

If you're using a Mac, boot it with Safe Boot. MacOS does not provide the full equivalent of Safe Mode. Macs always boot with networking enabled. Its Safe Boot does boot cleaner than a normal boot. To Safe Boot, follow these steps:

1. **Remove all USB drives, DVDs, CDs, floppies (yes, some people still have them), and any other external drives from your computer.**

2. **Shut down your computer.**

3. **Wait ten seconds and push the power button to start your computer.**

4. **While your computer is starting, hold down the Shift key.**

TIP

Older Macs (macOS versions 6–9) boot into a special superuser mode without extensions if a user presses the hold key during reboot. The advice to boot with Safe Boot applies only to Macs running more recent operating systems.

Backup

Hopefully you can ignore this section, because you paid attention to the advice in the chapter on backups, but if you have not backed up your data recently, do so now. Of course, backing up a compromised device is not necessarily going to save all your data (because some may already be corrupted or missing), but if you do not already have a backup, do so now — ideally by copying your files to an external USB drive that you will not attach to any other devices until it is properly scanned by security software.

Delete junk (optional)

At this point, you may want to delete any files that you do not need, including any temporary files that have somehow become permanent (a list of such files appears in the chapter on backups).

Why do the deletion now?

Well, you should be doing periodic maintenance, and, if you are cleaning up your computer now, now is a good time. The less there is for security software to scan and analyze, the faster it will run. Also, some malware hides in temporary files, so deleting such files can also directly remove some malware.

For users of Windows computers, one easy way to delete temporary files is to use the built-in Disk Cleanup utility:

1. In Windows 10, in the search box on the taskbar, type disk cleanup.
2. Select Disk Cleanup from the list of results
3. Select the drive you want to clean up and then click OK.
4. Select the file types to get rid of and then click OK.
5. Click on Accessories (or Windows Accessories).
6. Click on Disk Cleanup.

Run security software

Hopefully, you already have security software installed. If you do, run a full system scan. One important caveat: Security software running on a compromised device may itself be compromised or impotent against the relevant threat (after all, the security breach took place with the security software running), so, regardless of whether such a scan comes up clean, it may be wise to run the security software from a bootable CD or other read-only media, or, in cases of some products, from another computer on your home network.

TIP

Not all brands of security software catch all variants of malware. Security professionals doing a device "clean up" often run security software from multiple vendors.

If you are using a Mac and your Safe Boot includes Internet access, run the security software update routines prior to running the full scan.

Malware, or attackers, may add new files to a system, remove files, and modify files. They may also open communication ports. Security software should be able to address all of these scenarios. Pay attention to the reports issued by the security software after it runs. Keep track of exactly what it removed or repairs. This information may be important, if, for example, some programs do not work after the cleanup. (You may need to reinstall programs from which files were removed or from which malware-modified files malware was removed.) Email databases may need to be restored if malware was found within messages and the security software was unable to fully clean the mess up.

Security software report information may also be useful to a cybersecurity or IT professional if you end up hiring one at a later date. Also, the information in the report may provide you with clues as to where the attack started and what enabled it to happen, thereby also helping to guide you on preventing it from recurring.

TIP

Security Software often detects, and reports about, various non-attack material that may be undesirable due to their impact on privacy or potential to solicit a user with advertisements. You may, for example, see alerts that security software has detected tracking cookies or adware; neither is a serious problem, but you may want to remove adware if the ads bother you. In many cases you can pay to upgrade the software displaying the ads to a paid version that lacks ads. As far as recovering from an attack is concerned, these undesirable items are not a problem.

TIP

Sometimes, security software will inform you that you need to run an add-on in order to fully clean a system. Symantec, for example, offers its Norton Power Eraser, that it says "Eliminates deeply embedded and difficult-to-detect crimeware that traditional virus scanning doesn't always detect." If your security software informs you that you need to run such a scanner, you should do so, but make sure that you obtain it from the legitimate, official, original source. Also, never download or run any scanner of such a sort if you are told to do so not as the result of running security software. Plenty of rogue pop-ups will advise you similarly, but install malware if you download the relevant "security software."

Reinstall Damaged Software

There are experts who recommend uninstalling and reinstalling any software package that you know was affected by the attack, even if the security software fixed it.

Restart the system and run an updated security scan

For Windows computers, after you have cleaned the system, restart it in Safe Mode with networking using the procedure described above (but selecting Safe Mode with Networking rather than Safe Mode), run the security software, download all updates, and run the security software scan again.

If there are no updates, then you do not need to rerun the security software.

If you are using a Mac, Safe Boot already included networking so there is no reason to repeat the scan.

Install all relevant updates and patches. If any of your software has not been updated to its latest version and may contain vulnerabilities, fix this during the cleanup.

TIP

If you have the time to do so, run the security software full scan again after you have installed all the updates. There are several reasons for doing so, including the fact that you want it to check your system using its own most-up-to-date information on malware and other threats, as well as the fact that you want its heuristic analysis engine to have a baseline of what the system looks like with its latest updates.

Erase all potentially problematic System Restore points

System Restore is a useful tool, but it can also be dangerous. If a system creates a restore point when malware is running on a device, for example, restoring to that point will likely restore the malware! After cleaning up a system, therefore, be sure to erase all system restore points that may have been created when your system was compromised. If you are unsure if a restore point may be problematic, erase it. For most users, this means that it may be good to erase all system restore points.

To do this:

1. Click on the Start menu.
2. Click on Control Panel.
3. Click on All Control Panel Items.

4. **Click on Recovery.**

5. **Click on Configure System Restore.**

6. **Follow the prompts to delete the relevant system restore points.**

Restoring modified settings

Some attackers and malware may modify various settings on your device. What page you see when you start your web browser — for example, your web browser home page — is one common item that malware commonly changes. It is important to change the browser page back to a safe page as the malware's starting page might lead to a page that reinstalls malware or performs some other nefarious task.

The following sections walk you through the process for each browser.

REMEMBER

When using the phone or tablet versions of the browsers described in the following sections, the process will differ slightly, but should be simply discernable based on the instructions.

IN CHROME

To reset the Chrome browser:

1. **Click on the three-dot menu icon at the top right corner.**

2. **Click on Settings.**

3. **Scroll down to the On Startup section and configure it accordingly.**

IN FIREFOX

To reset the Firefox browser:

1. **Click on the three-line menu icon at the top right corner.**

2. **Click on Options.**

3. **Click on Home.**

4. **Configure the values in the New Windows and Tabs section accordingly.**

IN SAFARI

To reset the Safari browser:

1. **Click on the Safari menu.**

2. **Click on Preferences.**

3. **Click on the General tab.**

4. **Scroll down to the Homepage field and configure it accordingly.**

IN EDGE

To reset the Edge browser:

1. **Click on the three-dot menu icon at the top right corner.**

2. **Click on Settings.**

3. **Configure the Open Microsoft Edge with and Open new tabs with sections accordingly.**

Rebuild the system

Sometimes it is easier, instead of following the aforementioned processes, to simply rebuild the system from scratch. In fact, because of the risk of security software missing some problem, or of user mistakes when performing the security cleanup, many experts recommend that whenever possible one should rebuild a system entirely after a breach.

Even if you plan to rebuild a system in response to a breach, it is still wise to run a security software scan prior to doing so as there are some rare forms of malware that can persist even after a restore (such as BIOS reprogramming malware, certain boot sector viruses, and so on), and to scan all devices on the same network as the compromised device at the time of the compromise or afterwards, so as to ensure that nothing bad can propagate back to the newly restored device.

A guide to rebuilding systems from scratch appears in Chapter 14.

Dealing with Stolen Information

If your computer, phone, or tablet was breached, it is possible that sensitive information on it was stolen and may be misused by a criminal.

You should change any of your passwords that were stored on the device, for example, and check all accounts that were accessible from the device without logging in (due to your earlier setting of the device to "Remember Me" after a successful login) to ensure that nothing goes wrong. Obviously, if your passwords were stored in a strongly encrypted format the need to change them is less urgent than if they were stored in clear text or with weak encryption, but, ideally, unless you are certain that the encryption will hold up for the long term, you should change them anyway.

If you suspect that information may have been taken that could be used to impersonate you, it may be wise also to initiate a credit freeze and file a police report. Keep a copy of the police report with you. If you are pulled over by a police officer who informs you that there is a warrant out for your arrest in some location where you have never been, for example, you will have proof that you filed a report that private information that could be used to steal your identity was stolen from you. Such a document may not prevent you from having problems entirely, but it certainly may make your situation better in such a scenario than it would be if you had no such proof.

If you believe that your credit or debit card information was stolen, contact the relevant party at the phone number printed on the back of your card, tell them that the number may have been compromised, and ask them to issue you a new card with a new number. Also check the account for any suspicious transactions.

Keep a log of every call you make, when you made it, with whom you spoke, and what occurred on the call.

The more sensitive that information is, the more important it is to take action and to take it quickly.

Here are some ways to think of information:

>> **Not private, but can help criminals with identity theft:**

- Names, address, and home telephone number.

  This type of information is really available to anyone who wants it, even without hacking you. (Consider that a generation ago this type of information was literally published in phone books and sent to every home that had a phone line.) That said, this type of information can be used in combination with other information to commit all sorts of crimes, especially if unsuspecting other people make mistakes (for example, by allowing someone with this information to open a library card without ever producing identification documents).

- Other public-record information: The price that you paid for your home, the names of your children, and so on. While this information is public record, a criminal correlating it with other information that may be lifted from your computer could create issues for you.

>> **Sensitive:** Email addresses, cellphone numbers, credit card account numbers without the CVC code, debit cards account numbers that require a PIN to use or without a CVC code, ATM card numbers, student ID numbers, passport numbers, complete birthdays including the year, and so on. These items create security risks when compromised — for example, a stolen email address may lead to sophisticated phishing attacks that leverage other information garnered from your computer, attempts at hacking into the account, spam emails, and so on. Also, this type of stolen information may be used by a criminal as part of identity theft and financial fraud crimes, but may require combining multiple pieces of information in order to create a serious risk.

>> **More sensitive:** Social Security numbers (or their foreign equivalents), passwords to online accounts, bank account numbers (when compromised by a potential criminal as opposed to when displayed on a check given to a trusted party), PINs, credit and debit card information with the CVC code, answers to challenge questions that you have used to secure accounts, and so on. These types of information can often be abused on their own.

Paying ransoms

If you have proper backups, you can remove ransomware the same way that you remove other malware. If any data gets lost in the process, you can restore it from backups.

If you have been hit with over ransomware and do not have proper backups, however, you may face a difficult decision. Obviously, it is not in the common interest for you to pay a ransom to a criminal in order get your data back, but, in some cases, if your data is important to you, that may be the route that you need to go. In many cases, criminals will not even give you your data back if you do pay the ransom — so, by paying a ransom, you may not only waste money, but still suffer a permanent loss of your data. You will need to decide if you want to take that chance. (Hopefully, this paragraph will serve as a strong motivator for readers to back up proactively as discussed in the chapter on backups.)

Before paying a ransom, consult an information security expert. Some ransomware can be removed, and its effects undone, by various security tools. However, unless your security software tells you that it can undo the encryption done by ransomware, do not try to remove ransomware on your own once it has encrypted your data. Some advanced ransomware wipes the data permanently if it detects attempts to decrypt the data. Also, keep in mind that some advanced ransomware does not encrypt data, but rather removes it from the victim's device and only transmits it back if the ransom is paid. Such ransomware may be removable by security software, but security software cannot usually restore the data pilfered by the ransomware.

The best defense for home users against the impact of ransomware is to back up and keep the backups disconnected from anything else!

Learning for the future

It is important to learn from breaches. If you can figure out what went wrong, and how a hacker managed to get into your systems (either directly or by using malware), you can institute de facto policies and procedures for yourself to prevent future such compromises. A cybersecurity professional may be able to help you vis-à-vis doing so.

Recovering When Your Data Is Compromised at a Third Party

Nearly all Internet users have received notification from a business or government entity (or both) that personal data was potentially compromised. How you address such a scenario depends on many factors, but the following sections tell you the essentials of what you need to know.

Reason the notice was sent

Multiple types of data breaches lead to organizations sending notifications. Not all of them represent the same level of risk to you, however. Notifications may be sent when a company has

>> Knowledge that an unencrypted database containing personal information was definitely stolen

>> Knowledge that an encrypted database containing personal information was definitely stolen

>> Detected unauthorized activity on a computing device housing your information

>> Detected unauthorized activity on a computing device, but not the one that houses your information (but on one connected to the same or logically connected network)

>> Detected the theft of credit or debit card numbers as can occur with a skimming device or the hacking of a point-of-sale credit card processing device

>> Discovered that there were, or may have been, improperly discarded computers, hard drives, or other storage media or paper-based information

>> Discovered that there was, or may have been, improperly distributed information, such as sensitive information sent to the wrong parties, unencrypted email sent to authorized parties, and so on

In all these cases, action may be warranted. But if a company notifies you that an unencrypted database of passwords including yours was stolen, the need to act is more urgent than if it detects unauthorized activity on a system on the same network as another machine containing only an encrypted version of your password.

Scams

Criminals see when a breach receives significant attention and often leverage the breach for their own nefarious purposes. One common technique is for crooks to send bogus emails impersonating the breached party. Those emails contain instructions for setting up credit monitoring or filing a claim for monetary compensation for the pain and inconvenience suffered due to the breach. Of course, the links in such messages point to phishing sites, sites that install malware, and other destinations to which you do not want to go.

Criminals also act quickly. In February 2015, for example, the Better Business Bureaus started reporting complaints of emails impersonating Anthem, Inc., less than one day after the health insurance company announced that it had suffered a breach.

Passwords

One of the types of breaches most commonly reported in the mass media involves the theft of password databases.

Modern password authentication systems are designed to provide some protection in case of a breach. Passwords are usually stored in a *hashed format*, meaning that they are stored with one-way encryption. When you enter your password during an attempt to log in, what you type is hashed and then compared with the relevant hash value stored in the password database. As such, your actual password is not stored anywhere and is not present in the password database. If a hacker steals a password database, therefore, the hacker does not immediately obtain your password.

At least that is how things are supposed to work.

In reality, however, not all authentication systems are implemented perfectly; hashed password databases have multiple exploitable weaknesses, some of which can help criminals decipher passwords even when they're hashed. For example, if a criminal looks at the database and sees that the hashed password for many people is the same, it is likely to be a common password (maybe even "password"), which often can be cracked quickly. There are defenses against such attacks, but many authentication systems do not use them.

As such, if you are notified by a company that it has been breached and that an encrypted version of your password was stolen, you should probably reset the password. You don't need to panic, though. In most cases, your password was likely protected by the hashing (unless you selected a common, weak password, which, of course, you should not have). If, for some reason, you have reused the compromised password on other sites that you don't want have unauthorized parties to log in as you, you should reset your password there as well and don't reuse the new password this time!

Payment card information

If your credit card information or debit card information may have been compromised, take the following measures:

>> **Leverage credit monitoring services.** Breached firms often give those people potentially affected by the relevant breaches a free year or two of credit monitoring. While one should never rely on such services to provide full protection against identity theft, using such services does have benefit. Being that the cost to you is only a few minutes of time to set up an account, you should probably do so.

>> **Monitor your credit reports.** If you see any new accounts that you did not open, immediately contact the party involved. Remember, when it comes to fraud, the earlier that you report a problem, the less aggravation you are likely to suffer from it.

>> **Set up text alerts.** If your card issuer offers the capability to set up text alerts, use the feature. That way, you'll be notified when charges are made and can act quickly if something appears to be amiss.

>> **Check your monthly statements.** Make sure that you continue to receive your account's statements as you did before and that they are not being misdirected to someone else.

>> **Switch to e-statements.** If possible, set up your account to receive electronic monthly statements rather than physical statements and make sure that you receive an email and/or text message when each and every statement is issued. Of course, be sure to properly protect the email account and smartphone to which such messages are sent.

Government-issued documents

If your passport, driver's license, or other government-issued identity document has been compromised, you should contact the agency that issued the relevant document and ask how you should proceed. Document everything that you're told, including details as to who told you what.

You should also check online on the agency's website to see whether it offers instructions for such scenarios. In some cases, agencies will advise you to replace the document, which may necessitate a physical visit to an agency office. In other cases, the agency will advise you to do nothing, but will tag your account so that if the document is used for identification at other government agencies, those checking the ID will know to be extra vigilant (which, in itself, might be a reason to replace the document so that you do not encounter any extra aggravation when using it as ID).

School or employer-issued documents

If your school or employer ID information is compromised, immediately notify the issuer. Not only could this information be used to social engineer your school or employer, but it may potentially be used to obtain sensitive information about you from either one.

Social media accounts

If any of your social media accounts is compromised, immediately contact the relevant social media provider. All major platforms have mechanisms to address stolen accounts because all major platforms have had to deal with stolen accounts numerous times. Keep in mind that you may be asked to provide government ID to prove your identity as part of the account recovery process.

6
Backing Up and Recovery

Chapter **13**

Backing Up

W hile backing up your data sounds like a simple concept — and it is — actually implementing an efficient and effective backup routine is a bit more complicated.

To properly back up, not only do you need to know about your backup options, but you need to think about many other details, such as the location of your backups, encryption, passwords, and boot disks. In this chapter, you find out about all those backup details and more.

Backing Up Is a Must

In the context of cybersecurity, *backing up* refers to creating an extra copy, or extra copies, of data (that may consist of data, programs, or other computer files) in case the original is damaged, lost, or destroyed.

Backing up is one of the most important defenses against the loss of data, and, eventually, it's likely to save you from serious aggravation, as nearly everyone, if not everyone, will, at some point, want to access data to which he or she no longer has access.

In fact, such scenarios occur on a regular basis. Sometimes, they're the result of human error, such as a person inadvertently deleting a file or misplacing a computer or storage device. Sometimes, they're the result of a technical failure, such as a hard drive dying or an electronic device falling into water. And sometimes they're the result of a hostile action, such as a ransomware infection.

Sadly, many people believe that they back up all their data only to find out when something goes wrong that they do not have proper backups.

Don't let that happen to you. Be sure to back up on a regular basis — often enough that if you had to restore from a backup, you would not panic. In general, if you're in doubt as to whether or not you are backing up often enough, you aren't.

TIP

Do not think of backups as being there for you if you ever lose data. Think of them being there for you *when* you lose data. At some point, essentially every person who uses electronic devices on a regular basis will lose data.

Looking at the Different Types of Backups

Backups can be categorized in many different ways. One important way of distinguishing various types of backups from one another is based on what is being backed up. The following sections look at the different types of backups based on that approach.

Full backups of systems

A *full system backup* is a backup of an entire system, including the operating system, programs/apps, settings, and data. The term applies whether the device being backed up is a smartphone or a massive server in a data center.

Technically speaking, a full system backup includes a backup of all drives attached to a system, not just those mounted inside of it — although if some drives are attached to the system only from time to time and are not needed for the primary use of the system, some might exclude the contents of such drives from full system backups, especially if they're attached to other systems, or are backed up as part of the backup of other systems. For most home users, however, a full system backup means exactly what it sounds like: Backing up everything.

A full system backup is sometimes known as a *system image* because it essentially contains an image of the system as it existed at a particular point in time. If a device that you have an image of fails, you should be able to use the system image to re-create the entire system as it was at the time that the backup was made. When you use the rebuilt system, it should function exactly as the previous system did at the time of the backup.

Full system backups are the form of backup that typically is fastest to restore an entire system from, but they take longer to create than other forms of backup. They also usually require more storage space.

One important caveat: Because a system backup includes settings, hardware drivers, and so on, restoring from a system image does not always work well if you restore to a different device than the one that was originally backed up. If you imaged a laptop that runs Windows 7 as its operating system, for example, and then acquired a newer device intended to run Windows 10, which has different hardware in it, a restored system image of the first device may not work well on the newer device. The reverse is even more likely to be true: If you keep an old computer in your closet "just in case" and that just-in-case situation turns into reality, your attempts to restore the image from a newer machine to the older machine may fail fully or in part.

System images are sometimes referred to as *ghosts* (with ghost also being the verb for creating such images), especially among techies. The name originates from one of the original disk cloning software packages for PCs.

Original system images

One special case of system images is the original system image, also known as a *factory image.*

Many modern computing devices, whether laptops, tablets, or smartphones, come equipped with a factory image that can be restored. This means that when you acquire the device, it comes with an image of the original configuration that you receive — including the operating system, all the original software, and all the default settings — stored in a hidden partition or other storage mechanism not normally accessible to users.

At any point in time, you can perform a *factory reset* and set your device to look identical to the way that it did when it was new. When you do so, the device restores from the hidden image.

Two important caveats:

>> Some devices overwrite the factory reset image with new images in the event of certain operating system upgrades.

>> If you factory reset a computer, all security updates installed since the factory image was originally created will not be present on the restored device. Be sure to update your system ASAP after restoring and before going online for any other purpose!

Later system images

Some systems also create periodic images that you can restore from without having to go back to the original factory settings. Windows 10, for example, has such capabilities built in.

Never restore from an image unless you know that any problems that developed and caused you to need to restore did so after that image was made.

Original installation media

Original installation media is for programs that you acquire and install after you purchased your device.

If software came on a DVD or CD, saving the physical media that it came on allows you to reinstall the software in case of a problem.

Keep in mind, however, that if any updates for the software were issued and installed subsequent to the original installation, you will need to redownload and reinstall the updates. Doing so may happen automatically upon reinstallation, or it may require manual effort.

Downloaded software

If you've acquired programs since you purchased your device, it's likely that some or all of them were delivered to you via digital download.

When software is delivered as a download, the downloader does not receive a physical copy. However, if you received software via a download, you can store a copy of the installation file that you downloaded on one or more of many different types of media, such as a thumb drive or a CD or DVD. Alternatively, you can store the copy on a hard drive, but be sure to back up that drive if it is part of your computer infrastructure.

Additionally, some stores that sell downloadable software maintain copies of the software for you in a *virtual locker* so that you can download it at a later date. Such "backups" are useful, but be sure that you know how long the store will maintain the product in your locker. Some people have had serious problems because they relied on such "backups" only to find out that the software was not available to them at the time that they needed it.

For music and video files, the vendor's retention period is often theoretically forever, or at least as long as the material is available to purchase by others. For software, as new versions are released and old versions are *sunsetted* (the technical term for a software vendor phasing out and, ultimately, terminating support for an obsolete version of its software), the retention period may be far shorter.

Full backups of data

An alternative to performing a full backup of the entire system is to perform a full backup of the data on the system, but not of software and the operating system. (Configuration settings for both the operating system and various installed programs are often stored in data folders and included in such backups.) Performing a full data backup allows a user to restore all of his or her data in one shot if something goes wrong. Depending on the tool used to perform the backup, the user may be able to restore a subset of the data as well — for example, by choosing to restore only one particular file that he or she accidentally deleted.

Restoring from a full data backup will not restore applications. If a system has to be rebuilt entirely, recovering from full backups of data likely requires prior restorations to factory settings (or a later image of the computer) and reinstallation of all software. That is certainly more tedious than simply restoring from a system image. At the same time, it is also far more portable. The recovery can usually be done without any problems on many devices that vary quite a bit from the original device. Reduce the likelihood of your restored system suffering a security breach by updating the reinstalled software with the latest patches immediately after the relevant installations.

Incremental backups

Incremental backups are backups made after a full backup and that contain copies of only the portion of data (or, in the case of a system backup, the portion of the entire system) that has changed since the preceding backup (full or incremental) was run.

Incremental backups normally run much faster than full backups because, on most systems, the vast majority of data files do not change on a regular basis. For the same reason, incremental backups also use less storage space than do full backups.

To recover data, however, restoration must be done from the last full backup plus all the incremental backups performed since that last full backup.

If you decide to use incremental backups, consider limiting the number of such backups that you create after a full backup. For example, if you did only one full backup on the first day of the calendar month and performed incremental backups on all subsequent days until the next month began, then if something went wrong on the last day of the month, you would potentially need to restore from as many as 30 backups in order to recover your files.

Many people (and many businesses as well) choose to do full system backups on one of the days of the weekend and then do incremental backups during each other day of the week, thereby finding a happy medium between the efficiency gains during the backup process and the potential for a tedious recovering process.

Differential backups

Differential backups contain all the files that changed since the last full backup. (They are similar to the first in a series incremental backups run after a full backup.) A series of differential backups therefore requires more time to run and uses more storage space than incremental backups, but less than the same number of full backups. Recovering from differential backups can be faster and simpler than doing so from incremental backups because a restore needs to be done from only the last full backup and last differential backup.

If you decide to use differential backups, consider how many backups you should be making before making the next full backup. If the differential backup starts to grow quite large, there will not be much performance gains while making the backup, and any restoration will take far longer than if done from just a full backup.

Many people (and many businesses as well) choose to do full system backups on one of the days of the weekend, and then do differential backups during each other day of the week.

Mixed backups

Incremental and differential backups are made in conjunction with full backups, as shown in Table 13-1.

Do not mix incremental and differential backups within the same backup scheme, as doing so can create complexity and lead to confusion and costly mistakes.

TABLE 13-1

TABLE 13-1   A Comparison of Full, Incremental, and Differential Backups

	Full Backup	Incremental Backup	Differential Backup
Backup #1	All data	--	--
Backup #2	All data	Changes from Backup #1	Changes from Backup #1
Backup #3	All data	Changes from Backup #2	Changes from Backup #1

Continuous backups

Continuous backups refers to backups that run continuously. Every time that a change is made to data (or to a system and data), a backup of that change is made.

WARNING

Continuous backups are great in case of a hard drive failure in the primary system — the backup is available and up-to-date — but do little in the case of a malware infection or data destruction, as the malware typically propagates to the backup as soon as it infects the primary system.

One exception are complex backup systems that log each backup action and have the ability to reverse them. These backups can undo problematic portions of backups to the point that they occurred.

TIP

The process of continuously backing up is sometimes known as *syncing* (or *synchronizing*). You may see it described as such on your electronic devices or within various software packages.

Partial backups

Partial backups are backups of a portion of data. As opposed to full backups, partial backups do not back up all elements of data from a system. If a system were to be completely hosed, for example, you would have no way to fully recover all of its data contents from partial backups made earlier of that system.

Partial backups can be implemented in a full incremental-like model in which the first backup in a series includes all the elements that are part of the set included in the partial backup, and subsequent backups in the series include only items from that set that have changed.

Partial backups can also be implemented as always full-like — in which case, all elements of the set included in the partial backup are backed up each time, regardless of whether or not they have changed since the last backup.

REMEMBER

Partial backups are not intended to be full backups in case of a malware attack or the like. They are useful, however, in other situations, such as one in which a particular set of files needs to be backed up separately due to the needs of a particular individual or group or due to the sensitivity of the material. For example, while the IT department may do full and incremental backups of all files on a shared network drive, the accountant who needs constant access to a particular set of spreadsheets stored on that drive — and would be unable to work if those files become inaccessible — may set up his own backup of just those files. He can use his backup if something goes wrong when he is on the road or working from home on the weekend, without the need to bother members of the technical support department at his firm to work unnecessarily on a Sunday.

Folder backups

Folder backups, are similar to partial backups in situations where the set of items being backed up is a particular folder. While backup tools can facilitate folder backups, to the chagrin of many cybersecurity professionals and IT departments, many users perform such backups in an ad hoc fashion by manually making a copy of hard drive (or SSD) folders to USB drives at the end of each workday and consider such backups to be sufficient protection in case of problems.

Theoretically, of course, such backups work and can be used to recover from many problems. Reality dictates, however, that ad hoc backup procedures almost never result in proper backups: People forget on some days to back up or do not back up because they're hurried, neglect to back up some materials that they should have backed up, store the backups on insecure devices in insecure locations, or lose the devices on which the backups are stored — you get the idea!

If you want to be sure that you have proper backups when you need them — and, at some point, you are likely to need them — do not rely on ad hoc folder backups.

TIP

Never back up a folder onto the same drive as the original folder resides. If the drive fails, you will lose both the primary source of data as well as the backup copy.

Drive backups

A *drive backup* is similar to a folder backup, but for situations where an entire drive is being backed up instead of only a folder. Ad hoc backups of drives do afford some protection, but rarely deliver sufficient protection against risks of losing data.

Never store the backup of a drive on the same drive as the one being backed up. If the drive fails, you will lose the primary source of data and the backup copy.

Virtual drive backups

One special case of drive backup is that in which a person or organization uses an encrypted virtual drive. For example, a user may store his or her files within a BitLocker drive on Windows. BitLocker is a utility built in to many version of Windows that allows users to create a *virtual drive* that appears as any other drive to the user when it is in use, but appears as one giant encrypted file when not in use. To access the drive, the user must unlock it, normally by entering a password.

Backing up such drives is often accomplished by simply including the encrypted file within the full, incremental, folder, or drive backup. As such, all contents of the encrypted drive are copied without being referred to by name and remain inaccessible to anyone who does not know how to open the encrypted drive. Many backups tools offer drive backups in addition to more structured forms of backup.

Some software packages refer to the creation of an image of an entire disk as *cloning*.

While such a scheme protects the contents of the encrypted drive as they live in backups by using the same encryption as was used for the primary copies, note several caveats:

>> **Even if one small change was made to a single file within the virtual drive, the entire encrypted file will be changed.** As such, a 1KB change could easily lead to an incremental backup having to back up an entire 1TB file.

>> **The backup is useless for recovery unless someone knows how to unlock the encrypted drive.** While encryption may be a good defense mechanism against unauthorized parties snooping on sensitive files in the backup, it also means that the backup is not, on its own, fully usable for recovery. It is not hard to imagine problems developing as a result — for example, if someone attempting to utilize a backup several years after it was originally made forgets the access code, or if the person who created a backup is unavailable at the time that someone needs to restore from it.

>> **As with all encrypted data, there is a risk that as computers become more powerful — and, especially, as quantum computing takes hold — today's encryption may not offer sufficient protection against brute force attacks.** While production systems will, no doubt, be upgraded with

better encryption capabilities over time (as they already have been since the 56-bit encryption of the 1990s), backups that were made with old encryption technology and keys may become vulnerable to decryption by unauthorized parties. Hence, encryption may not forever protect your sensitive data contained in backups. You must store such backups in a secure location or destroy them when they are no longer needed.

Exclusions

Some files and folders do not need to be backed up unless you are imaging a disk (in which case the image must looks exactly like the disk).

Operating system paging files and other temporary files that serve no purpose if a system is restored, for example, need not be backed up.

The following are examples of some such files and folders that you can exclude from backups on a Windows 10 machine. If you're using backup software, the software likely comes with a built-in list of default exclusions that may resemble this list:

>> **The Recycle Bin,** which effectively temporarily backs up deleted files in case a user changes his or her mind about deleting them

>> **Browser caches,** which are temporary Internet files from web browsers, such as Microsoft Edge or Internet Explorer, Firefox, Chrome, Vivaldi, or Opera

>> **Temporary folders,** which are often called Temp or temp and reside in c:\, in the user directory, or in the data directory of software

>> **Temporary files,** which are usually named *.tmp or *.temp

>> **Operating system swap files,** such as pagefile.sys

>> **Operating system hibernation-mode system image information,** such as hyberfil.sys

>> **Backups** (unless you want to back up your backups), such as Windows File History

>> **Operating system files backed up during an operating system upgrade,** as usually found in C:\Windows.old on Windows computers that have had their operating systems upgraded

>> **Microsoft Outlook cache files (*.ost),** but Outlook local data stores (*.pst) should be backed up (in fact, in many cases, they may be the most critical files in a backup)

>> **Performance log files** in directories called PerfLogs

>> **Junk files** that users create as personal temporary files to hold information, such as a text file in which the user types a phone number that someone dictated to him or her, but that the user has since entered into his or her smartphone directory

In-app backups

Some applications have built-in backup capabilities that protect you from losing your work if your computer crashes, power fails, or you don't have battery power left.

One such program is Microsoft Word, which offers users the ability to configure how often files should be saved for AutoRecover. For most people, this feature is quite valuable. The author of this book even benefited from this feature while writing this book!

While the mechanism of configuring AutoRecover varies between some versions of Word, in most modern versions, the process is the following or something similar: Choose File ⇨ Options ⇨ Save and configure the options according to your taste.

TIP

In-app backups usually take just seconds to configure, normally run without your being actively involved, and can save you a lot of aggravation. In almost all cases, you should enable the feature if it exists.

Exploring Backup Tools

You can use multiple types of tools to create, manage, and restore from backups. Tools can automate various types of backups, for example, or can manage the process of a perpetual syncing backup. Backup tools come in wide variety of price ranges, depending on their robustness and scalability.

Backup software

Backup software is software designed specifically to run and manage backups and restorations from backups. You can find multiple vendors of such software, with exact features varying between products and between the platforms that they support (for example, features may vary between Windows and Mac versions of the same backup software package). Some offerings are intended for home users, some for large enterprises, and others for pretty much every level in between.

You can use backup software to manually or automatically backup — that is, you can configure it to backup specific systems, data, drives, or folders at specific times, using different backup models, such as full, incremental, and so on.

Backups can run only if a machine is on. So, be sure that your device to be backed up is on at those times! (Some backup software can be configured in cases of a missed backup to run the backup the next time that the device is booted or is idle.)

Backup software can take some time to set up, but after you do so, it can often make the process of creating proper backups much easier than any other method of backing up.

Ideally, you should configure your systems to automatically back up at specific times to make sure that you actually back up and don't neglect doing so while you do any of the many things that come up in life.

Do not confuse these manual and automatic options with manual and automated task copying.

If you just worked on some important project or spent many hours creating some new work on your computer, however, you may want to kick off an extra manual backup to protect your work and the time that you invested in it.

Beware of bogus backup software! Unscrupulous parties offer free backup software that contains malware of various severity, ranging from annoying adware to data-stealing infectors. Make sure that you obtain your backup software (as well as any other software that you use) from a reliable source.

Drive-specific backup software

Some external hard drives and solid state devices come with built-in backup software. Such software is often extremely intuitive and easy to use, and users may find it the most convenient way to set up their backup routines.

Three caveats, however:

>> Remember not to leave the drive connected to the system holding the primary data store.

>> If you use drive-specific versions of backup software, you may need to purchase all your backup drives from the same manufacturer in order not to complicate backup and restore procedures.

>> Drive-specific software is less likely to support newer technologies as they emerge from other vendors than is general backup software.

Windows Backup

Windows comes equipped with basic backup software built in. The software sports several features, and, for many people, may be sufficient. Using Windows Backup is certainly better than not backing up at all.

You can configure Windows Backup in two places:

>> In the Settings App, in the Update and Security Section.

>> Via the traditional Control Panel, which can be run from the Start Menu. Backup and Restore is an item in the traditional All Items view or in the System and Security section of the modern view.

Additionally, a Windows File Backup utility automatically backs up files as you modify them. You can access its configuration options via the Control Panel File History option. If you have plenty of disk space and work efficiently, make sure that your files are backed up quite often.

For more on restoring files from Windows File History, see Chapter 15.

Smartphone/tablet backup

Many devices come equipped with the ability to automatically sync your data to the cloud — a process that allows you to restore the data to a new device if your device is lost or stolen. Even devices that do not have this feature built in almost always can run software that effectively delivers these features for a specific folder tree or drive.

Using the sync feature provides great protection, but it also means that your data is sitting *in the cloud* — which, simply means that it is on someone else's computer — and potentially accessible to both the cloud–service provider (in the case of most smartphones, the provider would be Apple or Google), as well as to any government agencies that demand access to the relevant data while armed with a warrant, rogue insiders, or hackers who manage to somehow obtain access to it.

REMEMBER

Even if you haven't committed any crimes, the government may still demand your data as part of data collection procedures related to crimes committed by other people. Even if you trust the government not to abuse your data, the government itself has had several breaches and data leaks, so you have good reason not to trust it to adequately protect your information from being stolen by other parties who may abuse it.

Before you decide whether or not to use the sync, think about the pros and cons.

Manual file or folder copying backups

Manual backups are exactly what they sound like: backups performed manually, often by people copying files, folders, or both from their primary hard drive (or solid-state drive) to a network folder or thumb drive.

WARNING

Manual backups have their purpose, but using them on their own is not usually a good backup strategy. People inevitably do not perform such backups as frequently as they should, do not properly store such backups, and often do not back up all the items they should be storing copies of.

Automated task file or folder copying backups

Automated-task backups are essentially manual backups on steroids; they are manual backups that are run by a computer automatically instead of by people manually kicking them off. While automating the backup process reduces the risk of forgetting to back up or not backing up due to someone being hurried, file and folder copying is still risky because if some sensitive information is, for some reason, not stored in the proper folder, it may not be backed up.

One possible exception is the case of virtual drives. If someone automates the process of copying of the file containing the entire drive on which he or she stores all of his or her data files, such backups may be sufficient. For most home users, however, setting up an automated copying routine is not a practical solution. Using backup software is a far simpler, and better, option.

Third-party backups of data hosted at third parties

If you store any data in the cloud or use a third-party service to host any of your systems or data, the party that owns the physical and/or virtual systems on which your data resides may or may not back it up — often without your knowledge or approval. If you store data on a Google Drive, for example, you have absolutely no control over how many copies Google makes of your data. Likewise, if you use a third-party service such as Facebook, any data that you upload to the social media giant's servers — regardless of the privacy settings that you set for the uploads (or possibly even if you deleted them) — may be backed up by Facebook to as many backups as the firm so desires, in as many different locations as the firm desires.

In some cases, third-party backups resemble drive backups. While the provider has your data backed up, only you — the party who "owns" the data — can actually read it in an unencrypted form from the backup. In other cases, however, the backed-up data is available to anyone who has access to the backup.

That said, most major third parties have robust redundant infrastructure and backup systems in place, meaning that the odds that data stored on their infrastructure will remain available to users is extremely high when compared with data in most people's homes.

Knowing Where to Back Up

For backups to have any value, they must be properly stored so they can be quickly and easily accessed when needed. Furthermore, improper storage of backups can severely undermine the security of information contained within the backups. You've probably heard stories of unencrypted backup tapes that contained sensitive information on them getting lost or stolen.

That said, there is not a one-size-fits-all approach to proper storage of backups. You can back up in different places, which results in different storage locations.

Local storage

Storing a *local copy* of your backup — meaning somewhere near a home computer or readily accessible to the owner of a smartphone, tablet, or laptop — is a good idea. If you accidentally delete a file, you can quickly restore it from the backup.

REMEMBER

That said, you should never keep all your backups local. If you store your backups in your house, for example, and your house were to be severely damaged in a natural disaster, you could simultaneously lose your primary data store (for example, your home computer) and your backups.

Backups should always be stored in a secure location — not on a bookshelf. A fireproof and waterproof safe bolted down to the floor or fastened to the wall are two good options.

Also, keep in mind that hard drives and other magnetic media are less likely to survive certain disasters than solid-state drives, thumb drives, and other devices containing memory chips.

Offsite storage

Because one of the purposes of backing up is to have the ability to preserve data (and systems) even if your primary copy is destroyed, you want to have at least one backup *offsite* — meaning in a different location than your primary data store.

Opinions differ as to how far away from the primary store the backup should be kept. Essentially, the general rule is to keep the backups far away enough that a natural disaster that severely impacts the primary site would not impact the secondary.

TIP

Some people store a backup copy of their data in a fireproof and waterproof bag inside a safe deposit box. Bank safes typically survive natural disasters, so even if the bank is relatively close to the primary site, the backup is likely to survive even if it cannot be retrieved for several days.

Cloud

Backing up the cloud offers the benefits of offsite storage. If you lose all your equipment and systems to a natural disaster, for example, a copy of your data will almost always still exist in the cloud. Also, from a practical standpoint, the odds are that the information-security team at any major provider of cloud storage has much greater knowledge of how to keep data secure than do most individuals and have at their disposal tools that the average person cannot afford to purchase or license.

At the same time, cloud-based backup has its drawbacks.

When using cloud-based backup, you are relying on a third-party to protect your data. While that party may have more knowledge and better tools at its disposal, its primary concern is not you. If a breach occurs, for example, and large customers are impacted, its priorities may lie in addressing their concerns before addressing yours. Also, major sites are often major targets for hackers because they know that such sites contain a treasure trove of data, far greater than what they may be able to lift from your home PC. Of course, if the government serves the cloud provider a warrant, law enforcement agents may obtain copies of your backups — even, in some cases, if the warrant was served because it has demonstrated probable cause only that someone else (and not you) committed a crime.

That said, for most people, cloud-based backup makes sense, with the pros outweighing the cons, especially if you encrypt your backups, thereby making their contents inaccessible to the cloud provider.

REMEMBER

When it comes to computers, *cloud* really means "someone else's computers." Anytime you store sensitive data, including sensitive data within in backups, in the cloud, you're really storing it on some physical computer belonging to someone else. The cloud provider may offer better security than you can offer yourself, but do not expect that your using the cloud will somehow magically eliminate cybersecurity risks.

Network storage

Backing up to a network drive offers a blend of features from several of the prior locations for storing backups.

Like a local backup, a network backup is normally readily available, but, perhaps, at a slightly lower speed.

Like an offsite backup, if the network server on which the backup is located is offsite, the backup is protected from site problems at the primary data's site. Unlike offsite backup, however, unless you know for sure that the files are offsite, they may be in the same facility as the primary data.

Like cloud backup, network based backup can be restored to other devices on your network. Unlike cloud backup, it may be accessible to only devices on the same private network (which, may be a problem, or, in some situations, a good thing from a security standpoint).

Also, network storage is often implemented with redundant disks and with automatic backups, offering better protection of your data that many other storage options.

TIP

If you use network storage for backups, make sure that whatever mechanism you are using to run the backup (for example, backup software) has the proper network permissions to write to the storage. In many cases, you may need to configure a login and password.

Mixing locations

There is no reason to only back up to one location. From the perspective of restoring data quickly, the more places that you have your data securely backed up, the better. In fact, different locations provider different types of protection optimized for different situations.

Keeping one copy local so that you can quickly restore a file that you accidentally delete, as well as maintaining a backup in the cloud in case of natural disaster, for example, makes sense for many people.

Keep in mind, however, that if you do store backups in multiple locations you need to make sure all the locations are secure. If you can't be sure about the security of some form of backup, beware and do not back up there just because "the more backups, the better."

TIP

As different backup locations provide different strengths and weaknesses, utilizing multiple backup locations can protect you better against more risks than using just one site.

Knowing Where Not to Store Backups

Never, ever, store backups attached to your computer or network, unless you have another backup that you are willing to recover in case of a malware attack. Ransomware that infects your computer and renders the files on it inaccessible to you may do the same to your attached backup.

WARNING

After backing up, never leave backup hard drives or solid-state drives connected to the systems or networks that they are backing up. Any malware that infects the primary system can spread to the backups as well. Removing your backup from being connected to the material that it is backing up can make all the difference between quickly recovering from a ransomware attack and having to pay an expensive ransom to a criminal.

If you back up to write-once, read-many-times type media, which is most commonly found today in the form of CD-Rs and DVD-Rs, it is safe to leave the backup in an attached drive after you have finalized the backup recording and set the disk to read-only.

Encrypting Backups

Backups can easily become a weak point in the data protection security chain. People who are diligent about protecting their personal information, and organizations that are careful to do the same with their confidential and proprietary information, often fail to afford the same level of protection to the exact same data when it resides in backups rather than in its primary location.

How often do we hear news stories, for example, of sensitive data put at risk because it was present in an unencrypted form on backups tapes that were lost or stolen?

In general, if you're not sure if you should encrypt your backup, you probably should.

Be sure to encrypt your backups if they contain any sensitive information, which, in most cases, they do. After all, if data is important enough to be backed up, the odds are pretty good that at least some of it is sensitive and should be encrypted.

Just be sure to properly protect the password needed to unlock the backups. Remember, it may be a while before you actually need to use the backups, so do not rely on your memory, unless you practice using that password on a regular basis to test the backups.

From a practical standpoint, many professional system administrators who deal with multiple backups every day have never seen a backup that did not need to be encrypted.

Figuring Out How Often You Should Backup

No simple one-size-fits-all rule applies as to how often you should backup your system and data. In general, you want to ensure that you never lose enough work that it would cause you significant heartache.

Performing a full backup every day requires the most amount of storage space for backups and also takes the most time to run. However, doing so means that more total copies of data are available — so, if a backup were to go bad at the same time as the primary data store, less data is likely to be lost — and fewer backups are required to perform a system or data restoration.

Performing a full backup everyday may be feasible for many individuals, especially those who can run the backups after work hours or while they are asleep at night. Such a strategy offers the best protection. With storage prices plummeting in recent years, the cost of doing so, which was once prohibitive for most individuals, is now affordable to most folks.

Some people and organizations choose to perform a weekly full backup and couple that backup with daily incremental or differential backups. The former strategy provides the fastest backup routine; the latter offers the faster recovery routine and reduces the number of backups needed in order to perform a restore to a maximum of two instead of seven.

TIP

Additionally, consider using manual backups or an automated in-app backup scheme if you are working on important materials during the day. Using the in-app automated backups in Word, for example, can protect you from losing hours of work if your computer crashes. Likewise, copying documents to a second location can prevent losing significant work if your hard drive or SSD fails.

For apps that do not have in-app-auto-backup capabilities, some folks have suggested periodically using the Windows or Mac Send menu option to send to themselves via email copies of files that they are working on. While doing so is clearly not a formal backup strategy, it does provide a way of backing up work during the day between regular backups and often does so offsite, ensuring that if one's computer were to die suddenly, an entire day's worth of work would not be lost.

TIP

In general, if you are not sure if you are backing up often enough, you probably aren't.

Disposing of Backups

People and organizations often store backups for long periods of time — sometimes preserving materials for so long that the encryption used to protect the sensitive data on backup media is no longer sufficient to adequately protect the information from prying eyes.

As such, it is imperative that, from time to time, you either destroy your backups or re-create them.

REMEMBER

Both hardware and software formats change over time. If you backed up to tapes in the 1980s, to Bernoulli Boxes in the early 1990s, or to Zip drives in the late 1990s, you may have difficulty restoring from the backups today because you may have problems obtaining the necessary hardware, compatible drivers, and other software needed to read the backups on a modern computer.

Likewise, if you backed up data along with various DOS programs or early Windows 16-bit executables needed to process the contents of those backups, you may be unable to restore from the backups to many modern machines that may be unable to run the executables. Obviously, if you did a full system image of a machine 20 years ago, you are going to have difficulty restoring from the image today (you may be able to do so using virtual machines — something well beyond the technical skill level of most users).

Even some older versions of data files may not work easily. Word documents from the mid-1990s, for example, which can be infected with various forms of malware, do not open in modern versions of Word unless a user enables such access, which may be difficult or impossible to do in certain corporate environments. Files formats utilized specifically by software that has long since disappeared entirely from the market may be even harder to open.

As such, old backups may not have much value to you anyway. So, once a backup is no longer valuable or once its data protection may be at risk of compromise, get rid of it.

How should you dispose of the backup tapes, disks, and so on? Can you just throw them in the trash?

No. Do not. Doing so can totally undermine the security of the data in the backups.

Instead, utilize one of the following methods:

>> **Overwriting:** Various software programs will write over every sector of the storage media several times (the actual number of times depends on the security level that the user specifies), making subsequent recovery of data from the decommissioned media difficult, if not impossible.

>> **Degaussing:** Various devices containing strong magnets can be used to physically render data on magnetic media (such as hard drives and floppy disks) inaccessible by exposing the media to a strong magnetic field.

>> **Incineration:** Burning storage media in a high-temperature fire is often enough to destroy it. Do not attempt this on your own. If you want to pursue such a method, find a professional with experience. The incineration process varies based on the type of media involved.

>> **Shredding:** Cutting the media into tiny pieces. Ideally, such media should be totally pulverized into dust. In any case, shredding using an old-fashioned shredder that cuts media into strips is generally not considered secure disposal of media that has not been previously overwritten or degaussed.

TIP

I can't overstate the importance of properly storing and disposing of backups. Serious data leaks have resulted from backup media that was lost after being stored for quite some time.

Testing Backups

Many folks have thought that they had proper backups only to discover at the time that they needed to restore that the backups were corrupted. Hence, testing backups is critical.

While, theoretically, you should test every backup that you make and test that every single item within the backup can be restored, such a scheme is impractical for most people. Do, however, test the first backup that you make with any software, check the auto-recover files the first time that you use Word, and so on.

Some backup software comes with the capability to *verify* backups — that is, after making a backup, it checks that the original data and data in the backups match. Running such verification after making a backup adds significant time to the backup process, but is well worth running if you can do so because it helps ensure that nothing was improperly recorded or otherwise became corrupted during the backup process.

Conducting Cryptocurrency Backups

Because cryptocurrency (see Chapter 1) is tracked on a ledger and not stored in a bank, backing up cryptocurrency involves backing up the private keys used to control the addresses in the ledger at which one has cryptocurrency, not backing up the cryptocurrency itself. Often, keys are not maintained electronically. They're printed on paper and stored in a bank vault or fireproof safe.

For those who use hardware wallets to store the keys to their cryptocurrency, the backup for the wallet device is often a *recovery seed,* which is a list of words that allows the device to re-create the keys needed for the relevant addresses. It is generally accepted that the list of words should be written down on paper and stored in a bank vault and/or safe — not stored electronically.

Backing Up Passwords

TIP

Anytime that you back up lists of passwords, make sure to do so in a secure manner. For important passwords that do not change often and are not likely to be needed on an urgent basis, consider making no digital records of them at all. Instead, write them down on a piece of paper and put that paper in a bank safe deposit box.

Creating a Boot Disk

If you ever need to re-create your system, you will need the ability to boot the computer, so as part of the backup process, you should create a boot table disk. For most smartphones and tablets, creating a boot disk is not an issue because resetting the device to factory settings will make it bootable.

Such simplicity is not, however, always the case with computers, so when you perform your first backup you should ideally make a bootable disk that you know is safe to boot from (in other words, no malware and so on). Most backup software packages will walk you through this process, and some computer manufacturers will do the same on your initial startup of the system. Various security software packages are distributed on bootable CDs or DVDs as well.

Chapter **14**

Resetting Your Device

C hapter 13 talks about backing up and why it is a critical component of any and every cybersecurity plan. The odds are close to 100 percent that, at some point, you will lose access to some file to which you still need access, and restoring from a backup will be a "lifesaver."

In this chapter, I discuss resetting your computer and tell you what you need to know to successfully reset your device so that it's (almost) as good as new.

Exploring Two Types of Resets

Sometimes, the easiest way to restore — and to help ensure that none of the problems that forced you to restore in the first place remain — is to start over by resetting your device to factory settings and reinstalling your apps and copying your data files from a backup.

TIP

Some forms of malware can survive a factory reset. So, if your device was infected with malware, be sure to address that problem even if you plan to reset your device. Or consult with an expert.

Additionally, there will likely be times when your device crashes — that is, it becomes unresponsive and stops functioning normally. Such occasions can be scary for many nontechnical users, who assume that they may lose their data. Performing the proper type of reset in such occasions, however, is quite simple and will almost always preserve the user's files (although files currently being worked on may be preserved as they were last saved).

Resets come in two major flavors— soft and hard. It is critical to know the difference between them before you use either type.

Soft resets

A *soft reset* is the equivalent of physically turning a device off and then turning it back on. It does not wipe programs, data, or malware.

TIP

One common use of soft resets is to restart a device if it crashes and becomes unresponsive. It can also be useful after a Blue Screen of Death-type of crash (see Figure 14-1).

FIGURE 14-1:
One variant of
the infamous
Windows Blue
Screen of Death.
If you see this
screen, you need
to soft reset your
computer.

Older devices

Most modern computing devices have a soft reset capability, but some older devices do not. In such devices, however, the battery is often removable, so removing the battery and cutting off all power to the device achieves the same desired effect.

Windows computers

Most Windows computers can be soft reset by holding down the Power button for ten seconds to do a shutdown. Holding down the button cuts off power to the computer from both the battery and any connected AC adapters/mains (even if the battery is connected and fully charged) and shuts it down.

After the device shuts down, wait ten seconds and press the Power button once to restart the computer.

Mac computers

Various models of Mac computers can be soft reset through different means:

- ❯❯ Hold down the Power button for about five seconds, and the Mac should shut down completely. Let go of the Power button, wait a few seconds, and press it once again, and the Mac should reboot. On some Macs pressing and holding the Power button may display a menu, in which case you should press R for Reboot and reboot directly, rather than shutting down and restarting the device.

- ❯❯ Press and hold the Control + ⌘ key together with the Power button.

- ❯❯ Press and hold the TouchID button until the Mac reboots.

Android devices

The way to soft reset an Android device varies between manufacturers. One of the following methods is likely to work:

- ❯❯ Press and hold the Power button until you see a shutdown/restart menu and then press Restart. (Or press Power Off, wait a few seconds, and then press the Power button again to turn the phone back on.)

- ❯❯ Press and hold the Power button. If no menu appears, keep holding the Power button for 2 minutes. At some point the phone should turn off — when it does, wait 10 seconds and turn it back on.

- ❯❯ If you have a removable battery, remove it, wait ten seconds, put it back in, and turn on the phone.

iPhones

The way to soft reset an iPhone varies based on the model. In general, one of the following methods will work:

- ❯❯ Press and release the Volume Up button, then press and release the Volume Down button, and then press and hold the Side button (the Power button) until the Apple logo appears on the screen. Wait for the device to reboot.

>> Press and hold the Power button. While still holding it, press and hold the Volume Down button. When a Slide To Power Off prompt and slider appears on the screen, slide the slider to the right and turn the device off. Wait ten seconds and press the Power button to turn it back on.

>> Press and hold the Power button, and, while still doing so, press and hold the Volume Down button. Continue to hold both buttons as the iPhone powers off and back on. Release both buttons when the Apple logo appears on the screen and wait for the device to reboot.

WARNING

If you are using some versions of the iPhone X, following this option for performing a soft reset could end up calling emergency services (911 in the United States) because holding these particular buttons for longer than five seconds may be preprogrammed to issue an SOS signal from the device.

Hard resets

Hard resets reset a device to its factory image or to something similar. (For more on factory image, see Chapter 13.)

If you want to recover to the original factory image — to effectively reset your device to the way it was when it was new — you need to follow the instructions for your particular device.

WARNING

Hard resets are almost always irreversible. Once you run a hard reset and a device is set back to its factory settings, you typically cannot undo the reset. Anything that you previously installed on the device and any data that you stored on it is likely gone forever. (Advanced tools may, in some cases, be able to recover some of the material, but such recoveries are often incomplete, and, in many cases, impossible altogether.) As such, do not run a hard reset until you are sure that you have backups of all the material that you need on the device that you are hard resetting.

Also keep in mind the following:

>> In some cases, a factory reset will not reset your device to the way it was when it was new because during operating system updates, the recovery image was updated as well. Factory resetting such a device will set the device to the way the device would have looked (or quite similar to the way it would have looked) when it was new had you purchased it with the new operating system.

>> After performing a factory reset, one or more (or possibly all) patches and other security updates that you have installed on the device may be

gone — meaning that your device is more likely than not vulnerable to various compromises. So, immediately after restoring you should run the operating system update process (repetitively — until it finds no needed updates) as well as the update process for any security software (also repetitively until it finds no needed updates). Only after those steps have been completed should you begin to install other software or perform any other online activities.

Resetting a modern Windows device

Your modern Windows device likely offers one or more ways to reset it. The following sections describe three major ways.

METHOD 1

1. **In the Start menu, click on Settings or PC Settings, depending on your operating system version.**

2. **In Windows Settings, click on Update and Security.**

The Windows Update screen appears.

3. **Click on Recovery in the menu on the left side of the Window.**

4. **Click on the Get Started button in the Reset this PC section at the top of the window.**

At this point, you may be prompted to install the original installation CD on which you received Windows 10. If you receive that message, do so. If you do not receive it — and most users don't — just continue.

Windows then offers you two choices. Both remove programs and apps and reset settings to their defaults:

- **Keep my files:** Selecting this option leaves your data files intact (as long as they are stored in data folders).

- **Remove everything:** Selecting this option removes all your data files along with the apps and programs (this is the factory reset option).

5. **Select either reset option.**

TIP

If you're performing a full reset because your system was infected by malware or your data files may otherwise have been corrupted, ideally select Remove everything and restore your data files from a clean backup.

If you select to remove your files along with everything else, Windows presents you with two choices:

- **Just remove my files:** Selecting this option erases your files, but does not perform any drive cleaning. This means that someone who gains access to the drive may be able to recover the data that was in the files — in full or in part — even after the files are deleted by the rest. This option runs relatively quickly.

- **Remove files and clean the drive:** Selecting this option not only removes all your data files, it wipes the drive — that is, writes over every 1 or 0 in your file — to dramatically reduce the likelihood that anyone in the future could recover any data from the deleted files. Cleaning a drive is time-consuming; if you select this option the restore can take much longer than if you select the first option.

If you are resetting the system so that you can use a clean system after recovering from a malware infection, there is no reason to clean the drive. If you are wiping it before giving it to someone else, fully cleaning the drive is a good idea. (In fact, some would argue that you should wipe the entire drive with even better wiping technology than is provided through the reset option discussed in this chapter.)

At this point, you may receive a warning message. If your computer originally had a different operating system and was upgraded to Window 10, resetting the system will remove the recovery files created during the upgrade that allow you to downgrade back to the previously running operating system — meaning that if you reset the system you will have a Windows 10 computer that cannot be easily downgraded to another operating system. In most cases, this warning is not a significant issue — Windows 10 is relatively mature, and few people who upgrade to Windows 10 as of the data of this book's publishing choose to downgrade.

Of course, if you are resetting the system because it is not working properly after you performed an upgrade to Windows 10, do not proceed with the reset. Downgrade it to the older version of Windows using the relevant tool.

You then will see a final warning message that tells you that the computer is ready to reset — and which communicates what that means. Read what it says. If you do not want any of the things that it says will happen to happen, do not proceed.

6. **When you are ready to proceed, click on the Reset button.**

    You can probably go out for coffee. A reset takes quite some time, especially if you chose to clean your drive.

7. **After a while, if you receive a prompt asking you whether you want to continue to Windows 10 or to perform troubleshooting, click on Continue.**

METHOD 2

If you're *locked out* of your computer, meaning that it boots to a login screen, but you cannot log in — for example, if a hacker changed your password — you can still factory reset the machine:

1. **Boot your PC.**

2. **When the login screen appears, click on the Power icon in the bottom right-hand corner.**

   You are prompted with several choices. Do not click on them yet.

3. **Without clicking any choices, first hold down the Shift key and then click on Restart.**

   A special menu appears.

4. **Click on Troubleshoot.**

5. **Select Reset This PC.**

6. **Select Remove Everything.**

WARNING

Read the warnings, and understand what the consequences of running a hard reset are before you run it. This reset is likely irreversible.

METHOD 3

This method may vary a bit between various computer manufacturers.

To reset your device:

1. **Turn on your computer and boot into Windows 10.**

   If you have more than one operating system installed on your computer, select the Windows 10 installation that you want to reset. If all you have is one operating system — as is the case for most people — you won't have to select it because it will boot automatically.

2. **While the computer is booting, press and hold down the F8 key to enter the boot menu.**

3. **In the boot menu on the Advanced Boot Options screen that appears, click on Repair Your Computer and press Enter.**

4. **If you're prompted to choose a keyboard layout, do so and then click on Next.**

5. **Select your username, type your password, and click on OK.**

6. **From the System Recovery Options menu that appears, click on the System Image Recovery link and follow the onscreen prompts to do a factory reset.**

   If your menus appear differently after pressing F8 in the last step, look through them for a Factory Reset option.

TIP

Resetting a modern Android device

Modern Android devices come equipped with a Factory Reset feature, although the exact location of the activation option for it varies based on the device's manufacturer and operating system version.

I show you several examples of how to activate a hard reset on several popular devices. Other devices are likely to have similar options.

SAMSUNG GALAXY SERIES RUNNING ANDROID 9

On popular Samsung Galaxy phones running Android version 9 (or Android Pie, the latest version of Android as of early 2019), you can access the factory reset option by following these instructions:

1. Run the Settings app.
2. From the main Settings menu, click on General Management.
3. Click on Reset.
4. Click on Factory Data Reset.
5. Follow the instructions presented with the relevant warning.

SAMSUNG TABLETS RUNNING ANDROID 9

The popular Samsung series of tablets have menu structures for hard-resetting that are similar to those used for the Galaxy series, although with a different look and feel.

1. Run the Settings app.
2. From the main Settings menu, click on General Management.
3. In the General Management menu, click on Reset.
4. Click on Factory Data Reset.
5. Follow the instructions at the warning to continue.

HUAWEI DEVICES RUNNING ANDROID 8

Huawei phones, which are popular throughout Asia, can be reset using the following steps (or similar steps, in case of operating system version differences):

1. Run the Settings app.
2. From the main settings menu, click on System.

3. **In the System menu, click on Reset.**

4. **In the Reset menu, click on Factory Data Reset.**

5. **Follow the instructions at the warning to continue.**

Resetting a Mac

Before you hard reset a Mac, you should perform the following steps:

1. **Sign out of iTunes.**

2. **De-authorize any apps that are locked to your Mac.**

   Sign out of them so that you can relog-in from the newly restored device, which those systems may see as if it were a different device.

3. **Sign out of Messages.**

4. **Sign out of iCloud.**

   You can do this in the System Preferences app. You will need to put in your password.

While a hard reset will work without the preceding three steps, performing the steps can prevent various problems when you restore.

After you're signed out of iTunes, Messages, and iCloud:

1. **Restart your Mac in Recovery Mode by restarting your Mac and holding down the Command and R keys while it reboots.**

   You may be presented with a screen asking you in what language you want to continue. If you are, select your preferred language — for the sake of this book, I assume that you have selected English.

2. **Run the Disk Utility.**

3. **In the Disk Utility screen, select your device's main volume and click on Unmount then Erase.**

4. **Erase any other disks in the device.**

5. **Exit the Disk Utility by clicking Quit Disk Utility in the Disk Utility menu.**

6. **Click on Reinstall macOS and follow the steps to reinstall the operating system onto the primary disk within your Mac (see Figure 14-2).**

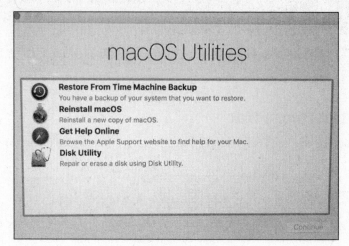

macOS Utilities

Restore From Time Machine Backup
You have a backup of your system that you want to restore.

Reinstall macOS
Reinstall a new copy of macOS.

Get Help Online
Browse the Apple Support website to find help for your Mac.

Disk Utility
Repair or erase a disk using Disk Utility.

Continue

FIGURE 14-2:
The Mac Recovery
Mode menu.

Resetting an iPhone

To hard reset a modern iPhone:

1. **Run the Settings app and choose General ➪ Reset ➪ Erase All Content and Settings.**

2. **If you're asked for your Apple ID and Password to confirm the erasure, enter them.**

3. **When you see a warning and a red Erase iPhone (or iPad) button, click on it.**

Rebuild Your Device after a Hard Reset

After you hard reset a device, you should

» Install all security updates

» Install all the programs and apps that you use on the device — and any relevant updates

» Restore your data from a backup

See Chapter 15 for more detail on these topics.

Chapter **15**

Restoring from Backups

Backing up is a critical component of any and every cybersecurity plan. After you reset a device to its factory settings as part of the recovery process (see Chapter 14), you can restore your data and programs so that your device will function as normal.

Because most people do not have to restore from backups regularly and because restoration is typically done after something "bad" happened that forced the restoration to be necessary, many folks first experience the process of restoring from backups when they are quite stressed. As such, people are prone to making mistakes during restoration, which can lead to data being lost forever. Fortunately, this chapter shows you how to restore.

You Will Need to Restore

The odds are close to 100 percent that, at some point, you will lose access to some file to which you still need access, and restoring from a backup will be a lifesaver. But restoring is not necessarily simple. You need to contemplate various factors before performing a restoration. Proper planning and execution can make the difference between recovering from lost data and losing even more data.

Restoring from backups is not as simple as many people think. Take the time to read this chapter before you perform a restore.

TIP

Wait! Do Not Restore Yet!

You noticed that some data that you want to access is missing. You noticed that a file is corrupted. You noticed that some program is not running properly. So, you should restore from a backup, right? Wait!

WARNING

Restoring without knowing why the problem occurred in the first place may be dangerous. For example, if you have a malware infection on your computer, restoring while the malware is still present won't remove the threat, and, depending on the type of malware and backup, may lead to the files in your backup becoming corrupted as well. If the malware corrupts the primary data store, you may lose your data and have nowhere from which to restore it!

For example, people who tried to restore data from backups on external hard drives have lost data to ransomware. The moment the external drive was connected to the infected computer, the ransomware spread to the backup and encrypted it as well!

WARNING

Malware can spread to cloud-based storage as well. Merely having the backup in the cloud is not a reason to restore before knowing what happened.

Even in the case of backups that are on read-only media, which malware cannot infect, attempting to restore before neutralizing the threat posed by the infection can waste time and potentially give the malware access to more data to steal.

Before you restore from any backups, make sure to diagnose the source of the problem that is causing you the need to restore. If you accidentally deleted a file, for example, and know that the problem occurred due to your own human error, by all means go ahead and restore. But if you're unsure what happened, apply the techniques described in Chapters 11 and 12 to figure out what you need to do to make your computer safe and secure prior to restoring from the backup.

Restoring from Full Backups of Systems

A *full system backup* is a backup of an entire system, including the operating system, programs/apps, settings, and data. The term applies whether the device being backed up is a smartphone or a massive server in a data center.

As such, the restoration process recreates a system that is effectively identical to the one that was backed up at the time that it was backed up. (This is not totally true in the absolute sense — the system clock will show a different time than the original system, for example — but it is true for the purposes of learning about system restoration.)

Restoring to the computing device that was originally backed up

System restoration from a system image works best when systems are restored to the same computing device from which the original backup was made. If your system was infected with malware, for example, and you restore to the same device from an image created before the malware infection took place, the system should work well. (Of course, you would lose any work and other updates done since that time, so hopefully you backed them up using one of the methods in Chapter 13.)

WARNING

Full system restores are often irreversible. Be absolutely sure that you want to run one before you do.

Restoring from a full system backup is likely the fastest way to restore an entire system, but the process can take dramatically longer than restoring just a few files that were corrupted. It is also far more likely to lead to accidentally erasing settings or data created since the last backup. As such, use a full system restore only when one is truly needed.

TIP

If you accidentally delete a bunch of files or even folders, do not perform a full system restore. Just restore those files from a backup using one of the techniques described later in this chapter.

Restoring to a different device than the one that was originally backed up

REMEMBER

System restoration from an image often won't work on a system with totally different hardware components than the system that was originally imaged. In general, the more different a system is from the system that was imaged, the more problems that you may encounter.

Some of those problems may autocorrect. If you restore a system with drivers for one video card to a system with another video card, for example, the restored system should realize that the wrong drivers are installed and simply not use them. Instead, it defaults to the operating system's built-in drivers and allows you to install the drivers for the correct card (or, in some cases, automatically download them or prompt you to do so).

Some problems may not autocorrect. For example, if the computer that was backed up used a standard USB-connected keyboard and mouse and the device to which you are restoring uses some proprietary keyboard that connects differently, it may not work at all after the restore; you may need to attach a USB keyboard to the system to download and install the drivers for your proprietary keyboard. Such situations are becoming increasingly rare due to both standardization and improvements in modern operating systems, but they do exist.

Some problems may not be correctable. If you try to restore the system image of a Mac to a computer designed to run Windows, for example, it won't work.

TIP

Some backup software packages allow you to configure a restore to either install separate drivers or search for drivers that match the hardware to which the restoration is being done to replace those found in the backup that are unsuitable. If you have such a feature and have difficulty restoring without it, you may want to try it.

A full system backup may or may not include a backup of all content on all drives attached to a system, not just those mounted inside of it. (Theoretically, all such drives should be included in a system image, but the term *system image* is often used to mean an image of the internal hard drives and SSDs.)

TIP

If a device for which you have an image fails, you should be able to use the system image to re-create the entire system as it was at the time that the backup was made. When you use the rebuilt system, it should function exactly as the previous system did at the time of the backup.

Original system images

If you want to recover to the original factory image of a system prior to restoring your data and programs, see Chapter 14, which is dedicated to performing such restorations.

After performing such a factory reset, one or more (or possibly all) patches and other security updates that you have installed on the device may be gone. Your device is likely vulnerable to various compromises. Immediately after restoring, you should, therefore, run the operating system update process (repetitively until it finds no needed updates) as well as the update process for any security software (also repetitively until it finds no needed updates).

Only after those steps are completed should you install other software, restore your data, or perform any other online activities.

Later system images

Before you restore from any system image, you must ascertain that whatever problem occurred that necessitated the restoration will not remain, or be restored, during the restoration. If your computer was infected with ransomware, for example, and you remove the malware with security software, but need to restore the criminally encrypted files from a backup, you do not want to end up restoring the ransomware along with the data.

If you know for certain that an image was made prior to the arrival of the problem, go ahead and use it. If in doubt, if possible, restore to an extra device and scan it with security software prior to performing the actual restoration. If you do not have an extra device to which you can restore and are unsure as to whether the backup is infected, you may want to hire a professional to take a look.

Installing security software

After you restore from a system image (whether factory settings or a later image), the first thing that you should do is check whether security software is installed. If it is not, install it. Either way, make sure to run the auto-updates until the software no longer needs updates.

TIP

Install security software before attempting to do anything online or read email. If you do not have security software in place before you perform such tasks, performing them could lead to a security breach of your device.

If you have the security software on CD or DVD, install it from there. If you created a USB drive or other disk with the security software on it, you can install it from there. If not, copy the security software to the hard drive from wherever you have it and run it.

Original installation media

For programs that you acquire and install after you purchased your device, you can reinstall them after you restore the original system image or even a later image that was created before the software was installed.

TIP

If you reinstall software from a CD or DVD, any updates to the software that were released after the CD or DVD was created will not be installed. Be sure to either configure your program to auto-update or manually download and install such updates. In some cases, software installation routines may also ask you whether you want them to automatically perform a check for updates immediately upon the completion of the installation. In general, answering affirmatively is a wise idea.

Downloaded software

The way that you reinstall programs that you previously purchased and installed at some point after you purchased your device depends on where the software is located:

>> **If you have a copy of the software on a thumb drive,** you can reinstall from the drive by connecting it into your device, copying the files to your hard drive, and running the install.

If there is any possibility that the thumb drive is infected with malware — for example, you're restoring due to a malware infection and may have inserted the thumb drive into your infected computer at some point in the past — make sure to scan it with security software before you run or copy anything from it. Do so from a device with security software running that will prevent infections from spreading upon connection from the drive to the machine being used for scanning.

>> **If you copied the software to a DVD or CD,** you can install from that disc. Make sure to install all necessary updates.

>> **If the purchased software can be redownloaded from a virtual locker,** do so. In some cases, software that is redownloaded will have been automatically upgraded to the latest release. In other cases, it will be the same version as you originally purchased, so make sure to install updates.

>> **If the software is downloadable from its original source** (public domain software, trialware that you activate with a code, and so on), feel free to redownload it. In some cases — for example, if newer versions require paying an upgrade fee —you may need to download the version that you had previously. In any case, make sure to install all updates for the version that you do install.

Restoring from full backups of data

In many cases, it makes sense to restore all the data on a device:

>> **After a restore from a factory image:** After restoring from a factory image and reinstalling all necessary software, your device will still have none (or almost none) of your data on it, so you need to restore all your data.

>> **After certain malware attacks:** Some malware modifies and/or corrupts files. To ensure that all your files are as they should be, after an infection, restore all your data from a backup. Of course, this assumes that you have a recent enough backup from which to do so without losing any work.

>> **After a hard drive failure:** If a hard drive fails, in full or in part, you will want to move your files to another drive. If you have a separate drive for data than for the operating system and programs — as many people do — performing a full restore of data is the easiest way to restore.

>> **When transitioning to a new, similar device:** Restoring from a backup is an easy way to ensure that you put all your data files onto the new device. Because some programs store settings in user data folders, copying the files directly or performing a selective restoration from a backup is usually a better way to go. But as people sometimes inadvertently leave out files when using such a technique, full restorations are sometimes used.

>> **After accidental deletions:** People occasionally accidentally delete large portions of their data files. One easy way to restore everything and not worry about whether everything is "back to the way that it should be" is to do a full restore of all data.

Unlike restoring from a full system backup, restoring from a full data backup won't restore applications. If a system has to be rebuilt entirely, recovering from full backups of data likely requires prior restorations to factory settings (or a later image of the computer) and reinstallation of all software.

TIP

The multi-step process of restoring from a factory image and then reinstalling applications and restoring data may seem more tedious than simply restoring from a more recent system image, but it also usually proves to be far more portable. Recovery can usually be done on devices that vary quite a bit from the original device, using images of those devices (or onto a new device), followed by the reinstallation of programs and the restoration of data.

Restoring from Incremental Backups

Incremental backups are backups made after a full backup and contain copies of only the portion of the contents being backed up that have changed since the preceding backup (full or incremental) was run.

TIP

Some simplistic backup software products use incremental and differential backups internally, but hide the internal workings from users. All users do is select which files or file types to restore and, if appropriate, which versions of those files, and the system works like magic hiding the merging of data from multiple backups into the resulting restoration.

Incremental backups of data

In many cases of home users, *incremental backup* refers to incremental backups of data. To recover data that was backed up using an incremental backup scheme requires multiple steps:

1. **A restoration must be done from the last full data backup.**

2. **After that restoration is complete, restoration must be performed from each incremental backup performed since that last full backup.**

Failing to include any of the incremental backups necessary in Step 2 may lead to corrupt data, missing data, data being present that should not be, or inconsistent data.

WARNING

Most modern backup software will warn (or prevent) you if you try to skip any incremental backups during an incremental restoration. Such software, however, sometimes does not, however, tell you if you're missing the final backup or backups in a series.

Incremental backups of systems

Incremental system backups are essentially updates to system images (or partial system images in the case of partial backups) that bring the image up to date as of the data that the backup was made. The incremental system backup contains copies of only the portion of the system that changed since the preceding backup (full or incremental) was run.

To restore from an incremental backup of a system:

1. **A restoration must be done from the last full system backup.**

2. **After that restoration is complete, restoration must be performed from each incremental backup performed since that system image was created.**

Failing to include any of the incremental backups necessary in Step 2 may lead to corrupt of missing programs, data, operating system components, and incompatibility issues between software. Most modern backup software will warn (or prevent) you if you try to skip various incrementals during a restore from an incremental backup. They often do not, however, tell you if you're missing the final backup or backups in a series.

Differential backups

Differential backups contain all the files that changed since the last full backup. (They are similar to the first in a series incremental backups run after a full backup.)

TIP

While creating a series of differential backups usually takes more time than creating a series of incremental backups, restoring from differential backups is usually much simpler and faster.

To recover from a differential backup:

1. **Perform a restoration from the last full system backup.**

2. **After that restoration is complete, perform a restoration from the most recent differential backup.**

Be sure to restore from the last differential backup and not from any other differential backup.

TIP

Many backup systems won't warn you if you attempt to restore from a differential backup other than the latest one. Be sure to double-check before restoring that you're using the latest one!

Table 15-1 shows the comparative restoration processes from full, incremental, and differential backups.

TABLE 15-1   **Restoration Processes**

	Full Backup	Incremental Backup	Differential Backup
After Backup #1	Restore from Backup #1	Restore from Backup #1 (Full)	Restore from Backup #1 (Full)
After Backup #2	Restore from Backup #2	Restore from Backups #1 and #2	Restore from Backups #1 and #2
After Backup #3	Restore from Backup #3	Restore from Backups #1, #2, and #3	Restore from Backups #1 and #3
After Backup #4	Restore from Backup #4	Restore from Backups #1, #2, #3, and #4	Restore from Backups #1 and #4

Continuous backups

Some continuous backups are ideal for performing system restore. Similar to a system image, they allow you to restore a system to the way that it looked at a certain point in time. Others are terrible for performing restores because they allow restoration to only the most recent version of the system, which often suffers from the need to be rebuilt in the first place.

In fact, the normal use of continuous backups is to address equipment failures, such as a hard drive suddenly going caput — not the rebuilding of systems after a security incident.

Furthermore, because continuous backups constantly propagate material from the device being backed up to the backup, any malware that was present on the primary system may be present on the backup.

Partial backups

Partial backups are backups of a portion of data. Likewise, partial backups are not intended to be full backups in case of a malware attack or the like. They are useful, however, in other situations, and you should be aware of how to restore from them.

If you have a particular set of files that are extremely sensitive and need to be backed up and stored separately from the rest of your system, you may use a partial backup for that data. If something happens and you need to rebuild a system or restore the sensitive data, you will need that separate partial backup from which to do the restore.

Digital private keys that provide access to cryptocurrency, email encryption/decryption capabilities, and so on, for example, are often stored on such backups along with images of extremely sensitive documents.

Often, partial backups of sensitive data are performed to USB drives that are then locked in safes or safe deposit boxes. Restoring from the backup would, in such cases, demand that the restorer obtain the physical USB drive, which could mean a delay in restoration. If the need to restore arises at 6 p.m. Friday, for example, and the drive is in a safe deposit box that is not available until 9 a.m. Monday, the desired material may remain inaccessible to the user for almost three days.

REMEMBER

Make sure that you store your partial backups in a manner that will allow you to access the backed-up data when you need it.

Another common scenario for specialized partial backups is when a network-based backup is used — especially within a small business — and a user needs to ensure that he or she has a backup of certain material in case of technical problems while traveling. Such backups should never be made without proper authorization. If permission has been obtained and a backup has been created, a user on the road who suffers a technical problem that requires restoration of data can do the restore by copying the files from the USB drive (after, presumably, decrypting the files using a strong password or some form of multifactor authentication).

Folder backups

Folder backups are similar to partial backups because the set of items being backed up is a particular folder. If you performed a folder backup using a backup tool, you can restore it using the techniques described in the preceding section.

The restore process is different if, however, you created the relevant backup by simply copying a folder or set of folders to an external drive (hard drive, SSDs, USB drive, or network drive).

Theoretically, you simply copy the backup copy of the folder or folders to the location of the original folder. However, doing so will potentially overwrite the contents of the primary folder, so any changes made since the backup will be lost.

Drive backups

A *drive backup* is similar to a folder backup, but an entire drive is backed up instead of a folder.

If you backed up a drive with backup software, you can restore it via that software.

If you backed up a drive by copying the contents of the drive somewhere else, you will need to manually copy them back. Such a restore may not work perfectly, however. Hidden and system files may not be restored, so a bootable drive backed up and restored in such a fashion may not remain bootable.

Virtual-drive backups

If you backed up an encrypted virtual drive, such as a BitLocker drive that you mount on your computer, you can restore the entire drive in one shot or restore individual files and folders from the drive.

Restoring the entire virtual drive

To restore the entire virtual drive in one shot, make sure the existing copy of the drive is not mounted. The easiest way to do so is to boot your computer and not mount any Bitlocker drives.

If your computer is booted already and the drive is mounted, simply dismount it:

1. **Choose Startup ⇨ This PC.**

2. **Locate the mounted Bitlocker drive.**

   The drive appears with an icon of a lock indicating that it is encrypted.

3. **Right-click on the drive and select Eject.** Once the drive is dismounted, it disappears from the This PC list of drives.

After the drive is unmounted, copy the backup copy of the drive to the primary drive location and replace the file containing the drive.

You can then unlock and mount the drive.

Restoring files and/or folders from the virtual drive

To restore individual files or folders from the virtual drive, mount the backup as a separate virtual drive and copy the files and folders from the backup to the primary as if you were copying files between any two drives.

Ideally, you should back up the backup of the virtual drive before mounting it and copying files and/or folders from it and mount it read-only when you mount it.

Always unmount the backup drive after copying files to the primary. Leaving it mounted — which inherently means that two copies of a large portion of your file system are in use at the same time — can lead to human mistakes.

Dealing with Deletions

One of the problems of restoring from any restore that does not entirely overwrite your data with a new copy is that the restore may not restore deletions.

For example, if after making a full backup, you delete a file, create ten new files, modify two data files, and then perform an incremental backup, the incremental backup may or may not record the deletion. If you restore from the full backup and then restore from the incremental, the restore from the incremental should delete the file, add the ten new files, and modify the two files to the newer version. In some cases, however, the file that you previously deleted may remain because some backup tools do not properly account for deletions.

Even when this problem happens, it is not usually critical. You just want to be aware of it. Of course, if you've deleted sensitive files in the past, you should check whether a restoration restored them to your computer. (If you intend to permanently and totally destroy a file or set of files, you should also remove it/them from your backups.)

Excluding Files and Folders

Some files and folders should not be restored during a restoration. In truth, they should not have been backed up in the first place unless you imaged a disk, but in many cases, people do back them up anyway.

The following are examples of some such files and folders that can be excluded from typical restorations done on a Windows 10 machine. If you're using backup software, the software likely excluded these files when creating the backup. If you are copying files manually, you may have backed them up.

>> Contents of the Recycle Bin

>> Browser caches (temporary Internet files from web browsers, such as Microsoft Edge or Internet Explorer, Firefox, Chrome, Vivaldi, or Opera)

>> Temporary folders (often called Temp or tem and reside in C:\, in the user directory, or in the data directory of software

>> Temporary files (usually files named *.tmp or *.temp)

>> Operating system swap files (pagefile.sys)

>> Operating system hibernation-mode system image information (hyberfil.sys)

>> Backups (unless you want to back up your backups) such as Windows File History backup

>> Operating system files backed up during an operating system upgrade (usually found in C:\Windows.old on Windows computers that have had their operating systems upgraded)

>> Microsoft Outlook cache files (*.ost — note that Outlook local data stores [*.pst] should be backed up; in fact, in many cases they may be the most critical files in a backup)

>> Performance log files in directories called PerfLogs

>> Junk files that users create as personal temporary files to hold information (for example, a text file in which the user types a phone number that someone dictated to him or her, but which the user has since entered into his or her smartphone directory)

In-app backups

Some applications have built-in backup capabilities that protect you from losing your work if your computer crashes, power fails and you don't have battery power left, and other mishaps.

Some such applications will automatically prompt you to restore documents that would otherwise have been lost due to a system crash or the like. When you start Microsoft Word after an abnormal shutdown of the application, for example, it provides a list of documents that can be autorecovered — sometimes even offering multiple versions of the same document.

Understanding Archives

The term *archive* has multiple meanings in the world of information technology. I describe the relevant meanings in the following sections.

Multiple files stored within one file

Sometimes multiple files can be stored within a single file. This concept was addressed with the concept of virtual drives earlier in this chapter and in Chapter 13. However, storing multiple files within one file does not necessitate the creation of virtual drives.

You may have seen files with the extension .zip, for example. *ZIP files,* as such files are called, are effectively containers that hold one or more compressed files. Storing multiple files in such a container allows for far easier transfer of files (a single ZIP file attached to an email is far easier to manage than 50 small individual files). It also reduces the amount (sometimes significantly) of disk space and Internet bandwidth necessary to store and move the files.

If you need to restore files from an archive, you can either extract all the files from the archive to your primary source, or you can open the archive and copy the individual files to your primary location as you would with any files found in any other folder.

Archive files come in many different formats. Some appear automatically as folders within Windows and Mac file systems and their contents as files and folders within folders. Others require special software to be viewed and extracted from.

Old live data

Sometimes old data is moved off of primary systems and stored elsewhere. Storing old data can improve performance. For example, if a search of all email items means searching through 25 years' worth of messages, the search will take far longer than a search through just the last 3 years. If nearly all relevant results will always be within the last few years, the older emails can be moved to a separate archive where you can access and search them separately if need be.

If you use archiving, factor that in when restoring data. You want to ensure that archives are restored to archives and that you don't accidentally restore archives to the primary data stores.

Old versions of files, folders, or backups

The term *archives* is also sometimes used to refer to old versions of files, folders, and backups even if those files are stored on the primary data store. Someone who has ten versions of a contract, for example, that were executed at different points in time, may keep all the Word versions of these documents in an Archive folder.

Archiving of this sort can be done for any one or more of many reasons. One common rationale is to avoid accidentally using an old version of a document when the current version should be used.

If you're archiving, factor that in when restoring data. Restore all the archives to their proper locations. You may see multiple copies of the same file being restored; don't assume that that is an error.

Restoring Using Backup Tools

Restoring using backup software is similar to the process of backing up using backup software.

To restore using the backup software that was utilized to create the backups from which you are restoring, run the software (in some cases, you may need to install the software onto the machine, rather than run it from a CD or the like) and select Restore.

When you restore, make sure that you select the correct backup version to restore from.

WARNING

Beware of bogus restoration prompts! Various forms of malware present bogus prompts advising you that your hard drive has suffered some sort of malfunction and that you must run a restore routing to repair data. Only run restores from software that you obtained from a reliable source and that you know that you can trust!

Many modern backup software packages hide the approach used to back up — full, differential, incremental, and so on — from users and instead allow users to pick which version of files they want to restore.

If you're restoring using the specialized backup and recovery software that came with an external hard drive or solid-state device that you use to back up your device, attach the drive, run the software (unless it runs automatically), and follow the prompt to restore.

Such software is usually simple to use; restoration typically works like a simplified version of that done using other backup software (see preceding section).

REMEMBER

Disconnect the drive from the system after performing the restore!

Restoring from a Windows backup

To restore from a Windows backup to the original locations from which the data was backed up, follow these steps:

1. Choose Start ⇨ Settings ⇨ Update & Security ⇨ Backup.

2. Click on Restore files from a current backup.

3. In the File System viewer, browse through different versions of your folders and files or type and search for the name of the file you're looking for.

4. Select what you want to restore.

5. Click on Restore.

Restoring to a system restore point

Microsoft Windows allows you to restore your system to the way it looked at a specific time at which the system was imaged by the operating system:

1. **Click on the Start button and select Settings.**

2. **Choose Control Panel ⇨ System and Maintenance ⇨ Backup and Restore.**

3. **Click on Restore My Files to restore your files or Restore All Users' Files to restore all users files (assuming that you have permissions to do so).**

Restoring from a smartphone/tablet backup

Many portable devices come equipped with the ability to automatically sync your data to the cloud, which allows you to restore the data to a new device if your device is lost or stolen.

Even devices that do not have such a feature built in almost always can run software that effectively delivers such features for a specific folder tree or drive.

When you start an Android device for the first time after a factory reset, you may be prompted if you want to restore your data. If you are, restoring is pretty straightforward. Answer yes.

While the exact routines may vary between devices and manufacturers, other forms of restore generally follow some flavor of the following process:

To restore contacts from an SD card:

1. **Open the Contacts App.**

   If there is an import feature, select it and jump to Step 4.

2. **Select Settings from the main menu (or click on the Settings icon).**

   If you aren't displaying all contacts, you may need to click the Display menu and select All Contacts.

3. **Select Import / Export Contacts (or, if that option is not available, select Manage Contacts and then select Import Contacts on the next screen).**

4. **Select Import from SD Card.**

5. **Review the file name for the backup of the Contact list then click on OK.**

   Contacts are often backed up (or exported to) VCF files.

To restore media (pictures, videos, and audio files) from an SD card:

1. Using File Manager, open the SD card.

2. Click to turn on check boxes next to the file or files that you want to restore.

3. To copy files to the phone's memory, go to the menu and select Copy ⇨ Internal Storage.

4. Select the folder to which you want to copy the files or create the folder and move into it.

5. Select Copy Here.

Restoring from manual file or folder copying backups

To restore from a manual file or folder copy, just copy the file or folder from the backup to the main data store. (If you are overwriting a file or folder, you may receive a warning from the operating system.)

REMEMBER

Disconnect the media on which the backup is located from the main store when you are done.

Utilizing third-party backups of data hosted at third parties

If you utilized the backup capabilities of a third-party provider at which you store data in the cloud or whose cloud-based services you utilize, you may be able to restore your relevant data through an interface provided by the third-party provider.

If you use a third-party cloud-based-service provider and you have not performed backups, you may still be able to restore data. Contact your provider. The provider itself may have backed up the data without notifying you.

TIP

While you should never rely on your cloud service provider performing backups that you did not order, if you are in a jam and contact the provider, you may (or may not) be pleasantly surprised to find out that they do have backups from which you can restore.

Returning Backups to Their Proper Locations

After you restore from a physical backup, you need to return it to its proper location for several reasons:

>> You do not want it to be misplaced if you ever need it again.

>> You do not want it to be stolen.

>> You want to ensure that you do not undermine any storage strategies and procedures intended to keep backups in different locations than the data stores that they back up.

Network storage

Ideally, when restoring from a network-based backup, you should mount the network drive as read-only to prevent possible corruptions of the backup. Furthermore, be sure to disconnect from the network data store once you are done performing the restoration.

TIP

Make sure that whatever mechanism you are using to run the restore (for example, backup software) has the proper network permissions to write to the primary data storage location.

Restoring from a combination of locations

There is no reason to back up to only one location. Restoration, however, typically will utilize backups from only one location at a time.

If you do need to restore from backups that are physically situated at more than one location, be extremely careful not to restore the wrong versions of files as some of the files may exist on multiple backups.

Restoring to Non-Original Locations

When it comes to restoring data, some folks choose to restore to locations other than original locations, test the restored data, and then copy or move it to the original locations. Such a strategy reduces the likelihood of writing over good data with bad data. You can make a bad day worse if you lose some of your data and discover that your backup of the data is corrupted. If you then restore from that backup over your original data and thereby corrupt it, you lose even more of your data.

Never Leave Your Backups Connected

WARNING

After restoring, never leave backup hard drives or solid-state drives connected to the systems or networks that they are backing up. Any future malware infections that attack the primary system can spread to the backups as well. Removing your backup from being connected to the material that it is backing up can make all the difference between quickly recovering from a ransomware attack and having to pay an expensive ransom to a criminal.

If you back up to write-once read-many-times media, such as CD-Rs, it is theoretically safe to leave the backup in an attached drive after you finalize the restoration, but you still should not do so. You want the backup to be readily available in its proper location in case you ever need it in the future.

Restoring from Encrypted Backups

Restoring from encrypted backups is essentially the same as restoring from non-encrypted backups except that you need to unlock the backups prior to restoration.

Backups that are protected by a password obviously need the proper password to be entered. Backups protected by certificates or other more advanced forms of encryption may require that a user possess a physical item or digital certificate in order to restore.

In most cases, security conscious home users protect their backups with passwords. If you do so (and you should), do not forget your password.

Testing Backups

Many folks have thought that they had proper backups only to discover when they needed to restore that the backups were corrupted. Hence, testing backups is critical.

While theoretically you should test every backup that you make and test every single item within the backup can be restored, such a scheme is impractical for most people. But do test the first backup that you make with any software, check the auto-recover files the first time that you use Word, and so on.

Some backup software comes with the capability to verify backups — that is, after making a backup, it checks that the original data and data in the backups matches. Running such verification after making a backup adds significant time to the backup process. However, it's well worth running if you can do so because it helps ensure that nothing was improperly recorded or otherwise corrupted during the backup process.

Restoring Cryptocurrency

Restoring cryptocurrency after it is erased from a computer or some other device it was stored on is totally different than any of the restore processes described in this chapter.

Technically speaking, cryptocurrency is tracked on a ledger, not stored anywhere, so the restoration is not to restore the actual cryptocurrency, but rather to restore the private keys needed in order to control the addresses within the ledger at which the cryptocurrency is stored. (I hate the term *digital wallets* as applied to cryptocurrency — we store digital keys, not cryptocurrency, in a digital wallet. The name *digital keyring* would have been far more accurate and less confusing.)

Hopefully, if you lost the device on which your cryptocurrency is stored, you have the keys printed on paper that is stored in a safe or safe deposit box. Obtain the paper, and you have your keys. Just don't leave the paper lying around; put it back into the secure location ASAP. (If you keep the paper in a safe deposit box, consider performing the restoration technique at the bank so that you never take the paper out of the safe deposit box area.)

If you store cryptocurrency at an exchange, you can restore your credentials to the exchange through whatever means the exchange allows. Ideally, if you properly backed up your passwords to a secure location, you can just obtain and use them.

For those who use hardware wallets to store the keys to their cryptocurrency, the backup for the wallet device is often a *recovery seed*, which is a list of words that allows the device to re-create the keys needed for the relevant addresses. It is generally accepted that the list of words should be written down on paper and stored in a bank vault and/or safe, not stored electronically.

Booting from a Boot Disk

If you ever need to boot from a boot disk that you created (as might be necessary during a system reset and restore process), boot your system, go into the BIOS settings, and set the boot order to start with the disk from which you want to boot. Then restart the system.

7

Looking toward the Future

IN THIS PART . . .

Explore cybersecurity careers.

Discover emerging technologies.

Chapter **16**

Pursuing a Cybersecurity Career

With a global shortage of competent cybersecurity professionals, there has never been a better time to pursue a career — especially since the shortage seems to grow with the passage of time.

As a result of an insufficient supply of cybersecurity professionals to satisfy the demand for people with relevant skills, compensation packages earned by cyber-security professionals are among the best found among technology workers.

In this chapter, you find out about some of the professional roles in the cyberse-curity field, potential career paths, and certifications.

Professional Roles in Cybersecurity

Cybersecurity professionals have a wide range of responsibilities that vary quite a bit based on their exact roles, but most, if not all, ultimately work to help either protect data and systems from being compromised, or, in the case of certain government positions, to breach the systems and compromise the data of adversaries.

No one, single career path called "cybersecurity" exists. The profession has many nuances, and different paths along which people's careers can progress.

Security engineer

Security engineers come in multiple types, but the vast majority are hands-on technical folks who build, maintain, and debug information security systems as part of organizational (corporate, government, or nonprofit) projects. Security engineers working in the professional services arms of vendors may also help ensure that software being deployed at clients is done so in a secure fashion.

Security manager

Security managers are typically mid-level management within larger enterprises who have responsibility for some specific area of information security. One security manager, may, for example, be responsible for all of a firm's security training, and another may be responsible for overseeing all of its Internet-facing firewalls. People in security manager positions typically perform less hands-on, technically detailed security activities than do the folks who report to them.

Security director

Security directors are the people who oversee information security for an organization. In smaller firms, the director is usually the de facto chief information security officer (CISO). Larger firms may have several directors responsible for various subsets of the firm's information security program; such folks, in turn, usually report to the CISO.

Chief information security officer (CISO)

The *CISO* is the person responsible for information security throughout an organization. You can think of the CISO role as being that of the chief of staff of the organization's information-security defensive military.

The CISO is a senior, C-level management position. Serving as a CISO usually requires significant management knowledge and experience, in addition to an understanding of information security.

Security analyst

Security analysts work to prevent information security breaches. They review not only existing systems, but study emerging threats, new vulnerabilities, and so on in order to ensure that the organization remains safe.

Security architect

Security architects design and oversee the deployment of organizational information security countermeasures. They often have to understand, design, and test complex security infrastructures and regularly serve as the security team member who is involved in projects outside of the security department as well — for example, helping to design the security needed for a custom application that an organization is designing and building or helping to guide networking folks as the latter design various elements of corporate IT networking infrastructure.

Security administrator

Security administrators are hands-on folks who install, configure, operate, manage, and troubleshoot information security countermeasures on behalf of an organization. These folks are the ones to whom nontechnical professionals often refer when they say "I am having a problem and need to call the security guy or security gal."

Security auditor

Security auditors conduct security audits — that is, they check that security policies, procedures, technologies, and so on are working as intended and are effectively and adequately protecting corporate data, systems, and networks.

Cryptographer

Cryptographers are experts at and work with encryption, as used to protect sensitive data.

Some cryptographers work to develop encryption systems to protect sensitive data, while others, known as *cryptanalysts*, do the opposite: analyzing encrypted information and encryption systems in order to break the encryption and decrypt the information.

As compared to other information security jobs, cryptographers disproportionately work for government agencies, the military, and in academia. In the United States, many government jobs in cryptography require U.S. citizenship and an active security clearance.

Vulnerability assessment analyst

Vulnerability assessment analysts examine computer systems, databases, networks, and other portions of the information infrastructure in search of potential vulnerabilities. The folks working in such positions must have explicit permission to do so. Unlike penetration testers, described in the next section, vulnerability assessors don't typically act as outsiders trying to breach systems, but as insiders who have access to systems and have the ability to examine them in detail from the start.

Ethical hacker

Ethical hackers attempt to attack, penetrate, and otherwise compromise systems and networks on behalf of — and with the explicit permission of — the technologies' owners in order to discover security vulnerabilities that the owners can then fix. Ethical hackers are sometimes referred to as *penetration testers* or *pen-testers*. While many corporations employ their own ethical hackers, a significant number of folks who work in such positions work for consulting companies offering their services to third parties.

Security researcher

Security researchers are forward-looking folks who seek to discover vulnerabilities in existing systems and potential security ramifications of new technologies and other products. They sometimes develop new security models and approaches based on their research.

WARNING

As far as ethics are concerned, and as far as most jurisdictions are concerned, a security researcher who hacks an organization without explicit permission from that organization is not a security researcher or an ethical hacker, but simply someone breaking the law.

Offensive hacker

Offensive hackers attempt to break into adversaries' systems to either cripple the systems or steal information.

In the United States of America, it is illegal for a business to go on the offensive and attack anyone — including striking back at hackers who are actively trying to penetrate the organization. As such, all legal offensive hacking jobs in the United States are government positions, such as with intelligence agencies. If you enjoy attacking and are not satisfied with just ethical hacking, you may wish to pursue a career with the government or military. Many offensive hacking positions require security clearances.

Software security engineer

Software security engineers integrate security into software as it is designed and developed. They also test the software to make sure it has no vulnerabilities. In some cases, they may be the coders of the software itself.

Software source code security auditor

Software source code security auditors review the source code of programs in search of programming errors, vulnerabilities, violations of corporate policies and standards, regulatory problems, copyright infringement (and, in some cases, patent infringement), and other issues that either must be, or should be, resolved.

Software security manager

Secure development managers oversee the security of software throughout the software's life cycle — from initial business requirements gathering all the way through disposal.

Security consultant

There are many different types of *security consultants.* Some, like the author of this book, advise corporate executives on security strategy, serve as expert witnesses, or help security companies grow and succeed. Others are hands-on penetration testers. Others may design or operate components of security infrastructure, focusing on specific technologies. When it comes to security consulting, you can find positions in just about every area of information security.

Security specialist

The title *security specialist* is used to refer to people serving in many different types of roles. All the various roles, however, tend to require at least several years of professional experience working in the information security field.

Incident response team member

The *incident response team* consists of the de facto first responders who deal with security incidents. Team members seek to contain and eliminate attacks, while minimizing the damage from them. They also often perform some of the analysis into what happened — sometimes determining that nothing requires any corrective activity. You can think of incident responders as roughly the equivalent of cybersecurity firefighters — they deal with dangerous attacks, but sometimes get called in to verify that there is no fire.

Forensic analyst

Forensic analysts are effectively digital detectives, who, after some sort of computer event, examine data, computers and computing devices, and networks to gather, analyze, and properly preserve evidence and deduce what exactly happened, how it was possible to happen, and who did it. You can think of forensic analysts as roughly the equivalent of law enforcement and insurance company inspectors who analyze properties after a fire to determine what happened and who might be responsible.

Cybersecurity regulations expert

Cybersecurity regulations experts are knowledgeable in the various regulations related to cybersecurity and help ensure that organizations comply with such regulations. They are often, but not always, attorneys who have prior experience working with various compliance-type matters.

Privacy regulations expert

Privacy regulations experts are knowledgeable in the various regulations related to privacy and help ensure that organizations comply with such regulations. They are often, but not always, attorneys who have prior experience working with various compliance-type matters.

Exploring Career Paths

Folks in information security can pursue multiple different career paths. Some involve becoming technical gurus focused on specific subsections of security, while others require broad knowledge of the discipline and interfacing with many different areas of a business. Still others focus on management.

TIP

People should consider their long-term goals as they plan their careers. For example, if you're looking to become a CISO, you may want to work in a variety of different hands-on positions, earn an MBA, and pursue promotions and certifications in areas of information security management, while if you want to become a senior architect, you'll likely be better off focusing on promotions into various roles involved in security analysis and design, doing penetration testing, and earning technical degrees.

The following sections give examples of some potential career paths.

Career path: Senior security architect

In the United States, security architects typically earn well over $100,000 — and, in some markets, considerably more — making this type of position quite attractive. While every person's career path is unique, one typical framework for becoming a senior security architect might be to follow a career path similar to the following:

1. **Do one of the following:**

   - Earn a bachelor's degree in computer science.

   - Earn a degree in any field and pass an entry-level certification exam in cybersecurity (for example, Security+).

   - Obtain a technical job while without a degree and demonstrate proficiency in the relevant technologies used as part of the job.

2. **Work as a network administrator or systems administrator and gain hands on security experience.**

3. **Obtain a slightly more focused credential (for example, CEH).**

4. **Work as a security administrator — preferably administering a range of different security systems over a period of several years.**

5. **Earn one or more general security certifications (for example, CISSP).**

6. **Become a security architect and gain experience in such a role.**

7. **Earn an advanced security architecture certification (for example, CISSP-ISSAP).**

8. **Become a senior level security architect.**

WARNING

Do not expect to become a senior-level architect overnight; it often takes a decade or more of relevant experience to achieve such a position.

Career path: CISO

In the United States, chief information security officers typically earn $150,000 or more (a lot more in certain industries), but, the jobs can be quite stressful — CISOs are responsible for corporate information security — which often involves dealing with emergencies. While every person's career path is unique, one typical framework for becoming a CISO might be to follow a career path similar to the following:

1. **Earn a bachelor's degree in computer science or in information technology.**

2. **Do one of the following:**

   - Work as a systems analyst, systems engineer, programmer, or in some other related hands-on technical position.

   - Work as a network engineer.

3. **Migrate toward security and work as a security engineer, security analyst, or security consultant — taking on various different roles within an organization, or as a consultant to organizations, thereby exposing oneself to various different areas of information security.**

4. **Obtain general certifications in information security (for example, CISSP).**

5. **Migrate toward management of security by becoming the manager of a security operations team. Ideally, over time, manage multiple information security teams, each that deals with different areas of information security that the others.**

6. **Do one of the following:**

   - Earn a master's degree in cybersecurity (ideally with a focus on information security management).

   - Earn a master's in computer science (ideally with a focus on cybersecurity).

   - Earn a master's in information systems management (ideally, with a focus on information security).

   - Earn an MBA.

7. **Do one of the following:**

   - Become a divisional CISO (de facto or de jure).

   - Become the CISO of a relatively small business or nonprofit organization.

8. **Obtain an advanced information security credential focused on information security management (for example, CISSP-ISSMP).**

9. **Become the CISO of a larger business.**

WARNING

The path to becoming a CISO can easily take a decade, or even decades, depending on the size of the organization in which the CISO serves.

Starting Out in Information Security

Many folks who work in information security began their careers in other areas of information technology. In some cases, the folks were first exposed to the amazing world of cybersecurity while serving in technical positions. In other situations, people took technical jobs not directly tied to information security, but did so with the intent of developing various skills and using the positions as stepping stones into the world of security.

TIP

Jobs in the fields of risk analysis, systems engineering and development, and networking are often good entry points. An email administrator, for example, is likely to learn plenty about email security and possibly also about the architecture of secure network designs and securing servers in general. People developing web-based systems are likely to learn about web security as well as about secure software design. And system and network administrators are going to learn about the security of the items that they are responsible to keep alive and healthy.

Some of the technical jobs that can help prepare you for cybersecurity-related roles include

>> Programmer

>> Software engineer

>> Web developer

>> Information systems support engineer (technical support hands-on specialist)

>> Systems administrator

>> Email administrator

>> Network administrator

>> Database administrator

>> Website administrator

Some nontechnical positions can also help prepare people for careers in the nontechnical roles of information security. Here are some examples:

>> Auditor

>> Law enforcement detective

>> Attorney focusing on cybersecurity-related areas of law

>> Attorney focusing on regulatory compliance

>> Attorney focusing on privacy-related areas of law

>> Risk-management analyst

Exploring Popular Certifications

Recognized cybersecurity certifications and, to a lesser degree, certificates showing successful completion of cybersecurity courses, can prove to an employer that your cybersecurity knowledge meets certain standards and help you advance along your desired career path.

Many different information-security certifications are on the market today. Some focus on specific technologies or areas of information security, while others are more broad.

While it is beyond the scope of this book to explore each and every possible certification available today, the following are five of the more popular — and better recognized — vendor-neutral certifications that may be ideal for folks relatively early in their cybersecurity careers.

CISSP

The Certified Information Systems Security Professional (CISSP) certification, initially launched in 1994, covers a broad range of security-related domains, delving into details in some areas more than in others. It provides employers with the comfort of knowing that workers understand important aspects of more than just one or two areas of information security; as components of information security are often highly interconnected, broad knowledge is valuable, and becomes absolutely necessary as one ascends the information-security management ladder.

The CISSP is intended to be pursued by people with several years of experience in the information security field — in fact, while you can take the CISSP exam without experience, you won't actually receive the credential until you work in the field for the required number of years. As a result, folks possessing CISSP credentials, who always have several years of experience under their belts, often command higher salaries than do both their uncertified peers and counterparts holding other certifications.

The CISSP credential, issued by the highly regarded (ISC)2 organization, is both vendor neutral and more evergreen than many other certifications. Study materials and training courses for CISSP exam are widely available, and tests are administered in more locations, and on more dates, than are most other, if not all other, cybersecurity certifications. Multiple add-ons to the CISSP are available for those interested in proving their mastery of information security architecture (CISSP-ISSAP), management (CISSP-ISSMP), and engineering (CISSP-ISSEP).

(ISC)2 requires that holders of the CISSP credentials accept to abide by a specific Code of Ethics and that they perform significant continuing education activities in order to maintain their credentials, which must be renewed every three years.

REMEMBER

The CISSP is not intended to test hands-on technical skills — and does not do so. People looking to demonstrate mastery of specific technologies or areas of technology — for example, penetration testing, security administration, auditing, and so on — may want to consider pursuing either a more technically focused, general certification or some specific product and skill certifications.

(For full disclosure, the author of this book holds a CISSP certification, as well as two add-on credentials — CISSP-ISSAP and CISSP-ISSMP — and authored (ISC)2's official study guide for the CISSP-ISSMP exam.)

CISM

The well-regarded Certified Information Security Manager (CISM) credential from the Information Systems Audit and Control Association (ISACA) has exploded in popularity since its inception a little under two decades ago.

Emanating from an organization focused on audit and controls, the CISM credential is, generally speaking, a bit more focused than is the CISSP on policies, procedures, and technologies for information security systems management and control, as typically occurs within large enterprises or organizations.

As with the CISSP, to earn a CISM, a candidate must have several years of professional information-security work experience. Despite the differences between the CISSP and CISM — with the former delving deeper into technical topics and the latter doing similarly for management-related topics — the two offerings also significantly overlap. Both are well respected.

CEH

The Certified Ethical Hacker (CEH), offered by the International Council of E-Commerce Consultants (EC-Council), is intended for people with at least two years of professional experience who are intent on establishing their credibility as ethical hackers (in other words, penetration testers).

CEH is a practical exam that tests candidates' skills as related to hacking: from performing reconnaissance and penetrating networks to escalating privileges and stealing data. This exam tests a variety of practical skills, including attack vehicles, such as various types of malware; attack techniques, such as SQL injection; cryptanalysis methods used to undermine encryption; methods of social engineering in order to undermine technical defenses via human error; and how hackers can evade detection by covering their tracks.

EC-Council requires CEH credential holders to acquire a significant number of continuing education credits in order to maintain a CEH credential — something quite important for an exam that tests practical knowledge — especially when you consider how rapidly technologies change in today's world.

Security+

Security+ is a vendor-neutral general cybersecurity certification that can be valuable especially for people early in their careers. It is offered and administered by the well-respected, technology-education nonprofit, CompTIA. While there is, technically speaking, no minimum number of years of professional experience required in order to earn a CompTIA Security+ designation, from a practical perspective, most people will likely find it easier to pass the exam after working in the field, and gaining practical experience, for a year or two.

The Security+ exam typically goes into more technical detail that either the CISSP or the CISM, directly addressing the knowledge needed to perform roles such as those related to entry-level IT auditing, penetration testing, systems administration, network administration, and security administration; hence, CompTIA Security+ is a good early-career certification for many folks.

Anyone earning the Security+ designation since 2011 must earn continuing education credits in order to maintain the credential.

GSEC

The Global Information Assurance Certification Security Essentials Certification (GSEC) is the entry-level security certification covering materials in courses run by the SANS Institute, a well-respected information-security training company.

Like Security+, GSEC contains a lot more hands-on practical material than the CISM or CISSP certifications, making this certification more valuable than the aforementioned alternatives in some scenarios and less desirable in others. Despite being marketed as entry-level, the GSEC exam is, generally speaking, regarded as more difficult and comprehensive than the test required to earn a Security+ designation.

All GSEC credential holders must show continued professional experience or educational growth in the field of information security in order to maintain their credentials.

Verifiability

The issuers of all major information security credentials provide employers with the ability to verify that a person holds any credentials claimed. For security reasons, such verification may require knowledge of the user's certification identification number, which credential holders typically do not publicize.

WARNING

If you earn a certification, be sure to keep your information in the issuer's database up to date. You do not want to lose your certification because you did not receive a reminder to submit continuing education credits or to pay a maintenance fee.

Ethics

Many security certifications require credential holders to adhere to a code of ethics that not only mandates that holders comply with all relevant laws and government regulations, but also mandates that people act appropriately even in manners that exceed the letter of the law.

WARNING

Be sure to understand such requirements. Losing a credential due to unethical behavior can obviously severely erode the trust that other people place in a person and can inflict all sorts of negative consequences on your career in information security.

Overcoming a Criminal Record

While a criminal record does not prevent someone from obtaining many cybersecurity-related jobs, a criminal record may be an insurmountable barrier when it comes to obtaining certain positions. Anything that prevents someone from obtaining a security clearance, for example, would disqualify that individual from working in certain government and government-contractor roles.

In some cases, the nature, timing, and age at which one committed past crimes may weigh heavily in an employer's decision. Some information-security organizations may be perfectly fine with hiring a reformed, former teenage hacker, for example, but may be averse to hiring someone who was convicted of a violent crime as an adult. Likewise, someone who served time in prison for a computer crime that he or she committed two decades ago, but whose record has since been clean, may be viewed quite differently by a potential employer than someone who was just recently released from prison after serving a sentence for a similar crime.

Looking at Other Professions with a Cybersecurity Focus

Besides working directly in cybersecurity, there are many opportunities to work in fields that interface directly with cybersecurity professionals, and which benefit from the global increase in attention to cybersecurity.

Lawyers may decide, for example, to specialize in cybersecurity-related laws or on firms' compliance with privacy regulations, and law enforcement personnel may develop expertise in the forensics that are utilized investigating cybercrimes.

The bottom line is that cybersecurity has created, is creating, and will continue to create for the foreseeable future many lucrative professional opportunities for people in multiple fields. You need not be a technical genius to benefit from the discipline's boom.

If you find cybersecurity fascinating, you may want to explore the opportunities that it may offer you.

IN THIS CHAPTER

» Understanding emerging
technologies and their potential
impact on cybersecurity

» Experiencing virtual reality and
augmented reality

Chapter **17**

Emerging Technologies Bring New Threats

The world has undergone a radical transformation in recent decades, with the addition of the benefits digital computing power to just about every aspect of human lives. Within the course of just one generation, Western society has evolved from single-purpose film cameras, photocopiers, closed circuit television, and radio-wave based music broadcast receivers to connected devices sporting the features of all these devices and many more — all within a single device. Simultaneously, new, advanced computing technology models have emerged, creating tremendous potential for even greater incorporation of technology into daily lives. Offerings that would have been considered unrealistic science fiction just a few years ago have become so totally normal and ubiquitously deployed today that children don't always believe adults when the latter explain how much the world has changed in recent years.

With the advent of new technologies and the digital transformation of the human experience, however, also comes great information security risks. In this chapter, you discover some technologies that are rapidly changing the world and how they are impacting cybersecurity. This list of emerging technologies is by no means comprehensive. Technologies constantly evolve and therefore constantly create new information security challenges.

Relying on the Internet of Things

Not that long ago, the only devices that were connected to the Internet were classic computers — desktops, laptops, and servers. Today, however, is a different world.

From smartphones and security cameras to coffeemakers and exercise equipment, electronic devices of all types now have computers embedded within them, and many of these computers are constantly and perpetually connected to the Internet. The *Internet of Things (IoT)*, as the ecosystem of connected devices is commonly known, has been growing exponentially over the past few years.

And, ironically, while consumers see many such connected devices marketed to them in stores and online, the vast majority of IoT devices are actually components of commercial and industrial systems. In fact, some experts even believe that as much as 99 percent of connected nontraditional-computer devices live in commercial and industrial environments. The reliability of utilities, factories and other manufacturing facilities, hospitals, and most other elements of the backbone of today's economic and social existence depends heavily on having stable, secure technology.

Of course, any and all computing devices — whether classic computers or smart devices of other types — can suffer from vulnerabilities and are potentially hackable, and exploitable for nefarious purposes. Internet-connected cameras, for example, which are designed to allow people to watch homes or businesses from afar, can potentially allow unauthorized hackers to watch the same video feeds. Furthermore, such devices can be commandeered for use in attacking other devices. In fact, in October 2016, the Mirai Botnet attack leveraged many infected IoT devices in unison, and took the popular Dyn DNS service offline. *DNS* is the system that converts human-names for computers into machine-understandable Internet Protocol numeric addresses (IP addresses). As a result of the attack on Dyn, many high-profile websites and services, including Twitter, Netflix, GitHub, and Reddit, suffered de facto outages as people could not reach the sites because the names in the URLs of the sites could not be translated to their proper Internet addresses.

Likewise, IoT creates tremendous potential for serious sabotage. Consider the possible effects of hacking an industrial system involved in the manufacturing of some medical equipment. Could people die if bugs or backdoors were inserted into the code that runs on the computer embedded within the device and then is exploited once the device were in use?

STUXNET

Sometime in 2009 or 2010, malware now known as Stuxnet crippled an Iranian uranium refinement facility that was believed to have been enriching uranium for potential use in building nuclear weapons. The sophisticated cyberattack was widely believed to have been launched by a joint team of cyberwarriors from the United States and Israel.

Stuxnet targeted the Siemens industrial control systems that the Iranians were using to operate and manage uranium-refining centrifuges. The malware caused the control systems to send improper instructions to the centrifuges while reporting that everything was running properly. The cyberattack is believed to have both inappropriately increased and decreased the speed of centrifuges. The inappropriate changes of speed caused the centrifuges' aluminum tubes to suffer from unexpected stress and to expand as a result, eventually causing them to come in contact with other portions of the machine and severely damage the device.

There is little doubt that Stuxnet's operational success will motivate other cyberwarriors to launch similar types of attacks in the future.

Hacks undermining systems controlled by connected devices are possible — even when such systems are not connected to the public Internet (see the nearby sidebar).

Could you see hackers demanding ransoms in exchange for not releasing video from people's home security cameras?

Could you see hackers demanding ransoms in exchange for not causing people's refrigerators to turn off and ruin their food — or even find criminals who turn off fridges when people leave for work and turn them on before the victims return home, causing food to spoil in an effort to poison targeted individuals?

As smart cars (which include essentially every vehicle made in the last decade or more) become more common, could criminals potentially hack them and cause crashes? Or blackmail people into paying ransoms in exchange for not crashing their cars? Before answering that question, consider that security researchers have demonstrated on more than one occasion how hackers can take control of some vehicles and cause brakes to stop working.

What about when self-driving cars and self-driving trucks are the norm? The stakes will only grow as technology advances.

IoT opens up a world of possibilities. It also dramatically grows the attack surface that criminals can exploit and increases the stakes if cybersecurity is not properly maintained.

Using Cryptocurrencies and Blockchain

A *cryptocurrency* is a digital asset (sometimes thought of as a digital currency) designed to work as a medium of exchange that uses various aspects of cryptography to control the creation of units, verify the accuracy of transactions, and secure financial transactions.

Modern cryptocurrencies allow parties who do not trust one another to interact and conduct business without the need for a trusted third party. Cryptocurrencies utilize *blockchain technology* — that is, their transactions are recoded on a distributed ledger whose integrity is protected through the use of multiple techniques that are supposed to ensure that only accurate transactions will be respected by others viewing a copy of the ledger.

Because cryptocurrencies are tracked via lists of transactions in ledgers, there are technically no cryptocurrency wallets. The currency is virtual and not stored anywhere, even electronically. Rather, cryptocurrency owners are the parties who control the various addresses on the ledger that have cryptocurrency associated with them after performing all the transactions to date on the ledger.

For example, if Address 1 has 10 units of a cryptocurrency and Address 2 has 5 units of a cryptocurrency and a transaction is recorded showing that Address 1 sent 1 unit of cryptocurrency to Address 2, the result is that Address 1 has 9 units of cyrptocurrrency and Address 2 has 6 units of cryptocurrency.

To ensure that only legitimate owners of cryptocurrency can send money from their addresses, cryoptocurrencies typically utilize a sophisticated implementation of PKI where every address has its own public-private key pair, with the owner being the only one to possess the private key. Sending cryptocurrency from an address requires the signing of the outgoing transaction with its associated private key.

Because anyone with knowledge of the private key associated with a particular ledger address can steal whatever amount of cryptocurrency is recorded in the ledger as belonging to that address, and because cryptocurrencies are both liquid and difficult to track back to their real-life human or organizational owners, criminals often attempt to steal cryptocurrencies via hacking. If a crook obtains the private key to a cryptocurrency address from someone's computer, the crook can quickly and easily transfer his victim's cryptocurrency to another address that the criminal controls. In fact, if the criminal obtains the key in any way, he or she can steal the cryptocurrency without hacking anything. All he or she has to do is issue a transaction sending the money to some other address and sign the transaction with the private key.

Because cryptocurrencies are not managed centrally, even if such a theft is detected, the legitimate owner has little hope of recovering his or her money. Reversing a transaction would, in most cases, require an unachievable consensus of a majority of operators within the cryptocurrency's ecosystem and is exceedingly unlikely to happen unless enough cryptocurrency was stolen to undermine the integrity of the entire currency. Even in such cases, the forking of a new cryptocurrency may be required to achieve such a reversal, and many operators will still likely reject the undoing of transactions as being an even greater threat to the integrity of the cryptocurrency than is a major theft.

Besides providing hackers with an easy way to steal money, cryptocurrencies have also facilitated other forms of cybercrimes. Most ransoms demanded by ransomware, for example, are required to be paid in cryptocurrency. In fact, cryptocurrency is the lifeblood of ransomware. Unlike payments made by wire transfer or credit card, smartly made cryptocurrency payments are exceedingly hard to trace back to real life people and are effectively irreversible once a transaction has settled.

Likewise, criminals have the ability to *mine* cryptocurrency — that is, to perform various complex calculations needed to both settle cryptocurrency transactions and create new units of the cryptocurrency — by stealing processing power from others. Cryptomining malware, for example, surreptitiously commandeers infected computers' CPU cycles to perform such calculations and, when new units of cryptocurrency are generated, transfers control of them to the criminals operating the malware. Cryptocurrency mining provides a simple way for criminals to monetize their hacking. Hacked computers can thus be used to "print money" without the involvement of victims as is typically needed for many other forms of monetization, such as ransomware.

Criminals have also benefited from the dramatic rise in the value of cryptocurrency. For example, those who accepted Bitcoin as payment for ransomware ransoms several years ago and who did not entirely cash out their cryptocurrency enjoyed amazing returns — sometimes growing their dollar-value holdings by a factor of hundreds or even thousands. Some such criminals likely cashed out a portion of their cryptocurrencies during the 2017 market frenzy and may be sitting on small fortunes that they are now investing in creating new cybercrime technologies.

The blockchain technology that serves as the underlying engine that powers cryptocurrencies also has potential uses within cybersecurity countermeasures. A distributed database may prove to be a better way to store information about backup servers and redundant capabilities than are existing structures because the distributed nature dramatically increases the number of points of failure necessary to take down the entire system. Likewise, distributed defenses against DDoS (distributed denial-of-service) attacks may prove to be both more effective and cost efficient than the present model of using single massive infrastructures to fight such attacks.

Blockchain also offers a way to create transparent records of transactions or of activities — transactions that are viewable by anyone, but not modifiable by anyone, and with only authorized parties able to create appropriate new transactions.

Optimizing Artificial Intelligence

Artificial intelligence, technically speaking, refers to the ability of an electronic system to perceive its environment and take actions that maximize its likelihood of achieving its goals, even without prior knowledge about the specifics of the environment and the situation in which it finds itself.

If that definition sounds complicated, it is. The definition of artificial intelligence from a practical perspective seems to be a moving target. Concepts and systems that were considered to be forms of artificial intelligence a decade or two ago — for example facial recognition technologies — are often treated as classic computer systems today. Today, most people use the term artificial intelligence to refer to computer systems that learn — that is, they mimic the way that humans learn from past experiences to take specific courses of action when encountering a new experience. Instead of being preprogrammed to act based on a set of specific rules, artificially intelligent systems look at sets of data to create their own sets of generalized rules and make decisions accordingly. The systems then optimize their own rules as they encounter more data and see the effects of applying their rules to that data.

Artificial intelligence is likely to ultimately transform the human experience at least as much as did the Industrial Revolution. The Industrial Revolution, of course, replaced human muscles with machines — the latter proving to be faster, more accurate, less prone to becoming tired or sick, and less costly than the former. Artificial intelligence is the replacement of human brains with computer thinking — and it will eventually also prove to be much faster, more accurate, and less prone to illness or sleepiness than any biological mind.

The era of artificial intelligence has several major impacts on cybersecurity:

>> An increased need for cybersecurity

>> The use of artificial intelligence as a security tool

>> The use of artificial intelligence as a hacking tool

Increased need for cybersecurity

As artificially intelligent systems become increasingly common, the need for strong cybersecurity grows dramatically. Computer systems can make increasingly important decisions without the involvement of humans, which means that the negative consequences of not adequately securing computer systems could increase dramatically. Imagine if a hospital deployed an artificially system to analyze medical images and report diagnoses. If such a system or its data were hacked, incorrect reports could occur and cause people to suffer or even die. Unfortunately, such a problem is no longer theoretical (see the nearby sidebar).

Of course, such research represents just the tip of the iceberg. Industrial AI systems can be manipulated to alter products in ways that increase danger, and artificially intelligent transportation technology designed to optimize routes and improve safety could be fed data that increase danger or create unnecessary delays.

AI CAN ALREADY FALSIFY MRI IMAGES AND PRODUCE INCORRECT MRI RESULTS

In 2019, Israeli researchers found that artificial intelligence technology could successfully modify medical images in such a way that it would consistently trick both radiologists and artificial intelligence systems designed to diagnose medical conditions based on scans, including reporting cancer when none existed and overlooking it when it did. Even after the researchers told the radiologists involved that AI was being used to manipulate the scan images, the radiologists were still unable to provide correct diagnoses and incorrectly found cancer in 60 percent of the normal scans to which tumors had been artificially added and did not find cancer in 87 percent of the scans from which the AI had digitally removed tumors.

Furthermore, because evildoers can undermine the integrity of artificially intelligent systems without hacking the systems but rather by simply introducing hard-to-find small changes into large data sets and because the decisions made by artificially intelligent systems are not based on predefined rules known to the humans who create the system, protecting all elements of such systems becomes critical. Once problems are introduced, humans and machines will likely not be able to find them or even know that something is amiss.

The bottom line is that for artificial intelligence projects to be successful, they must include heavy-duty cybersecurity.

Use as a cybersecurity tool

One of the biggest challenges facing cybersecurity operations professionals today is that it is practically impossible to dedicate sufficient time to analyze and act on all alerts produced by cybersecurity technologies. One of the first major uses for artificial intelligence in the realm of cybersecurity is as an agent that helps prioritize alerts. This agent first learns how systems are typically used and what types of activities are anomalous, as well as which old alerts actually indicated serious issues rather than benign activities or minor issues. Future iterations of such artificially intelligent systems will likely involve the AI itself actually acting upon the alerts rather than referring them to humans.

Use as a hacking tool

Artificial intelligence is not just a defensive tool; it can also be a powerful weapon in the hands of attackers. For obvious reasons, I don't provide details in this book as to how to use AI to launch advanced attacks, but I do discuss several general examples.

AI systems can, for example, be used to scan and analyze other systems in order to find programming errors and configuration mistakes. AI systems may also be used to analyze organization charts, social media, corporate websites, press releases, and so on in order to design — and perhaps even implement — maximally effective social engineering attacks.

AI can also be utilized to undermine authentication systems. For example, a system that is given a recording of a person saying many different things may be able to trick a voice-based authentication system by mimicking the relevant human — even if the authentication system asks the AI to enunciate words for which the AI has no recording of the human speaking.

REMEMBER

The bottom line is that when it comes to the use of AI as a cybersecurity tool, it's likely a spy-versus-spy battle between cyberattackers and cyberdefenders, with each trying to build better and better AIs so as to defeat one another.

Experiencing Virtual Reality

Virtual reality refers to an experience taking place within a computer-generated reality rather than within the real world.

Current virtual reality technology typically requires users to wear some sort of headset that displays images to the user and that blocks the user's vision of the real world. (In some cases, in lieu of wearing a headset, a user enters a special room equipped with a projector or multiple projectors, which achieves a similar effect.) Those images, combined with sounds and, in some cases, physical movements and other human-sensible experiences, cause the user to experience the virtual environment as if he or she were actually physically present in it. A person using virtual reality equipment can usually move, look, and interact with the virtual world.

Virtual reality typically incorporates at least visual and audio components, but may also deliver vibrations and other sensory experiences. Even without additional sensory information, a human may experience sensations because the human brain often interprets what it sees and hears in a virtual environment as if it were real. For example, someone riding a roller coaster in a virtual environment may feel his or her stomach drop when the roller coaster makes a sharp drop, even though, in reality, he or she is not moving.

Immersive virtual environments can be similar to or completely different from what a person would experience in the real world. Popular applications of virtual reality already include tourism (for example, walking through an art museum without actually being there), entertainment (first-person vantage point gaming), and educational purposes (virtual dissection).

Virtual reality systems, of course, are computer-based and, as a result, have many of the same security issues as other computer-based systems. But virtual reality also introduces many new security and privacy concerns:

» Can someone hack VR ecosystems and launch visual attacks that trigger seizures or headaches? (Flashing strobe lights in various cartoons and other displays have been known to cause seizures.)

- Can others make decisions about your physical abilities based on your performance in VR applications? Can governments, for example, refuse to issue drivers' licenses to people who perform poorly in VR driving games? Can auto insurance companies surreptitiously gather data about people's driving habits in the VR world and use it to selectively raise rates?

- Can hackers digitally vandalize a virtual environment — substituting obscene content for art, for example, in a museum offering virtual tours?

- Can hackers impersonate an authority figure, such as a teacher in a virtual classroom, by creating an avatar that looks similar to one used by that person and thereby trick other users into taking harmful actions (for example, by asking people for the answers to their tests, which the crooks then steal and pass off as their own to the real teacher)?

- Likewise, can hackers impersonate a coworker or family member and thereby obtain and abuse sensitive information?

- Can hackers modify virtual worlds in ways that earn them money in the real world — for example, by adding tolls to enter various places?

- Can hackers steal virtual currency used in various virtual worlds?

- Can hackers usurp control over a user's experience to see what he or she experiences or even to modify it?

In theory, when it comes to new risks created by virtual reality, I can compile a list that would take up an entire book — and time will certainly tell which risks emerge as real-world problems.

Transforming Experiences with Augmented Reality

Augmented reality refers to technology in which computer-generated images sounds, smells, movements, and/or other sensory material are superimposed onto a user's experience of the real world, transforming the user's experience into a composite of both actual and artificial elements. Augmented reality technology can both add elements to a user's experience — for example, showing a user the name of a person above the person's head as that individual approaches the user — as well as remove or mask elements, such as converting Nazi flags into black rectangles with the words "Defeat hate" written on them.

GOOGLE GLASS

Google Glass is a smart glasses technology consisting of a display and camera device embedded within a pair of eyeglasses. A user wearing a pair of Google Glass eyeglasses sees information superimposed over his or her field of vision and can communicate with the glasses by speaking commands.

Google's first release of Google Glass in April 2013 generated controversy related to the potential privacy implications created by people wearing and utilizing such devices.

Google Glass is an example of an early attempt at consumer-focused augmented reality that was a bit too early to market. Pokémon Go, on the other hand, was an example of a game using augmented reality that was a massive success.

Augmented reality is likely to become a major part of modern life over the next decade. It will introduce many of the risks that virtual reality does, as well as risks associated with the merging of real and virtual worlds, such as configuring systems to improperly associated various elements in the real world with virtual data.

As with all emerging technologies, time will tell. But, if you decide to invest in AR or VR technology, be sure to understand any relevant security issues.

POKÉMON GO

Pokémon Go is an augmented reality game for mobile devices that was first released in July 2016 as a result of a collaboration between Niantic, Nintendo, and The Pokémon Company. The game, which is free to play but offers in-game items for a fee, became an immediate hit and was downloaded more than half a billion times by the end of 2016. It uses a mobile device's GPS to locate, capture, battle, and train virtual creatures, called Pokémon, which appear on the device's screen within the context of the player's real-world location, superimposed on the image that would result if the player were aiming his or her camera at some area within the field of view.

As of early 2019, the game is believed to have been downloaded more than 1 billion times and to have generated more than $3 billion in worldwide revenue.

8

The Part of Tens

Find out how you can improve your cybersecurity without breaking the bank.

Learn from others' mistakes.

Learn how to safely use extremely convenient public Wi-Fi.

Chapter **18**

Ten Ways You Can Improve Your Cybersecurity without Spending a Fortune

Not all security improvements require a large outlay of cash. In this chapter, you discover ten ways that you can quickly improve your cybersecurity without spending a lot of money.

Understand That You Are a Target

People who believe that hackers want to breach their computers and phones and that criminals want to steal their data act differently than people who do not understand the true nature of the threat. Internalizing today's reality will help introduce into you healthy skepticism, as well as impact your attitude and behavior in numerous other ways — many of which you may not even consciously realize are being affected.

For example, when you believe that you're a target of cyberattackers, you're less likely to blindly trust that emails that you receive from your bank were actually sent by the bank, and, as such, you're less likely to fall prey to phishing scams than are people who believe that they are not targets. People who believe that criminals are after their passwords and PIN numbers are also more likely to better protect these sensitive pieces of data than are people who believe that crooks "have no reason to want" their data.

Use Security Software

All computer devices (laptops, phones, tablets, and so on) that house sensitive information or that will be attached to networks with other devices do need security software. Several popular, inexpensive packages include antivirus, firewall, antispam, and other beneficial technologies.

Portable devices should have remote wipe capabilities and software optimized for mobile systems; remember to enable such features as soon as you get the device. Many phones come with security software preinstalled by providers — make sure you enable and use it. (For more details on securing mobile devices, see Chapter 5.)

Encrypt Sensitive Information

Store all sensitive data in an encrypted format. If you have doubts as to whether something is sensitive enough to warrant encryption, it probably does, so err on the side of caution and encrypt.

Encryption is built in to many versions of Windows, and plenty of free encryption tools are available as well. It is amazing how much sensitive data that has been compromised could have remained secure if the parties from which it was stolen had used free encryption tools.

Also, never transmit sensitive information unless it is encrypted. Never enter sensitive information to any website if the site is not using SSL/TLS encryption, as evidenced by the page loading with HTTPS, and not HTTP, a difference easily seen by looking at the URL line of a web browser.

Encryption involves complex mathematical algorithms, but you don't need to know any of the details in order to utilize and benefit from encryption.

One point that you should be aware of, however, is that two major families of encryption algorithms are used today:

>> **Symmetric:** You use the same secret key to encrypt and decrypt.

>> **Asymmetric:** You use one secret key to encrypt and another to decrypt.

Most simple encryption tools utilize symmetric encryption, and all you need to remember is a password to decrypt your data. Throughout the course of your professional career, however, you may encounter various asymmetric systems that require you to establish both a public key and a private key. The public key is shared with the world, and the private key is kept secret. Asymmetric encryption helps with sending data:

>> If you want to send information to John so that only John can read it, encrypt the data with John's public key so that only John can read it, because he is the only party who has John's private key.

>> If you want to send information to John and want John to know that you sent it, encrypt the data with your own private key and therefore, John will decrypt it with your public key and know that you sent it because only you have the private key that goes along with your public key.

>> If you want to send information to John in a format that only John can read and in a format that John will know that you sent it, encrypt with both your own private key and john's public keys.

In reality, because asymmetric is processor intensive, it is rarely used for encrypting entire conversations, but, rather it is utilized to encrypt special *session keys* —that is, to convey to the parties to a conversation the keys that they need for symmetric encryption. Additional discussions regarding asymmetric encryption are beyond the scope of this book.

Back Up Often

Back up often enough that if something goes wrong, you won't panic about how much data you lost because your last backup was days ago.

TIP

Here is the general rule: If you're not sure whether you're backing up often enough, you probably aren't. No matter how convenient doing so may seem, do not keep your backups attached to your computer or even to your computer network (see Chapter 13). If you do keep backups attached in such a fashion, you run a serious risk that if ransomware or other malware somehow manages to infect your network, it can corrupt the backups as well, which would undermine the reason for backing up in the first place!

Ideally, have both backups stored both onsite and offsite. Onsite storage lets you restore quickly. Offsite storage helps ensure that backups are available even when a site becomes inaccessible or something else devastates all the computer equipment and digital data at a particular site.

One more thing: Make sure that you regularly test that your backups actually work. Backing up is worthless if you can't actually restore from your backups.

Do Not Share Passwords and Other Login Credentials

Every person accessing an important system should have his or her own login credentials. Do not share passwords for online banking, email, social media, and so on with your children or significant other — get everyone his or her own login.

REMEMBER

Implementing such a scheme not only improves the ability to track down the source of problems if they occur, but, perhaps more importantly in the case of families, creates a much greater sense of responsibility and encourages people to better protect their passwords.

Use Proper Authentication

You have likely heard the conventional wisdom to use complex passwords for all systems, but do not overdo it. If using too many complex passwords is causing you to reuse passwords on multiple sensitive systems or to write down passwords in insecure locations, consider other strategies for forming your passwords, such as combining words, numbers, and proper names, such as custard4tennis6Steinberg. See Chapter 7 for more details.

For extremely sensitive systems, if stronger forms of authentication, such as multifactor authentication, are available, take advantage of the offerings and use them.

For systems to which passwords do not really matter, consider using weak, easy-to-remember passwords. Don't waste brainpower where it does not need to be used.

Alternatively, use a password manager — but, not for your most sensitive passwords because you don't want to put all your eggs in one basket.

Use Social Media Wisely

Oversharing on social media posts has caused, and continues to cause, many problems, such as leaking sensitive information, violating compliance rules, and assisting criminals to carry out both cyber and physical attacks.

Be sure that your phone does not autocorrect anything to sensitive material when posting and don't accidentally cut and paste anything sensitive into a social media window.

Segregate Internet Access

Nearly all modern Wi-Fi routers allow you to run two or more networks — use this feature. If you work from home, for example, consider connecting your laptop to the Internet via a different Wi-Fi network than the one that your children use to browse the web and play video games. As discussed in Chapter 4, look for the Guest feature in your router's configuration pages — that is where you will typically find the ability to set up the second network (often referred to as the Guest network).

Use Public Wi-Fi Safely

While public Wi-Fi is a great convenience that most people utilize regularly, it also creates serious cybersecurity risks. Because of the benefits that public Wi-Fi provides, however, cybersecurity practitioners who preach that people should refrain from using public Wi-Fi are about as likely to succeed in their effort as they would be if they instructed people to abandon insecure computers and revert back to using typewriters.

As such, it is important that you learn how to use public Wi-Fi safely and understand multiple techniques for improving your odds of defending yourself against mischievous parties (see Chapter 6).

Hire a Pro

Especially if you're starting or running a small business, getting expert advice can be a wise investment. An information-security professional can assist you in designing and implementing your approach to cybersecurity. The minimal cost of a small amount of professional help may pay for itself many times over in terms of time, money, and aggravation saved down the road.

REMEMBER

The folks who will attack you — cybercriminals and other hackers — have, and utilize, technical expertise. If you'd hire a lawyer if you were charged with a crime, go to a doctor if you felt a virus coming on, or hire an accountant if you were audited by the IRS, hire a cyberpro.

Chapter **19**

Ten Lessons from Major Cybersecurity Breaches

Learning from the experiences of others can save people from unnecessary pain and suffering. In this chapter, I discuss five breaches that teach ten lessons. I specifically chose these five because they directly impacted either myself or a member of my family and, due to the breaches' respective magnitudes, are likely to have impacted you and yours as well.

Marriott

In November 2018, Marriott International disclosed that hackers had breached systems belonging to the Starwood hotel chain as far back as 2014 and had remained in the systems until September 2018 — about two years after Marriott acquired Starwood.

At the time of the disclosure, Marriott estimated that the breach may have impacted as many as 500 million customers and that the data compromised ranged from just the name and contact information for some customers to far more detailed data (including passport numbers, travel data, frequent traveler numbers, and so on) for others. Marriott also estimated that 100 million people's credit card numbers — along with expiration dates, but without CVC codes — were compromised, but that data was in an encrypted database, and Marriott saw no clear indication that the hackers who had obtained the data were able to decrypt it.

Evidence suggests that the attack against Marriott was carried out by a Chinese group affiliated with the Chinese government and was launched in an effort to gather data on U.S. citizens. If such an attribution is correct, the Marriott breach would likely be the largest known breach to date by a nation-state funded organization of personal, civilian data.

In July 2019, the Information Commissioner's Office of the United Kingdom (ICO) announced that it intended to impose a fine of the equivalent of $123 million on Marriott as a penalty for the failure to properly protect consumer data as mandated by the European Union's General Data Protection Regulation (GDPR). (See Chapter 9 for more on GDPR.) According to an SEC filing by Marriott, the firm intends to appeal the penalty once the fine is formally filed, which had not happened at the time of writing.

While many lessons can be learned from the Marriott incident, two stand out:

>> **When anyone acquires a company and its information infrastructure, a thorough cybersecurity audit needs performed.** Vulnerabilities or active hackers within the acquired firm can become a headache to the new owner, and government regulators may even seek to hold the acquiring company responsible for the failures of a firm that it acquires.

As the UK's Information Commissioner, Elizabeth Denham, put it: "The GDPR makes it clear that organisations must be accountable for the personal data they hold. This can include carrying out proper due diligence when making a corporate acquisition, and putting in place proper accountability measures to assess not only what personal data has been acquired, but also how it is protected."

Don't rely on acquired companies to disclose cybersecurity problems; they may not be aware of potentially serious issues.

REMEMBER

>> **From an intelligence perspective, foreign governments — especially those engaged in competition with the United States and other Western powers — value data about civilians.** Such governments may seek to find and use information to blackmail folks into spying, look for people with financial pressure who may be amenable to accepting money in exchange for illegal services, and so on.

Target

In December 2013, the giant retail chain Target disclosed that hackers had breached its systems and compromised about 40 million payment card numbers (a combination of credit and debit card numbers). Over the next few weeks, Target revised that figure. Altogether, the breach may have impacted as many as 110 million Target customers, and the information accessed may have included not only payment card information, but other personally identifiable information (such as names, addresses, telephone numbers, and email addresses) as well.

Hackers entered Target by exploiting a vulnerability in a system used by a third-party HVAC contracting company that was servicing Target, and that had access to the retail company's point-of-sale systems.

As a result of the breach, Target's CEO and CIO both resigned, and the company estimated that the breach inflicted about $162 million of damage to the firm.

Two lessons from the Target incident stand out:

» **Management will be held responsible when companies suffer cyberattacks.** Personal careers can be harmed.

» **A person or organization is only as cybersecure as the most vulnerable party having access to its systems.** Like a weak link in a strong chain, an inadequately secured third party with access to one's systems can easily undermine millions of dollars in cybersecurity investment. Home users should consider the moral of the Target story when allowing outsiders to use their home computers or networks. You may be careful with your personal cyberhygiene, but if you allow someone who is not careful to join your network, malware on his or her device can potentially propagate to your machines as well.

Sony Pictures

In November 2014, a hacker leaked confidential data stolen from the Sony Pictures film studio, including copies of as-of-yet-unreleased Sony films, internal emails between employees, employees' compensation information, and various other personal information about employees and their families. The hacker also wiped many computers within Sony's information infrastructure.

The leak and wiping occurred after hackers had been stealing data from Sony for as long as a year — potentially taking as much as 100 terabytes of material; Sony's executives also apparently dismissed as spam various demands that the hackers had communicated via email. Sony's cybersecurity plan, procedures, and countermeasures either did not detect the large volume of data being transferred out, or took grossly insufficient action upon detection.

After the breach, a party claiming to be the hackers threatened to carry out physical terrorist attacks against theaters showing Sony's then-upcoming film, *The Interview*, a comedy about a plot to assassinate North Korean leader Kim Jong-un. With the attackers' credibility and capabilities clearly asserted via the breach, cinema operators took the threat seriously, and many major American movie theater chains stated that they would not show *The Interview*. As a result, Sony canceled the film's formal premiere and theatrical release, instead offering the film only as a downloadable digital release followed by limited theatrical viewings.

While some cybersecurity experts were at least initially skeptical about the attribution, the United States government blamed North Korea for the hack and subsequent threats and, in September 2018, brought formal charges against a North Korean citizen that it claimed was involved with carrying out the hack while working for the North Korean equivalent of the Central Intelligence Agency.

Here are two lessons that stand out:

>> Depending on what technology Sony actually had in place, this breach either shows the need for implementing data loss prevention technology or shows that cybersecurity technology can be terribly ineffective, if not utilized properly.

>> Nation-states may use cyberattacks as a weapon against businesses and individuals whom they view as harmful to their goals, interests, and aspirations.

Office of Personnel Management

In June 2015, the United States Office of Personnel Management (OPM), which manages personnel processes and records for the U.S. federal government, announced that it had been the victim of a data breach. While the office initially estimated that far fewer records were compromised, the eventual estimate of the number of stolen records was more than 20 million.

The stolen records included personally identifiable information, including Social Security numbers, home addresses, dates and places of birth, and so on, of both current and former government employees, as well as of people who had undergone background checks, but who were never employed by the government. While the government initially believed that the contents of sensitive SF-86 forms — which contain all sorts of information used in background checks for security clearances — were not compromised, it ultimately disclosed that such data may have been accessed and stolen, meaning that the attackers may have obtained a treasure trove of private information about people with all sorts of security clearances.

The OPM breach is believed to actually be a combination of more than one breach — one likely began around 2012 and was detected in March 2014 and another began in May 2014 and was not detected until April 2015.

Many lessons can be learned from the OPM incident, but two stand out:

>> **Government organizations are not immune to serious breaches** — and even after being breached once, may still remain vulnerable to subsequent breaches. Furthermore, like their civilian counterparts, they may not detect breaches for quite some time and may initially underestimate the impact of a particular breach or series of breaches.

>> **Breaches at an organization can impact people whose connections with the organization have long since ended** — some folks may not even remember why the organization had their data. The OPM breach impacted people who had not worked at the government in decades or who had applied for clearances many years prior, but who never ended up working for the government.

Anthem

In February 2015, Anthem, the second-largest health insurer in the United States, disclosed that it had been the victim of a cyberattack that had compromised personal information of almost 80 million current and former customers. Data that was stolen included names, addresses, Social Security numbers, dates of birth, and employment histories. Medical data was not believed to have been pilfered, but the stolen data was sufficient to create serious risks of identity theft for many people.

The breach — likely the largest in the history of the American healthcare industry — was believed to have initially taken place sometime in 2014, when one worker at a subsidiary of the insurer clicked on a link in a phishing email.

Two lessons stand out:

>> **The healthcare industry is increasingly being targeted.** (This is also apparent from the tremendous number of ransomware attacks directed at hospitals in recent years, as discussed in Chapter 3.)

>> **While people often imagine that breaches of major corporations require sophisticated James Bond-like techniques, the reality is that many, if not most, serious breaches are actually achieved using simple, classic techniques.** Phishing still works wonders for criminals. Human mistakes are almost always an integral element of a serious breach.

Chapter **20**

Ten Ways to Safely Use Public Wi-Fi

You may not realize that you can do a few things to protect yourself while using public Wi-Fi. In this chapter, you discover ten ways to keep your devices safe while accessing Wi-Fi in public.

Use Your Cellphone as a Mobile Hotspot

If you have an unlimited cellular data plan, you can avoid the risks of public Wi-Fi by transforming your cellphone into a mobile hotspot and connecting your laptop and any other devices that lack cellular data service to your cellphone, rather than to public Wi-Fi.

Turn Off Wi-Fi Connectivity When You're Not Using Wi-Fi

Turning off Wi-Fi connectivity will prevent your device from (without notifying you) connecting to a network with the same name as one you have previously connected to. Criminals can, and have, set up Wi-Fi access points with names similar to popular public Wi-Fi networks, in an effort to lure people into connecting to poisoned networks that route their victims to phony sites or distribute malware to connected devices. As an added bonus, turning off Wi-Fi will also conserve battery power.

Don't Perform Sensitive Tasks over Public Wi-Fi

Do not bank online, shop online, or access medical records online while using a public Wi-Fi connection.

Don't Reset Passwords When Using Public Wi-Fi

You should avoid resetting any passwords over public Wi-Fi. In fact, you should refrain from resetting any passwords while in a public location, regardless of whether or not you're using public Wi-Fi.

Use a VPN Service

If you can't use a cellular connection and must use the public Wi-Fi connection for a sensitive task despite the recommendation not to do so, at least consider using a VPN service, which adds multiple security benefits. Many popular VPN services are available today.

There is a tradeoff to using a VPN service, however. You may notice that your communications are slightly slower or suffer from greater latency than without the VPN running.

Use Tor

If you don't want your browsing history to be tracked by anyone, consider browsing using Tor (see Chapter 4), which bounces your communications through many servers and makes tracking exceedingly difficult. There are even Tor browsers for smartphones. Like a VPN, Tor may slow down your communications.

Use Encryption

Use HTTPS instead of HTTP for all web pages that offer it, to prevent other users on the network from seeing the content of your communications.

Turn Off Sharing

If you're using a computer or device that shares any of its resources, turn off any and all shares before connecting to the public Wi-Fi. If you're unsure if your device shares resources, check it. Don't assume that it does not.

Have Information Security Software on Any Devices Connected to Public Wi-Fi Networks

For computers security packages must include, at a minimum, antivirus and personal firewall capabilities. For smartphones and tablets, use an app designed specifically to secure such devices. And, of course, make sure that the security software is up to date before connecting to public Wi-Fi.

Understand the Difference between True Public Wi-Fi and Shared Wi-Fi

Not all public Wi-Fi is equally risky. There is usually a much lower risk of being misrouted to phony sites or of malware being delivered to your device if you use the password-protected Guest network at a client site, for example, than if you use unprotected free Wi-Fi offered by a public library. That does not mean that you should fully trust the network; other guests at the site still pose risks.

Index

A

AARP (American Association of Retired Persons), on passwords, 124

access control, as component of Crime Prevention Through Design (CPTD), 91

access devices
  checking access device lists, 109
  securing of, 107

access management, 181, 184

accounts
  accessing of only when you're in safe location, 109
  audible access to corporate accounts, 158
  limiting access to corporate accounts on social media, 158–159
  monitoring of, 103–104
  reporting suspicious activity on, 104
  securing data associated with user accounts, 101
  securing of, 99–113
  securing of external accounts, 100
  setting appropriate limits regarding, 109
  use of alerts on, 109

advanced attacks, 40–42

advanced persistent threats (APTs), 42

adware
  alerts regarding, 216
  as cyberattack, 35
  defined, 35
  as malware, 32, 35

adware malware, 35, 205

alarms
  false alarms, 136–137
  as physical security method, 92
  as remotely triggerable, 93
  use of, 172

Alcoa, hacking of, 48

alerts
  about tracking cookies or adware, 216
  prioritizing of, 308
  responding to fraud alerts, 110
  setting up text alerts for payment card information, 224
  signing up for from bank, 83
  triggering fraud alerts, 109
  use of on your accounts, 109

algorithms (for encryption)
  asymmetric algorithm, 317
  symmetric algorithm, 317

Allegheny Technologies, hacking of, 48

Amazon AppStore, as reputable app store, 101

American Association of Retired Persons (AARP), on passwords, 124

American Superconductor, 31

Android devices
  hard resets on, 260
  soft resets on, 255

Anthem, Inc.
  cybersecurity breach, 325–326
  impersonation of, 223

Apple App Store, as reputable app store, 101

Apple Pay, 102

APTs (advanced persistent threats), 42

archives, understanding of, 276–277

artificial intelligence (AI)
  as able to falsify MRI images, 307
  defined, 306
  optimizing of, 306–309
  use of as hacking tool, 308–309

assets
  information asset classification and control, 183
  inventorying of, 70–71

asymmetric algorithm, for encryption, 317

Burr, Bill (author), 120
business
    conducting of with reputable parties, 101
    cybersecurity and big businesses, 175–187
    cybersecurity and small business, 155–173
business continuity plans (BCPs), 176, 185–186
business data theft, 31–32
business risks, as mitigated by cybersecurity, 20
BYOD (Bring Your Own Device) policy, 160,
        167–169

C

calculated attacks, 39
carve outs, 164
cellphone numbers
    caution in publicizing, 80
    protection of, 111–112
CEO fraud, as cyberattack, 27
certifications
    adherence to code of ethics as required by, 299
    Certified Ethical Hacker (CEH), 298
    Certified Information Security Manager (CISM), 297
    Certified Information Systems Security Professional
        (CISSP), 296–297
    in cybersecurity, 296–299
    digital certificates as form of authentication, 104
    Global Information Assurance Certification Security
        Essentials Certification (GSEC), 298–299
    Security+, 298
    TLS/SSL certificate, 171, 316
    verifiability of, 299
Certified Ethical Hacker (CEH), 298
Certified Information Security Manager (CISM), 297
Certified Information Systems Security Professional
        (CISSP), 296–297
Cheat Sheet, 4
chief information security officer (CISO)
    career path of, 294–295
    role of, 182–187, 288
China, as known for performing cyberespionage, 109
CIA (Confidentiality, Integrity, and Availability), 18
CIA triad, 18–19
Cialdini, Robert Beno (social psychologist), 137
claimed destruction, as overt breach, 193–194
class action lawsuits, from data breaches, 180

classified information
    defined, 87
    protection of, 86
Clinton, Hillary (former U.S. Secretary of State), 86
cloning, 237
cloud
    in the cloud, 241
    storage of backup on, 244–245
communication, impact of covert breach on, 197
compliance
    for big businesses, 177–180
    on biometric data, 167
    breach disclosure laws, 166, 179
    CISO's responsibility for, 186
    cybersecurity regulations expert, 292
    General Data Protection Regulation (GDPR), 166
    Health Insurance Portability and Accountability Act
        (HIPAA), 167
    industry-specific regulations and rules, 179–180
    Payment Card Industry Data Security Standard (PCI
        DSS), 165, 178
    private regulations expert, 292
    public company data disclosure rules, 179
    Sarbanes Oxley Act of 2002 (SOX), 177–178
    Small Business Administration as source of
        guidance on, 164
    for small businesses, 164–167
CompTIA, 298
computer viruses, 32
computer worms, 33, 45
computer(s)
    as basic element of protection, 71, 74
    locking, 106
    resets on, 253–262
    storage of at businesses, 173
    use of separate, dedicated one for sensitive
        tasks, 106
    using your own, 106
confidentiality, as part of CIA triad, 18
Confidentiality, Integrity, and Availability (CIA), 18
construction, contingencies during, 93
consultants, considerations about in big businesses,
        181–182
continuity planning, 57, 176, 185–186
continuous backups, 235, 272
corporate accounts, limiting access to, 158–159

distributed denial-of-service (DDoS) attacks
described, 19, 22–24
protecting against, 306
DNS (domain name system), 37
DNS poisoning, 37
DoS (denial-of-service) attacks
described, 22
protecting against, 171
double-locking, 164
downloaded software
backup/backing up, 232–233
restoring of, 268
drive backups, 236–237, 273
drive-by downloads, as cyberattack, 38
drive-specific backup software, 240–241
DRPs (disaster recovery plans), 57, 177, 185–186

E

EC-Council (International Council of E-Commerce Consultants), 298
economic model, shifts in as impact on cybersecurity, 13
education, evaluating security measures regarding, 77–78
802.11ac Wi-Fi protocol, 72
802.11n Wi-Fi protocol, 72
Einstein, Albert (scientist), 44
election interference, as political ramification of cybersecurity, 14–15
emails
cautions in clicking on links in, 112–113
tantalizing emails as type of social engineering attack, 136
employees
considerations about in big businesses, 181–182
enforcing social media policies for, 162–163
giving everyone his or her own credentials, 157–158
implementing cybersecurity policies for, 160–162
incentivizing of, 157
limiting access of, 157
monitoring of, 163
protecting employee data, 164–165
watching out for, 156–163

employer-issued documents, compromise of, 225
encryption
of all private information, 81
of backups, 245, 246–247
end-to-end encryption, 81
for guest users, 73
one-way encryption, 223
ransomware as often encrypting user files, 33, 192, 221
of sensitive information, 316–317
use of, 76, 80, 94, 122, 123, 127, 162, 164, 329
of virtual drives, 237–238, 273
of Wi-Fi network, 72
end-to-end encryption, 81
environmental risk mitigation, as physical security method, 92–93
ethical hacker, role of, 290
ethics, code of, 299
expunged records, as no longer really expunged, 59–60
external accounts, securing of, 100
external disasters
manmade environmental problems, 57
natural disasters, 57

F

Facebook
authentication capabilities provided by, 121
backups of data by, 242–243
basic control and audibility on, 158
for business, 158
cautions in listing family members on, 141
celebrity accounts as verified on, 151
criminals as creating fake profiles on, 144, 149
friend requests from as red flags, 147
number of connections on as red flag, 146
red flags on, 39, 146, 147, 150
requests from celebrities on as red flag, 150
use of to find someone's mother's maiden name, 61, 79
factory image, 231
Fair Credit Reporting Act (FCRA)
as impotent, 58–59
limitations of, 116

Huawei devices running Android 8, hard resets on, 260–261

human errors

  as greatest cybersecurity danger, 55

  as No. 1 catalyst for data breaches, 156, 181

humans

  as Achilles heel of cybersecurity, 55–56, 77

  as always coming first regarding safety and security, 95

I

ICO (Information Commissioner's Office of the United Kingdom), 322

icons, explained, 3–4

identity and access management, 184

impersonation, as cyberattack, 25–29, 135–136

in the cloud, defined, 241

in-app backups, 239, 276

inbound access, handling of, 169–171

incident response plan, 185

incident response team member, role of, 292

incineration, as way of disposing of backups, 249

incremental backups, 233–234, 269–270, 271

incremental system backups, 270

indirect financial fraud, as way to monetize cyberattackers actions, 51–53

industry-specific regulations and rules, for big businesses, 179–180

Influence: The Psychology of Persuasion (Cialdini), 137

information

  bogus information, 151

  classified information, 86, 87

  credit card information, 52–53, 102, 103

  dealing with stolen information, 219–222

  financial information, 140

  insider information, 52

  personal information, 141

  private information, 102

  sensitive information, 102, 106, 107, 221, 316–317

  stolen information, 219–222

  that is not private but can help criminals with identity theft, 220–221

information asset classification and control, 183

Information Commissioner's Office of the United Kingdom (ICO), 322

information security

  defined, 8

  standards of, 165

  starting out in, 295–296

  strategy of, 184

  training in, 156, 181–182

Information Systems Audit and Control Association (ISACA), 297

insider information, as technique of cyberattackers, 52

insiders, as posing greatest risk, 94

Instagram

  for business, 158

  celebrity accounts as verified on, 151

  criminals as creating fake profiles on, 144, 148

  impersonation on, 136

  usage level as red flag on, 148

insurance

  cyber insurance, 163–164, 187

  evaluating security measures regarding, 77

integrity, as part of CIA triad, 18

intellectual property (IP), theft of, 31

interception, as cyberattack, 29–30

internal politics, dealing with, 181

International Council of E-Commerce Consultants (EC-Council), 298

Internet

  handling access of in your small business, 167–172

  impact of on cybersecurity, 10

  segregating access to, 319

Internet of Things (IoT)

  being careful with IoT devices, 172

  defined, 11

  potential problems of regarding cybersecurity, 69, 83–84

  relying on, 302–304

investigations, CISO's responsibility for, 186

IP (intellectual property), theft of, 31

iPhones

  hard resets on, 262

  soft resets on, 255–256

iris scanners/readers, 129

ISACA (Information Systems Audit and Control Association), 297

text message (SMS)-based authentication, 105, 128, 130, 131, 159, 201

text messages, cautions in clicking on links in, 112–113

thefts
business data theft, 31–32
of intellectual property (IP), 31
of password databases, 223–224
personal data theft, 30

threats
advanced persistent threats (APTs), 42
dealing with nonmalicious ones, 54–62
emerging technologies as bringing new ones, 301–311

TLS/SSL certificate, 171, 316

Tor Browser Bundle, 80, 114, 115, 329

Trojans, as cyberattack, 33

2016 Presidential election (U.S.), 47

Twitter
authentication capabilities provided by, 121
for business, 158
celebrity accounts as verified on, 151
criminals as creating fake profiles on, 149

U

uninterruptible power supply (UPS), 173

United States Office of Personnel Management (OPM), cybersecurity breach, 324–325

updates, installing of to reduce exposure to vulnerabilities, 107–108

U.S. Supreme Court, National Socialist Party of America v. Village of Skokie, 45

USB-based authentication, 132

user accounts, securing data associated with, 101

V

verifiability, of certification, 299

video cameras, as physical security method, 92

viral trend, 143

virtual credit card numbers, use of, 103

virtual drive backups, 237–238, 273–274

virtual kidnapping scams, 61, 140

virtual locker, 232

Virtual Private Network (VPN)/VPN service, 9, 68, 114, 115, 171, 328–329

virtual reality, 309–310

virus hoax, as type of social engineering attack, 137

viruses, as cyberattack, 32

vishing, as cyberattack, 28

Vivaldi, privacy mode, 81

voice login passwords, 111

voice-based authentication, 130

VOIP number, 159

vulnerability assessment analyst, role of, 290

W

WannaCry, 34

water holing, as type of social engineering attack, 137

Westinghouse, hacking of, 48

whaling, as cyberattack, 28

white hat hackers, 50

Wi-Fi
cautions with performing sensitive tasks over public Wi-Fi, 108, 328
cautions with using public Wi-Fi for any purpose in high-risk places, 108–109
recommended protocols for, 72
turning off Wi-Fi connectivity when not using Wi-Fi, 328
understanding difference between true public Wi-Fi and shared Wi-Fi, 330
using public Wi-Fi safely, 319, 327–330

Windows AutoUpdate, 107–108

Windows backup, 241, 278

Windows Blue Screen of Death, 254

Windows computers
hard resets on, 257–259
soft resets on, 254–255

wiper attacks, 25

work environment, potential problems of regarding cybersecurity, 70

worms, as cyberattack, 33, 45

WPA-2 standard, 72

Z

zero day malware, as cyberattack, 36

zombies, 24–25

About the Author

Joseph Steinberg advises businesses in the cybersecurity and emerging technologies sectors, helping them grow and succeed. He also serves as an expert witness and consultant on related matters.

Joseph previously led businesses and divisions within the information-security industry for more than two decades, has been calculated to be one of the top three cybersecurity influencers worldwide, and has written books ranging from *Cybersecurity For Dummies* to the official study guide from which many Chief Information Security Officers (CISOs) study for their certification exams. He is also one of only 28 people worldwide to hold the suite of advanced information security certifications(CISSP, ISSAP, ISSMP, and CSSLP), indicating that he possesses a rare, robust knowledge of information security that is both broad and deep; his information-security-related inventions are cited in more than 400 U.S. patent filings.

Joseph is also one of the best read columnists in the cybersecurity field and a respected authority on other emerging technologies, having amassed millions of readers as a regular columnist for *Forbes* and *Inc.* magazines. Within three months of going independent in April 2018, his column — now published exclusively on JosephSteinberg.com — reached 1 million monthly views. His writing reflects his passion for exploring the impact of emerging technologies on human society, making complex technical concepts simple to understand and helping people focus on the technology issues and cybersecurity risks that truly impact them.

Joseph can be reached at https://JosephSteinberg.com.

Dedication

Many summers ago, when I was 8 years old, my parents arranged for me to take a programming class, giving me my first exposure to the then-emerging world of personal computers. Unbeknownst to any of us at the time, the moment at which I wrote my first line of code by typing on the chicklet keyboard of the school's Commodore PET marked the start of what would become my lifelong fascination with computer technology. That childhood interest ultimately blossomed from a hobby into a college major, a graduate course of study, and a career.

On that note, as I stand in my office looking at the almost four-decades-old cassette tape containing software that I wrote that summer, I dedicate this book to my parents, Dr. Edward and Sandra Steinberg.

Also, as my youngest daughter, Tammy, was not yet born when I dedicated a prior book to my wife and children, I also dedicate this work to her, the first digital native born into our family.

Author's Acknowledgments

Cybersecurity is of paramount importance in today's world, but few modern-day adults learned from their parents or in school about mitigating against today's major cybersecurity risks. Couple that lack of formal education with the combination of information overload, the proliferation of oft-repeated impractical advice, technical terms, and the constant barrage of news stories about cyberattacks and breaches, and it is no surprise that, when it comes to cybersecurity, many folks feel confused, fatigued, and scared.

As a result, there has never been a greater need for a book that brings basic, practical cybersecurity knowledge to "nontechnical people" than there is today.

It was with the aim of satisfying that need in mind that Wiley approached me about writing this book, and it was the importance of delivering on such a goal that led me to accept the opportunity. As such, I would like to thank Ashley Coffey and the team at Wiley for both agreeing to provide the public with a resource that it so desperately needs, and for giving me the opportunity to collaborate with them on this important effort.

I would also like to thank my editor, Kelly Ewing, and my technical reviewer, Daniel Smith, whose input and guidance helped improve the book that you are now holding, optimized it for readability, and ensured that it delivers to you its maximum informational value.

Thank you also to my wife, Shira, and to my daughters, Penina, Mimi, and Tammy, for their support and encouragement throughout the time-intensive process of developing and writing this work.

And, finally, while there were no cybersecurity classes when I went to school, several great professors helped me hone my understanding of the building blocks of computer science that I ultimately assembled and applied in order to develop expertise in my field. I wish to single out and specifically recognize two of my instructors, Matthew Smosna and Aizik Leibovitch, both of who, unfortunately, did not live to see this book published, but whose influence on my thinking resonates throughout it.

Publisher's Acknowledgments

Acquisitions Editor: Ashley Coffey

Project Editor: Kelly Ewing

Technical Editor: Daniel Smith

Editorial Assistant: Matthew Lowe

Sr. Editorial Assistant: Cherie Case

Proofreader: Debbye Butler

Production Editor: Siddique Shaik

Cover Image: © NicoElNino/Shutterstock